ENG

MODERN WARS IN PERSPECTIVE

General Editors: *H.M. Scott and B.W. Collins*

This ambitious new series offers wide-ranging studies of specific wars, and distinct phases of warfare, from the close of the Middle Ages to the present day. It aims to advance the current integration of military history into the academic mainstream. To that end, the books are not merely traditional campaign narratives, but examine the causes, course and consequences of major conflicts, in their full international political, social and ideological contexts.

ALREADY PUBLISHED

Mexico and the Spanish Conquest
Ross Hassig

The Anglo–Dutch Wars of the Seventeenth Century
J.R. Jones

The Wars of Louis XIV
John A. Lynn

The Wars of Frederick the Great
Dennis Showalter

The War of the Austrian Succession, 1740–1748
M.S. Anderson

The Wars of Napoleon
Charles J. Esdaile

The Spanish–American War: Conflict in the Caribbean
and the Pacific 1895–1902
Joseph Smith

China at War, 1901–1949
Edward L. Dreyer

The Wars of French Decolonization
Anthony Clayton

A Noble Cause? America and the Vietnam War
Gerard J. DeGroot

The Northern Wars
Robert I. Frost

ENGLAND'S COLONIAL WARS 1550–1688

Conflicts, Empire and National Identity

BRUCE P. LENMAN

Longman

An imprint of **Pearson Education**

Harlow, England · London · New York · Reading, Massachusetts · San Francisco
Toronto · Don Mills, Ontario · Sydney · Tokyo · Singapore · Hong Kong · Seoul
Taipei · Cape Town · Madrid · Mexico City · Amsterdam · Munich · Paris · Milan

Pearson Education Limited
Edinburgh Gate
Harlow
Essex CM20 2JE
England

and Associated Companies throughout the world

Visit us on the World Wide Web at:
http://www.pearsoneduc.com

First published 2001

© Pearson Education Limited 2001

ISBN 0 582 06297 7 (csd)   0 582 06296 9 (ppr)

British Library Cataloguing-in-Publication Data
A catalogue record for this book is available from the British Library

Library of Congress Cataloging-in-Publication Data
A catalog record for this book is available from the Library of Congress

10 9 8 7 6 5 4 3 2 1
05 04 03 02 01

Typeset by 35 in 11/13 pt Baskerville MT
Produced by Pearson Education Asia Pte Ltd
Printed in Singapore

CONTENTS

List of Maps vii

Acknowledgements ix

Introduction: Give war a chance 1

PART ONE. THE TUDOR CROWN, THE ENGLISH NATION,
AND THE HERITAGE OF ANGLO-NORMAN EXPANSIONISM
c. 1550–1603

1. Colonial Englishmen face up to the Tudors 23

2. The Gaidhealtachd and the colonial enterprise 41
   The Gaidhealtachd, the Lordship, and the Crowns of England and
   Scotland to 1558 41
   Making a bad situation worse: early Elizabethan Ireland 59

3. Feeding frenzy: marginal courtiers and perceived opportunities,
   1578–1590 73
   The New English, asset seizure, and instability on the land frontier 73
   Entrepreneurial violence on the sea frontier after 1568 82

4. Nadir of statesmanship: the origins of the last Elizabethan
   colonial war 100

5. The bankruptcy of Elizabethan imperialism and the fatal
   fracturing of the Englishry 125

PART TWO. THREE-KINGDOM MONARCHY AND EMPIRE
1603–1688

6. Reluctant warriors: James I, Charles I, appeasement and
   the aborting of a three-kingdom overseas empire 147
   The shaping of a triple monarchy after 1603 147
   The aborting of the overseas dimension of triple kingship 168

7. No enthusiasts for empire: the English East India Company
   and the struggle for maritime trade in seventeenth-century
   Asia to 1689 182
   Breaking in or the East India Company as the trader armed before 1660 182
   The rise and fall of Stuart imperialism in Asia after 1660 196

8. War in the New English marchlands in North America
   1607–1676 217
   The violent genesis of plantation society on the Chesapeake 1607–1644 217
   The bankruptcy of integration in New England by 1676 235
   Conclusion 249

9. The clash of European states and the rise of the imperial
   factor in the Caribbean and North America 255
   The Caribbean cockpit 1586–1688 255
   Anglo–Dutch and Anglo–French competition in North America 1664–1688 ... 272

Conclusion: The fracturing of the Englishry, the marginality of
colonial enterprise, and the erratic impact of war 283

Further reading 294
   Imperial context 294
   Military background 294
   Naval 295
   Regional studies 295

Index 299

LIST OF MAPS

Map 1 Dominions of the Crown of England under the Tudors,
       c. 1540   22

Map 2 The expansion of the Lordship and Kingdom of Ireland,
       1525–1603   42

Map 3 The Western Isles, Ulster and Man, *c.* 1600   151

Map 4 The English East India Company in the trading world
       of seventeenth-century Asia   183

Map 5 Eastern North America, *c.* 1680   218

Map 6 The West Indies, *c.* 1680   256

Map 7 Principal routes of the fur trade in the later seventeenth
       century   273

ACKNOWLEDGEMENTS

Though the ultimate responsibility for what is in this book rests with the author, he must express his gratitude to people and institutions whose assistance was vital in bringing the major enterprise of which this volume is the first part to a conclusion. Andrew MacLennan, then of Addison Wesley Longman, was the editor who originally had the courage to commission a work so different and wider in scope than was normal for his 'Modern Wars in Perspective' series. It has taken so long to bring the commission to fruition that he has retired, in so far as so dynamic a man can. However, I remain proud to have been associated with someone who is by common consent one of the great creative Humanities editors of our time. I have also been grateful that within the wider embrace of Pearson Education I have experienced the efficient and amiable editorship of his worthy successor Heather McCallum. My academic editor and good colleague Professor Hamish Scott, has been a model of patience with a project which has been on my mind for over twenty years and which has taken over a decade to write. His constant generous assistance and unobtrusive suggestions have been indispensable. Dr Jane Dawson helped enormously by making available to me both her formidably precise scholarship and some of the material on the evolution of the western Highlands in the sixteenth century which she has accumulated for her forthcoming important monograph on the evolution of Clan Campbell in the early-modern period.

Research of the kind embedded in this book is, of course, so heavily indebted to previous scholarship that adequate acknowledgement is impractical. Acknowledgements have perforce been selective. I can only apologise to the many others who might have been cited in more general terms. It is however appropriate to say that I am very conscious of what I owe to former colleagues in the College of William and Mary in Virginia especially those associated with the Omohundro Institute of Early American History and Culture. In the Asian sphere, Dr Andrew Cook and Tony Farrington of the Oriental and India Office Collections in the British Library have done much to keep up my morale and guide my steps. The understanding support of my own Department of Modern History here in St Andrews has been matched by the generosity of the School of History with leave and grants for travel. By the excellence of the research atmosphere they constantly uphold both have done much to compensate for the inevitable loneliness of one of the few early-modern imperial historians working in a Scottish, or for that matter a UK university. The current vitality of the field long ago ceased to be matched by the number of academic posts generating that vitality.

I recall writing the first pages of this book in the Folger Shakespeare Library in Washington DC, another body to which I cannot repay my debts. This volume was largely completed in the library of the University of Emory. Along with the John Carter Brown Library and the Huntington Library in San Marino, California, these American institutions combined with the National Library of Scotland and the British Library to give me the basic resources on which this sort of study must be based.

Finally it behoves me to express my deep gratitude to the kindness of two people. Nancy Bailey offered me much more than excellent editorial and secretarial services. She, her family, and indeed her extended family have done much to support me in recent very difficult years. Dr Julian Crowe, the best of all IT consultants, has over the years also shown me great kindness, not least in repeatedly saving me and other colleagues in the Faculty of Arts from the consequences of our own ignorance and ineptitude. I dedicate the book to Roderick, not because he will read it, but out of relief that he will be around to look at it.

Bruce Lenman
St Andrews
May 2000

Give war a chance

Colonial warfare is a concept which sits easily on the modern tongue. Indeed, the word 'colonial' is often used far too freely, having become, as *The Oxford English Dictionary* reminds us, an adjective with a pejorative edge to it. In raucous mouths its various forms compete too often with variations on the word 'fascist' as a substitute for rational analysis. All of this is comprehensible, though not excusable, after the wars of decolonisation which loomed so large in the history of the twentieth century. It is, however, important to grasp that the adjective 'colonial' gained general currency quite late in the early-modern period, which stretches roughly from the late fifteenth to the late eighteenth centuries. It did not feature in Dr Samuel Johnson's great *Dictionary of the English Language* in any of its versions between 1755, when it first appeared, and the fourth edition, revised by the author and published in 1773. What Johnson did have as an entry was the noun 'colony', but that had a very specific meaning, much narrower than the modern usage, as Johnson's examples show. It was very close to its classical origin, the Latin *colonia* – which meant a body of persons sent by the mother country to inhabit a distant place, and the specific site which they inhabited. Thus Dr Johnson could cite Carthage, a city, as a 'Trojan colony', but that did not imply, even allowing for the bad history in the example, that what moderns might call Tunisia had become a colonial country. Only by the late eighteenth century had it become fashionable to use it, at first most commonly with reference to the colonies in British America – as Edmund Burke did in his famous speech *On Conciliation with the Colonies* – and then more generally, as in Burke's 1796 reference to 'all our colonial councils'. The far commoner word in the sixteenth, seventeenth, and early eighteenth centuries for what post-1800 commentators would have called a colony was 'plantation'. It is cognate with the other term in the sense that colony derives through French from the Latin verb *colere*, which means to cultivate. 'Plantation' derives from the Latin *plantare*, which means to plant. The two terms were seen as exchangeable in the early seventeenth century, but the dominance of 'plantation' in the literature is marked. In English usage it was, in fact, much more appropriate, for it conveyed a clear dual message to the effect that these were communities planted by enterprise deriving from the national community, and also that their job was to plant and raise commercially desirable commodities.[1]

To define colonial wars purely with reference to such a narrow, if precise, definition of the arena would be as indefensible as the modern bad habit of slapping the adjective 'colonial' on a war of which the commentator particularly disapproves. In the sixteenth, seventeenth, and eighteenth centuries Western European states, whether republican or monarchical, often came into close contact with societies which were radically alien to their own political and cultural norms. They could do this on their own territorial margins, or through the consequences of long-range trade with or exploration of distant regions. The results of these contacts varied, but in a significant number of cases it proved possible to establish by persuasion, force, or settlement – or most often a mixture of the three – some form of supremacy over areas or activities which had not been traditionally part of the concern of the European parent-state. Where, as in the Orient, Europeans were normally incapable of conquest or where, as in West Africa, they were incapable of settlement for health reasons, they still strove to establish supremacies over the seaborne trade of these vast territories. Plantations were only one of the techniques used to establish or underpin these ascendancies. The successful seizure of control over alien populations by an invading warrior elite from the European state did not in itself constitute what contemporaries would have called a plantation, nor did it necessarily lead on to plantation unless the original inhabitants were destroyed or displaced and agriculturalists from the parent-state set up in their place. Those agriculturalists did not need to be peasants. They could be entrepreneurs using a slave labour force.

A good example of this attitude is provided by the 'consideration on the plantations' offered by Malachy Postlethwayt, a voluminous writer on commercial matters and policy in mid-eighteenth-century England, in one of his books, published in 1757. By then it was becoming commoner to talk about colonies rather than plantations, so his text moves between the two terms. A staunch opponent of systems of trade monopoly, Postlethwayt insists that 'No plantation colony ever did or ever will thrive under such management.' His view was that it was by vigorous competition amongst merchants and by competitively low costs assisted by such factors as 'cheapness of negroes' that plantations flourished.[2] The original Spanish conquests in the larger Caribbean islands went from being exploitative ascendancies over conquered populations to being plantation societies using slave labour, because the nature of early Spanish rule led to genocide of the indigenous inhabitants. Despite the spectacular fall in the size of the native population in what is now central Mexico and the less severe but still horrendous population loss in Peru in the first century of Spanish rule, the great mainland viceregalities of Spain in the Americas always remained areas in which the Spaniards provided, or bred, an elite which dominated local populations, so they were dominions rather than plantations.

Colonial wars in the early-modern era of European history were the episodes of violence associated with the establishment of these dominions (usually but not always overseas), trading supremacies on oceanic routes, and plantations or colonies; as well as the subsequent struggles between European states and their rival subjects for control of or access to such imperial prizes. The latter conflicts were almost invariably, until well into the eighteenth century, the by-products of massive military confrontations in Western Europe generated by duels between states or coalitions of states fighting for or against potential political or economic hegemony. Nevertheless, as wars, colonial campaigns – even when linked to European conflict – were different from what went on in Europe. They involved far smaller armies. The extreme cases of the conquest of the Aztec Empire by Hernan Cortes in 1519–21 with a force of only about 500 Spaniards with 14 cannon and 16 horses, or of the fall of the Inca Empire in 1531–33 to an even smaller force of 168 Spaniards with 4 cannon and 67 horses, may be dismissed as deceptive. The Inca territories were weakened by disease and split by civil war, while the Aztecs were overthrown primarily by large armies of revolting subject peoples who seized on the Spaniards as allies, and were subsequently betrayed by them.[3]

The whole concept of a military revolution leading to a vast expansion in military establishments in early-modern Europe is controversial. Military changes did occur in the era, as they had in the military culture of all others, but their effects were spread over very long periods and only fully affected a handful of states, basically the Western European hegemon, its challenger, and cockpit areas where the two champions fought it out. Exceptions like Sweden tended to fall by the wayside owing to lack of resources to play the great power game indefinitely. Total numbers of troops funded by one of the greater monarchies in time of war went up by about 1700 into the low hundreds of thousands. It has to be said that field army sizes before the wars of the French Revolution and Napoleon never approached such figures. On any one front, it was difficult to feed and otherwise supply a force of over about 50,000, and such a force required a vast logistical tail which severely limited its mobility. Large forces were fielded for the odd crucial battle, but Frederick the Great never led an army larger than the 65,000 men he commanded before Prague in 1757, and he fought four of his major engagements with armies under 25,000 strong. The best generals of the period around 1750 were unanimous in saying that 40,000–50,000 troops were about as many as a commander could effectively control.[4] Compared with such a figure, even the armies which fought the climacteric colonial campaigns of the old Europe were very small. In the Battle of the Plains of Abraham fought outside Quebec on 13 September 1759, the opposing generals, the French marquis de Montcalm and the British Major General James Wolfe, both commanded, so far as historians can judge, about the same number of troops – 4500.[5]

These were very large forces indeed by the standards of English commitment in other and earlier colonial conflicts. England was, of all Western European early-modern monarchies of any significance, for long the one which was least affected by the pressures of unavoidable military competition with a formidable and neighbouring state. It had lost its natural Anglo-French orientation, which it had had since the Norman Conquest of 1066, when Lancastrian France, the proud heritage of the victories of Henry V, had collapsed in the fifteenth century. There was no need for a standing army after that. English administrators developed the habit of thinking of their monarchy as an island. Shakespeare's 'sceptered isle' is merely one expression of a concept which was total nonsense, and which has been repeated *ad nauseam* because scholars have a tendency to be fixated by resounding rubbish in an easily available source high in the literary canon. Tudor England had a highly centralised form of government well adapted to the unique circumstances of the centre and south-east of England, but the monarchy and the English ethnic community had distant extensive and extremely difficult land frontiers. The most obvious one was the 110 miles of Anglo–Scottish border situated 300 miles from London, which was the core of the political establishment's social world. Vastly longer were the hundreds of miles of frontiers between England in Ireland, the Lordship of Ireland, and the complex of units which made up the Irish part of the Gaidhealtachd, the kinship-based world of the autonomous Gaelic-speaking peoples. There was also a convoluted internal ethnic frontier within Wales, not to mention a lesser one of the same kind in a Cornwall where a Celtic tongue was still widely spoken. The borders with Scotland and the Irish Gaidhealtachd were extremely unstable. Neither ,the king of Scots (as his defeat and death at Flodden in 1513 underlined) nor *a fortiori* the chiefs of the Gaidhealtachd could endanger the core territory of the English monarchy, but raiding across the frontiers of the Englishry was endemic. From the 1490s, the new Tudor dynasty cooperated closely with great regional marcher magnates such as the Percys and the Lords Dacre on the north-west frontier and the earls of Kildare in the Lordship of Ireland, itself essentially an English marcher land, reinforcing the considerable local power which these men could place at the service of the Crown with royal authority and resources. It was an economical and sensible course to follow, but a breakdown of relations between the Crown and two regional noble dynasties in 1534–35 was the first sign of a major crisis. This was between the increasingly faction-ridden royal administration, cocooned in the south-east of England while pouring millions into a futile bid to re-create the Anglo-French empire of Henry V, and the neglected frontiers of the English nation.

The first crisis with Kildare and Dacre was more the result of a unique mixture of accident and intrigue than part of a preconceived executive plan. Both families to some extent recovered politically after the death of Henry VIII. Nevertheless, it is significant that the new deputy sent out to replace Kildare as the governor of the Lordship of Ireland was originally intended to be supported by 150 troops and a pretentiously titled pamphlet. That was a more accurate measure of Crown commitment to a part of English territory where low-level colonial war on the frontiers was endemic than the larger number of troops which eventually had to be sent to contain the internal rebellion engineered by the disgruntled Gerald Fitzgerald, ninth Earl of Kildare.[6] Even long after the development of very extensive English plantations in North America, it was most unusual for the Crown to accept any large-scale military commitment there. The force of over 1000 redcoats which Charles II despatched to Virginia in 1676 to contain the effects of Bacon's rebellion was much the largest force which any English monarch had ever landed in a North American colony. Bacon's rebellion was not in fact a rebellion against the Crown as such. Bacon was dead by the time the troops landed, and they were removed fairly quickly on the grounds that there really was not enough for them to do.[7] Even allowing for the fact that much colonial fighting was done by militias and other irregular formations, it remains striking that such small forces produced on the whole much more decisive results than the large armies which fought protracted wars in the cockpits of Western Europe.

It has been argued that 'After the Renaissance . . . much of Western Europe seemed locked into a military system in which offence and defence were almost exactly balanced'.[8] Much of this argument hinges on the spread of the elaborate bastion-defended artillery forts with thick, low walls sunk behind moats, which reached their peak of development under Louis XIV in the complex of frontier defences designed for him by the greatest of French military engineers, Marshal Vauban. Certainly, these defences could impose massive delays on the progress of early-modern armies. In 1940, Vauban's 200-year-old forts around Bergues and Gravelines played a key role in delaying Hitler's divisions and allowing a large part of the British Expeditionary Force to escape from Dunkirk, another place fortified by Vauban.[9] Yet the whole idea that European war in the early-modern era became more and more indecisive has been queried, with some justice, for there were indeed decisive battles, campaigns, and wars. Monarchs entertained very extreme military ambitions. Louis XIV, for example, set out in 1672 to erase the Dutch Republic from the map of Europe. France had by the 1680s dethroned Spain as the hegemonic Western European power, and Sweden was decisively demoted from great power status by the peace settlement of 1721 at the end of the Great Northern War. On the other hand, as Louis XIV found in 1672, it was virtually impossible to achieve total, obliterative victory over a rival in Western Europe, if only because other states became very worried about the implications of this for the general structure of international power.

Much more dramatic and irreversible changes of fortune occurred in colonial wars of every kind. Spaniards totally destroyed the great Amerindian ascendancies which they attacked, thrusting their mental worlds into an irrecoverable past. The English in Virginia reduced the once numerous coastal Algonquin Indians to mere shadows on the land long before the end of the seventeenth century. In the eighteenth century, the British were permanently to conquer the French colonial empire on the St Lawrence, and they also decisively destroyed the French as a power in India. There were cases, and important ones, where expectations of dramatic change through violence in a colonial context proved delusive. Thus, the Dutch, French, English, and later the British were to find it virtually impossible to wrench from imperial Spain control over the mixed-blood or mestizo cultures which had been created on the ruins of the conquered Amerindian empires of Central and South America. Nevertheless, the generalisation holds in more cases than not that small forces in a colonial context produced more decisive results than much larger ones in Europe. This was particularly significant for a monarchy like England which for all of the sixteenth and most of the seventeenth century just did not have a serious standing army by continental European standards. Nor did it in the sixteenth century participate in such developments as the new artillery-age bastion-based fortification techniques, apart from installing them in Berwick-upon-Tweed and a couple of places on the south coast of England.

The lack of a large professional army was to some extent compensated for by the existence of a relatively big English navy. Throughout the sixteenth century, the Tudor Navy Royal seldom consisted of more than 30 ships. Henry VIII, who was genuinely interested in naval issues, built up the biggest royal fleet of the sixteenth century by 1546, when it could muster 58 ships, but this growth was funded by the confiscated wealth of the monasteries and was unsustainable when that source of revenue ran dry. In 1588, in the face of the Great Armada of Philip II of Spain, the English Crown had only 34 royal ships, and only 197 altogether in Crown pay. The other 163 in service either volunteered or were levied from specific ports. The Navy Royal was seen not as a national institution so much as the personal property of the monarch. The Jacobean and Caroline periods in the early seventeenth century saw no fundamental change in the situation, and the next phase of naval expansion in England came with the English Civil War and the Commonwealth, when confiscated royalist properties enabled a republican regime to build large numbers of specialist warships and fight a naval war against the Dutch. Even this phase of expansion began to run into fiscal trouble when the sale of royalist assets started to tail off. It was in fact a long and complex path to the professional British Royal Navy of the Napoleonic era with its over 1000 specialised warships served by some 130,000 men.[10]

What made the Tudor Navy Royal formidable from the days of Henry VIII to the era of the Great Armada, despite its extremely modest proportions, was the absence of rival European navies of comparable size. The king of Spain did maintain substantial galley forces in the Mediterranean Sea, where he faced a permanent naval challenge from the Ottoman Turks, but prior to 1570 he had in fact no permanent Atlantic fleet at all. In that year was established an Atlantic squadron of 12 small galleons known as the *Armada Réal de la Guarda de la Carrera de las Indias*. Its function, as its name suggests, was to guard the *flotas* which sailed between Seville and the Indies, and which on their return voyages carried the vital bullion cargoes. They proved very successful in their main function. Only in the late 1570s and early 1580s did Philip II embark on a building programme in northern Spain which produced eventually the eight larger galleons which were to form the squadron of Castile in the 1588 Armada. Designed to stay at sea for six months if need be during escort or piracy suppression missions, they sacrificed speed and armament to endurance. Indeed, Philip was lucky that his accession to the throne of Portugal in 1580 had given him the nine two-decker heavily gunned oceanic warships of the squadron of Portugal which included the awesome bulk of the 1000-ton *San Martin*. They were the core of the fighting section of an armada which in 1588 was essentially an escorted convoy.[11]

The defeat of the optimistically named 1588 *Felicissima Armada* by a combination of English action and weather did not mark the end of Spanish oceanic naval power: quite the reverse. Between 1589 and 1598, the Spanish Crown financed the building of forty-odd galleons, starting with the 'Twelve Apostles' built from 1589 to 1591. Galleons for Atlantic service were built for Spain in the Mediterranean, though not all proved seaworthy.[12] England's naval power went into relative decline. As one author has put it: 'The Armada marked the rebirth, not the extinction, of Spanish sea power as the lost ships were replaced with better ones, and the Spanish Main refortified against attack.'[13] So there is no way the slippery concept of naval supremacy can be used as a *deus ex machina* to explain the pattern of England's colonial wars in the sixteenth and seventeenth centuries. Only in the 1690s, when the French abandoned the attempt to create a superior battlefleet and concentrated on a *guerre de course* by privateers against English commercial shipping, can it be said that a sort of naval supremacy lay in the hands of 'the Maritime Powers' (i.e. England and the United Netherlands). That the early nineteenth century saw an unprecedented degree of naval supremacy in British hands does not mean that such a supremacy can be taken as axiomatic throughout even much of the eighteenth century.

In any case, very large concentrations of ships, whether royal or private, were comparatively rare in colonial waters. Many of the biggest and most heavily gunned early-seventeenth-century battleships were not good sailors, and hardly fit for oceanic operations outside the summer season and the Narrow Seas on the approaches to Western Europe. This was particularly true of the crankier battleships of the Jacobean and Caroline English Navy Royal. Obviously, English naval power owed a huge debt to private shipping, whether operating autonomously or on hire to the Crown. Yet the most aggressive and predatory of private operators did not usually operate on a large scale; whilst the English maritime corporate body which did operate on the largest scale, the East India Company – chartered by Queen Elizabeth in 1600 – was genuinely anxious to avoid unnecessary violence and after 1604 did keep its focus firmly on trade, not dominion. In eastern waters in the seventeenth and early eighteenth centuries it became most unusual to see formidable concentrations of European ships and guns bent on aggressive purposes. Most states were not inclined to hazard the game of forcible power-projection on a substantial scale over vast distances. In an age of wind and sail it was a hazardous enough game even in European waters, as Philip II found out when he assembled three more armadas after that of 1588. He managed to launch two of them, one in 1596, one in 1597. Both were blown to pieces by Atlantic gales. The one exception to all of this in Asian waters was the Dutch East India Company, which was founded in 1602. Sir William Temple, the former English ambassador at The Hague who published in 1673 a celebrated set of *Observations upon the United Provinces of the Netherlands*, remarked in what were almost a set of platitudes on 'the mighty advance they have made towards engrossing the whole Commerce of the East-Indies'. He knew that this had been achieved by war, the forcing of exclusive trade contracts on native regimes, and massive fortifications to secure footholds. Temple then very shrewdly stressed the way in which the Dutch were here the exception which proved the general European rule for their:

> East Indy Company . . . have managed it like a Commonwealth rather
> than a Trade; and thereby raised a State in the Indies, governed indeed by
> the Orders of the Company, but otherwise appearing to those Nations like
> a Soveraign State, making War and Peace with their greatest Kings, and
> able to bring to Sea Forty or Fifty Men of War, and Thirty thousand men
> at Land, by the modestest computations.[14]

By the eighteenth century it is possible to argue with a great deal of plausibility that 'Decisiveness in conflict among European states was most clearly demonstrated in naval conflict', and that comment is quite compatible with an admission that obliterative victory in sea battles was still an extreme rarity until the very latest part of the eighteenth century and the beginning of the nineteenth.[15] The ability to access sea routes and possession of the resources needed to use them could be decisively important when combined with an ability to deny such facilities to others. However, for most of the early-modern period England was far from being an oceanic hegemon, and – although historians have traditionally dated the origins of the British Empire to the late Tudor period, with heavy stress upon growing national self-consciousness – there is much to be said for the opposite point of view: that there was little or no significant overseas imperial development before the death of Elizabeth and that one English identity is a naive concept in the face of the violent conflict of different English identities within that ethnic community in the sixteenth century. Literary scholars devoted to 'the new historicism' have somewhat arbitrarily conscripted vast ranges of contemporary Elizabethan writing into a 'generational enterprise' in which sundry 'discursive communities' hammered out together, with inevitable contradictions in minor detail, a new sense of imperial Englishness, of whose scope it is alleged that 'England's overseas expansion depended on the participation of merchants, so mercantile interests were included'.[16] It has been justly pointed out that this sort of argument is essentially circular.[17]

Francis Bacon, Viscount St Albans, a former lord chancellor of England, published in 1625 the most complete edition of his *Essays*, with a fulsome piece of flattery of the Duke of Buckingham, Lord High Admiral of England, in his Epistle Dedicatory. Bacon claimed that this, his most popular work, came 'home to men's business and bosoms'. The essay 'Of Empire' has nothing in it which would have stirred the heart of a Victorian British imperialist. It is about kingly power and its exercise in the face of rival monarchs and potentially subversive subjects. Behind this interpretation of the term lies the Latin source *imperium*, which means 'power to command'. Bacon also included an essay 'Of Plantations' which is mainly about the difficulty of establishing an overseas agricultural colony. There is very little in it about war, apart from advice to avoid being used by indigenous peoples as a tool in their own internal struggles. Behind the essay patently lies the experience of the infant Virginia, especially in such advice as not to establish settlement in unhealthy low-lying places. A better description of Jamestown, Virginia's first capital, would be difficult to find.[18] Of the 1622 Indian rising and massacre there is no mention. Nevertheless, it is clear that the experience of wars on the peripheries of Englishness – wars which modern historians would regard as colonial, and which were marked on occasion, for a complex set of reasons, by an unusual degree of decisiveness despite the comparatively modest forces involved – did deeply influence the endless struggle to define English identity. The crucial point to grasp is that this was not a linear process going from strength to strength. That was a view largely manufactured in the late nineteenth and early twentieth centuries. For example, Sir Henry Newbolt, a lawyer turned poet, made his literary name when he published his poem 'Drake's Drum' in the *St James's Gazette* in 1896. He followed it up with a collection of verse whose title *Admirals All* underlined the extent to which he saw a succession of imperial wars as the key to the rise of the Victorian identity of, to quote the title of another of his verse collections, *The Island Race*. Anyone familiar with the refrain of 'Admirals All' (which starts 'Admirals all for England's sake') will be aware that the identity in question was English.

This concept of an apostolic succession of identity-forging imperial warriors running continuously from the Elizabethan era was taken up and propagated by a myriad writers, but perhaps by none with more spirit and panache than the imperialist boys' writer G.A. Henty (1832–1902), whose novels run the gamut from *Under Drake's Flag* (1883) to *With Roberts to Pretoria (A Tale of the South African War)* – which came out in the year of his death. In between, the Victorian boy could visit vicariously the battlefields of Culloden or Plassey, not to mention being thrilled *By Sheer Pluck* during the Ashanti War – English pluck, of course.[19] We know, thanks to the illuminating scholarship of Professor John Mackenzie,[20] that these imperial resonances were assiduously propagated by the Westminster executive of the United Kingdom until deep into the 1950s, when that executive, which had never been willing to sink its autonomy into a wider imperial federal structure, knew full well they were anachronistic irrelevances. The British Empire–Commonwealth had become an incoherent strategic liability by the 1930s, one that the UK would on balance have been better without, but the 'Land of Hope and Glory' syndrome encouraged deference to their government on the part of those who remained British, and that was the name of the game.

When the imperial theme became too much of a nonsense to be plausibly sounded, there were other well-established historical traditions which served the same purpose of buttressing acquiescence towards a particular political tradition. Two men of conservative and authoritarian convictions, both of central European origins, sum it all up. Both fell deeply in love with the English Establishment. Sir Lewis Namier spent a lifetime encouraging an obsessive pursuit of the history and prosopography of the lower house of a parliament whose function is to rubber-stamp and legitimise the actions of the executive which controls it. Sir Geoffrey Elton more straightforwardly preached the gospel that the executive had always ruled and that the main virtue of the English was that they did what their government told them to do. This relentless drive to give Westminster an 800-year ancestry is matched by the very similar attempt by other historians to give the nationalist regime in Dublin an 800-year ancestry. Whether the attempt be to create a triumphalist ideology going back to Brian Boru or to Alfred the Great, the aggressive cultural imperialism implicit in both is similar in purpose: to enable an existing and powerful political tradition to stamp on and eliminate alternative and reasonable views and traditions. Ironically, those who most doggedly resist criticism of their selective plundering of the past to serve contemporary political manipulation in Ireland have been known to cite the activities of that adopted modern English nationalist Elton as justification, on the grounds that they are playing a version of his game. It is rather a case of the pot using the kettle to prove they are both black.[21]

These traditions are disastrous in the context of an attempt to understand the role of colonial conflicts in shaping the identities, several of them English, to be found within the orbit of the Crown of England, later of Britain and Ireland, in the early-modern era. They deprive us of the basic human dignity of a critical insight into the mental prison which is the 'imagined community' of a given definition of national identity at a particular time. They do this by a teleological approach whose tunnel vision fails, in the words of that mordant commentator P.J. O'Rourke, to 'give war a chance'. War is the most dangerous of *djinns* once it escapes from the magic lamp. Often enough it is an uncontrollable spirit, not a dramatic prop in a play with only one possible ending. It is therefore crucially important to grasp that the origins of the early-modern English monarchy lay in a medieval society structured for war, a society itself intrinsically colonial in nature.

The Tudor Crown was the heir of the Norman Conquest of 1066. It was a creole regime shaped by denizened heirs of medieval barons from continental Europe who had brought feudal kingship to the offshore archipelago.

In feudal England and in Ireland, as it began to develop about a century later, their conquest was similarly the point of reference at which relevant history began. There is nothing odd about this, exactly the same world viewpoint which saw the conquest as the point of reference from which relevant politics begins was typical of the creole patriots who are now seen as the fathers of the independent nations of Latin America.[22] Despite official modern propaganda about the creation of a mestizo or mixed Spanish–Amerindian culture in colonial Mexico, the whole point is that colonial Mexico was a conquest-derived hierarchy, not a blend. Different groups even ate different cuisines to confirm their places within that hierarchy. Wheat and partridges were for the heirs of the conquerors; maize for Amerindians.[23]

Conquest was inherent in the nature of the feudal society which dominated that part of Christendom which adhered to the Latin rite and the papal supremacy in the medieval era. Its warrior aristocracy was originally centred on the old Frankish territories which had been the core of Charlemagne's empire, which means they may be described in modern terms as central West Europeans. From there a military technology based on the armoured mounted knight, the castle, crossbows to defend it, and siege engines to attack it, enabled them to expand and colonise new territories on almost every front from the tenth century onwards. With them they carried their intolerant creed, their characteristic silver coinage, and their Latin administrative language. It was an aristocratic society practising primogeniture whose younger sons were always potential predators. Since many of their original military techniques were over time transferable to their enemies, the process of expansion was uneven and complex. When dynastic states emerged as the dominant political form in the early-modern era they still were served by aristocratic elites whose marginal members preserved the ethos of a predatory feudal warrior class. There was ironic justice in the fact that the sixteenth-century Chinese term for the Spanish and Portuguese Europeans who reached China by sea was borrowed from the Arabic word *faranga*, which derived from the Frankish knights whom the Islamic world had met in the Crusades, the first Western European bid for overseas conquest.[24]

By the accession of Henry VII to the English throne in 1485, the heroic ages of feudal expansion seemed to be over. There was no question of knights conquering whole kingdoms for their prince, as Norman knights had conquered England and Sicily in the Middle Ages. Nor was it possible for individual barons to carve out fresh ascendancies as the Normans had on the Welsh marches. The conquest of all Wales was an accomplished fact. Equally, the sensational and independent progress made by Norman-Welsh barons in Ireland in the period 1169–71 was not going to occur again. They were invited over by Dermot MacMurrough, King of Leinster, and their success in gaining control of Leinster and Meath had forced the Plantagenet monarch Henry II to cross over from England in October 1171, not to conquer Ireland but to ensure that an independent Norman principality did not emerge on his flank. The logical next step would have been for its ruler to turn his back on the poor lands of the west and use his new resources to start playing for higher stakes back in England.[25] By the end of the fifteenth century, the Lordship of Ireland which Henry II erected in 1171 was still very much there, but transfer of military technology on its frontiers had created a state of virtual deadlock between the descendants of Norman barons and the still autonomous Gaelic principalities.

The Europe of the Renaissance was not only a place where exciting cultural developments were occurring, but also an extremely violent place. Intellectuals from the French courtier and ambassador Philippe de Commines around 1500 to the English courtier, soldier, and poet Sir Philip Sidney in 1581 lamented the fact that armed conflict appeared to be universal. Kings of France like Henry II and Henry III in the second half of the sixteenth century openly endorsed the common contemporary view that foreign wars were a way of controlling population and keeping potentially seditious nobles busy. On a central core of rivalry between France and the Habsburgs, and assisted by the religious clashes generated by the Reformation and Counter-Reformation, the great European monarchies raised a culture of constant conflict.[26] The large professional armies generated by the early-modern warfare state were an ideal habitat for the warrior caste who, far from fading away before 'the rise of the bourgeoisie', officered these forces on a more and more exclusive basis right up to 1800, and beyond in certain cases. Especially for the numerous poorer gentry or lesser nobility, violence, in royal service, remained by far the most promising, if hazardous, fast track to material advancement and enhanced noble status.[27] The trouble with England in such a world was that normally it hardly had an army, and certainly not much of a standing one by the standards of other Western European monarchies. Englishmen started fighting one another in 1642 over control of the county militias, because they were the only sub-stantial bodies of armed men in the country. How then did the natural tendency for aspiring lesser gentry or impoverished nobles to seek salvation through violence find expression?

Part of the answer must be: 'with difficulty'. Opportunities did occur in the sense that when the Crown's demands provoked a regional aristocracy to rebellion – as in Cornwall in 1497 and 1549, over taxation and the new English prayer book respectively – the predominantly Cornish-speaking gentry of this still distinctive land was superseded by or assimilated to a new

English gentry like the Carews, Courtenays, Pollards, Tremaynes, and Killigrews. These were to keep close links with the court under Elizabeth and play a key role in the naval war against Catholic Spain after 1585, a war which offered them private profit on a limitless sea frontier. The exploitation of court connections in a period of turmoil by one section of the aristocracy to enable them to eat another section was to be a recurring theme in the Elizabethan era, notably in the plantation of Munster, but whether this should be seen as the inevitable expansion of something called 'the Renaissance State' may be doubted.[28] It could verge on political anarchy and certainly had a cannibalistic dimension to it.

Wales is an extremely interesting case in point. By escheat, forfeiture, and purchase the marcher lords had largely been replaced by the Crown by the time Wales was formally united with England after 1536. There were few great magnates in Wales and though the second Earl of Pembroke, as lord president of the Council of Wales and the Marches, was an important figure in the Elizabethan administration of Wales, there was no replacement for him of comparable stature after he died in 1601.[29] The sixteenth and seventeenth centuries were an age when a Welsh gentry invented itself from the much more numerous ranks of those who claimed some form of gentility. In a wild scramble for office and revenues, the lucky ones turned themselves into the cooperating class without which the Tudors or Stuarts could not administer Wales. Inevitably, this meant that the Welsh gentry class exploited its Crown connections to thrust into every frontier of perceived potential profit. Sir John Perrot was no Welshman, but he had extensive estates in south Wales, and when he went to Ireland as deputy he took with him a phalanx of 'Castle Welshmen' whose prominence in the Dublin administration understandably enraged the resident Old English nobility. Welsh gentry were prominent in the Munster plantation in the 1580s, though it has to be said that one of them, Sir William Herbert, finally denounced those who had turned it into a brutal and anarchic racket. The Ulster war at the end of Elizabeth's reign took a heavy toll of Welsh lives, yet there was substantial backing in south Wales (where he had important estates) for the Earl of Essex, the Elizabethan faction leader who openly sought to dominate royal government with the spirit and personnel of a warrior nobility. Court faction politics was essentially a form of gambling for those who attached themselves to the protagonists. The rebellion, fall, and execution of Essex in 1601 was a heavy blow to the hopes of many Welsh gentry. They were fortunate indeed that by 1603 the English throne was occupied by a new Scots monarch who had been an Essex sympathiser, James I.[30]

King James was most unusual in sharing the views of that minority of Christian humanists led by Erasmus which had pointed out the contradiction implicit in the worshippers of a pacific incarnation being habitual practitioners of murderous violence. Normally the legitimacy of war, if only as an arena where the God of battles could pass judgement, was not questioned. Popes praised military virtue and sought their ends by force. Gunners invoked St Barbara as they loaded their cannon.[31] Anglicans were not admirers of popes nor likely to rely much on St Barbara, but most of them shared the majority view of humanist culture that heroic virtue in war was a desirable trait. Erasmian pacifism was dead in Elizabethan England. The pulpits denounced the outrageous heresies of the only surviving pacifist sect – the anabaptists. Though England was an unmilitary country in which it was difficult to raise armies, the church taught in the spirit of Roger Ascham, who wrote in his treatise on archery that 'God is well pleased with wyse and wittie feates of warre'. Provided the war was a just one licensed by the prince, the spoils of war were not a theological problem, for Richard Bernard preached that 'God allowed Israel to take what they did win in their just wars'.[32] The bulk of King James' loyal subjects were firmly in this hitherto orthodox tradition. In so far as they were aware of their monarch's pacific views, they must have regarded them as yet another sign of His Sacred Majesty's extreme eccentricity, if not indeed of his cowardice, which was blatant.

Captain John Smith, a famous name in the history of early Virginia, not least because of his own relentless self-advertisement, published in the third book of his *Generall Historie of Virginia, New England and the Summer Isles* (1624) a passage which expresses unconsciously exactly what the violent adventurers who hung around courts hoped for. It comes in a continuous narrative of the settlement of Virginia assembled by 'William Simons, Doctour of Divinitie'. The good doctor felt obliged to explain that:

> It might well be thought, a Countrie so faire (as Virginia is) and a
> people so tractable, would long ere this have beene quietly possessed, to
> the satisfaction of the adventurers, & the eternizing of the memory of
> those that effected it. But because all the world doe see a defailement; this
> following Treatise shall give satisfaction to all indifferent Readers, how the
> business hath bin carried: where no doubt they will easily understand and
> answer to their question, how it came to passe there was no better speed
> and successe in those proceedings.[33]

Behind the negative image which is to be explained away lies the positive, ideal image of a royal licence to lands currently enjoyed by others; a quick seizure against just enough violence to sustain a claim to heroic stature; acquiescence by a docile peasantry; and then the noble life sustained by their work and sweetened by the sycophantic histories of humanist scholars.

In the English case matters seldom worked out that way, as the passage cited testifies. Instead of seeing England's colonial wars throughout the early-modern period as the inevitable outward expansion of a taut homo-genous nation under the best of governments, it is much more consonant with the evidence to realise that very often the reverse is the case. For an extensive people with deeply seated regional variations in their culture, the English had rather a bad government which combined to a bizarre degree metropolitan arrogance and south-east of England parochialism. It had a mischievous and destructive tradition of over-centralisation of decision taking without a willingness to consult interests which might press for modification in the policies first mooted at the centre. The high-handed demands of the Crown were often therefore deeply divisive, and to make a bad situation worse, were often not backed by sufficient power to push them through quickly and irreversibly but rather persisted in stubbornly over lengthy periods without decisive backing, in such a way as to maximise opposition and resentment. Colonial settlement was as often as not a result of the divided nature of an English nation whose identity was in turmoil. Colonial wars were more frequently the consequence of failure and miscal-culations than of purposeful planning.

Any series of decisive military victories tends to be interpreted by those who later identify with the victors as either providential, or the product of ingrained social and moral superiority. As that master of the concise, penetrating phrase about British imperial history, Archie Thornton has said: 'Every doctrine of imperialism devised by men is a consequence of their second thoughts. But empires are not built by men troubled by second thoughts.'[34]

Whatever late-Victorian British jingoists may have believed to the con-trary, discontinuity and defeat were commonplace in the story of English and then British overseas settlement and trade before 1800, and the United Kingdom's 'mid-Victorian pinnacle'[35] of imperial influence, was the prod-uct of exceptional, transitory circumstances, not of inexorable destiny. All empires mythologise. A more enduring imperial structure, the United States of America, is no exception. The future president Andrew Jackson's victory over British forces in the Battle of New Orleans in 1815 was hailed as a triumph of hawk-eyed, leathery-faced, democratic frontiersmen with their Kentucky rifles, mowing down the British ranks coming at them and thus defending a new, egalitarian society. In fact, the battle was won by cannonfire and visibility at the height of the action was so poor that no 'Kentucky hunter' could have seen well enough to exercise his legendary talents. Nor were they needed, since the tactical incompetence of the British commander, the Irish General Pakenham, presented American cannon and musket fire with a massed, largely immobile target.[36] Jackson was, as ever, a very lucky as well as a very brave man. Nor was American society in the Jacksonian era egalitarian. Income differences, even between white people in different social classes, were huge. The very rich had fortunes fully comparable with those of their richest European contemporaries. Intragenerational social mobility was very limited, and though the common man was courted at elections, America was run by a propertied elite, of which General Jackson was an exceptionally formidable member.[37]

So we must beware of the imaginative reconstruction of events, especially military events, by either imperialist apologists or apologists for successor regimes reaching out for moral hegemony, often with a barely concealed agenda of cultural genocide for elements in their society of which they disapprove, or more accurately, hate. The English colonial wars of the early-modern era underline the autonomy of the war experience; the fallible nature of man; and the transitory, deceptive quality of his self-images. The plasticity of identities is an unpopular doctrine in Washington DC, Westminster, or Dublin, but a fact in the history of the English-speaking peoples. Those who started or blundered into these wars can often be seen in retrospect to have had only a limited understanding of where they were going or who they might be when they came out, if they came out, at the other end. In studying them, we must give war a chance to be its unpredictable self.

Notes and references

1. *The Oxford English Dictionary* (Clarendon Press, 2nd edn, Oxford, 1989), Vol. 3, entry for 'colonial', and Vol. 11, entry for 'plantation'. Eric Partridge, *Origins: A short etymological dictionary of modern English* (Routledge and Kegan Paul, London, 1958), entry for 'colonial'.

2. Malachy Postlethwayt, *Britain's Commercial Interest Explained and Improved* (eds. D. Browne *et al.*, 2 vols., London, 1757), Vol. I, pp. 153, 159, and 161.

3. Ross Hassig, *Mexico and the Spanish Conquest* (Longman, London, 1994).

4. Christopher Duffy, *The Military Experience of the Age of Reason* (Routledge and Kegan Paul, London, 1987), pp. 15–16.

5. C.P. Stacey, *Quebec, 1759: The siege and the battle* (Macmillan of Canada, Toronto, 1959), pp. 140–41.

6. Steven G. Ellis, *Tudor Frontiers and Noble Power: The making of the British state* (Clarendon Press, Oxford, 1995).

7. Stephen Saunders Webb, *1676: The end of American independence* (Alfred A. Knopf, New York, 1984).

8. Geoffrey Parker, *The Military Revolution: Military innovation and the rise of the West, 1500–1800* (Cambridge University Press, Cambridge, 1988), p. 14.

9. Vincent Scully, *Architecture: The natural and the man made* (Harvill, London, 1991), pp. 308–10.

10. Michael Duffy, 'The Foundations of British Naval Power' in Michael Duffy, ed., *The Military Revolution and the State 1500–1800* (Exeter Studies in History No. 1, University of Exeter, 1980), pp. 49–81.

11. Colin Martin and Geoffrey Parker, *The Spanish Armada* (Hamish Hamilton, London, 1988), pp. 35–37.

12. The best overall survey of these matters is to be found in the introductions by M.J. Rodriguez-Salgado to the relevant sections of the official catalogue, *Armada 1588–1988. An international exhibition to commemorate the Spanish Armada* (Penguin Books in Association with the National Maritime Museum, London, 1988). There is now a detailed study by David Goodman, *Spanish Naval Power 1589–1665: Reconstruction and defeat* (Cambridge University Press, Cambridge, 1997).

13. Felipe Fernandez-Armesto, *The Spanish Armada: The experience of war in 1588* (Oxford University Press, Oxford, 1988), p. 269.

14. Sir William Temple, *Observations upon the United Provinces of the Netherlands* (printed by A. Maxwell for Sa. Gellibrand, London, 1673), pp. 203–04.

15. Jeremy Black, *European Warfare 1660–1815* (UCL Press, London, pbk edn, 1994), pp. 78–79.

16. Richard Helgerson, *Forms of Nationhood: The Elizabethan writing of England* (University of Chicago Press, Chicago, IL, 1992), *passim*, the quotation is on p. 11.

17. *Vide* the trenchant review of Helgerson's *Forms of Nationhood* by Simon Adams in *Times Literary Supplement*, 30 October 1992, p. 23.

18. *Vide* essays XIX, 'Of Empire' and XXXIII, 'Of Plantations' in the 1625 edition reprinted in *Bacon's Essays* (Library of English Classics, Macmillan, London, 1900).

19. Guy Arnold, *Held Fast for England: G.A. Henty, imperialist boys' writer* (Hamish Hamilton, London, 1980).

20. John M. Mackenzie, *Propaganda and Empire: The manipulation of British public opinion 1880–1960* (Manchester University Press, Manchester, 1984).

21. *Vide* the wrath of Brendan Bradshaw against Steven G. Ellis, and especially the citation of Elton's bizarre Cambridge inaugural as justification by Bradshaw, in *English Historical Review*, 114 (1989), pp. 472–74.

22. D.A. Brading, *The First America: The Spanish monarchy, creole patriots and the liberal state 1492–1867* (Cambridge University Press, Cambridge, 1991).

23. Rachel Laudan and Jeffrey M. Pilcher, 'Chiles, Chocolate, and Race in New Spain: Glancing backward to Spain or looking forward to Mexico?', *Eighteenth Century Life*, 23, n.s., 2 (1999), pp. 59–70.

24. Robert Bartlett, *The Making of Europe: Conquest, colonization and culture change 950–1350* (Penguin Books, London, 1994).

25. J.C. Beckett, *The Anglo-Irish Tradition* (Faber and Faber, London, 1976), pp. 13–18.

26. John Hale, *The Civilization of Europe in the Renaissance* (HarperCollins, London, pbk edn, 1993), pp. 94–106.

27. Christopher Storrs and H.M. Scott, 'The Military Revolution and the European Nobility, *c.* 1600–1800', *War in History*, 3 (1996), pp. 1–41.

28. A.L. Rowse, *The Expansion of Elizabethan England* (Macmillan, London, 1955), is the classic statement of the view that Elizabethan expansion was an inevitable consequence of the development of a modern Renaissance state.

29. Hugh Thomas, *A History of Wales 1485–1660* (University of Wales Press, Cardiff, 1972), pp. 48–49 and 183; and Glanmor Williams, *Recovery, Reorientation and Reformation: Wales, c. 1415–1642* (Oxford History of Wales, Oxford and Cardiff, 1987).

30. A.H. Dodd, *Studies in Stuart Wales* (University of Wales Press, Cardiff, 1971), Chaps. 1 and 3.

31. J.R. Hale, 'War and Public Opinion in Renaissance Italy', reprinted in J.R. Hale, *Renaissance War Studies* (Hambledon Press, London, 1983), pp. 359–87.

32. *Idem*, 'Incitement to Violence? English Divines on the Theme of War, 1578 to 1631', *ibid.*, pp. 487–517.

33. This passage is conveniently available in the anthology edited by Mary Ann Radzinowicz, *American Colonial Prose: John Smith to Thomas Jefferson* (Cambridge University Press, Cambridge, pbk edn, 1984), p. 42.

34. Archibald P. Thornton, *Doctrines of Imperialism* (Wiley, New York, 1965), p. 47.

35. The phrase is from R.K. Webb, *Modern England from the 18th Century to the Present* (Dod, Mead and Co., New York, 1968), p. 366.

36. John William Ward, *Andrew Jackson – Symbol for an Age* (Oxford University Press, New York, pbk edn, 1962), pp. 3–29.

37. Edward Pessen, *Jacksonian America: Society, personality and politics* (Dorsey Press, Homewood, IL, revised edn, 1978), pp. 77–100.

PART ONE

The Tudor Crown, the English Nation, and the Heritage of Anglo-Norman Expansionism 1550–1603

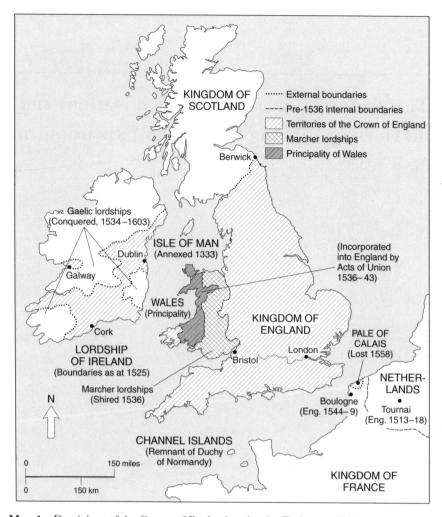

Map 1 Dominions of the Crown of England under the Tudors, *c.* 1540

CHAPTER ONE

Colonial Englishmen face up to the Tudors

The Tudor dynasty seized control of the Crown of England and of its core territory almost by accident. No rational observer can have been sure of the outcome when the young Henry Tudor, the future Henry VII, invaded England through Wales as the sole surviving viable leader of the aristocratic Lancastrian faction opposed to King Richard III. Of national identity in the modern sense, he was no clear-cut example, being by birth one quarter Welsh, one quarter French, and half English. His army at the decisive Battle of Bosworth had a large French contingent in it. This was not surprising as he had invaded from France, with significant aid from its monarch, Charles VIII. That there were a thousand soldiers from England's other traditional enemy, Scotland, in his ranks, owed much to the presence of Scots mercenaries in the service of the French Crown. Welsh supporters naturally came in, though not in the numbers Henry might have hoped for. There were exiled English nobles and their followers in the invasion force, and other noble adherents of Henry's Lancastrian faction joined him later, but Henry, like his army, was a product of cosmopolitan neo-feudal political banditry. His claim to the throne was dubious. Backing him was an extreme form of risk-taking in the field of redistributive industry.

That the gamble came off was due to the fact that his opponent, Richard III, proved to be an even bigger gambler than Henry, who had been forced into this invasion by the collapse of all other options. Richard chose to try to snatch a quick victory by heading a charge against the heart of his rival's army. It was not a necessary decision by a desperate man, as the Tudor propaganda of Shakespeare's *Richard III* would have us believe. It was a reckless throw by a very brave one. It nearly came off. Henry's standard-bearer was killed, and his dragon standard bit the dust. Henry himself came close to death, but in the event it was Richard III who was killed. Unhorsed, his crown was knocked from his helmet, his body was hacked to pieces, and his helmet smashed into his skull.[1]

The kingship which the inexperienced Henry so luckily seized that day in August 1485 was recognisably the feudal lordship of England established by force of arms at the Norman Conquest of 1066. Yet it was radically different from that lordship in the sense that it did not draw strength from or add crucial resources to continental metropolitan territories. That was the main significance of the original conquest of 1066 in European terms. That was why William the Conqueror was plunged for the rest of his life into war with an alarmed king of Scots and a deeply threatened king of France.[2] The Angevin counts who succeeded the Norman dukes as lords of this cross-Channel territorial complex were even greater rulers than their predecessors. King Henry II, the ablest head of their Plantagenet dynasty, was lord of a feudal empire very much made in France. Culturally he was French. England was a province.[3]

The Crown of England which Henry VII gained was the mere wreckage of this once great feudal structure. He was technically still duke of Normandy, but only in that surviving scrap of the once autonomous duchy which was the Channel Islands, and even they had been annexed to the Crown of England by his predecessor Henry III. Purely technically, the kings of England maintained a claim to the throne of France until the early nineteenth century. Originally, between 1316 and 1328, King Edward III of England had had a very good claim to the hereditary succession to the kingdom of France. In that sense, the arguments of Shakespeare's archbishop of Canterbury in the first act of *Henry V* to the effect that the French had manufactured false precedents to keep the English monarch off their throne have substance behind them. Yet in 1485 this was such an academic point that Charles VIII of France had granted Henry facilities to recruit troops. It was clear that Henry was no threat to France.

What was much less clear was the nature of the bounds of the community of the realm which in practice gave substance to the concept of the Crown of England. Allegiance is about the only word which can be used to describe the sense of 'Englishness' implied by such a body, and then only if used in a broader sense than the purely feudal, though that feudal relationship was still very important for large sections of the ruling classes within the community of that realm. The subjects of English kings were a complex of interlocking communities using different forms of law, speaking several different languages, and adhering to different customs, but they were united by a common status as subjects of the Crown of England and from that status they derived a common identity. It was seldom their only identity, but it was important to them.[4]

The regions subject to this monarchy were roughly patterned into core and peripheries. About the core there was no doubt, for it was south-east England. One of the factors which had destabilised the regime of Richard III was that his own power-base was a northern one and he lacked support in the south-east. Partly the south-east was dominant because of its agricultural wealth in an age of ineffective drainage techniques which made its lighter soils very desirable. There were, however, other reasons – such as the unique urban development which was London, and the continental background and obsessions of the royal court and government – which made proximity to France and the Low Countries of paramount importance to them. Some peripheries were more peripheral than others. On the mainland of Britain only the north of England was a true frontier zone, and it was a zone confronting a long-established Scottish kingdom with the same sort of feudal framework as England.

Internal frontiers had existed in other marginal regions of England-in-Britain, but by the early Tudor era these frontiers had really closed. Cornwall, for example – despite the survival, especially in its west, of the ancient Celtic tongue – had been for centuries securely associated with the English Crown. The Cornish rebellion of 1497 had been against taxation for the defence of the northern frontier against the Scots, and the Cornish rising of 1549 was against the imposition of radical Protestant usages by the government of Edward VI. These were essentially arguments about the terms of association. The defeat of both rebellions and the replacement of uncooperative conservatives among the local ruling class by a new gentry oriented towards the Tudor court and government settled the argument on the terms of the royal government.[5] The fact that the Council of Wales and the Marches survived into the seventeenth century did not mean that even in the sixteenth century there were autonomous marcher lordships, militarised to take advantage of a frontier of expansion and exploitation against what was perceived as the alien, fractured world of the Welsh principalities. Edward I had destroyed the Welsh princes. The council was an instrument of royal rule. The government of Henry VIII, helped by an underlying native Welsh tendency to identify with the perceived 'Welshness' of the Tudors, was able to carry through a systematic legislative union of Wales with the English Crown between 1536 and 1543. Such were the advantages to the Welsh nobility and gentry of closer association with government that the union proved very stable.[6]

On the other hand, in the Lordship of Ireland the community of the Crown of England had a genuine frontier march in the sixteenth century. Like the medieval barons of the Welsh marches, from whom they were often descended, the magnates of England-in-Ireland abutted onto societies which were perceived as being absolutely outwith the community of the realm – as indeed they were, not so much because they spoke Gaelic as because they, in practice, defied the concept of any meaningful political community beyond the bounds of the regional ascendancies into which they were divided. The Old English magnates of the Lordship were very much an active part of the community of the realm owing allegiance to the Crown of England. The trouble was that they were disproportionately disposed to support the Yorkist side, which was ultimately defeated in the struggle for the throne by the rival Lancastrians led by Henry VII. Of course, the English in Ireland claimed the same privileges as Englishmen in England. They denied they might be taxed without the expression of their consent in an appropriate and convenient legislative assembly. It was a view subsequently held by the English in Virginia. Since the barons of Ireland were of French extraction, they naturally thought of a parliament as the appropriate assembly. That the king might have several parliaments in his realm was not in the least odd. The French kings had representative Estates in many of their provinces, and an Estates-General for the whole of the realm.

Nor was it at all unreasonable for the Irish parliament to insist that it could not be bound by the legislation of a parliament held in, say, Westminster. Parliament had normally very limited functions. The Common Law was the king's law, prescribed by custom and usage universal amongst the Englishry, and unalterable in fundamentals, even by the king. Mainly, parliaments were about exceptional taxation and certain aspects of judicial activity. A parliament was a high court, indeed the king's highest court of law. Above all, the king was parliament. It was an aspect of his sovereignty. The whole notion of the sovereignty of parliament beloved of later Westminster politicians was a perversion. It was clearly stated in the by then meaningless formulas of United Kingdom statute even in the early twenty-first century that it is the monarch who legislates, with advice. That the Irish parliament in 1460 tried to limit the king's writ in Ireland under the guise of restating platitudes about its own powers was intolerable, for the aim of the exercise was to protect Richard, Duke of York, a claimant to the throne. It was not a declaration of independence. No parliament could be independent of the reigning monarch who was its most important part, either in person or by representative. It was a move in a civil war.[7] Nor had the Yorkist sympathies of the Irish magnates vanished by the time of Bosworth, as they proved by providing the springboard for the first serious strike against Henry's fragile new regime.

With leadership from the powerful Earl of Kildare, the whole Lordship apart from the city of Waterford went over to the first serious Yorkist pretender, Lambert Simnel, who pretended to be the imprisoned Earl of Warwick, in 1487. Simnel had actually been crowned king of England in

Christ Church Cathedral, the cathedral of Norse Dublin founded in 1038 by King Sitric, the local Viking ruler. Its bishops had originally been consecrated at Canterbury. Simnel, in this great church of the Lordship, claimed its crown – England's. With 2000 German mercenaries supplied by Margaret, dowager Duchess of Burgundy, and support in Cornwall and Lancashire, the Irish Yorkists invaded England with their associates Lords Lincoln and Lovell in June 1487. Landing in Lancashire, they were defeated at Stoke by King Henry within a matter of days.[8]

As late as the 1950s and 1960s English historians who mentioned these events in their texts were liable to repeat the then accepted interpretation that this proved how anxious 'Ireland' was to throw off 'English' rule. This was a bizarre misreading of evidence which clearly shouted exactly the opposite. The fact that Sir Thomas Fitzgerald, chancellor of Ireland, died fighting against Henry VII at Stoke in the Midlands of England underlines just how clearly he and his fellow Old English noblemen from the Lordship saw themselves as integral parts of the English political community; so much so that they were following the classic ploy of trying to use forces created on the periphery of the political system to seize power at the centre. It was a hard-fought field, and *The Great Chronicle of London* records the grim resolution of Martin Schwartz, commander of the German mercenaries, when he realised that the Earl of Lincoln had been unable to rally to the Yorkist standard more than a fraction of the forces he had promised. Both Lincoln and Schwartz died fighting. As a bid for power, this episode was far more serious than, say, Buckingham's rising against Richard III in 1483, a rising in which the future Henry VII, then nobody's candidate for the throne, had played an abortive role.[9]

In an age when water united and land divided, the Irish Sea was the great inland sea of the English communities, and no monarch could afford to ignore what went on on its western shore. The ease with which the Yorkists had invaded Lancaster after crowning Simnel king of England in Dublin underlined that. It is true that the next pretender to plague Henry VII, the young man Perkin Warbeck who claimed to be the dead Richard, Duke of York, was at his most dangerous during the substantial period when he was entertained and backed by James IV of Scotland. Yet Warbeck's extraordinary political career, which ended on a gallows at Tyburn in 1499, had begun in the city of Cork in 1491, where he had succumbed to heavy local pressure to assume the role of a Yorkist pretender. He spent the winter of 1491–92 in Munster, beginning to learn to speak English among other ploys. He was later to become the focus of a great deal of discontent in England proper, so it is interesting to note that his original backers were in no wise deterred by the fact that he did not yet speak English. The language of the Common Law, in Dublin as much as London, was that eccentric survival of Norman French known as Law French. Most of the Welsh nobility was bilingual in Welsh and English, and the magnates of the Englishry of Ireland were by the sixteenth century as often as not as comfortable in Irish Gaelic as in the slightly archaic Chaucerian English of the Lordship. The most prestigious language among the ruling class of the domains of the Crown of England was probably French, which admittedly few spoke as a native tongue but many knew passing well. Warbeck's last, disastrous foray against Henry VII took the form of a landing in the far west of Cornwall in late 1497, an area where Cornish was still very much the dominant language.[10]

So any attempt to see 'Ireland' as 'England's first colony' around 1500 entirely misses the point that the Lordship was a march of the kingdom of England. Equally, the Gaelic lordships against which it was set, and with which it interpenetrated, were not bits of 'Ireland' waiting to be more securely attached, but independent regions of a Gaidhealtachd united by culture, by a common cultural language, and by a common repudiation of the concept of the centralised state – even in the very tentative form it had reached in the greater monarchies of Western Europe. United by the galleys which coursed the convenient seas between its regions, that Gaidhealtachd stretched from Kerry to Cape Wrath in the north of Scotland, with a very important detached section in the Wicklow hills and adjacent coast of Leinster. Even here the Irish Sea provided convenient direct access to the rest of the Gaidhealtachd, whether to the north or west. Yet if the modern connotations of the word 'colony' are singularly unhelpful in explaining the nature of the Lordship, there is an important sense in which that Lordship faced the new Tudor dynasty with the only part of the ruling class of their dominions which can be described as colonial Englishmen. These aristocrats were still attracted by the idea of expansion into the lands of Gaelic rulers. Their ancestors had probably been amongst those feudatories most resentful of control, which is one reason why they moved further away from their monarch, to try to re-create the conditions which had obtained in the feudal community of England before the powerful, diabolically clever, and constantly innovative Angevin Henry II succeeded to its throne.[11] Nevertheless, their protestations of loyalty were not insincere, for they needed the ultimate resource of the power of the Crown of England should the fortunes of local war run too disastrously against them. The sixteenth-century Englishry of the Lordship were both loyal and defensive of local autonomies. They were very like metropolitan Englishmen in some respects, very different in others. One crucial difference between them and eighteenth-century American Englishmen was that they had transferred a genuinely aristocratic social order to their new homes. Their leading magnates were comfortable in the royal court, except when they were actively trying to overthrow a given monarch. In other respects, their political position prefigured that of future frontier elites created by the territorial expansion of English subjects.

On the other hand, the aristocratic social structure of the Lordship was crucial in shaping its politics. Around the seat of royal government in Dublin, the strict equivalent of London-Westminster down to the duplication of the major organs of administration and the four central courts of the Common Law, there lay the only truly arable territory in the Lordship, the four fertile counties of Dublin, Kildare, Meath, and Louth. This was the Pale, where direct royal administration of a society very like southern England was feasible. Outwith the Pale the Lordship was organised on the only basis on which it could possibly have been run, which was by delegation of authority to the palatine jurisdictions of the great feudatories of whom the earls of Kildare, Ormonde, and Desmond were the mightiest and longest enduring. The low-lying areas of Munster and Leinster were the heart of the feudal Lordship, and in large parts of them an English type of manorial economy survived, often with a mixed agricultural population, though one in which the substantial landowners were usually English in stock. Though the Lordship was no more urbanised than most of the rest of the king's realm outside the London area, towns were important to it and usually very loyal to it. Given their desire to keep a measure of independence from surrounding noble power, and their extremely close economic links with other English towns by sea, this was hardly surprising. Dublin may have had 8000 inhabitants in 1540, which would have made it the size of a town like Norwich; while Drogheda, Waterford, Cork, Limerick, and that most detached part of the Lordship Galway, were smaller but significant, and so considered by the Dublin administration.

In 1494–95, Henry VII for the first and last time in his reign sent a substantial armed force across to Dublin commanded by the able Sir Edward Poynings. The incentive appears to have been the need to discourage support for Perkin Warbeck, of which there was potentially a great deal in the Lordship, but Poynings also seized the opportunity to discountenance the inveterate tendency of the magnates to feud with one another, instead of defending the marches against the Gaelic princes, and to try to reinforce the very feeble degree of effective royal control. His best-known achievement was Poynings' Law, which lasted much longer than anyone can have expected and was latterly used for purposes quite contrary to its original intention, but that intention was wholly reasonable in so far as it insisted that proposed legislation of any parliament held in Ireland in the customary but not hitherto invariable absence of the monarch had to be submitted to the king in council in England. Since the monarch was parliament, or rather a parliament was a particular aspect of the royal sovereignty, it was essential to stop magnates usurping that sovereignty to pursue feuds with rivals or a Yorkist coup through a parliament in the Lordship. Militarily, Poynings never had the strength to pursue an aggressive policy towards the Gaidhealtachd once he fell out with and arrested the Earl of Kildare. The Lordship had had a fiscal deficit for a long time. Poynings' expedition – which in the winter of 1494–95 amounted to a mere 653 troops, with half a dozen senior administrators – did not help the deficit, so in December 1495 the army was cut to 330 English troops and 100 Gaelic kerne or light infantry, with the chancellor replacing the recalled Poynings as governor.

Once Poynings had crushed signs of Yorkist support in Munster, the Lordship posed no real danger for King Henry. With Warbeck marginalised, the sensible and economic way to administer the Lordship was through delegation to a local magnate great enough to deploy the resources needed for the job. The eighth Earl of Kildare, who served either as justiciar or as deputy lieutenant of the Lordship of Ireland between 1477 and 1492 and again from 1496 to 1513, was the obvious choice. Attempts by twentieth-century nationalist historians to turn this man into a forerunner of de Valera after 1932 were grotesquely anachronistic. As one of the most perceptive of historians of medieval Ireland remarked after surveying contemporary notarised evidence which effectively cleared Kildare of the charges of con-spiring with Gaelic chiefs against the peace of the realm, 'it is as impossible for us as it was for his contemporaries to maintain further the accusation of treason against the earl of Kildare'. He went on to stress that it was cooperation with the monarch which offered Kildare maximum advantage, and that the concept of Kildare ruling 'not in the interests of England but in the interests of Ireland' was beside the mark and of no contemporary relevance.[12]

For a serious challenge to the dynasty to emerge from the western side of the Irish Sea, three conditions had to be met. One was a consensus within the Lordship on an alternative candidate for the throne. The second was significant support from magnates whose power lay far closer to the seat of royal government than the Lordship. The third was substantial assistance in the form of professional soldiers, money, and munitions from a foreign power. After 1500, when the Yorkist cause had ceased to be plausible or viable, the first two conditions were inconceivable and foreign sovereigns were to show comparatively little interest in intriguing with malcontents in the Lordship of Ireland. Of course there were endemic problems for a monarch who was not prepared to pump more money into the Dublin administration, for this implied reliance on magnate power for local defence. The discountenancing of the retaining of armed followers by nobles, which was a natural royal instinct, was impractical. The parliament which passed Poynings' Law had to accept that on the marches of the Lordship retaining was essential, and could only try to make magnates register or 'book' their retainers. In practice frontier areas are always zones of contact and cultural blending, at least in a colonial context, and the retention of Gaelic septs or aristocratic kinship groups as military dependents by the great frontier families was another necessity. Legislation did try to curb magnate power by forbidding the use of handguns or artillery save by licence of the royal governor.

There was an element of perennial optimism in all legislation. The restriction on handguns in the Lordship can be seen as part of a sustained and hopeless campaign by the monarchy to control and discourage the new weapons. Apart from anything else, they were deemed to have a bad effect on the cultivation of the longbow 'by reason whereof as well our said sovereign lord the King as also his noble progenitors have had and obtained great and triumphant victories against their enemies', as a royal proclamation by Henry VIII put it in 1528. Yet that proclamation, which sought to secure enforcement of existing statutes on archery, handguns, and unlawful games, sums up the futility of the legislation in its own words:

> In consideration whereof and for the better maintenance and good
> continuation of the said archery and shooting in longbows, divers good and
> politic statutes have been made, established, and devised as well in the time
> of our sovereign lord the King that now is as also in the days of his noble
> progenitors, Kings of this realm. Yet that notwithstanding, for lack of good
> and effectual execution of the laws and the statutes, the said archery and
> shooting in longbows is sore and marvelously decayed and in manner
> utterly extinct; And specially by the new fangled and wanton pleasure that
> men now have in the using of crossbows and handguns, whereby also great
> number of people be given to felonies.[13]

It was the timeless language of paranoid conservatism, and it was futile.

On the other hand, the attempt to secure for the Crown control amounting to operational monopoly of artillery in the territories of the Lordship and elsewhere was successful, not because of inherent respect for law but because of practical considerations. The sheer cost of a battering piece for a siege train was beyond the resources of most nobles. Even if it were not, they normally did not have access to the plant and expertise needed to cast such pieces. Arranging to buy in such massive artefacts from abroad posed impossible problems of security, not to mention transportation. If the king was not informed of any such ploy by his diplomatic agents, he was sure to be informed by the magnate who could see that his castle was the likely first target for his rival's new toy. Henry VIII was to find himself a major beneficiary of this situation, though he at his accession in 1509 at the age of 17 had no reason to think of the Lordship as constituting any particularly acute problem. Its nobles had a high degree of autonomy, but others of his subjects had more, notably the Stanley earls of Derby. English rule had only been established unequivocally in the Isle of Man in 1333, but by 1406 the kingship of Man had been transferred to the Lancashire landowner Sir John Stanley and his heirs in perpetuity. In 1505 the second Stanley Earl of Derby styled himself, admittedly in Latin, king of Man and the Isles. For once, legal opinion summed up the realities when it held Man no part of the realm of England, though in subjection to and owing homage to it.

Henry VIII at first had no need to be a particularly active ruler in his Lordship of Ireland. He did have an atypical burst of activism in 1520–22, when he sent across one of his best generals, the Earl of Surrey, with a siege train containing three battering pieces and what turned out to be a not very appropriate force of household troops. Surrey did write important memoranda on the question of dealings with the Gaelic areas, but he was underfunded and in the end achieved little despite being given the prestigious title of king's lieutenant. This was a typical substitution of rhetoric for reality. Adequate funding for more than the six-month period originally allowed for would have been more useful than a fancy title. All he contrived were a series of pretty standard police actions to deal with noble feuds and frontier security. It was really the Kildare rebellion of 1534–35 which demonstrated the decisive role of royal artillery.

Like most feudal rebellions, this one was a complex web involving miscalculation on the part of all parties, but at its core lay the fears of 'Silken Thomas', the young heir to the earldom of Kildare and leadership of the Fitzgerald or Geraldine interest, that his father's detention under examination in England might be the prelude to the loss of the long-standing family connection with the office of deputy. The old earl was not executed, nor probably in great danger of being executed. He died of natural causes in England, by which time the new Earl of Kildare was committed to a rebellion, supported by his Fitzgerald family's traditional Gaelic dependants, and with some links with conservative court dissidents such as Lord Dacre. Even so, there was no chance of a coup, and a rising which originally may have been a means of placing pressure on Henry to accede to Fitzgerald demands became a desperate business when the king sent William Skeffington out as governor, with the comparatively speaking huge force of 2300 men to crush the rebellion. In a castle-using aristocracy, it was natural for Kildare to retreat into his castle of Maynooth after following scorched-earth tactics and in the hope that he could sit out Skeffington until a combination of logistical and fiscal problems compelled him to go away. Skeffington's guns enabled him to take the castle in ten days in March 1535, killing the garrison. He thereby broke the rebellion, though it took time and executions to seal its failure.

Since some of the administrative correspondence connected with the equipping of the deputy's forces survives, we can say a good deal about the weaponry Skeffington deployed. Though his troops used arquebuses, in the early form known as 'hagbushes', he also carried yew bows and sheaves of arrows for the skilled archers who, when they could be obtained, were still in a class of their own. Light man-killing ordnance such as falcons and falconets were shipped for the campaign, but the truly important provision was for heavy siege guns and heavy horses from Northamptonshire to pull them. Maynooth was on a plain, accessible by roads. Carts, artificers, and abundant shot and powder were essential. Sir William Skeffington's own account of the capture of Maynooth says that roughly two-thirds of the garrison were 'gunmen', though there were also archers. The defenders had light ordnance which they mounted on the highest part of the keep or donjon to gain range to keep besiegers at a distance. It was not an uncommon ploy, most impressively displayed in the titanic curtain wall which is the fourteenth-century Douglas fortress of Tantallon in East Lothian in Scotland. There a sea cliff is the rest of the defence and the wall is so massive as to take substantial guns. Tantallon only fell to bombardment in 1651. Maynooth was less resistant. Skeffington first destroyed its ordnance by bombarding the top of the donjon, and then set up the 'great battery' on its north side which enabled him to breach and storm the outer defences or 'base court'. From there he assaulted and took the donjon. The episode showed that the nobility of the Lordship, even the greatest of them, could not seriously shake their king.[14]

Of course, the fact that Henry VIII was at the time of the Kildare rebellion moving into more and more radical confrontation with the papacy, normally the Crown's reliable ally in Ireland, enabled the Earl of Kildare to claim that he was leading a crusade for orthodox religion. Those few foreigners who heard of the rebellion tended to believe him. Few locals did, for in the last analysis his motives were neither religious nor nationalist, but dynastic. Henry had little difficulty in securing the passage through what historians call the Irish Reformation Parliament of 1536–37 of the bulk of the ecclesiastical measures he had already passed through a Westminster parliament. There was little opposition in the Lordship to a declaration of royal supremacy in the church, and such steps as the dissolution of the monasteries had to be passed through a parliament in the Lordship which, if cooperative, was not subservient, so the nobility benefited as much as the king from the financial implications. As long as religious rituals remained untouched, as they largely did under Henry's conservative caesaropapism, the traditional loyalism of the nobles kept the Lordship politically quiet. Government activism set in with a high-powered reform commission in 1537–38, but its first military decision, which was one of its initial decisions, was to reduce the garrison despatched and funded by the Crown from 750 to 300 men. This was a risible force which could not even hold the frontiers in the absence of the support of the Kildare following. By 1537, Henry's new deputy, Lord Leonard Grey, found himself facing a major security crisis manufactured by his master's grim determination to cut costs in a deficit area of the realm.

As it happened, Grey turned out to be energetic and a first-class soldier. He reinforced his always inadequate forces by levies from the Pale and funded them partly by that extremely unpopular form of military exaction known as the cess, with which he turned back what at one time looked like a lethal resurgence of raiding by the Irishry of the Gaidhealtachd. Cannon were used most skilfully against the castle strongholds of Gaelic border chiefs, and in encounter battle Grey had that most invaluable of the attributes of generalship – luck. It did not extend to the murderous politics of the fully factionalised court of Henry VIII, where the Butlers, the hereditary enemies of the Fitzgeralds, were industriously spreading the not totally unfounded story that Grey was trying to build up a personal following among the former adherents of the fallen Earl of Kildare. In 1540 Grey became politically vulnerable with the sudden fall from power and execution of his patron, Thomas Cromwell, victim of the rival Norfolk faction and their allies at court.

In January of that year Grey had, not unreasonably, been hoping to reap reward for his services. He was arranging for a list of the contracts and agreements which had been made under his aegis with different Gaelic chiefs, some of which were still in the hands of the bishop of Meath and Justice Aylmer, to be forwarded to the king. These were the evidences of the securing of the marches. He was also touting the idea that the king might arrange a profitable marriage for him. In April the very letter from Henry which announced increased pay for the troops also announced the 'temporary' recall of Grey.[15] Replaced by a new deputy, Sir Anthony St Leger, Grey was tried and executed in 1541. Ironically, 1539–40 saw King Henry also reluctantly accept the need to reinforce the tiny army Grey had led so brilliantly.

Since identity was so tied up with the monarchy, it is perhaps sensible to see what Henry VIII thought he governed. There is an unequivocal statement in a royal proclamation which he issued in March 1538 in connection with revaluing the currency. The subject was a murky one because of the crisis created by shortage of means to pay Skeffington's forces at the height of the Kildare revolt in 1534–35. It was decided to break with tradition and strike a distinct coinage for the Lordship of Ireland. In a pattern which was to be repeated again and again in regions where the English central government felt it faced political unrest, control was centralised. The coins were struck within the Tower of London, under conditions of extreme secrecy – which was just as well, for the government was hoping to pass this new silver coinage off as of sterling standard, which it was not, being only 10 ounce fine or in a ratio of 833 to the 925 parts in a thousand of pure silver which was sterling. The debasement was predictably soon carried much further. Just as the Westminster government was to experiment with the unpopular concept of a poll tax in the 1980s in Scotland, where it had few supporters to alienate, as a prelude to implementing the same policy in its areas of indispensable support in England, so the debasement of the currency in the Lordship was in fact a dummy run for the policies of debasement which the Crown was to implement on a much wider basis in England after 1544. The 1538 proclamation cunningly devotes most of its space to the gold coinage, which was rare and least susceptible of discreet debasement. It stressed the king's will that uniform currency values be respected 'within all places throughout this his realm of England, Ireland, Wales, Calais, and the Marches of the same'. That summed up reality neatly: Henry ruled one realm which had marches on its land frontiers in France (around Calais), against Scotland, and in Ireland on the edges of the Gaidhealtachd.[16]

Historians have pursued the origins of English or British identity in the reign of Henry VIII with a wilfully selective and parochial vision. Indeed, the strict English equivalent of the Gaelic Sinn Fein, the name of a Catholic nationalist party in modern Ireland, has been deemed an appropriate part title for a section of a monograph devoted to the theme of monarch and people in Tudor England: 'Ourselves Alone'.[17] Yet it is clear enough that the reign of Henry VIII generated wildly different, often contradictory experiences for any of his subjects in search of an identity other than that of subject. Perhaps the vast programme of fortification on the Channel coasts, begun under threat of French invasion in 1539, gave those who lived in proximity to those forts a sense of being apart from the continent on the other side of the Channel, or so some scholars have thought. The need for fortification was in fact a sign of just how closely the politics of both sides of the Channel intermeshed, and of how deeply Henry and his court were influenced by French culture. Anne Boleyn, Henry's second wife and a crucial figure in the breach with Rome and the first penetration of evangelical theology into elite court circles, was wholly French in education, which was why she was bilingual.[18] Henry devoted vast amounts of energy and even more resources to trying to re-create the Anglo-French Channel state. Henry V, the one medieval English king to make good his claim to the French throne, was his hero, and the so-called *First English*

Life of that monarch was published in 1513, on the occasion of Henry VIII's invasion of France, as a model of what might be.[19]

In the face of all the mountains of scholarly work devoted to the administrative history of the Henrician regime, we are liable to lose sight of the fact that as late as 1545, two years before his death, Henry VIII was planning to partition France with the Emperor Charles V, taking for himself Boulogne, Normandy, and Guienne. His more intelligent counsellors, from Wolsey to Thomas Cromwell, had been aware that this had long ceased to be a realistic objective. Nevertheless, that was where the assets which had been stripped from the church and which might well have solved the very real underlying fiscal crisis of the Crown went.

Between 1543 and 1547, it is reckoned that the staggering sum by sixteenth-century standards of £2,000,000 sterling was poured into war by land and sea against France.[20] The army which Henry VIII led was still an army royal rather than a national army in the sense that though of course it contained many mercenaries hired by the Crown, its core consisted of contingents raised by the great magnates. By 1542, the garrison which Grey had once commanded in the Lordship had been reduced to a mere 500 men. Henry was actually recruiting more Irish infantry than that by far with the assistance of both Old English and Gaelic lords to serve in his continental and Scottish wars after 1544. This shows that he related to these magnates as to any others in some ways. So convenient was the arrangement that the successor administrations under his son Edward VI kept Irish troops in their French and Scottish garrisons until 1550.

By 1544, however, Henry was king of Ireland, having been so declared in June 1541. It is often said to have been part of the struggle with the papacy, repudiating any idea of papal grant of authority over Ireland, but this is not so. Henry very sensibly deemed his sovereign authority to be rooted everywhere in the British Isles in Norman or Angevin conquest. He subsequently complained that his Irish council had foisted on him a title without any funds to sustain it. The members of that council, to the king's understandable displeasure, had always regarded the change of title as a way of committing their liege lord to a more activist policy with respect to the absorption of the Irishry of the Gaidhealtachd. In a sense, Henry had no more objections in principle to successful aggression there than the average early-modern king had to successful aggression on his behalf anywhere. It could always be rationalised in retrospect. What he objected to was an attempt to deprive him of control over the pace and scale of his own commitment. The whole episode was less a constitutional revolution – though a case has been argued for so describing it –[21] than yet another example of the utter confusion which could be created when a faction successfully manipulated the authority of a king who, however formidable, made up his own mind much less often than appeared on the surface to be the case.

Certainly, many of the large loyalist population in the old Lordship, quite rightly, did not see how a piece of paper could change the historic identity to which they continued to cling as the Englishry of Ireland. Henry and his advisers did not fail to become mired in the inherently confusing nomenclature which was one of the many less than desirable results of the change. In a proclamation issued at Westminster early in 1542, Henry was made to say that he was taking the title and name of king of Ireland, but then the proclamation instantly added that of course title and realm 'should be united and annexed to our imperial crown of our realm of England'. So it was a change which was not a change.[22] In the same proclamation Wales was referred to separately as a 'dominion', despite the great Act of 27 Henry VIII, *c.* 26 of 1536, which had incorporated Wales into England. Henry himself continued to think in perfectly realistic terms about the limits of his effective power in Ireland, stressing in the letter to the deputy and his council in which he complained there was no revenue to support the royal title that it would be necessary to try to enforce different conditions in treaties with the Irish on the marches from conditions acceptable in dealing with those Irish who were more remote. Clearly this meant not all the inhabitants of the island but those of the Gaidhealtachd.[23]

Though the change of royal title in 1541 left a heritage of expectation, it can be seen primarily as a monument to manipulation of the royal will by faction and as a fruitful source of muddle and confusion rather than as one of the hinges of history. Those hinges were turning indeed but in response to the pressures of new circumstances after the defeat of the rebellion of 'Silken Thomas' and his Geraldine faction. After 1535 there was no magnate in the Lordship capable of offering the Crown the support of forces strong enough to hold most of the frontiers in order to free Crown troops to deal with an exceptional danger at any specific point on the marches, let alone to conduct punitive strikes into the Gaidhealtachd. These were the essential deterrent without which ever larger areas of the Lordship would end up paying blackmail to Gaelic chiefs all too happy to supplement their revenues with tribute from the fertile lowlands of Leinster and Munster. The period between 1470 and 1534 had seen a remarkable recovery in the Lordship. By forcing its nobility to defend themselves in large measure, with only a stiffening of royal troops and occasional expeditions of reinforcement at times of military or political crisis, the Crown had in fact revitalised the admittedly demoralised Lordship of the later medieval era. There had been a long period of comparative peace and prosperity. These were mutually reinforcing concepts. Wealth bred power both to hold the marches and even to take out small Gaelic lordships which lived by raiding into the Lordship.[24] Of course, the logic of the situation demanded that the Crown cooperate with a largely, but not quite, self-funding community. Royal government only worked through loyalist magnates. The Kildares were probably too powerful, but it was then the sovereign's duty to restructure the nobility of this particular marcher area of the realm so that the Crown could find within readjusted parameters of local power men with whom it could cooperate in governance. In August 1539 the Ulster chiefs raided deep into the Pale itself, driving off vast herds of cattle. As it happened, Grey pursued them with half the garrison and Pale levies and decisively routed them at Bellahoe, south of Carrickmacross, but the lucky victory was inherently less significant than the challenge to the heart of the economy of the Lordship.

This could not go on. Yet by the death of Henry VIII in January 1547 in Whitehall – one of the sixty-odd residences he had accumulated to outshine numerically predecessors and successors alike – royal government had developed in ways which made it potentially an even more dangerous form of government for an extensive monarchy. Quite unnecessarily, it had plunged deep into debt in pursuit of strategic lunacies in France. A fraction of the resources so wasted would have made a vast difference to many a hard-pressed deputy in Dublin. Worse still was the way politics had evolved into bloody faction fights at the centre to control the voice speaking from behind the royal mask. Increasingly, the factions were ideologically driven, or at least identified with an ideological position in that most lethal of areas – religion. It was only a question of time before the shifts of court politics drove significant loyalist elements into reluctant confrontation with a group which was driving unacceptable policies through on the back of their ascendancy in the central counsels of the Crown. Ironically, the Gaidhealtachd, no longer the menace it had been in the fourteenth and fifteenth centuries, played a central role in triggering first passive, then active rebellion by the much provoked colonial Englishry of Ireland. But to grasp that complex sequence of events it is essential to turn to the Gaidhealtachd, and not just to that part of it which happened to lie in the island of Ireland.

Notes and references

1. Ralph A. Griffiths, *King and Country: England and Wales in the fifteenth century* (Hambledon Press, London, 1991), Chap. 7: 'Henry Tudor: The training of a king', pp. 114–36.

2. David C. Douglas, *The Norman Achievement 1050–1100* (University of California Press, Berkeley and Los Angeles, CA, 1969), p. 49.

3. John Le Patourel, *Feudal Empires: Norman and Plantagenet* (Hambledon Press, London, 1984), Chap. 7: 'The Plantagenet Dominions'.

4. Griffiths, *King and Country*, Chap. 3: 'The English Realm and Dominions and the King's Subjects in the Later Middle Ages'.

5. A.L. Rowse, *The Expansion of Elizabethan England* (Macmillan, London, 1955), pp. 31–44.

6. Steven G. Ellis, 'Tudor State Formation and the Shaping of the British Isles', in *Conquest and Union: Fashioning a British state 1485–1725*, eds. Steven G. Ellis and Sarah Barber (Longman, London, pbk edn, 1995), pp. 55–56.

7. For an extremely unconvincing exercise in reading the king out of a body whose very name said it was the king talking to his barons, *vide* James Lydon, '"Ireland corporate of itself" The Parliament of 1460', *History Ireland*, Summer 1995, pp. 9–12.

8. Geoffrey R. Elton, *England under the Tudors* (Methuen, London, 1967 reprint), pp. 22–23.

9. J.R. Lander, *The Wars of the Roses* (St Martin's Press, New York, 1990), pp. 185–88 and 200–06.

10. Ian Arthurson, *The Perkin Warbeck Conspiracy 1491–1499* (Alan Sutton, Stroud, 1994).

11. Marie T. Flanagan, *Irish Society, Anglo-Norman Settlers, Angevin Kingship* (Clarendon Press, Oxford, 1989), p. 304.

12. George O. Sayles, 'The Vindication of the Earl of Kildare from Treason', reprinted in his *Scripta Diversa* (Hambleton Press, London, 1982), pp. 89–95. The quotations are on pp. 94–95.

13. Westminster, 4 December 1528, 20 Henry VIII, printed in Paul L. Hughes and James F. Larkin (eds.), *Tudor Royal Proclamations.* Vol. I: *The Early Tudors (1485–1553)* (Yale University Press, New Haven, CT, 1964), No. 121, pp. 177–81, the quotations are on p. 178.

14. By far the best and most convenient guide to this and other episodes in the Tudor military history of the Lordship is Steven G. Ellis, *Tudor Ireland: Crown, community and the conflict of cultures 1470–1603* (Longman, London, 1985). Now republished in a second edition: *Ireland in the Age of the Tudors, 1447 [sic] to 1603: English expansion and the end of the Gaelic rule* (Longman, London, 1998).

15. Calendar of State Papers (hereafter CSP) Ireland, 1509–73, p. 51 (entries for 2 and 16 January) and p. 52 (entry for 1 April).

16. Westminster, 27 March 1538, 29 Henry VIII, in *Tudor Royal Proclamations*, Vol. I, p. 261. For the complexities of the monetary history see Michael Dolley, 'The Irish Coinage, 1534–1691', in T.W. Moody *et al.* (eds.), *A New History of Ireland*, Vol. III: *Early Modern Ireland 1534–1691* (Clarendon Press, Oxford, 1976), pp. 408–09.

17. P.S. Crowson, *Tudor Foreign Policy*, Part IIC, 'Monarch and People – "Ourselves Alone"' (Adam and Charles Black, London, 1973).

18. David Starkey, *The Reign of Henry VIII: Personalities and politics* (George Philip, London, 1985), pp. 91–94.

19. G.L. Harriss (ed.), *Henry V: The practice of kingship* (Oxford University Press, Oxford, 1985), p. 134.

20. David Loades, *The Tudor Navy: An administrative, political, and military history* (Scolar Press, Aldershot, 1992), p. 138.

21. Brenden Bradshaw, *The Irish Constitutional Revolution of the Sixteenth Century* (Cambridge University Press, Cambridge, 1979).

22. Westminster, 23 January 1542, 23 Henry VIII, in *Tudor Royal Proclamations*, Vol. I, p. 307.

23. Henry VIII to Lord Deputy and Council, York, 23 September 1541, in CSP Ireland, 1509–73, p. 60.

24. Steven G. Ellis, *Reform and Revival: English government in Ireland, 1470–1534* (Boydell Press, Woodbridge, 1986), pp. 49–66.

CHAPTER TWO

The Gaidhealtachd and the colonial enterprise

The Gaidhealtachd, the Lordship, and the Crowns of England and Scotland to 1558

If the Lordship of Ireland was in many ways a pragmatically defined survival of a Norman conquest which had only very partially succeeded, its theoretical commitment to outward expansion remained. However Gaelicised they might be in their personal culture, the whole rationale of the baronage was the defence and expansion of the Lordship in general, and their own lordships in particular. The obvious device to set the pattern of conquest rolling forward again was to persuade or manipulate the king into sending regular supplies of troops and money to fuel the renewed advance. Though no doubt his subjects in the Lordship would have made a contribution to this exercise, they saw no reason why the rest of the English community should not contribute to this common enterprise. It was the king's job not to be conned into thus paying for the acquisition of real estate by the barons of the Lordship at rates cheap for them but ruinous for him in a frontier march already running at a loss. The lieutenancy of the Earl of Surrey in 1520–22, in a period when the Earl of Kildare was out of favour, was one in which these issues became a matter of debate between the king and his lieutenant. Henry VIII, like every other contemporary monarch, was intrigued by the idea of conquest on the cheap. Surrey was sent over the Irish Sea with six months' funding and vague instructions to arrange for the conquest of the Gaidhealtachd on a self-financing basis. The concepts were contradictory. Surrey was costing Henry £10,000 a year to do little more than hold the marches and establish control when in June 1521 he sent his monarch a memorandum, reminding him that Edward I had

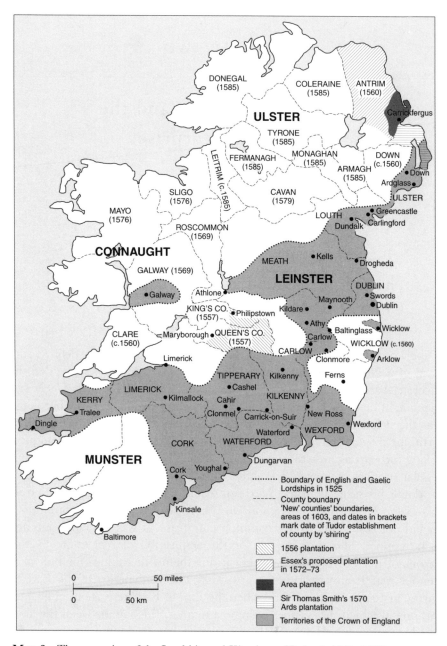

Map 2 The expansion of the Lordship and Kingdom of Ireland, 1525-1603

needed ten years to conquer Wales and insisting that any attempt to conquer the Gaidhealtachd in Ireland with as small a force as 2500 men would
last indefinitely, even if it did not provoke a general Gaelic confederacy
which might render the exercise impractical. Surrey's view was that what
was needed was a wholly funded royal army of 6000, with of course a programme of castle and town building and loyalist immigration. Henry VIII
made it quite clear that he preferred persuasion, political guile, and concessions as means to advance recognition of his claims by Gaelic lords.

With the arrival in 1540 of a new governor, Sir Anthony St Leger, it
can be argued that the Tudor state did in fact commit itself to trying to
establish a measure of control over the whole island of Ireland, though by
the politic method of what historians have called 'surrender and regrant'.
By this procedure, Gaelic chiefs agreed to recognise the authority of the
Crown in exchange for assurances that the monarch would abandon his
unrealistic claims on their lands. They were to be granted a feudal title; were
to cease the use of their Gaelic ones; and were to turn up when summoned
to a parliament, an institution whose essence remained its original French
one of the monarch or his surrogate talking to the barons.

Between 1540 and his recall in 1546, St Leger, with the support of
locally born officials such as Lord Chancellor Thomas Cusack, made real
progress with this policy, even persuading Conn Bacagh O'Neill to become
earl of Tyrone. There was much to be said for the argument that this was
infinitely preferable to the alternative of war in the very difficult terrains of
the Gaelic chiefdoms, many of them dominated by woodland, mountain,
and bog. Nor had the Dublin administration the necessary geographical
knowledge to function efficiently in these regions. Before 1558 few lord
deputies had made extensive journeys throughout Ireland. Well after 1600
Ulster was largely *terra incognita* to the officers of the state. Even the mightiest of the Gaelic lords were usually reluctant to travel through the territory
of another, preferring sea journeys to more distant destinations if they could
be arranged. The learned orders moved round the Gaidhealtachd, maintaining it as a cultural unit; merchants operated under safe-conduct, when
they could get it; peasants were surprisingly mobile – but this was a culture
which combined wide mental horizons with ferocious elite regionalism,
especially in military matters. Conflict was regional or inter-regional, but
it was almost continuous, and the tempo of violence seems to have been
accelerating in the early sixteenth century.[1]

Violence was an important part of the political repertoire of a Gaelic
leader. After several centuries of dealing with Anglo-Norman state structures, they had nearly all learned the basic lessons for survival in military
units that did not normally have the wealth to generate the heavy battle
equipment which a Tudor royal army could field. They avoided set-piece

43

battle with such an opponent. Their own military power depended on two elements. The first was the obligation to a general hosting or rising-out against invasion (in Gaelic *gairm sluaigh*). In practice, this fell into two parts: one was a cavalry force supplied by the substantial landowners of the septs which elected the regional kings or bosses. Riding without stirrups on a quilted saddle, these horsemen could not sustain shock action in the shape of a massed charge. They wielded javelins overhead rather than couching lances after bracing themselves on long stirrups, as all European lancers of the period did. Each cavalryman was lightly armoured, carried sword and dagger as well as javelin, and was accompanied by a couple of servitors. So automatic was this role of the aristocracy that in the O'Neill's country the O'Hagans, Quinns, and Devlins of his core territories were known as his 'horsemen'. Light infantry or *kerne* were supplied by the rising of able-bodied freemen affluent enough to carry arms as a matter of course. Unarmoured, they were either sword and buckler men or missile troops with javelins or bows and arrows. These troops were ideal for raiding or for harassing an invader and cutting off sections of his forces as he withdrew baffled.

Such was the relentless arms race between rival lords that by the sixteenth century some regional princes were employing bands of professional infantrymen known as *kerne*[2] organised by hereditary captains. Originally, this would have been a pattern only expected of the heavy infantry element in the armies of the Gaelic lords: the gallowglasses. Whether settled on a given lord's lands or freelance bands, gallowglasses were by definition mercenary soldiers who served for reward. Coins did change hands increasingly as the sixteenth century advanced, but it was always the case that the bulk of the expense of maintaining a gallowglass force was offloaded onto the long-suffering peasantry by a system of billeting known as *buannacht* in Gaelic, a term usually Anglicised as 'bonaghts'. These forced contributions to a lord's billeted troops formed a system commonly called 'coign and livery' which was universal amongst Gaelic chiefs and feudal barons alike.

Gallowglass infantry with their helmets and knee-length armour and their heavy blade weapons were the shock element in set-piece Gaelic battle, though increasingly this was a kind of battle which the lords of the Gaidhealtachd only indulged in between themselves. Firearms became increasingly common among the kerne from the early sixteenth century, both as hand weapons and for use in the sieges of the castles which the Gaelic lords had learned from their feudal enemies how to build. The earls of Kildare had pioneered the use of light artillery pieces in the late fifteenth century.[3] Truly formidable bombardment pieces capable of smashing the heaviest defences remained, all over Europe, the final argument of the king (*ultima ratio regis*), as German field artillery proclaimed on its barrels as late as the 1914–18 war.

Standing armies were, however, becoming very common everywhere in the Irish part of the Gaidhealtachd in the sixteenth century, and not just in the hands of the greater regional princes. Chiefs such as O'Sullivan Beare in Leinster, who would have been fined by his acknowledged superior MacCarthy More if he had failed to produce contingents on time, logically enough began to create their own standing forces of kerne and gallowglasses. The whole system began to be pushed to extremes in the later fifteenth century with the importation of vast numbers of lighter infantry known as redshanks from the Highlands of Scotland. Hired on three-month summer contracts for campaigns in Ulster and elsewhere, they were a fearful additional burden on an already stressed countryside. Turlough Luineach O'Neill, who received 8000 redshanks as dowry with his Scottish bride in 1569, used these troops to reinforce his authority and to compensate for the shrinkage of his power south of the River Blackwater. The O'Cahan was so oppressed by the consequences that he at one point wanted to migrate across the Bann into Clandeboy, where he could hold his land at a known rent from the queen and 'be rid of Turlough and the Scots'.[4]

By the late sixteenth century, the weapon and troop mix available to a substantial chief anywhere in the Scottish or Irish Gaidhealtachd was sophisticated and practice in handling these resources appropriately was freely available. Old and new weapons coexisted, not because of technical backwardness so much as because of the limitations on the performance of any particular weapon. Firearms were widely used but were not normally accurate at any significant range. Nevertheless, when – in the course of a dispute over the guardianship of the young seventh Earl of Argyll – John Campbell of Ardkinglas became part of a conspiracy to assassinate John Campbell of Calder in February 1592, he equipped the chosen assassin, Gillipatrick Oig Mackellar, with a 'reid stockit hagbit', which hagbut with the red stock was then charged with three bullets. The victim was despatched by a shot through a window whilst sitting peaceably by the fireside. Campbell of Cabrachan, who was also involved in the plot and who was Mackellar's employer, found it necessary to be in Ireland that summer. Both he and the assassin were in the end to be executed, but Campbell of Ardkinglas eventually escaped judgement. His own in selecting a triple-charged firearm for a close-range hit was excellent – the chances of at least a couple of lethal wounds were high.[5] On the other hand, there was still a place very much later for the skilled archer, whose accuracy and rate of fire enabled him totally to outclass the average soldier armed with some form of firearm, at least in skirmishing and ambush work, well into the seventeenth century. In 1627 the MacNaughtan of that Ilk was commissioned to raise 200 Highland archers to join the Duke of Bucking-ham's ill-fated expedition to relieve La Rochelle in the course of Charles I's war with France. Raise them he did, for they were shipped out of Lochkerran in December of that year.[6]

Though the Scottish and Irish Gaelic-speaking areas were very much part of a single cultural area, which was why military culture was pretty uniform throughout the Gaidhealtachd, there were fundamental differences in the way they related to the adjacent territories which had been deeply influenced by Anglo-Norman feudalism. Within that feudal frame those territories had experienced the vigorous development of gentry, peasant, and burgher cultures derived from either the northern or the southern Anglo-Saxon tradition. It has been shown that in the twelfth and thirteenth centuries there was little sign that the inhabitants of an admittedly deeply regionalised Scottish realm saw the Highlands and Islands as in any way alien or exceptionally different from other parts of a culturally plural king-dom. The Gaelic language was not just the standard vernacular of the Hebridean islands and of the western seaboard, but elsewhere north of the Forth it had become confined largely to the upland parts of the counties bordering on the North Sea. Nevertheless, feudal forms had penetrated many Gaelic-speaking areas profoundly. Those areas were actively involved in the complex, often internecine strife of the Scottish wars of independence against Edward I and Edward II of England, which culminated in King Robert the Bruce's great victory at Bannockburn in 1314.

At the turn of the thirteenth and fourteenth centuries, and especially under Robert the Bruce, a policy of feudalising the western Highlands was pursued with a substantial measure of success.[7] Autonomy and loyalty were therefore not necessarily competing concepts in the Scottish part of the Gaidhealtachd, the more so in that many of the larger jurisdictions accepted or granted by the king carried with them regalian rights. Their holders, who were to include Highland magnates such as the earls of Argyle and Atholl, were in Scots nobiliary law *sub reguli*; that is, sub-kings with exclusive jurisdiction in all matters below high treason. Their royal status was so far from nominal that they possessed the right to bestow titles of nobility.[8]

Multiple identities are commonplace in most complex social realities. Historically, they have tended to enrage the powers-that-be in an ambitious state anxious to monopolise politically significant loyalties. Ecclesiastical authorities have nearly always responded with near apoplexy to the appear-ance of an often very reasonable mixture of religious identities. Yet the realities of God's creation kept denting simpler theories. Thus, the Crown of England had to deal with people on its border with Scotland in the six-teenth century who simply defied and indeed resented definition in national terms. These northern counties were in many ways similar to the Lordship of Ireland, complete with a heavily devolved administration and endless frontier clashes. Between 1333 and 1503 there was no peace between Scotland and England, just intermittent truces. Yet frontier lineages intermarried in such a way that by the start of the sixteenth century there were English branches of the Scottish Armstrong and Graham clans, settled in Bewcastle and Eskdale respectively. These Grahams derived from one William Graham who had simply squatted on the English side of the Esk after making Scotland too hot to hold him around 1516.[9]

Within the Scottish area of the Gaidhealtachd it seems that the prominent chiefs normally had no doubts about their Scottish identity. This was certainly the case with the most powerful of the principalities to emerge from the endless rise and fall of competitive kin-based groups – the Lordship of the Isles. At its height this particular structure embodied the greatness of Clan Donald, a clan which after the forfeiture of the Lordship in 1493 was to break into several smaller units functioning as distinct clans. In the fifteenth century the Lordship was by far the most powerful of the Scottish provinces, controlling not only all the Western Isles but also mainland territories such as Kintyre, Knapdale, Morvern, Ardgour, Ardnamurchan, Moidart, Knoydart, and Lochaber. Well did its ruler bear the title of *Ri Innse Gall*, king of the Hebrides. From the coastal territory of Lochalsh in Ross the lords of the isles also advanced a bitterly contested claim to the earldom of Ross. On occasion, the idea of challenging for the kingship of the Scots may have passed through their minds, though in fact it was the Scottish Crown which was to destroy the Lordship, indeed eventually felt it had to after 1462. In February of that year John, Lord of the Isles, and James, Earl of Douglas, conspired with Edward IV to partition Scotland between them. The short-term objective of the Scots conspirators was probably English gold, for which provision was made in the treaty with Edward IV, but of course intrigue with another monarchy was the one form of autonomy which the Crown could not tolerate. Even so, it was only in 1493, at a time when the Lordship was under exceptionally ineffective leadership, that James IV of Scotland forfeited the Lordship permanently. The ability of the Crown to enforce its decree was an entirely different matter. The upshot was fifty years of turbulence in the Western Isles, at the end of which it looked very much as if Donald Dubh, grandson of the forfeited John, would re-create the Clan Donald principality. Others were beginning to treat him as if he had indeed emerged as *Ri Innse Gall* when he unexpectedly died, and with him the hopes of the restoration of the Lordship.

When under strong leadership, the Lordship was capable, as it showed on several occasions, of defeating a royal army invading its territories. Even after the forfeiture, the Crown could not establish in this vast maritime province forces capable of imposing the royal will on a continuous basis. It could hope to influence the outcome of kinship struggles in the province, but it had ultimately to live with their outcome, whatever that might be.[10] Nor could the Scottish kings hope to set more than the broadest of limits to the external contacts sustained by such a province. It was sea-based, and sea was the great facilitator of contact and movements usually much more difficult by land. The Lordship's central administrative activity was the granting of feudal charters to its major landholders. Their survival has been predictably erratic, and only one in Gaelic is extant. The great bulk are in Latin. However, two of the Latin charters which survive specify galley service to the Lord of the Isles. One is dated 1463, relates to lands in Sleat in Skye, and is to a brother of the then holder of the dignity. The other, dated 1488, confirms land in Mull to Hector Maclean with service of a ship of 22 oars. Each oar would have had at least two men pulling it, and the largest galleys mentioned in other sources seem to have been of 40 oars.[11]

The west Highland galleys were descendants of the Viking longships, but they had, naturally, evolved over time. For example, by the fifteenth century they had replaced the steering sweep of Norse days by a conventional stern rudder. Though there were no burghs in the western Highlands, seaborne trade appears to have been vigorous, and as well as importing luxuries the elites of the western seaboard derived income from sending agricultural surpluses to Lowland consumers, often by sea up the Firth of Clyde. Socialising, elite burials (often on sacred islands) and, of course, raiding were all facilitated by galleys. The narrow waters between the southern Hebrides and Ulster, better seen as a unifying Dalriadian Sea, were much traversed. Often raiding was a purely economic venture. In 1582 Angus Macdonald of Islay descended on Ireland bent on plunder, but his galleys were intercepted by an English fleet which he escaped only by running into a storm that caused heavy loss in his fleet. A Maclean raid into what is now Donegal was much luckier, sweeping the MacSweeney country clear of cattle. In 1589 Hebridean galleys pillaged Mayo and Ulster. The MacNeill of Barra about the same time made summer sweeps down the Irish Sea, hovering off the coast of Munster with an eye to profit. In many ways he was essentially a professional pirate. Cattle might sound difficult from the point of view of seaborne raiders, but they could be slaughtered and shipped back quickly over the shorter raiding routes, or they could be skinned and hides and tallow shipped after such meat as was needed by, say, the 2000 Macleans who attacked the MacSweeneys had been consumed.[12]

There were significant changes on the western seaboard of the Scottish Highlands even before the downfall of the Lordship. The rise of Clan

Campbell in Argyll, for example, was marked by two developments which effectively moved the frontier of the Lordship into the sea and deprived its inhabitants of their former ability to strike deep into the Scottish mainland. One was the building of a cordon of strategic seaboard castles which screened the Campbell lands in Argyll, as well as the nearby ancestral lands of their royal allies the Stuarts, from the threat of galley-borne attack. Between the middle of the twelfth century and 1330 the strategically important areas of the Firth of Lorne, Sound of Mull, and the Clyde estuary were defended by a series of stone castles. The earliest of all Scottish medieval stone castles lies outside these limits in the shape of Castle Sween by Loch Sween in Knapdale, almost certainly named for Suibne, who gave his name to the MacSweens, but it is a square version of a shell-keep style emulated only a little later by the Stuarts in their circular shell keep at Rothesay on the Isle of Bute. Most of these castles had anchorages or boat landings, though none perhaps quite matched the sheltered bay in Loch Etive which served the great Campbell fortress of Dunstaffnage.[13] Parallel with this hardening of the sea margins went a steady development by the Campbells of a complex of land routes ranging from drove roads for cattle which were essentially broad rights of way to more formally defined tracks. The effect of these was to pull Argyll firmly into the heart of Scottish commercial and political life and to abolish by the seventeenth century the old distinction between the west and east Highlands.[14]

As opportunities for Clan Donald narrowed in some areas, fresh opportunities arose elsewhere. Political fragmentation made Clan Donald South, otherwise known as Clan Ian Mor, an autonomous unit. One of its principal seats in Scotland was Dunaverty Castle at the south end of the Mull of Kintyre, controlling the narrow waters between Scotland and Ulster. However, these MacDonalds had formed a marriage alliance with the Bisset family, which claimed to be heir to the old Norman earldom of the de Courcys in Ulster, and more particularly heir to the Glynnes or Glens of Antrim. With a following wind in the single square sail of a galley, the Antrim coast was a bare couple of hours from Kintyre, and indeed not much further from Islay, where Dunyveg Castle was the ancestral seat of Clan Ian Mor. Before the construction of a coastal road which linked them to Belfast in the early nineteenth century, the Antrim glens were fertile slots in the coast which looked over the sea to the Hebrides and Kintyre rather than backwards onto the windswept plateau of Antrim, let alone to the south. By the 1530s, when James MacDonnell,[15] sixth of Dunyveg and the Glynnes, was an ornament of the Scottish court, the MacDonald empire in Antrim was a fact of Ulster life. The marriage of James of Dunyveg and the Glynnes to Lady Agnes Campbell, daughter of Colin, third Earl of Argyll, in 1545 linked MacDonald and Campbell power in the west and was probably not unwelcome to the Scottish Crown when Henry VIII of England was intriguing with the claimant to the Lordship of the Isles, since it reminded Henry that two could play at that game. From almost precisely the middle of the sixteenth century the greatest of all the leaders of Clan Donald South in Antrim was to emerge as one of the main figures in Gaelic Ulster. This was Sorley Boy MacDonnell. His surname was simply one of many variations on MacDonald, but the Gaelic form of his other names 'Somhairle Buidhe', which mean 'yellow-haired Somerled', are a reminder of his Hebridean Gaelic–Norse origins.[16] To regard this crucial relationship between the south and west of Scotland and Gaelic Ulster as an intrusion into the self-contained history of 'Ireland' is unhistorical nonsense. People had been moving to and fro across these narrow waters for a thousand years before 1500: close interconnection was normal.

This was as true of Clan Campbell as it was of Clan Donald. If one examines the power-base of the fifth Earl of Argyll, for example, it is clear that this great prince of the Gael disposed of amphibious military power on a scale which made him virtually impregnable. Even in relation to the power of the state, he was formidable. He could raise 5000 fighting men with an effort, and more in a desperate emergency. Though short on cavalry, he was endowed with mobility across the innumerable seaways of the west by his possession of a big galley fleet. He himself maintained resident families of shipwrights working for him on Loch Awe and Loch Fyne, and of course he could add to their galleys those of his kin and allies. Nor was that all. Friendly ports lent him merchant ships – as, for example, Ayr did in 1555 and 1559. In 1560, when negotiating with the English government, he made it clear that he could possibly offer them the support of an expeditionary force of 3000 in Ireland. That was twice the size of the English standing force in Ireland. Argyll was a power in Lowland politics. He was a staunch Protestant, but a supporter of Mary, Queen of Scots, in the bitter civil war between her adherents and those of the young James VI in the years 1567 to 1573. The Queen's Men lost, yet the victors felt it essential to buy Argyll's good will with high office at the end of the war. Campbell involvement in Ulster politics was underlined by the fact that in 1569 the formidable Agnes Campbell, widow of MacDonnell of the Glynnes, married Turlough Luineach O'Neill, a Gaelic prince whose power and aspirations in Ulster matched those of the chief of Clan Campbell in the west of Scotland.[17]

The Dublin administration was understandably nervous about the depth of the Scottish connection in the north of Ireland. In 1580 Sir Nicholas Malbie warned Sir Francis Walsingham, a more hawkish individual by far than his rival William Cecil, later Lord Burleigh, that the Lady Agnes, her daughter, and Sorley Boy MacDonnell between them were threatening to turn Ulster into a new Scotland.[18] It was an alarmist view, probably designed to suggest the need for action and expenditure from which Malbie might benefit. He was a classic marginal beneficiary of court factional patronage. He developed into a good soldier and administrator. Surprisingly, he also became a notably fair judge. His background, however, was criminal. He had been convicted of coining in 1562 and pardoned on condition he offered military service in France. Through that service, he became an adherent of the Dudley faction at court. Nevertheless, the earls of Argyll were a pervasive and significant influence in the north of Ireland, above all because they could to a large extent control the flow of redshank infantry from the western Highlands. The fifth earl had an unusually complex military life. As Lord Lorne, he had campaigned in 1555–56 with Calvach O'Donnell, who was on the way to establishing his supremacy in Tyrconnell by the time-honoured device of ousting his own father. In the turmoil of the Wars of the Congregation in Scotland between 1559 and 1560, the fifth earl was prominent on the Protestant side. Always royalist in sympathy since their rise under Robert the Bruce, Clan Campbell contributed to Queen Mary's forces at the Battle of Corrichie in 1562, opposed her in the Chaseabout Raid of 1565–66 alongside her half-brother the Earl of Moray, and then fought for her in the long civil war between the Queen's Men and the King's Men between 1567 and 1573, with particularly heavy involvement in 1568 and 1570.[19] Apart from the odd threat to cut up awkward in Ireland if Elizabeth did not show more sympathy for the Queen's Men, this particular MacCailein Mor (to give him his Gaelic title) was too preoccupied latterly to do much there.

His life was further complicated by the outbreak of conflict between Campbell of Glenorchy and Clan MacGregor. Like the Macleans, the MacGregors had long served as a virtually satellite clan enhancing the military muscle of the Campbells. Because the honour of MacCailein Mor was involved, he had to help Glenorchy when this relationship disintegrated into war. It was not an easy war, for Argyll in the 1560s was short of the matchlock muskets known as hagbuts. Indeed he at one stage tried to negotiate with Queen Elizabeth for a supply of hagbutters as part of his price for giving her military support in Ireland. The fifth earl found that it required large numbers of troops to contain the hit-and-run tactics of the MacGregors. Glenorchy also complained that the MacGregors were better equipped with armour and the light muskets known as calivers than were the Campbell levies he was fielding against them.[20] Such was the intimacy and complexity of the Scoto–Irish relationships within the Gaidhealtachd that in 1564 James MacDonnell of Dunyveg can be found apologising frantically to Colin Campbell of Glenorchy because his brother Sorley Boy had, unknown to him, provided a group of MacGregors led by their chief with a season of employment as mercenaries in Ulster.[21] In September of that year Agnes Campbell can be found telling Glenorchy that Sorley Boy had finally terminated his contract with the MacGregor chief and that her husband James MacDonald had declined to transport the MacGregors to Scotland[22] – not that that presented any problem to the MacGregors, given the volume of movement by sea between Scotland and Ulster. The final letter in this fascinating correspondence was from Archibald, Earl of Argyll, to Campbell of Glenorchy telling him that he had gathered in Edinburgh that the MacGregor and eighty men had landed in Ayrshire and were walking home. The town of Ayr had – one wonders why – refused admittance to this cheerful band of seasonal workers, but that did not stop them returning home to Breadalbane to pick up their most important war where they had left it when they needed to earn a little elsewhere.[23]

The sixth and seventh earls of Argyll were in many ways more infuriating to the Tudor regime, for they did indeed become great purveyors of mercenaries in Ireland. That honest and ancient trade flourished as never before. In 1575 even the aggressive Earl of Essex accepted that Turlough Luineach needed to have a bodyguard of Scots of the Earl of Argyll's surname. When the O'Donnell and the O'Neill were confronting one another on either side of Loch Foyle in 1581, their inability to build up their troop numbers quickly was put down to the fact that 'The great army of Red Shanks' had been 'twice stayed' by Argyll. This was probably because of the close relationship between Argyll and the O'Docherty, who sat rather uncomfortably in the Innishowen peninsula between the two antagonists and who, since he was reported as paying cess to the Scots, was almost certainly entitled to protection from Argyll.[24]

There was nothing odd about this situation. It reflected the reality of intimate linkage facilitated by easy sea passages. The windy rhetoric of the common lawyers and the Tudor Crown was remote from reality when it tried to impose itself on the situation in the north of Ireland. Lord Deputy Perrot, when he heard that the sixth Earl of Argyll had died, urged that the time had come to test the devotion of the young Scottish king to Queen Elizabeth. He wanted Elizabeth to write to James and send an ambassador to demand, not for the first time, that the Scottish Crown stop its people invading Ireland.[25] First, the concept of James, as great an egotist as Elizabeth, showing devotion to her was optimistic. Secondly, James did not have the power to tell Argyll or the Clan Donald South what they should or should not do in the western Gaidhealtachd. Last and most fundamental of all, the concept of Scots 'invading' a political unit called 'Ireland' was simply fatuous. Gaelic Scots were only technically aliens in Ulster. The legal hostility of the Dublin government could be awkward for elite figures like Sorley Boy, who devoted a lot of energy to trying to secure at least denizen status – which would have removed many legal disabilities, though it would not have naturalised him as a subject of the Crown of Ireland. To humbler people the issue was irrelevant. Some lived there and more were seasonal workers in its regional military labour markets. The ultimate comment on Perrot's dream world of 1584 was an Irish state paper by Ambrose Lacy dated 1587 in which he surveyed the realities of the Earl of Tyrone's virtually independent government, his definitely non-Anglican religion, his Gaelic personal culture, his extensive diplomatic contacts with Scotland, and his 'confederacy' with Argyll for the supply of 4000 redshanks.[26] Ulster was an effectively independent world, linked primarily to other parts of the Gaidhealtachd.

The argument against any all-out offensive by either the English or the Scottish monarchies into the Gaidhealtachd was that almost by definition such a policy was bound to involve more effort, particularly financial effort, than it could possibly be worth. The guerrilla tactics of the Irish Gaelic chiefs were in effect a 'poison pill' defence against any takeover. There was, however, no squeamishness on the part of such chiefs when it came to using force to extend their own regional empires. The O'Neill was constantly trying to terrorise lesser Ulster chiefs into accepting his supremacy over them, and usually locked in mortal conflict with the O'Donnell, who saw himself with some justice as a wholly independent regional prince in his own right in Tyrconnell (roughly modern Donegal). In the Scottish Gaidhealtachd the three most powerful clans after the fall of the Lordship of the Isles – the Gordons, the Mackenzies, and the Campbells – were all aggressive and expansionist. They all, however, had special relationships with the Stuart monarchy. Their equivalents in Ireland were the earls of the Lordship. Crown relations with the Gaelic chiefs were extremely difficult. Even the surrender and regrant policy, designed to improve them, bred trouble almost at once because of the clash between the feudal concept of succession by primogeniture through legitimate heirs, which sat ill with the decidedly casual Gaelic approach to matrimony, preference for partible inheritance, and practice in political units of tanistry – whereby the most appropriate kinsman emerged as heir.

The most immediate problem, particularly after the Crown became reluctant to cooperate closely with the Earl of Kildare, was the lack of security in the Pale proper due to the proximity of the midland areas of Leix and Offaly, which virtually cut the old Lordship area in two and relentlessly terrorised its western boundaries. Payment of protection money or 'black rent' to the O'Mores and O'Dempseys of Leix or the O'Connors of Offaly was not acceptable indefinitely. It merely encouraged these entrepreneurs in redistributive industry to display more enterprise. Geographically they were so situated as to be able to make it difficult for a deputy to visit much of the Lordship and indeed in 1528 Brian O'Connor actually captured the lord deputy. There was a very powerful case for saying that this was the one area of the Gaidhealtachd which had to be permanently broken as a military power even if the sole objective of royal policy was to live in peace with as many Gaelic lordships as possible. Coexistence of the English and Gaelic polities was not feasible until the midlands of the Lordship were safe. In 1537 the deputy's forces marched into areas of Offaly which had been spared retribution before, captured Dengen Castle, razed it, and massacred its garrison. There were suggestions at the time that punitive columns, however heavy handed, made no long-term difference, and that permanent garrisons should be established in both Leix and Offaly. They were likely to be drowned in the surrounding sea of Gaelic hostility, so nothing was done, but the outbreak of serious trouble in the midlands in 1546–47, which saw fierce fighting between Crown forces and the O'Connor and the O'More, provoked the new regime of Protector Somerset into sending Sir Edward Bellingham to Ireland to impose a military solution. Campaigns were mounted which allowed the creation of a network of forts controlling the midlands. The cost of all of this was heavy. Some form of settlement was essential.

There was from an early stage a reasonable intention to settle military colonies on a limited scale around the new forts, of which the most import-ant were at Dangan and Ballyadams – first named Forts Governor and Protector respectively and then (when Queen Mary succeeded Edward VI) re-christened Philipstown and Maryborough after the queen and her con-sort, Philip II of Spain. There was little point in building these essential forts unless their immediate surrounds were friendly, which meant they had to be farmed by representatives of the Englishry, whether born in England or within the old Lordship in Ireland. Loyalist opinion expected further settlement to be done in association with local magnates, especially since the heir to the Earl of Kildare had been restored to the title and estates. There was much to be said for this in practical terms. Not only had these lords private power to supplement that of the Crown, but some of the greatest baronial houses had a hereditary knack of detaching Gaelic septs from the followings of recalcitrant chiefs by fitting them into their own. In the event the Marian regime opted for the drastic solution of confiscating and planting two-thirds of Leix and Offaly. Both areas were to be turned into shires, and displaced O'Mores, O'Connors, and O'Dempseys were to be moved into the remaining third, along the Shannon. The upshot was fifty years of bitter border war, which most loyalist opinion deemed un-necessary, not in the sense that the area did not need to be bridled – that was agreed – but in the sense that they thought that there were infinitely more sensible ways of doing it.

By the 1540s, loyalist opinion both in the Pale and in the wider fiefdoms of Munster and Leinster was finding itself plunged into a political and fiscal nightmare which continually faced it with insoluble dilemmas and imposs- ible choices. The increasingly drastic changes of regime and policies which emanated from the Palace of Westminster and other haunts of the royal court passed a crucial point with the aggressively Protestant regimes of Protectors Somerset and Northumberland. The evidence is clear that within certain conservative limits the Englishry of Ireland were willing to go along with the Crown in accepting religious change, but they were dependent on an instinctive consensus, which was there for most of the reign of Henry VIII between them and their monarch, that change could not, espe- cially in matters of public ritual, go too far without becoming distasteful. The dizzy rate of change in official religious policy in the 1540s destroyed that assumption. The ability of parliaments held in Ireland to check ex- ecutive policy initiatives in the military sphere also collapsed. Parliamentary taxation in Ireland was in desperate need of reform, but as deficits in Irish government soared from £4700 in 1542 to £34,700 in 1552, any possible contribution from the community that supported parliaments in Ireland became an irrelevance. From 1547 the government chose to rely on an enhanced garrison, which rose to 2600 men by 1551, and on the systematic extension of military exactions on a scale which destroyed the traditional assumptions about the need for consent to taxation. Thus purveyance, the standard if limited feudal obligation to supply the household of the monarch or his representative – known in the Lordship as cess – was pushed to unprecedented limits to sustain the civil and military establish- ment. The obligation of loyal subjects to rise in a hosting to defend the marches against Gaelic raids – a sensible, economic, and necessary device – was extended unreasonably and then commuted into payments which were used to fund policies not supported by the traditional community of the realm in Ireland.

There was a general tendency on the part of the executive to ignore that community's opinions as much as those of the Gaelic princes, and to scorn the demands of the baronage for some measure of partnership in and therefore control over policy formation. As a result, the loyalist community found itself taxed relentlessly to pay for an ill-thought-out, unsuccessful, and dismally expensive confrontation with the Gaidhealtachd. Since debasement of the currency, which generated inflation, was another favourite mode of financing military activity, it is not surprising that parliaments ceased to be summoned in Ireland. Religious change in the reigns of Edward VI and Mary was handled by royal proclamation. Between 1543 and 1613 only four parliaments were summoned in Ireland, and of these only two saw attempted dialogue between Crown and community. In 1569–71 leading opponents of the Crown left parliament for the battlefield, as a place more likely to produce results, and in the parliament of 1585–86 the Crown deservedly lost most of its proposed legislation.

Sir Thomas Radcliffe, Lord Fitzwalter and later earl of Sussex, who succeeded St Leger as deputy after the latter's second spell in office came to an end in 1556, was the epitome of the courtier cum military entrepreneur who was to dominate the later sixteenth-century deputyship, with lethal results. He came with no local knowledge, but with Sir Henry Sidney, his kinsman – the first of many to take office – as under-treasurer. He seems to have accepted all existing lines of action initiated by his immediate predecessors, but drove them simultaneously with a vigour which in the short run generated a flow of funds to Ireland to sustain his forces, and generated jobs for his incoming relatives and dependants. Increasingly, the old loyalist community was referring to itself as the Old English, to distinguish itself from this new band of upstarts, themselves increasingly identified as the New English. Movement between different parts of the English community was, of course, natural and right, but this new group from close to the levers of court power offered contempt and hostility to their established kinsmen, whom they excluded from decisions. Despite fierce criticism from the Old English and St Leger, who represented them at court, Sussex launched heavy-handed action on three fronts. One was the midland plantation, where his actions belied the hopes of the Old English that they should control the end game in Leix and Offaly. The other two were in Ulster.

The penetration of Antrim by Highland Scots who did not pretend to be subjects of the Tudors absolutely enraged both Mary and Elizabeth, partly because of the Scots connection with a hostile France, and partly because of an inability to distinguish between rhetoric and reality in the Gaidhealtachd. Since Dublin could not control north Antrim, it mattered little which Gaelic chief did, as long as he was not the O'Neill, whose power was already too great too close to the Pale. Governor James Croft nevertheless had proclaimed a hosting against the MacDonnells in 1551, to discover that they withdrew to Scotland as he advanced from Carrickfergus (returning as he left, of course), and that he did not have the naval power to take their island stronghold of Rathlin, off the north-east coast of Antrim.

The other debacle which Sussex embraced with enthusiasm was that created by the paradoxical effect of the policy of surrender and regrant in Ulster. Succession under Gaelic law was not necessarily from father to eldest son, which is not to say that such succession did not occur. Powerful Gaelic dynasts often preferred to confine the succession to their closest relatives, so in the MacCarthy More family son succeeded father for two hundred years. The Maguires of Fermanagh, more or less permanently squeezed between the O'Neill and the O'Donnell, both anxious to dominate them, were strong enough to ensure that leadership passed from father to son for seven generations. Military strength was often the key to ability to keep the succession in the ruling family. Scottish mercenaries would be imported in large numbers if it looked as if a rival candidate was gathering strength among the septs. The MacWilliam Burkes not only used this device themselves to contain internal conflict, but over generations seem to have become the principal brokers in Scottish mercenaries to the northern and western chiefs. The availability of overwhelming force in hands resolute for an otherwise reasonable exercise in primogeniture ensured that there was seldom any need to use it.

So far from dogmatically insisting on the strict primogeniture of Common Law in the surrender and regrant procedure, the terms of agreements made by the Crown in the 1540s often showed considerable flexibility to local situations in these and other respects. Thus, Murrough O'Brien, it was agreed, was to be succeeded by his tanist, his nephew Donogh, rather than his eldest son. Catastrophically, Conn O'Neill seized the opportunity offered by the process of surrender and regrant to nominate as his successor an illegitimate son, Matthew, who was created Baron of Dungannon rather than the O'Neill's extremely able son Shane, the accepted tanist.[27] Shane moved fast. Matthew was assassinated. Conn was driven out of Ulster by force, to take refuge in the Pale, where he died. Shane had himself proclaimed O'Neill by the septs at the traditional inauguration site of Tullahogue in east Tyrone. A sensible government might have accepted this as a fact of life, particularly as pedigree making and faking was a major industry everywhere in the Gaidhealtachd and legitimacy or its reverse often a matter of taste. Given the hereditary ambitions of the O'Neill, any Dublin administration needed to bridle and weaken him, but for that there were allies to hand. A tacit alliance between the Crown and the O'Donnell survived from the 1540s to the 1580s, on that solidest of all foundations – mutual self-interest. The septs of south Ulster were always anxious to escape O'Neill's exactions, and the Scots MacDonnells in Antrim were potential allies rather than a threat, for the O'Neill's megalomaniac ambition to lord it over all Ulster threatened them as much as the O'Donnell. Despite the existence of these options, Sussex tried simultaneously to crush Shane and the Scots.

In Shane he faced a man who understood the need for unprecedented mobilisation. He immediately brought over 1500 redshank mercenaries, Campbells, McLeans, MacLeods, and McKays from Kintyre and Islay. Then he went further than any Gaelic prince had gone: he started to arm and train 'all the peasants of his country, the first that ever did so of an Irishman'. War in the Gaidhealtachd had hitherto been the prerogative of social and military elites. Now the O'Neill disposed of forces far greater than the 300 cavalry, 800 regular infantry, and 300 of the 'queen's kerne' which were all Sussex could field. To make a bad situation worse, Sussex had tried to discourage Scottish intervention in Ulster by devoting the last autumn of Queen Mary's reign to an amphibious offensive against the MacDonald heartland in Scotland. Weather conditions prevented him from reaching Islay but he ravaged Kintyre, Arran, Bute, and the Cumraes. It was possible for Sussex to argue that conflict with Shane and Sorley Boy's MacDonnells was inevitable, because of their intrigues with the French, and more particularly with the Scottish government of Mary of Guise – regent for her daughter Mary, who was married to the heir to the French throne – but this was specious. Both the Scots and the O'Neill would have been happy to go through some form of feudal homage to Elizabeth as queen of Ireland in order to obtain a secure title to their position and possessions. The problem was that Shane knew Sussex loathed him and had marked him for destruction, while the Antrim Scots would have been fools indeed not to grasp that the policy of the Dublin administration was to drive them out of Ireland.

As if these problems were not enough, the new Queen Elizabeth inherited a religious situation in Ireland which, if not totally impossible, was certainly much more difficult than it had been at the death of Henry VIII in 1547. That monarch was the first king of England to be addressed as 'Majesty' (the previous usage had been 'Your Grace', later resurfacing for the ducal order). He became, reluctantly, the first king of Ireland, and progressed from Defender of the Faith to Supreme Head of the Church. In Ireland the abolition of the monasteries, themselves not very active in social work or spiritually very dynamic, had passed off with relatively little incident. As long as the Crown remained Catholic in usage, simply moving towards a territorial church headed by the monarch – who had always had extensive, if debated, powers over the church in his dominions – there was no widespread resistance on purely religious grounds. But the reign of Edward VI had seen drastic innovation by an English government controlled by ideologically driven Protestants. Their attempt to use royal prerogative to bring in an unmistakably Protestant church settlement, certainly enforced in Dublin churches by 1550, was dangerous.

The conservative monastic orders may have lacked vigour but Ireland had a far stronger tradition of reformed Observant Franciscans than England, and these austere mendicants were a potential core of resistance to a perceived heretical government. This does not mean that the cause of the Reformation was predestined to failure, in either the old Lordship lands or the Gaelic areas. Many conservative clergy accepted the need for royal leadership to achieve church reforms, which were clearly overdue in some fields. Papal links with the Gaels were not very strong. Even under Edward VI the Reformation made some progress in Ireland and there are some indications that this progress was maintained, at a lowish level due to linguistic obstacles in Gaelic areas, in the early years of Elizabeth. She certainly did not face as much principled opposition to the re-establishment of the royal supremacy among Irish bishops as amongst English ones. Reluctant conformity with the Crown's wishes continued to characterise the Englishry of the Lordship lands. There was a lot of ambiguity and hedging of bets from the highest levels down but, drifting into the 1560s, the Elizabethan regime could hope for slow acceptance of an Anglican Church of Ireland. By the mid-1570s the situation was much more disturbing. The Old English were beginning to patronise the militant Counter-Reformation. Protestants had failed to control pre-university education, and wealthy merchants' sons were beginning to go to continental universities rather than Oxford. Nevertheless, it seems clear that in the crucial transition between 1580 and 1641 which made the Old English the core of a Roman Catholic culture on which modern Catholic nationalism was to be built, war and its impact on the Old Irish loyalist community under the later Elizabethan regime was the decisive trigger.[28]

Making a bad situation worse: early Elizabethan Ireland

When Elizabeth came to the throne in 1558, she inherited a dire situation on several fronts, and Ireland was no exception. The loss of Calais to France in the last days of Mary may have been a blessing in disguise, but it made plain to all that the military pretensions of the English monarchy to parity with the great continental powers were a thing of the past. They had been sustained under Henry VIII by vast infusions of expensive foreign mercenaries into his field armies, but his heirs were now near to insolvency.[29] In Ireland Sussex was acutely aware of agitation against him at court by allies of his Old English critics. In 1558 and 1560 he headed for court to protect his position, coming back both times confirmed in his governance, but at a price. He had to produce unrealistic plans for the conquest of Gaelic Ireland, on which his own patronage system depended, and for the crushing of the autonomy of the great Old English earls, whilst at the same time radically reducing expenditure. Until the French were expelled from Scotland in 1560, he could use the threat of a French invasion of Ireland to still the doubts of a parsimonious and sceptical queen, but his bogus prospectus brought its own nemesis with it. The Northamptonshire gentleman Sir William Fitzwilliam whom he had made vice treasurer and treasurer at war in Ireland in 1559, and who held the reins in Dublin for him as a Lord Justice when he was in England in 1560, was relentlessly totting up the soaring figures for the war against Shane – as well he might, for he himself was to leave his treasurerships an ill and impoverished man. The army came expensive. Cavalrymen cost ninepence a day, arquebusiers eightpence, archers sixpence, and kerne a very reasonable threepence. Their officers were entrepreneurs who supplied their own troops, and were paid accordingly. 'Frauncis Crosby generall over the sayd kerne' was paid three shillings a day for his activities as general (secured by letters patent), and another three shillings and fourpence daily for leading his own band of 100 kerne. As well as the several hundred kerne normally retained, there had to be a topping up of the establishment with 'Cearten kerne reteined by order of the lord lieutenante and counsell in the warres againste Shane ONeyle'. Debts owed to officers and men alike mounted remorselessly. Kerne were discharged unpaid, which in the long run would make further recruitment near impossible. By the end of December 1562, Fitzwilliam reckoned that since the last full pay day, which had been in May 1560, the queen had accumulated debts of nearly £40,000 to her forces and their suppliers in Ireland.[30]

Between 1560 and 1562 Sussex had failed to produce results. In 1560 Shane's troops were ravaging the northern Pale and threatening Dundalk. The next year saw his power massively enhanced when Lady O'Donnell, formerly countess of Argyll, betrayed her husband Calvach O'Donnell to him. She became Shane's mistress. Calvach was imprisoned in chains, while Shane's power peaked, though at the price of bitter hostility from the O'Donnells. Sussex had Shane proclaimed a rebel and traitor (which implied confiscation of his lands), and tried to break him with successive invasions of Tyrone. Using Newry as a base, he penetrated deep. Taking advantage of the talents of 'the extraordynare bandes of kerne' brought into the queen's service for these campaigns, he was able in one march down the Mourne–Stroule valley to Loch Foyle to capture 4000 cattle and a stock of brood mares, most of which had to be slaughtered, for there was no means of moving them out. Faced with this cruel level of destruction of economic resources, it was a great tribute to Shane's tactical intelligence that he refused to be drawn into formal battle. His fabian tactics wore down Sussex, just as the destruction wrought by Sussex was one factor in persuading Shane to pay a visit under safe conduct to the court of Queen Elizabeth early in 1562. Significantly, he insisted on being accompanied by the Geraldine earls of Kildare and Desmond, to whom he was related. Both Elizabeth and Shane put on performances of a high theatrical order for the occasion without quite getting the measure of the other, but Shane left with a tacit deal that he would concentrate on attacking that other object of royal ire, the MacDonnells.

Sussex was appalled by the very idea of a rapprochement with Shane. In 1563 there was another invasion of Shane's lands by Sussex. It demonstrated little more than the fact that Shane's forces were now making an extensive use of arquebuses. Though there were no urban developments of any significance on Shane's lands, trade was obviously vigorous in agricultural produce and timber with the west of Scotland and the lands of the Pale. It was possible for Shane to use surplus wealth to arm himself in the latest fashion, no doubt greatly assisted by the fact that Scottish merchants had a special relationship with the Netherlands, a major centre of the production of arms and munitions. In despair, the Dublin authorities connived at an attempt to poison the hard-drinking Shane with a gift of doctored wine. The plan failed. In September 1563 a treaty was negotiated whereby Shane was recognised by the Crown as the O'Neill, though not as earl of Tyrone. He could even afford to release Calvach O'Donnell, a broken old man whose appeals elicited no concrete aid from either Dublin or Elizabeth's court, where he went to plead his case. The queen regarded Shane's campaigns against the MacDonnells, now led by James MacDonnell and his younger brother Sorley Boy, as good service to her.

Shane's official line in the grandiloquent Latin letters he sent to the Dublin administration and the queen was that he was consumed with a desire to do her a signal service. Guided by his correspondence with her favourite the Earl of Leicester and her great minister Sir William Cecil, he had decided that there were no traitors like the Scots traitors in Antrim.[31] In reality, he served nobody but himself. He began by trying and failing to storm Sorley Boy's position at Coleraine, which guarded the strategic crossing on the lower Bann. Then in 1565 he mounted a direct attack overland on north Antrim, where the MacDonnells had confirmed their grip in 1558 by subjugating the MacQuillans of the Route. Reinforced from Scotland, the 'robbers of the Hebrides' stood and fought at Glenshesk, only to be bloodily defeated. Of their leaders, James was captured, his wounds were callously neglected and he died. Sorley Boy, already wounded in the Coleraine fight, was also captured and would have been starved publicly to death by Shane outside Dunluce Castle had not the MacDonnell defenders elected to surrender.

Royal policy had been incredibly expensive, and almost unbelievably imperceptive. It had neglected friends like the O'Donnell. It had alienated potential allies like the MacDonnells, and on top of that it had actively encouraged the expansion of the power of an O'Neill always proud as the devil but now puffed up to the point where megalomania began to over-ride judgement. Deficit financing had created a cash flow in the Irish administration which attracted the courtier-racketeer, and pressure to reduce expenditure did not discourage them. Rather it encouraged them to make unrealistic contract bids when the queen tried to semi-privatise Irish administration.

They had then, of course, to count on enriching themselves with every courtier's dream of heaven – extensive confiscations of 'traitors'. Given the aggrandisement of Shane, passivity was not a viable policy. What was needed was adequate force and moderate objectives. Elizabeth's policies guaranteed miserably inadequate forces allied to unrealistic but wildly provocative policies that persuaded most Gaelic chiefs that their lands were not safe.

After an interlude of conciliatory but weak government under Nicholas Arnold, Sussex was succeeded as deputy by his former subordinate Sir Henry Sidney. There seems to have been no fundamental change in policy between the two men: that was the trouble. Sidney, like Sussex, was committed to controlling the midlands by making the exercise in plantation in Leix and Offaly work. He was also committed to breaking Shane, driving the Scots out of Ulster, and confirming these achievements with limited strategic plantation in that province. It was back to 1562, with the difference that Sidney insisted on adequate forces, funding, and support from the privy council before he would take the job. He had been appointed lord president of the Council for Wales and the Marches in 1560. The fact that he did not resign that post reflected his declared opinion that he had the solution to the problems of Ireland. He expected to have solved them in three years, when he would resign the deputyship to return to appropriate rewards in land and title.[32] Even if he had not been short-changed on his conditions, as he absolutely predictably was, the presumption implicit in the promise of a quick fix with a programme which had already effectively failed was alarming.

Sidney was undoubtedly a man of ability and energy, and Shane's antics had reached the point where punitive action was imperative. Intriguing at the Scots court was pretty standard behaviour for an O'Neill, but posing as the defender of the faith against a heretic queen and offering the throne of Ireland to Charles IX of France in exchange for troops was to invite the invasion which Sidney launched in September 1566. Starting from Drogheda with his lieutenant Humphrey Gilbert, Sidney marched by way of a ruined Armagh to Loch Neagh, where he stormed and subsequently garrisoned the fortress on Coney Island which was Shane's treasury. He then marched by Clogher to repeat Sussex's drive down the Mourne–Stroule valley of 1561, but this time the operation was part of a pincer movement whose other arm was a landing by Colonel Randolph on the west shore of Loch Foyle where he built a fort at Derry and then moved up river to meet Sidney. Sidney had restored the Maguire power on his way in. On his way out he restored the O'Donnell by marching through his country before returning by Sligo and Athlone. Subsequent attacks on Randolph's fort failed, but had the good luck to kill him. When the powder magazine accidentally blew up in April 1567, the garrison had had enough and withdrew by sea to Carrickfergus.

Nevertheless, the whole episode had a withering effect on Shane's prestige. He had been unable to stop the devastation of his own heartland. Naval patrols had interrupted the usual rush of contract military workers from Scotland which would have strengthened him, and his prime regional protection racket had paid, at the hands of a more ruthless exponent of terror than he, the price for hubris and over-extension. Instead of licking his wounds, the O'Neill decided to try to crush the newly independent O'Donnells. The result was that in May 1567 Hugh O'Donnell lay waiting for him behind earthworks near Letterkenny on the River Swilly. Shane's impetuous assault across the ford failed in the Battle of Farsetmore, and as the estuary filled with the rising tide, many of his retreating troops drowned. An extraordinarily injudicious attempt by the defeated Shane to recruit support from the MacDonnells, who summoned a galley fleet from Kintyre to meet the tattered forces of the victor of Glenshesk at Cushendun, proved disastrous. Sorley Boy, whom Shane had kept prisoner since that battle, was released, but clearly retained a sharp memory of being nearly starved to death before Dunluce. Shane was stabbed to death during negotiations with the MacDonnells, and his head was sent, pickled, as a present to Sidney in Dublin.[33] Shane exited shabbily the scene he had once adorned. Elizabeth congratulated her deputy at the news that Shane's head was displayed on a pole in Dublin Castle. It was a standard display of royal vengeance on traitors. It was also particularly meaningless. The MacDonnells, not Sidney, had killed him and for their own reasons. Besides, the trouble was that the head had ceased to function in even a moderately sensible way some time before it was separated from the body which went with it. The straightforward succession of Shane's tanist, the infinitely cannier but not soft Turlough Luineach, was a great gain to all the peoples of Ulster. Sir James Ware later calculated that Elizabeth spent £147,000 Irish (the £ Irish was at a one third discount to the £ sterling) and lost 3500 men in her wars against Shane. Two years later the sovereignty of the O'Neills in Ulster was officially 'abolished' again by the queen's government (Shane's sovereignty had been 'abolished', but in a fit of commonsense the matter had not been raised at Turlough Luineach's accession). This gesture showed that nothing had been learned from such an appalling waste of resources to little purpose in an almost pointless colonial war.

To advertise an intention to grab O'Neill lands on the back of destroying their political structure, when Turlough Luineach was more than capable of looking after himself, was to secure the worst of all possible worlds. Already, the cost of the Ulster wars had deeply alienated the Old English loyalists. They had been put under high-handed, arrogant direct rule. Though some had hoped Kildare might be made deputy at the start of the reign, it had become increasingly clear that they were to be denied any real influence, let alone control, over their own governance. New English, too many of them ruthless chancers from court circles, were winning the dutch auctions which the queen conducted in order to cut the cost of governing in Ireland. Cessed to death without consent, even the ultra-loyalist Palesmen were increasingly desperate. They were an extreme case, but not at all a unique one. The Tudors were often the most disruptive force in their own dominions, especially when they interfered in long-established regional ascendancies, such as that of the Percys in the north of England, thrusting new and voraciously greedy court candidates for loaves and fishes into an area with its own established patronage networks. Percy patronage in the north of England was no more anarchic than royal patronage. There was an elaborate structure of royal government in the north, from the warden-ships of the marches to the Council of the North. Yet it was a system which required cooperation from local magnates if it was to operate smoothly. After the Dacres and Percys ceased to be acceptable for major local office, there was a long period of tension in the affairs of the region, culminating in the reluctant revolt of the northern earls, Northumberland and Westmorland, in 1569 – a revolt closely connected with their being on the losing side in faction battles in court and council.[34] They went down to defeat, not least because Berwick was one of the most up-to-date and heavily garrisoned fortresses in the queen's dominions. They did not fall alone, for in that same year Sir Edmund Butler, a cadet of the Ormondes, and Sir James Fitzmaurice Fitzgerald, cousin of the Earl of Desmond, rose in revolt in Munster.

It was another case of the unsettling effect of a power vacuum. The earls of Desmond and Ormonde had actually met in formal battle at Affane in 1565, thereby offending the queen. As a result, both were summoned to England, where Desmond was effectively kept under house arrest until 1573, leaving powerful Geraldine interests without a head at a time when the Butler Earl of Ormonde, though detained at court for three and a half years, was known to be cultivating the good will of the queen only too successfully. Sir James had been chosen 'captain' in Gaelic fashion by local Geraldines, who needed a leader. A group of arrogant and ruthless west country oppor-tunists, of whom the most notorious were Sir Peter Carew, Humphrey Gilbert, and Richard Grenville, were trying to take advantage of the exclusion of the local aristocracy from government and the disfavour of the earls to advance dubious legal claims to lands. Sir James Fitzmaurice does seem to have been an early adherent of the Counter-Reformation, passionately hos-tile to a heretic sovereign, but the core issue of the rising was insecurity over land, which is why it was joined by Gaelic lords like the MacCarthy More, recently created Earl of Clancarthy by surrender and regrant.

Only a minority of the Old English of Munster rose. The towns re-mained loyal. Sidney was swift to react and Gilbert, placed in command of the army in Munster, proved to be murderously efficient. His open terrorism, complete with avenues of severed heads before his tent, and his emphasis on the unfettered power of the prince, were totally incompatible with traditional English liberties. The stress on princely absolutism was that of a politician not only sure that he could use that authority to serve his own ends, but also totally confident that his prospective victims in Munster had no chance of accessing the source of sovereignty. It was a classic early-modern European recipe for political disintegration. Sir Edmund Butler had risen, insisting that he did not rebel against the Crown of England, to which his august house had been loyal for centuries, but against those 'who banish Ireland and mean conquest'. It was a very fair comment. Manageable though the crisis proved, the combination of Gaelic and Old English forces should have given the executive pause.

Curbing the unacceptable tendency to internecine strife among the baronage, and making the midland plantation stable, both tasks most easily accomplished by aiming at partnership with the Crown's traditional aristocratic allies, was about the limit of what could constructively be accomplished with the resources Elizabeth would willingly commit. Certainly, before the 1590s there was no programme for a 'conquest' of an alien and hostile Ireland. Large parts of it were not alien, and in any case Elizabeth was probably too mean to make the necessary resources available for such a policy, even if she had them in the first place. There was a permanent army in Ireland which between 1556 and 1578 averaged about 1800 men. It had a small administrative staff of whom the marshal dealt with discipline, the treasurer at wars with pay, the master of the ordnance with equipment and supplies, and the clerk of the checks with musters. Normally, a large proportion of these troops was tied up in garrisons commanded by constables or seneschals, or as part of the units always attached to senior military officials. The marshal had over 100 men in attendance, and such figures as the lords president – who were theoretically permanently resident in Connaught and Munster after 1569 – both had military retinues of 50. Captains were the highest regular field appointments. The company of 100 men was the basic unit. Companies were usually scattered in penny packets acting as security guards and enforcers of Common Law court decisions, especially in those marginal areas where the main thrust of the post-1541 policy of extending Common Law jurisdiction lay. None of this was necessarily provocative. It all depended how it was done. Gaelic Connaught, for example, seems to have had no great difficulty in absorbing the concept of the presidency, not as the product of alien conquest so much as of the endless rise and fall of regional powers.

Even the process of demilitarising relations between the great magnates of the old Lordship and their tenants was not necessarily a source of lethal friction. The system of coyne and livery, whereby these men, like Gaelic chiefs, extracted necessary obedience, supplies, and military support from subordinates, was not very satisfactory. Almost all magnates used it, but few profited much from it, and many would have gained by conversion to monetised rent, which would still have allowed them to employ bands of retainers as enforcers, preferably with the consent of the government.[35] To secure that, they needed to be part of it. Members of what became known as the Old English community did indeed hold key positions within the Tudor administration in Ireland, particularly in the Irish privy council. They had their own pervasive networks of patronage. Yet the pattern after 1562 was one in which even they saw the high policy decisions, and especially the expensive military ones, relentlessly clawed back into the hands of the queen and her central group of advisers. The results could be hair-raising. What drove the queen was the knowledge that military expenditures absorbed two-thirds of her Irish budget. However, by refusing adequate resources at the start of a crisis she usually allowed it to get out of hand, and ended up with costs running out of control. There were three drives for troop reductions between 1572 and 1578. By 1579, with a very serious Munster rising threatening to break out into the other provinces, Elizabeth was still pushing, with a stubbornness worthy of the modern UK treasury, for reductions in garrisons. Narrowing the basis of discussion before high-level decisions were taken could only be justified if the outcome was the placing of adequate means behind sensible policies.[36]

Instead, the queen's government persisted with unintelligent attempts to cut costs, including the licensing of private adventures whose sponsors had to be offered other men's lands as inducement. Sir Thomas Smith, a classic example of a renaissance humanist in politics, had had a chequered career because of his close association with Protector Somerset, ending up a state prisoner in the Tower of London at one point, but under Elizabeth he enjoyed an Indian summer as privy councillor and ambassador to France. In 1571 he secured a grant to settle the Ards peninsula in east Ulster. The rhetoric of Roman imperialism was mother's milk to a humanist. Indeed, it permeated the political language of educated Western Europeans.[37] Smith's propaganda about sending out the equivalent of Roman colonists to bring civility to the barbarians of the Ards was more than usually unreal. Most of the locals were descended from Norman colonists introduced by the medieval de Courcy earls of Ulster. Smith has been depicted as one of the fathers of English colonial theory. The concept can be objected to on almost every ground. Colonial theory the English state had never had, nor should such a concept be confused with the 'tissue of propaganda and special pleading so characteristic of most Elizabethan projects'.[38] Rank lunacy was not at all unheard of in this sort of promotional literature, which can be found later in the century suggesting that two English families from every parish should be moved to Ireland, to be replaced by five families from each Irish parish, moving the other way. Sir Brian McPhelim O'Neill, the Lord of Clandeboy, knew Smith for what he was: an optimist trying to parlay court favour into fortune by seizing large parts of Sir Brian's ancestral lands under guise of grant. The tired tropes of Smith's humanist rhetoric were neither here nor there, as Smith soon found. His illegitimate son, who led an inadequate force of 100 men to try to settle in the Ards in 1572, lost the fight against Sir Brian and his own life to a hit man who very sensibly used a gun. After a pause, his father emitted another cloud of sycophantic rhetoric about establishing a walled city to be called 'Elizabetha'. When the lady herself told him to get on with it or forfeit the grant, all he could do was send 150 men, a totally inadequate force against the Clandeboy O'Neills. Smith transferred his rights to the Earl of Essex, another courtier blinded by greed to the fact that the queen, who would only lend him money for his Ulster venture on the security of his estates, was offering him something not hers to give and well beyond his strength to take.

Almost everyone with a grasp of realities was aghast at the policies emerging by default through court-engineered grants. At a time when the Fitzmaurice rising was fielding forces with '1400 galloglas, 400 pikes with shirts of mail, 400 gunners, and 1500 kerne' under the walls of Kilkenny,[39] it was, as the Earl of Ormonde told Cecil, bizarre to let loose in Munster a claim-jumper like Sir Peter Carew, who was guaranteed to alienate all the lords and loyalists.[40] The 'enterprise of Ulster', as Elizabeth blithely called the activities of Smith and Essex, just appalled her experienced local commanders like William Piers, constable of 'Knockfergus' (i.e. Carrickfergus) from 1556 to 1578. He knew that news of land grants to the egregious Smith in the Ards and elsewhere in Ulster would generate a Gaelic rising. Indeed, when the news came out he forged a deputy's letter denying the whole scheme.[41] He was wasting his time. Sir Brian read the granting away of lands in an original publication,[42] which it has to be said the Dublin administration thought it wanton provocation to publish. Deputy Fitzwilliam, who had succeeded Sidney in 1571, told Cecil, now Lord Burghley, that he deemed Smith a dangerous windbag.[43] His successor, the first Earl of Essex, was an extreme case of a court-backed chancer. He came with support from Burghley, Sussex, and Leicester, and after gambling a large proportion of his assets on the venture. He always meant to use force on an unprecedented scale, accumulating in advance 6 pieces of artillery, a great deal of gunpowder and slow match for firelocks, entrenching tools, 150 light muskets known as calivers, and 60 ordinary muskets, plus the services of 200 archers and 2 surgeons. His arrival in Antrim in August 1573 was calculated to make a bad situation much worse.[44]

More or less simultaneously, Essex launched into violent aggression against the MacDonnells, Sir Brian McPhelim O'Neill, and Turlough Luineach O'Neill. That the queen gave Essex the title of governor of Ulster was another piece of self-deceiving rhetoric, but also a chilling warning that the sort of presidential military regimes which had been tried out in the southern provinces might lie in store for Ulster. There was no excuse for the Essex debacle. Burghley was warned in the plainest possible terms in late 1573 that the episode had given the Ulster chiefs all the fury of desperation. They just could not believe that the queen could be so stupid. Indeed, it was widely believed that Essex was conducting the war on his own private initiative. Besides, the assumptions on which the venture was based, as Burghley's informant pointed out, were all patently bogus. The rhetoric of a sharp division between 'civility' and 'savagery' was glib stupidity in an Ulster where Sir Brian could access the public prints as easily as anyone else. If Gaelic influences bit deep into the lands of the old Lordship, the opposite was also true: English culture and government influence permeated large parts of the Gaidhealtachd. The total cynicism with which the neoclassical humanist vocabulary of civility was twisted to serve the selfish ends of opportunist politicians was amusingly demonstrated in a brief phase when Essex thought that the Lady Agnes might play along with what he wanted of her husband, the O'Neill. She suddenly became in his discourse a wise and civil woman, an instrument of peace. This odour of sanctity did not suit her and she was soon back to being 'lewd' and a menace in the eyes of the lord deputy.[45] Even in Ulster, where government influence was at a minimum, Burghley was reminded that the Gaels had long ago learned the techniques of fortification and had much the same range of modern weapons as anyone else. The folly of reactivating a colonial war on the traditional frontiers of the Englishry of Ireland violated one of the basic principles of entrepreneurial violence: there has to be a reasonable prospect of success without disproportionate sacrifice. As Burghley was told, in so many words, the English were soft and unwarlike compared with the peoples they were proposing to assault.[46]

Essex tried to compensate with savagery for his inadequate funding base. He needed results quickly, so when Turlough Luineach wisely ignored his imperious summons to a meeting, he invaded and devastated Tyrone. It was a totally counter-productive gambit. The unfortunate Sir Brian McPhelim O'Neill tried to be conciliatory. For his pains, he was kidnapped by Essex and, after he had seen his entourage massacred before his face, he was shipped to Dublin with his wife and brother for judicial butchery. A fresh offensive against the O'Neill by Essex was actively encouraged by the queen, but then she turned round and told him that there was no question of financial assistance from the Crown. Essex resigned as governor of Ulster in high dudgeon. Turning against Clan Donald South, he drove Sorley Boy out of Clandeboy, but found it impossible to strike effectively at his positions in the Glynnes or the Route. As a preliminary to these campaigns, Sorley Boy had moved his clan's non-combatants to a camp of refuge on Rathlin Island, whose allegiance was singularly vague as between the Scottish and English monarchies. There, in August 1575, a surprise amphibious assault was launched by a squadron under John Norris, sent by Essex from Carrickfergus. Francis Drake commanded the *Falcon* on an expedition which benefited from Sorley Boy's failure to set watch on the Antrim headlands. After storming the old castle and killing its 200 defenders, the landing force massacred between 300 and 400 women and children, as well as destroying 11 galleys, 300 cattle, 3000 sheep, 300 brood mares, and a year's food supply for 300 men. It was traumatic for Sorley Boy to watch what was happening from the shore, though his decision not to hazard his main force in a hopeless rescue bid was militarily correct.

Essex had shot his final, dreadful bolt. He was financially broken and his campaigning days were over. He died in Dublin in 1576, his last days rendered hideous by manic depression and dysentery. Arguably, by the end of his nightmarish intrusion into Ulster in 1575, it had become clear that Elizabeth was offering to Old English and Gael alike such atrociously bad lordship that her experienced servants in the Dublin administration could not overcome the handicap of serving such a ruler. Her meanness and her mulish obstinacy in pursuit of superficially cheap privatised solutions sold to her by court syndicates combined to store up dreadful trouble for the future. The unity of the English nation, not to mention the coherence of her dominions, was coming under shearing stress. Fitzwilliam has been denounced as a purely reactive ruler. There is truth in this. Sidney's first period as deputy had been terminated partly because of continuing high military charges, and Fitzwilliam had seen his own military establishment cut to an inadequate 1300 men. He could do little. Yet behind this lay a totally rational despair, which he communicated frankly to Burghley.[47] He feared the judgment of God on himself for so much unnecessary effusion of innocent blood, and he had no way of accessing effectively the circles round the queen from which emerged the policies which manufactured grievances and hatred, not to mention a high likelihood of long-term failure.

Notes and references

1. Nicholas P. Canny, *The Elizabethan Conquest of Ireland: A pattern established 1565–1576* (Harvester Press, Hassocks, 1976), Chap. 1.

2. 'Kerne' is from the Middle Irish *ceithern*, meaning a band of foot soldiers.

3. Colm Lennon, *Sixteenth-Century Ireland: The incomplete conquest* (Gill and Macmillan, Dublin, pbk edn, 1994), pp. 54–57.

4. *Ibid.*, p. 275.

5. J.R.N. MacPhail (ed.), 'Papers Relating to the Murder of the Laird of Calder', in *Highland Papers*, Vol. 1 (Scottish History Society, 2nd Series, 5, Edinburgh, 1914), pp. 141–94. The heiress of Calder was abducted by the Campbells in 1499. She married Sir John Campbell, third son of the second Earl of Argyll, and from them are descended the Campbells of Calder, whose head was created Baron Cawdor in 1796. The Tower of Calder was added to by the Campbells and took the name Cawdor Castle.

6. 'Roll of M'Nachtane's Soldieris schipped at Lochkerran, 11th December 1627 – fra then to the 28th of December inclusive', in *ibid.*, pp. 114–16.

7. Geoffrey W.S. Barrow, 'The Highlands in the Lifetime of Robert the Bruce', Chap. 13 in his *The Kingdom of the Scots* (Edward Arnold, London, 1973), pp. 362–83.

8. Patrick Rayner, Bruce Lenman, and Geoffrey Parker (eds.), *Handlist of Records for the Study of Crime in Early Modern Scotland (to 1747)*, List and Index Society, Special Series, Vol. 16 (Swift Printers, London, 1982), Chap. 9: 'Franchise Courts'.

9. Steven G. Ellis, *The Pale and the Far North: Government and society in two early Tudor borderlands* (O'Donnell Lecture, 1986, published for the National University of Ireland by Officina Typographica, Galway, 1988), pp. 13 and 20–21.

10. John W.M. Bannerman, 'The Lordship of the Isles', Chap. 10 in Jennifer M. Brown (ed.), *Scottish Society in the Fifteenth Century* (Edward Arnold, London, 1977).

11. Jean Munro and R.W. Munro (eds.), *Acts of the Lords of the Isles 1336–1493* (Scottish History Society, 4th Series, 22, Edinburgh, 1986), Nos. 80 and 121.

12. John MacInnes, 'West Highland Sea Power in the Middle Ages', *Transactions of the Gaelic Society of Inverness*, 48 (1972–74), pp. 518–53.

13. Jane E.A. Dawson, 'Argyll: The enduring heartland', review article in *Scottish Historical Review*, 74 (1995), pp. 75–98.

14. *Ibid.*, 'The Origins of the "Road to the Isles": Trade, communications and Campbell power in early modern Scotland', in Roger Mason and Norman Macdougall (eds.), *People and Power in Scotland* (John Donald, Edinburgh, 1992), pp. 74–103.

15. The forms MacDonald, MacDonnell, and MacDonnel are all variant versions of the name of Clan Donald. MacDonald may be substituted for any of the other two and there was never any consistency in spelling the other two forms.

16. J. Michael Hill, *Fire and Sword: Sorley Boy MacDonnell and the rise of Clan Ian Mor 1538–90* (Athlone Press, London, 1993), provides a convenient summary of events.

17. Jane E.A. Dawson, 'The Fifth Earl of Argyll, Gaelic Lordship and Political Power in Sixteenth-Century Scotland', *Scottish Historical Review*, 77 (1988), pp. 1–27.

18. CSP Ireland, 1574–85, Sir Nicholas Malbie to Walsingham, 17 August 1580, p. 245.

19. I am deeply indebted to Dr Jane Dawson of the Department of Ecclesiastical History of the University of Edinburgh for sharing with me her profound knowledge of the Clan Campbell and the earls of Argyll in the sixteenth century. Without her help, this section could not have been written.

20. 'Grey' Colin Campbell of Glenorchy to Archibald, Fifth Earl of Argyll, 7 June 1570, Scottish Record Office (hereafter SRO), GD112/39/7/8. My access to this correspondence is entirely due to the generosity of Dr Dawson, who made it available from the material she is preparing for a very important edition of letters between Argyll and Glenorchy for the Scottish History Society.

21. James MacDonnell of Dunyveg to Colin Campbell of Glenorchy, 6 June 1564, SRO, GD112/39/3/6.

22. 'Agnes Campbell ladye off Dunnevaig and Glennes' to Colin Campbell of Glenorchy, 11 September 1564, SRO, GD112/39/3/7.

23. Archibald, Fifth Earl of Argyll, to Colin Campbell of Glenorchy, 8 October 1564, SRO, GD112/39/3/8.

24. CSP Ireland, 1574–85, Patrick Culan to the Knight Marshal Bagenall, enclosure in Lord Deputy to Walsingham, 10 December 1581, p. 333.

25. *Ibid.*, Lord Deputy Perrot to Walsingham, 16 November 1584, p. 537.

26. *Ibid.*, 1586–88, information by Ambrose Lacy concerning abuses, 10 December 1587, pp. 450–51.

27. Mary O'Dowd, 'Gaelic Economy and Society', in Ciaran Brady and Raymond Gillespie (eds.), *Natives and Newcomers: The making of Irish colonial society 1534–1641* (Irish Academic Press, Dublin, pbk edn, 1986), pp. 133–36.

28. The latest summary of the history of the Reformation in Ireland is in Steven G. Ellis, *Ireland in the Age of the Tudors 1447–1603* (Longman, London, rev. enlarged edn 1998), Chaps. 8–9. There is also a review article by K. Bottigheimer and Lote Neumann, 'The Irish Reformation in European Perspective', *Archiv für Reformationsgeschichte*, 89 (1998), pp. 268–309.

29. Gilbert J. Millar, *Tudor Mercenaries and Auxiliaries 1485–1547* (University Press of Virginia, Charlottesville, VA, 1980).

30. 'Ireland. A Full Paye 1560–1562', printed in A.K. Longfield (ed.), *Fitzwilliam Accounts 1560–65 (Annesley Collection)* (Irish Manuscripts Commission, Dublin, 1960), pp. 54–78.

31. CSP Ireland, 1509–73, the O'Neill to the Lord Justice and Council, 18 August 1564, and same to the Queen, 28 July 1565, pp. 244 and 268 resp.

32. Canny, *Elizabethan Conquest of Ireland*, p. 47.

33. Ciaran Brady, 'The Killing of Shane O'Neill: Some new evidence', *Irish Sword*, 15 (1982–83), pp. 116–23.

34. B.C. Beckingsale, 'The Characteristics of the Tudor North', *Northern History*, 4 (1969), pp. 67–83.

35. Ciaran Brady, *The Chief Governors: The rise and fall of reform government in Tudor Ireland 1536–1588* (Cambridge University Press, Cambridge, 1994), pp. 172–74.

36. Jon G. Crawford, *Anglicizing the Government of Ireland: The Irish privy council and the expansion of Tudor rule, 1556–1578* (Irish Academic Press, Dublin, 1993), *passim*, but esp. Chap. 5.

37. Anthony Pagden, *Lords of All the World: Ideologies of empire in Spain, Britain and France c.1500–c.1800* (Yale University Press, New Haven, CT, 1995), Chaps. 1 and 2.

38. David B. Quinn, ' "A Discourse of Ireland" (*circa* 1599): A sidelight on English colonial policy', in *Proceedings of the Royal Irish Academy*, 47 (1941–42), Section C, p. 159.

39. CSP Ireland, 1509–73, Suffrein and others, of Kilkenny, and Captain William Collyer to Lord Deputy, 21 July 1569, p. 414.

40. *Ibid.*, Earl of Ormonde to William Cecil, 24 July 1569, pp. 414–15.

41. *Ibid.*, Captain Piers to Lord Deputy, 3 January 1572, p. 463.

42. *Ibid.*, Sir Brian McPhelim O'Neill to Privy Council, 27 March 1572, p. 469.

43. *Ibid.*, Lord Deputy to Burghley, 25 September 1572, p. 484.

44. Grenfell Morton, *Elizabethan Ireland* (Longman, London, 1971), p. 38. In general, this unpretentious little book is a masterly exercise in clarifying the complexities of its subject.

45. CSP Ireland, 1574–85, articles of peace with Turlough O'Neill and considerations which moved Essex, 27 June 1575, p. 73. For the lewdness of the lady, see Lord Deputy to Privy Council, 17 March 1577, p. 107.

46. *Ibid.*, 1509–73, Thomas Wilsford to Burghley, 1 December 1573, p. 530.

47. *Ibid.*, Lord Deputy to Burghley, 21 October 1572, p. 486.

CHAPTER THREE

Feeding frenzy: marginal courtiers and perceived opportunities, 1578–1590

The New English, asset seizure, and instability on the land frontier

The risk of foreign intervention in Ireland was a recurring fear of the Crown, and a continual source of hope for those who fell into conflict with it. Apart from the intimate connection with Scotland rooted in the nature of the Gaidhealtachd and functioning in ways which were geared to its needs, these hopes and fears were usually grossly exaggerated. The French threat in the reign of Edward VI and early in the reign of Elizabeth could only have come from Scotland, and the maintenance of French power there proved beyond the capacity of the Valois dynasty, despite the existence at one point of a dynastic alliance with the Stuarts which made the Valois seriously hope to make Scotland a French province. With the religious changes introduced by the Tudors, the possibility of support from the great monarchs of Europe who adhered to the Roman fold was a recurring phantom for opponents of Tudor power in Ireland. Especially after it became clear that the Elizabethan regime was a Protestant one, it became standard practice for those in arms against her to demand aid from France or Spain, the only two powers even faintly capable of mounting an expedition. Shane O'Neill had postured as a defender of the faith, though few believed that faith was his central interest. Gaelic Ireland was in fact much slower to be affected by that mighty current of Catholic reform and anti-Protestant militancy known as the Counter-Reformation than were the Old English, and even they as a group were not intransigent on the religious front until quite late. It was in the mid-1580s when even the conservative Palesmen made it clear that they were not going to budge from their papal allegiance, though they also made it clear that this did not mean that they were going to abandon their allegiance to the Crown. It had become clear to them that they were being permanently excluded from the political process, and that therefore there was no point in tacking or compromising with a government which intended to offer them nothing real in return. Instead, they went over to a policy of firm passive resistance, both in politics and in religion.[1] An obvious advantage of this form of loyalist revolt was that it offered no openings for the court sharks for ever on the cruise for other men's lands.

One reason why in 1571 Sir James Fitzmaurice Fitzgerald had, with his kinsman the seneschal of Imokilly, surrendered to Sir John Perrot, the first lord president of Munster, was disappointment at his inability to mobilise international support. Perrot had even managed to intercept and drive back the traditional influx of Scottish mercenaries summoned to assist the rebellion. Fitzmaurice's appeals to Philip II of Spain had never been likely to elicit hard support. For much of the early part of Elizabeth's reign Philip was actively supporting her against the danger of a French challenge, and his agents worked overtime to stop the papacy from formally excommunicating her. In 1570 papal patience snapped. Pius V issued the bull *Regnans in Excelsis*, which not only excommunicated Elizabeth but also called on the faithful to depose her, thereby placing her many loyal Catholic subjects in an impossible dilemma. Gregory XIII, the successor to Pius V, was deemed to have partially suspended the deposition in 1580 when he ruled that Catholics need not take action until it was likely to be effective, but his deeds up to that point belied his words, for he tried very hard to set off a war of religion in the queen's dominions. He licensed a not untypical English projector-cum-pirate from Devon called Thomas Stukeley to invade Ireland with a papal force. Stukeley had started off with a 1562 licence to establish a settlement in Florida, but found that piracy off Munster was more immediately rewarding. Unable to go home without a fair chance of hanging in chains, he visited Spain, where he awarded himself the title of duke of Ireland, and picked up a knighthood from Philip II. After fighting the Turk, he led his papal expeditionary force as far as Lisbon, where he diverted it into an enterprise totally in tune with his own normal levels of lunatic optimism. He died in 1578 with young King Sebastian of Portugal, fighting in that monarch's doomed Moroccan crusade. Stukeley, it has to be said, was not unlike other Elizabethan bravos who pursued fame and fortune on the other side of the confessional divide, many of whom came as deservedly unstuck as he. James Fitzmaurice, a serious fellow by comparison, was left with the scrapings from the bottom of the Stukeley barrel, which were duly shipped with him in charge into Dingle in Kerry. Sir Humphrey Gilbert was supposed to be guarding the Kerry coast with a squadron, but in an age of wind and sail no coast could be secured against a small expedition. Fitzmaurice was soon entrenched in Smerwick, but his ships could now be located and attacked, and he himself faced a difficult situation. The Earl of Desmond, who had returned to Ireland in 1573, was at best equivocal. Sir John of Desmond became one of the few significant early supporters of the rising.

Fitzmaurice was no more a spokesman for a precocious form of conscious nationalism than Stukeley was, though the Irish component in his identity was infinitely more genuine. He was appealing to his fellow Old English of the Lordship to rise, not against England – which was part of their identity, as of his – but against heresy. His proclamation was clear:

> This war is undertaken for the defence of the Catholic religion against the heretics. Pope Gregory XIII hath chosen us for general captain in this same war, as it appeareth at large by his own letters patent, which thing he did so much rather because his predecessor Pope Pius V had before deprived Elizabeth, the patroness of the aforesaid heresies, of all royal power and dominion, as it is plainly declared by his declaratory sentence, the authentic copy whereof we also have to show. Therefore now we fight not against the lawful sceptre and honourable throne of England, but against a tyrant which refuseth to hear Christ speaking by his vicar.[2]

Fitzmaurice, whom even Sir John Perrot admitted to be a man of stature, had the ill-fortune to fall in a skirmish with local Burkes. That Sir John of Desmond could carry on the rising was a commentary on the pathetic level of government troops facing him. Lord Justice Sir William Drury was trying to contain an extremely explosive situation with 400 infantry and 200 cavalry. The Earl of Desmond, understandably bitter about his long detention in England and disturbed by the relentless pressure against the traditional autonomy of his estates, vacillated until the prospect of a new and unsympathetic lord justice finally drove him over the edge. With the seneschal of Imokilly, he sacked Youghal in November 1579. The die was cast. His motives were very different from those of the papal nuncio who had landed with Fitzmaurice. Not the brightest of men, Desmond could still smell the decay of all he most valued in his life-style if the pace and shape of change continued to be wholly outwith his control. At least by coming out he could reassert leadership over his own two brothers, who were already fighting and losing battles against Crown forces, literally under the banner of religion.

Militarily, Desmond could not cope with set battles once government reinforcements came in, as they did inevitably. He was beaten again and again, but for the bulk of four years he emerged apparently as strong as ever. Though troops from England were prominent in the first couple of years, when government forces devastated Desmond's estates and seized his castles, usually massacring their garrisons, the war latterly took the form of a civil war between loyalist and non-loyalist factions among the Munster lords. By and large, the Gaelic septs stood aside.[3] Unable to pin the earl down and aware that the rising's leaders counted on the inability of the queen's government to 'abide the chardges of a generall warre',[4] the government had the wit to transfer control of the campaign to Desmond's hereditary rival, the Butler Earl of Ormonde. Unlike his predecessors in command, Ormonde did not confuse indiscriminate savagery with military efficiency. He issued pardons freely, thus isolating Desmond. The earl was on the point of surrender when in mid-September 1580 a papal and Spanish force of 600 Italian soldiers with Spanish officers arrived at Smerwick carrying 6000 stands of arms and some money, as well as two papal emissaries. As reinforcement it was too little, too late. The expedition could not even fight its way out of the Dingle peninsula in the face of Ormonde.

On the other hand, the intervention was calculated to cause maximum grief. It heightened the paranoia of a Protestant Tudor regime, whilst protracting the Desmond rising beyond any hope of a negotiated settlement. Admiral Winter, who had been refitting in England, reappeared off the coast, thus closing escape lines and ensuring that with an effort ordnance could be moved into position to blast the fort at Smerwick, recently refurbished by Fitzmaurice and now the last resort of the papal forces. To professional eyes, it was clear that there was no hope for the garrison once Lord Deputy Lord Grey of Wilton was in position before it. The garrison surrendered unconditionally. The Spanish officers were spared, but 600 others were put to death by two companies of Grey's troops, one commanded by Sir Humphrey Gilbert's half-brother Walter Raleigh. There were precedents such as the indiscriminate massacre with which the Spaniards finally crushed French attempts to establish a settlement in Florida in the 1560s, but that was a case of tiny European minorities playing for high stakes in a dangerously unknown continent. The Smerwick massacre was another attempt to discourage future challenges by terror, but the papal source of the challenge was perhaps crucial.

These were beaten, outnumbered men. It was not like the situation which arose in 1588 when more Spaniards were landing on the west coast of Ireland from wrecked ships of the Spanish Armada than Elizabeth's local commanders had men. It was fear which made the lord deputy, Sir William Fitzwilliam, at that time order the governor of Connaught, Sir Richard Bingham, to execute all survivors from the six or so Spanish vessels wrecked on his shores. Fitzwilliam was already in a state of panic about reports of the large number of Spaniards who had landed in Donegal. Bingham was regarded as a counter-productively violent man by significant sections of the Dublin administration, and attempts had been made to remove him. His violence was geared to self-enrichment and advancement, so even he wanted to hold at least the richer Spaniards for ransom, but the conscientious Fitzwilliam was so alarmed that he would not hear of this.[5] A better military analogy with Smerwick was the Spanish garrison captured at Kinsale in December 1601, which was repatriated. In 1583 the already doomed Desmond rising sputtered out. First, Sir John of Desmond was killed in action in January, and then in November Desmond literally lost his head in Glenageenty near Tralee at the hands of an O'Moriarty whose family had been maltreated and whose cattle had been stolen by the earl's followers.

Much of the sickening barbarism which had marked the activities of the Crown forces in the early stages of the conflict had almost certainly been motivated by the desire to kill landowners at all levels and thus clear the way for royal grants of their properties to those on the inside track at court. With the death of Desmond, not only were all his vast properties forfeit for treason, but also, as a high proportion of Munster lesser gentry and nobility had at some point joined the rising, a quite chillingly high proportion of these men were dead. It was a potential bonanza for a particular kind of Elizabethan courtier, of whom Walter Raleigh was an example. He came from an old Devon family, one indeed which went back to the Norman Conquest, but it had fallen on hard times, which meant he was initially as poor as he was proud. He was also a half-brother to Sir Humphrey, Sir John, and Adrian Gilbert. In December 1577 he described himself as 'of the court', to which he would have had access through Sir Humphrey Gilbert, a personal servant of the queen in the days when she had been the Princess Elizabeth. The Gilberts also seem to have staked their devastatingly handsome sibling for the expensive gamble of hanging around the court in the hope that the queen would notice him.[6] At an early stage he showed signs of being pathologically violent, and he developed – like all the Elizabethan courtier-projectors, from the Catholic Stukeley to his fellow Protestant Humphrey Gilbert – into a compulsive propagandist for ideas which often bore little or no relationship to reality. Raleigh lived and died by the court. In the shape of Bess Throckmorton, a courtier from a family of courtiers, he was even to marry into it, to the fury of a jealous queen. That lay ahead in the rush for grants after the collapse of the Desmond rising, and Raleigh emerged with a grant of 12,000 of the most fertile acres around Cork and Waterford.

The plantation of Munster after 1583 was a piecemeal affair because of the piecemeal nature of the forfeitures. From the start it was all about court favour, partly because widespread confusion over land titles placed a premium on ability to bend or manipulate the law. With characteristic arrogance, Raleigh later spelled out the rules of the game when he fell foul of Sir William Fitzwilliam, who returned as lord deputy between 1588 and 1594, and who did not favour Raleigh's debatable claim to hold a lease of Lismore. In December 1589 Raleigh told Sir George Carew that as for Fitzwilliam:

> I take myself far his better by the honourable offices I hold, as also by that nearness to her majesty which still I enjoy and never more. If in Ireland they think I am not worth the respecting, they shall much deceive themselves. I am in place to be believed not inferior to any man, to pleasure or displeasure the greatest; and my opinion is so received and believed as I can anger the best of them.[7]

Raleigh was only one of a swarm of insufferably arrogant court opportunists attracted by the forfeitures. Most of them were men whose birth gave them pretensions but few concrete prospects. They were marginal in the sense that they had no hope, due to lack of political weight or flaws of character or both, of the bigger plums in the queen's gift.

Even Raleigh, who was to rise higher than most as captain of the royal guard and a virtual viceroy in Cornwall and Devon, could never make it into the central elite of the council – not just because of Burghley's hostility, but crucially because the queen did not trust his judgement. Ralph Lane, an equerry of the great stable – which was a minor household post under the authority of the master of the horse – almost made Raleigh look like a shrinking violet. He too hoped by dint of military service in Munster to carve out the vast estates he did not have except in fantasies. He took a post in Kerry late in 1584, and instantly advanced outrageous demands. Sir Henry Wallop, vice treasurer of Ireland, remarked acidly after Lane had sailed for America that Lane was insufferable and seemed to think he should be given all the good land in Kerry outright, and should control the letting and setting of all the rest. This was on the strength of commanding 'twentie horsemen and fourtie footmen'.[8] Lane was close to Raleigh and Sir Richard Grenville. The latter had had an early stab at making his fortune in Munster in the late 1560s, but had in fact lost money in the destruction caused by the first rising of James Fitzmaurice. He came back into Munster twenty years later in 1588, after the great Desmond power was broken, riding on the back of the St Leger family into which he had married. In between he made a reputation as a financer of privateers and played an important part in Raleigh's American ventures.[9] A Spaniard described him as 'the most arrogant man in the world'. As Don Ricardo de Campoverde, he was both feared by Spaniards and admired for his *arrogancia*, the almost insane pride of the true noble. Others saw it differently. Ralph

Lane, himself pushy, demanding, violent, and greedy, actually complained of Grenville's 'intolerable pride and insatiable ambition'.[10]

Grenville's end in a tremendous but hopeless sea fight off the Azores in 1591 was scarcely that of a sane man, as several eminent contemporary Englishmen said. His reputation benefited enormously from an account of the last fight of his galleon, the *Revenge*, written by his kinsman and friend Sir Walter Raleigh as pro-war propaganda. At the time it set the dominant tone, but had to cope with a persistent undercurrent which saw Grenville as a martyr to his own crazy obstinacy. Victorian Britons, wholly misunderstanding their own warped and indirect connections with the lost world of Grenville, saw him as a flawless exemplar of all that was best in them, which he was not. Like other members of this prominent but utterly atypical group, he was a pathological personality. Almost without exception, they were physically extremely brave, but they were nearly all ruthless gamblers in politics, and compulsive killers as well as habitual liars. To treat these men as defining 'English identity' is to insult the intelligence of their contemporaries.[11]

Lane's superiors clearly could not get him out of Munster fast enough, and Sir Walter Raleigh was detested by Londoners as the unacceptable face of the court elite's presumption and arrogance. Such characters could only hope to achieve their more extreme ambitions under unusual circumstances. Large-scale forfeiture was one favourable conjuncture, from their point of view. Munster was particularly attractive to them because the estates there were worth seizing. If one compares these men's outlook with that of Edmund Campion, a future Jesuit martyr in England in 1581, the comparison is illuminating.

Campion was patronised by the Earl of Leicester and went to Dublin to work with Lord Deputy Sidney, with a particular interest in helping to establish a university there. He was moved to compose a *History of Ireland* which remained in manuscript between 1571 and 1633, but which was widely read none the less. He was clear that the Gaidhealtachd was a separate civilisation and its inhabitants 'mere Irish'. However, that did not make him an ill-informed observer. On the contrary, he was aware of the huge gap between the immensely archaic and artificial written Irish of the learned orders and the Gaelic dialects actually spoken. Of course he identified with 'our English in Ireland', the Old English, as indeed he should have, but he was as conscious as anyone of the permeability of cultures on the marches of the old Lordship, and one of his motives for wanting to push for the establishment of a university in Dublin was precisely the need to strengthen English culture in the island. Although twentieth-century American scholarship seems to find these very natural attitudes perplexing, they were what one would expect.[12] The disruptive force to which there was no answer and which by 1571 had turned Campion into a fugitive was a product of the government which most deplored its consequences. The Tudor quarrel with the papacy in itself was just another manifestation of a recurring conflict endemic in Western European society, but the assertion of royal supremacy in the church deeply fractured the English ethnic community, and by no means on a single plane.

To many of the New English who swarmed to Munster in the wake of the Desmond rising, these deep divisions were not a political tragedy but a personal opportunity. Sustained violence was desirable. That was an attitude common to contemporary soldiers. Captured letters written by a Spanish soldier on the Armada of 1588 expressed fear that the English might surrender quickly and thereby deprive him of his hopes of plunder. He urged his correspondent to pray God to grant 'that in England He give me a house of some very rich merchant where I may place my ensign, which the owner thereof do ransom of me in thirty thousand ducats'. A culture of aggressive religiosity did not change basic human motivation: it merely made available an intricate vocabulary to rationalise that motivation self-righteously. From the Philippines to Peru, the dream of the Spanish soldier was not just the quick loot of a day's plundering, but violence so visceral and sustained as to lead to social upheaval and *repartimiento*: the seizure by right of conquest of the great immovable sources of permanent wealth which in a hierarchical society where social climbing was difficult could overnight catapult a poor captain up to noble status.[13] That was what Lane was after in Munster. Even the man who rightly deemed Lane impossible, Sir Henry Wallop, was up to the same game. His despatches to ministers of the Crown tried to knock out alternative beneficiaries of royal generosity by relentlessly running down the loyalist Old English, and every now and then he would conclude a whining account of his sufferings in office as vice treasurer and treasurer at war with a prayer that he be granted some rebel lands.[14]

Before the eyes of the human kites and carrion crows who flapped ominously around the edge of every major court there were always the precedents of the swordsmen who had overrun two empires in Mexico and Peru in the early sixteenth century in the name of the Habsburg Emperor Charles V. These were, of course, exceptional cases which had enjoyed a combination of outstanding leadership and favourable circumstances that never recurred. Though a great deal of intellectual energy had to be poured into justifying their military conquests, there was never any question of repudiating them. Much more common a scenario was, however, the exploitation by men of violence either of conflict between European monarchs or of internal rebellion, something which the confessional splits of the sixteenth century made more frequent and more traumatic. A monarchy which succeeded in crushing a confessionally based rebellion was always liable to make a clean sweep of dissenting landowners, without whose leadership resistance was far more difficult to organise. An unusual feature of the conquests of Mexico and Peru had been the primacy of the swordsmen in the initial share-out of wealth. The bureaucrats who eventually tamed the swordsmen came in afterwards. In Europe the reconstruction of a rebellious and defeated nobility was usually a joint venture between royal bureaucrats and entrepreneurs in violence such as the immigrant military adventurers, including Catholic Scotsmen and Irishmen, who shared the spoils of victory with royal officials after the defeat of the Bohemian revolt against the Habsburgs at the Battle of the White Mountain in 1620.

Such swift and drastic changes as were enforced in Bohemia after 1620 were quite beyond the capacity of Elizabethan government. It lacked the physical and fiscal strength even to think of expropriating all Catholic landowners on the lands of the Lordship. The Munster confiscations were unusual and were a patchwork, not a clean sweep. In waging colonial campaigns against the autonomous units which composed the Gaidhealtachd, the government simply did not have the sort of edge in weapons technology which in some cases had greatly simplified the work of Spanish *conquistadores* in the Americas. Indeed, as the chiefs of the Gaidhealtachd steadily converted their kerne into musketeers and their gallowglass into pikemen in the later sixteenth century, the only area in which the Elizabethan regime had any kind of edge was its monopoly of heavy ordnance, which made its forts virtually impregnable.

That was why there were endless vain appeals to European rulers by the leaders of every major rising to send heavy artillery to Ireland. Queen Elizabeth herself was well aware of this fact of military life. In the course of her endless cheese-paring on the Irish accounts she insisted in 1567 that in building forts 'no superfluity of chargs be therein employed but that they be made agreable to withstand the common force of that countrcy, without sumptuous and gross bilding to withstand great artillerye, which is not there commonly to be doubtid [i.e. expected]'.[15] This was a fair point, but building forts was still horribly expensive when allowance was made for garrisoning them and the experience of the experiment at Derry underlined the difficulty of finding materials to build and then repair them. Until late in the century not much was attempted in terms of fort building; even less was permanently achieved. The main forts and garrisons at Newry, Carrickfergus, Maryborough, Philipstown, and Athlone were frontier defences essential for the long-term security of the Lordship lands rather than springboards for the reduction of the autonomous Lordships of the Gaidhealtachd.[16]

In this complex, essentially very difficult and ambiguous situation, the quack, the projector, the political con artist, and all the other varieties of *terribles simplificateurs* had a field day. So anxious was the government to believe that there might be a cheap solution that men on the make kept trying to sell it such. One of the hazards of serving on the Dublin privy council was to have to read regularly such drivel as the 'plat for governing Ireland without charge to England, after the first year or so' which came before it on 12 November 1578.[17] The trouble was that when a quack like Sir Thomas Smith secured grants of land on the back of an unrealistic project, both he and his successor automatically turned to phys-ical savagery rather than face up to failure. They were politicians. There was always therefore a twisted connection between the projectors and the quasi-criminal men of violence, partly because they were occasionally the same men.

Entrepreneurial violence on the sea frontier after 1568

More often, entrepreneurial violence was pragmatic and quick to cut per-ceived losses to move on to another frontier of plunder. In particular, there had always been a sea option for those of a predatory disposition. Almost from the accession of Elizabeth her subjects had been preying on Spanish trade in the Channel and on the Atlantic approaches to it. They did this with commissions from foreign authorities, often French. The effect of such commissions was to change them from pirates to privateers: technically aggrieved parties seeking compensation for registered and unrequited injur-ies. From the start there had been a sectarian edge to this because friction between the Spanish authorities and the English merchant community seems to have started as early as the reign of Henry VIII and to have been the result of the harassing of Protestant merchants by the Spanish Inquisition. Neither the Crown nor the bulk of the very important merchant interest trading with the Iberian peninsula wanted conflict with Spain. There was too much to lose.[18]

Two sets of factors nevertheless drove the English state towards conflict with the Spain of Philip II. One was the passionate desire of merchants like John Hawkins of Plymouth to gain access to the vast trading potential of the Spanish Empire in the Americas, something which in the 1560s he clearly thought might be arranged in exchange for an offer of armed service against the French privateers, predominantly Huguenot, who were running rampant in the Caribbean. If Philip chose instead seriously to uphold his formal exclusion of all foreign merchants from the Americas, it was obvious that he would be, like the Portuguese in Africa, trying to grasp too much for other European maritime communities willingly to accept his claims. So confident was Elizabeth in this logic that she invested significantly in the enterprise of Hawkins, which was based on supplying the Spanish settlers in the Caribbean with the West African slaves they needed to replace the collapsing indigenous populations if commercial agriculture and mining were to have any future at all. The destruction of Hawkins' squadron by a Spanish viceregal fleet at San Juan de Ulua in 1568 drew a line under this gambit. In any case, Hawkins was in the long run probably not capable of competing with other illegal traders like the French, who continued to supply Spanish settlers with a mix of goods that included slaves but was much broader, and who could offer markets for Caribbean products such as hides. To make matters worse, the situation in both England and the Low Countries deteriorated dangerously with the arrival in England of Mary, Queen of Scots, as both a refugee and a focus for endless plotting, and with the ruthlessly successful assertion of Spanish power over the traditional autonomy of the Netherlands nobility and towns. By 1569–72 the Elizabethan regime was positively encouraging its subjects to take privateering licences from all and sundry and a wave of licensed violence swept the Channel and Caribbean. There were thirteen identifiable English expeditions to the Caribbean in 1570–77 alone.[19]

The situation in the Netherlands faced Elizabeth with two policy imperatives, both of which she conspicuously failed to achieve, and that for the usual reason that she did everything by halves, searching frantically for cheap alternatives whose failure – as in Ireland – left her exposed to far more expense and danger than need have been the case. The first necessity was to stop Philip II from installing a military government rationalised and justified by a militant Counter-Reformation ideology in any large part of a Netherlands so close to eastern England as to be part of its strategic outworks. The other, of which she repeatedly said she was aware, was the need to keep the Netherlands from falling prey to an aggressive France potentially as dangerously ambitious as Spain. Both necessities required unequivocal and generous support for the Prince of Orange in the late 1570s when he had a fair chance of holding the northern and southern Netherlands together, with the crucial backing of the great Walloon noble dynasties. Such a union had the inherent strength, especially in its advanced urban economy in the south, to check France. Elizabeth only reluctantly committed herself unequivocally against Philip in the Netherlands in 1585, and continued to try to renege on her commitment right up to the eve of the Armada in 1588. The consequences were simply appalling. By 1588 Philip had crushed resistance in Flanders, where his biggest army had a secure base too close to London by half. In the future, once Spanish power started to move downhill, lay centuries of European instability due to the lack of an adequate

counterbalance to France on her northern frontier.[20] In the short run, failure to act decisively to check the centralising ambitions of King Philip in
the Netherlands in the later 1570s was but the prelude to another massive
blow to English interests in the shape of the successful Spanish takeover
of Portugal and its extensive overseas empire in 1580. Claiming the Portuguese throne, Philip defeated the Portuguese claimant Dom Antonio in a
brief campaign whose combination of brilliance and atrocities bore all the
hallmarks of his outstanding senior general, the Duke of Alva. To the
significant resident English mercantile community in Portugal the episode
was a disaster. Many were identified with Portuguese resistance and had
to flee, as did Dom Antonio. Neither France nor England was capable of
maintaining Dom Antonio on Portuguese soil, though the French tried
hard in the Azores, but the French and English privateers happily accepted
commissions from him. In the English case quite a few even had genuine
unredressed grievances.

The fact that the outbreak of open war between Elizabeth and Philip
had been preceded by the arrest of English merchant ships in Spanish
harbours in May of 1585 was vital in removing merchant opposition to all-
out naval war with Spain. Ironically, Philip's motive seems to have been
fear that the English, already in a state of undeclared naval war against
him, were about to mount a major offensive against crucially important
bullion fleets, the *flotas*, as they assembled in the West Indies. His fears were
understandable, but in fact the English themselves seem to have been
uncertain about what they wished to do. In the event, Elizabeth's most
striking response was to send Sir Francis Drake at the head of a powerful
squadron to the West Indies. That voyage probably originated in late 1583
as a plan for a primarily commercial voyage to the East Indies. By 1584 it
had evolved into a much more aggressive plan to attack Portuguese establishments and shipping there under the flag of Dom Antonio, the Portuguese claimant. Only early in 1585 was this voyage suspended and the
expedition taken into royal control. So Philip ascribed much more clarity of
strategic vision to the English than was realistic, but as a result he took
measures which destroyed the position of those in England who wanted to
argue for good relations with Spain.[21] In a port such as Bristol with very
strong Iberian connections privateering became the standard way of trying
to keep some profit moving through the embargoed part of the shipping
interest.

Formal war was never declared and open war did not break out before
1587, but long before then a combination of predatory gentlemen and
bellicose merchants had created a massive privateering industry. The formidable financial resources of a London which was relentlessly engrossing more and more of English overseas trade were made available for

privateering through syndicates which both spread the risk and broadened the financial base of the industry. Some of the leading participants have been described as amateurs, like the third Earl of Cumberland, an independently wealthy court figure who in the end lost money on his voyages. Cumberland funded large squadrons capable of taking heavily defended Spanish Caribbean cities like San Juan de Puerto Rico. The great bulk of the thousand or so prizes probably captured by English privateers during the war was snapped up by smaller units exploiting the fact that by the time Philip II had arranged effective convoy for the vital bullion fleets, he had exhausted the bulk of his available naval cover for Spanish and Portuguese Atlantic commerce. Cumberland's overheads were too high, but he did his best to make his voyages pay, and was up to most of the tricks of the trade. He and his wife cultivated Sir Julius Caesar, judge of the High Court of Admiralty (which adjudicated prize cases), by every device from presents of venison to giving Caesar's brother Thomas a family pocket burgh when he wanted to be an MP.[22] Cumberland was just as ready to strip the ordnance off prizes for resale to the Dutch as he was to pursue gold and jewels.

Allowing that some people proved better at it than others, the privateering war was, for the overwhelming majority of its participants, all about making money. That very much included Elizabeth's lord admiral, Charles Howard, later earl of Nottingham. He has been described as 'a capitalist seeking a profit in the maintenance of public safety'. His Admiralty Court was a vast feudal franchise which Sir Julius Caesar, who presided over it, could – as he kept telling Howard – manipulate to make his master fabulously wealthy in time of war, if he were so inclined. Were a ship deemed a lawful prize, the admiral automatically had his share of one tenth of its value. He could also benefit hugely from the confiscations of ships and goods which could follow other judgements. On top of all of this the admiral issued letters of marque and reprisal which turned pirates into patriotic privateers. In theory a letter of reprisal was issued only after a judicial inquiry requiring proof of damages, with appropriate witnesses; but in practice nobody who paid Howard his fee was ever refused, and half the matelots of England would have died laughing if anyone had suggested that someone might be penalised for recovering more than his original losses. It is true that the ports of the south of England and their maritime communities had a stronger Protestant tradition than most of the rest of the realm, partly because of their early proximity to continental Protestant ideas, but the idea that the privateers were Protestant crusaders is nonsense. Like the lord admiral and his chief judge, they were primarily cheerful thieves. Howard, best known for much of his life as Howard of Effingham, was a kindly, garrulous but canny conservative who had moved calmly from Protestant to Catholic to Protestant religious positions as regimes changed.[23] If stealing from someone like Turlough Luineach O'Neill or Sorley Boy was rather like trying to make a living by holding up Jesse James, privateering was a rational occupation. Barbary, West African, and Levant merchants could combine it with legitimate trade in goods and slaves, but the bulk of the English privateers who swarmed over the Atlantic and into the Caribbean did not even bother with a spot of honest slaving.

By definition, most unescorted merchant ships were easy meat for an appropriate privateer since they could not carry the weight of ordnance nor the big crews of the privateers without themselves becoming commercially non-viable. Nor did they usually fight hard. There was no point. If what was going to happen to them when they could not outrun their pursuer was inevitable, the sensible course was to relax at least to the point where their captors could get what they wanted without turning really nasty. On his 1577 outward voyage Francis Drake called in at the Portuguese-controlled Cape Verde Islands, mainly to seek provisions, but off one of them he gave chase to a ship which turned out to be carrying a welcome cargo of wine. The account of the episode later published by Richard Hakluyt makes two interesting points. One is that Drake's men 'in the end boarded her with a ship-boat without resistance'. The other is that once Drake had the wine and the ship's pilot, he 'sent the rest away with his Pinesse, giving them a Butte of wine and some victuals, and their wearing clothes'. It was hard on the owners, and a shock to the crew, but not at all a lethal one.[24] All sensibly organised expeditions had with them a pinnace which either crossed the Atlantic as a tender to a larger boat or in the hold in sections. It was used for cutting out small victims in inshore waters. Andrew Barker of Bristol, who was harassed and beggared by the Inquisition in the Canaries, went privateering in 1576 with a view to redressing the account. Richard Hakluyt's narrative mentions Barker's capture off 'the Isle of Margarita' of 'a small Spanish ship having in her certaine pitch and thirty tuns of Canarie wines whereof we reserved 4 or 5 tunnes to ourselves, dismissing them without any further damage'. No skipper wanted enough wine aboard to make his crew permanently drunk. Techniques could be much rougher when elite prisoners were suspected of secreting small valuables, though that was a case where excessive respect for personal space was not compatible with best business practice.[25]

Semi-official expeditions against the Spanish Caribbean undoubtedly became more destructive of both ships and settlements as the war ground on into the embittered 1590s. Christopher Newport set out from London in January 1591 with three ships and a pinnace, returning to England after a foray into the West Indies in which Hakluyt boasted 'they tooke and burnt upon the coast of Hispaniola, within the bay of Honduras, and other places,

3 townes, and 19 sail of shippes and frigats'. Some of the land fighting was stiff, but the pattern at sea was different. Chasing 'a frigat of the iland of Cuba of 30 tunnes', Hakluyt's informant, John Twitt of Harwich, who was corporal on *The Golden Dragon*, reported that 'after a shot or two made at her, she yeelded unto us'. It was a very sensible decision, for the English merely took the tobacco and hogs which were the cargo 'and sent the men away with their frigat'.[26] On the return haul in late 1592 Newport's squadron joined up with a fleet sent out by Sir Walter Raleigh with backing from the queen and London capitalists to do some very bloody sea fighting indeed, in the course of which they captured the vast 1600-ton Portuguese Indian carrack the *Madre de Dios*. Here everyone knew that the stakes were astronomically high, for the carrack's cargo was later valued at £150,000 sterling. Even so, the balance between risk and gain was one which had to be debated literally up to the last minute of the fight, when Sir Robert Cross persuaded his crew that if they did not make one more bid to board the carrack, they would lose a fortune. Sir John Burrough, who commanded the fleet for Raleigh, sent the defeated Portuguese home 'in certaine vessels furnished with all kinds of necessary provision'. If they had fought so hard to defend much less, it might have been a different story, but by and large seamen knew the unwritten rules and showed sympathy for enemies who lived by them.[27]

By definition, the real professionals in this game wanted as low a profile as possible, especially since they tended to have an incorrigible inability to distinguish between Spanish and Portuguese shipping and tempting vessels which did not owe allegiance to those crowns. Serious self-advertisers were invariably from the court circle, falling into two distinct though interconnected categories. There were courtiers who were not literally hungry for favours, because they were men of independent means. Cumberland would have liked to touch Elizabeth for a contribution, but that was because he had already spent so much of his own money. Thomas Cavendish, who belonged to the Raleigh circle at court and shared in his Virginia enterprise, was well-off, but an extreme example of the insane pursuit of honour and reputation. In 1586–88 he led the third expedition after Magellan's and Drake's to sail round the world. Instead of battening on the richer streams of Spanish colonial commerce, he developed plans to seize the Philippines and a penchant for assaulting fortified Spanish and Portuguese positions. In 1591, when dreadful weather and a mutinous crew prevented him from penetrating the Pacific by means of the Strait of Magellan, he willed himself to death on the homeward voyage, leaving a manuscript which makes it clear that he could not face the thought of returning to England after failing. Because these unbalanced oddities have tended to leave literary remains, the silent majority tends to be ignored by modern scholarship. It is worth stressing that when Cavendish urged his starving, frozen, battered crew:

> that they would cheerfulli goe forewarde to atempte either to make them
> selues famous in resalutelie dyeinge, or in liveing to performe that which
> wilbe to theire perpetuall reputations & telled them the more wee
> attempted beinge in so weke a case the more if wee performed woulde be
> to our honours, but Contrarie wise if wee dyed in atempeing wee did but
> that which wee Came for, which was either to performe or dye[28]

they had the sense to treat him like the lunatic he had become. Grenville was like Lord Louis Mountbatten in the twentieth century, an example of the perils of adrenalin, and like him culpably careless with the lives of other people.[29]

The idea of sapping Spanish war-making capacity by a sustained assault on Spanish and Portuguese commerce on both sides of the Atlantic was obvious. There was a natural tendency to exaggerate the overall import-ance of the flow of American bullion to the finances of the Spanish monarchy. At least one English merchant commentator writing in the 1560s, when Philip II was still an ally of Elizabeth, had been clear that the bullion of the Americas was nothing like as important to Philip as the revenues he drew from a united and prosperous Netherlands.[30] By November 1577, when Sir Humphrey Gilbert was laying a discourse before the government on 'How Hir Majestie May Meete With and Annoy the King of Spain', it was possible for Gilbert just to assert that the West Indies were the most valuable possessions of King Philip. Since he believed that they were also weakly defended, it was here that he thought the queen could best annoy Spain 'With leste charges'. The phrase sounds reasonable but was in fact the shrewd pitch of the projector to a notoriously frugal queen. What followed was in many ways a masterpiece of glib folly. Gilbert suggested that forces be sent to conquer Hispaniola and Cuba, the two biggest of the Spanish Caribbean islands. This he blithely stated 'may easely be done'.[31] Any appearance of words implying cheap and easy solutions to major prob-lems in documents designed for the queen should warn historians of the nature of the minds they may be dealing with. Fortunately, Gilbert's plan was politically out of the question in 1577, when Elizabeth was desperate to avoid open war with Spain. It was also logistically unsustainable, a fiscal trap, and a strategic insanity, for it would have provided the Spaniards with a sitting target for an obliterative counter-stroke.

It was, in short, very typical of a category of plans which kept emerging from the Gilbert–Raleigh connection, and which have been taken far more seriously by posterity than they deserve. Selling himself, Gilbert developed the incorrigible optimism of the compulsive salesman. He fitted into the second rough category of court-connected venturer: the ones with no independent financial base. As the second son of a relatively modest Devon squire, Gilbert had been lucky to make a court connection in the Princess Elizabeth's household. Thereafter, he rose by ruthlessness and by selling projects. He was a projector – the word was well established in the Elizabethan vocabulary by the time the Earl of Essex in 1596 announced that he thought an action 'such as it were disadvantage to be thought the projector of it'.[32] In *The Devil is an Ass*, a comedy acted in 1616, Ben Jonson has as a leading character 'the wit, the Brain, the great projector', one Meerecraft. When the rustic Squire Fitzdotterel of Norfolk enquires, 'But what is a projector?', he receives, from Engine, a broker, the answer 'Why, one sir, that projects Ways to enrich men, or to make 'em great.' Rich and great was certainly what men like Gilbert and Raleigh wanted to be.

The trouble was that the means they used to accelerate their progress towards greatness tended to be the violent and unscrupulous exploitation of the extremely vague royal patents which represented the limits of their political clout. Gilbert's attempt to seize control of Newfoundland in 1583 was a classic case. His long-standing obsession with an attack on the foreign fishermen on the Newfoundland Banks was a crude expression of the underlying bandit ethos of ambitious lesser noblemen in most continental countries. His intervention was unnecessary, for the English fishermen, making common cause with the French loyalists in the period when Henry IV was fighting as Elizabeth's ally in his struggle to assert his rights to the French throne, were able to discourage Iberian ships. By 1600 the French and English effectively shared the rich fishery which was a major source of supplies and seamen for both the privateers and the Navy Royal.[33] Gilbert moved in to seize the harbour of St John's; he then absolutely predictably started making notional land grants. His associate Edward Hayes argued that the 'common opinion' that the climate made Newfoundland unsuitable for colonisation was wrong. According to him the southern parts had to have much the same climate as Brittany, Anjou, or Poitou in France.[34] Common opinion was broadly correct in sixteenth-century circumstances. Gilbert was lost with his ship on the return voyage, but not before he had told Hayes, who was sceptical about funding for further voyages, that he was confident the queen would loan him £10,000.[35] Anyone with that sort of confidence in Elizabeth Tudor was not living in the real world. The crew of his ship the *Squirrel* knew that. They had compelled him to turn back from his crazy voyage, but they still drowned with him, nor did Hakluyt record their names.

There is no reason to doubt the ardent Protestantism of most of the more articulate exponents of naval war against Spain, and of the linked plans for various kinds of settlement in the Americas. Gilbert was a notably pious Anglican. Richard Hakluyt the younger, the arch-publicist of the group, was an Anglican divine. Drake was the son of a lay reader to the navy. Yet to see Elizabethan religion as the cornerstone of an incipient 'empire', imparting a decisive sense of destiny to Elizabethan imperialists,[36] is to underrate the way early-modern men could weave together their material ambitions and their religious vocabularies. Christopher Columbus himself is perhaps the extreme example. The man who by accident gave Spain a New World spent much of his subsequent life weaving round himself a web of increasingly hysterical religious mysticism, all ultimately in the service of his lust for power, recognition, and gold.[37] The same mixture of religion, mysticism, geographical curiosity, and material self-interest which drove Columbus was available in Elizabethan England, notably in the person and circle of the Welsh mathematician, geographer, alchemist, and visionary John Dee.

Dee was a product of the integration of Wales into the wider political and economic world of Tudor monarchy. His father Roland Dee had held a minor court appointment under Henry VIII and sent his son from a grammar school to Cambridge University, where his brilliance guaranteed an academic career. Though Dee's first marriage had been into the City, it is significant that his third underlined his court links, for it was to a gentlewoman of the retinue of Lady Howard. The ladies of the privy chamber to Elizabeth were a group with whom Dee successfully cultivated warm relations, and the poet and courtier Edward Dyer often acted as his contact man with the good and great.[38] As well as being an authority on navigation and geography consulted by most of the better-known Elizabethan oceanic voyagers, Dee was a Hermetic magus, a philosopher–magician in the continental tradition he had studied at first hand in Brussels and Prague. His extensive writings advocating a 'British empire', with which he bombarded the queen, must not be taken as a precursor of the Victorian British Empire. On the contrary, they depicted Elizabeth as the heir to a totally mythical Arthurian empire through, of course, her Tudor Welsh (i.e. ancient British) blood. One of the reasons why Elizabeth found Dee useful was that he could cook up a claim to sovereignty over almost anywhere for her (not that the cautious lady necessarily wanted to do anything with all these claims). Dee eventually raised the mythical Welsh prince Owain Gwynedd in 1580 to assist his friend Sir Humphrey Gilbert's plans for settlement in America. This intrepid Welsh prince had crossed the Atlantic three hundred years before Columbus and settled in America, thus establishing a most convenient precedent for the subjects of the Tudors, the only reigning dynasty of Welsh extraction. When Dee summoned spirits from the vasty deep, they came. For this he was rewarded in not quite spectral currency, for Gilbert at one point promised him vast land grants north of 50 degrees latitude, which would have given Dee most of what is now Canada and control of the fabled north-west passage to Cathay.[39]

Such grants of permanent assets beyond the effective control of the granter were like the papal grants of most of the world to Spain and Portugal by Pope Alexander VI in the later fifteenth century. They did no harm until the grantee tried to implement them, when they were often fatal for him and always fatal for many of the inhabitants of the area concerned. There was an element of wild impracticality even in the proposals of the two Richard Hakluyts, who of all these men were probably the ones least interested in personal gain. The elder Hakluyt, a lawyer of the Middle Temple who transmitted to his cousin and namesake his passionate interest in geography some time before 1570, was obsessed with the idea that English agricultural colonies could profitably be established in such unlikely sites as Newfoundland. In 1577–78 Hakluyt had been in contact with Anthony Parkhurst, a merchant of Bristol who had ventured to St John's and the St Lawrence for two or three years. The underlying attraction was the fact that there were the great cod fisheries on the Banks off Newfoundland, but Parkhurst depicted an earthly paradise where benign weather and immense natural fertility would enable both arable and pastoral farming to be pursued in a climate of abundance. These views fed straight into the pamphlets which Hakluyt was currently writing on behalf of Gilbert, with predictable results.[40]

The younger Hakluyt also relied heavily on first-hand accounts from participants in major voyages. He seems to have been galvanised into writing on any scale by the failure of the Portuguese succession, which made a vast expansion in the empire of Philip II very likely. Having quizzed Thomas Griggs, the steward of John Winter's ship the *Elizabeth* which had just returned from the Strait of Magellan, he wrote in 1579 a manuscript discourse on that strait which duly became a published pamphlet in which he argued that it was essential to check the power of Spain by three steps, all of which were impractical. First was the seizure and fortification of the strait. Second was to be the seizure of an island base off Brazil. Thirdly, the search was to be put in hand at once for the north-east passage to Cathay. The plan for occupying and fortifying the strait included a quite mad proposal to transplant there as auxiliaries to the English garrison several thousand of the 'Symerones' or Cimarrones, the members of the negro communities founded by escaped slaves who had assisted Francis Drake in his remarkable and lucrative raids on the cities and bullion trains of the Isthmus of Panama in 1572–73. The idea that they would have allowed Drake or anyone else to move them was almost as unreal as the basic concept of a happily self-sustaining English colony in the Patagonian winter. Certainly, every single member of the Spanish expedition which tried to set up a base there died. In true projector fashion, Hakluyt was sure his proposal for the strait could be executed 'with small charges', whilst the Brazilian island of St Vincent was 'easely to be wonne'.[41]

Hakluyt did not see these as more than the beginnings of the benefits to be derived from the execution of his plan for the strait. The operation was so to beggar King Philip by interrupting a (non-existent) flow of trade that the Portuguese pretender Dom Antonio, to whom he hoped to be sent as ambassador, would 'be esely restored to his kingdom and become a perpetual friend'.[42] As ever, the repeated occurrence of varieties of the word 'easy' was a bad sign. Fortunately, no action was taken on these proposals. By 1584 the younger Hakluyt was working for a new patron, Sir Walter Raleigh, who had in 1583 obtained by royal patent most of the rights granted in 1578 to Sir Humphrey Gilbert for settlement and exclusive privileges in North America. The year 1584 saw Hakluyt produce the work known as the *Discourse of Western Planting*, which is openly an attempt to persuade the queen to put state resources behind a plan for extensive colonisation designed to spread true religion, forestall other European powers like the Dutch and French, revive England's flagging export trade, and undermine the power of Spain.

Elizabeth was too frugal to throw money in a direction where so many had already failed, and the only part of the *Discourse* which was to prove a guide to the objectives of the colony which Raleigh started to try to establish, through expeditions led by his associates from the summer of 1585, was the section which explicitly envisaged using it as a base for attacks on the Spanish West Indies. Hakluyt emphasised the weakness of the Spanish forces in the Americas, which he described as 'feble scarr crowes', and he reproduced a list of 'rich Townes lienge along the sea coaste' which he reported were 'rarely and simply manned and fortified', from which he deduced that 'the Inlande is moche more weake and unmanned'.[43] It was a privateer's prospectus.

The Spanish government faced almost insuperable problems in the Caribbean, the most popular haunt of the privateers. Utterly ruthless and able admirals like Pedro Menendez de Aviles tried to use fast galleons to cleanse the region of privateers, but wind conditions alone made it very difficult. With prevailing easterly trade winds, the Caribbean was a one-way system and privateers who found themselves to windward of the galleons were effectively immune. Galleons eventually had to concentrate on protecting the bullion flows from the collection and assembly ports of Catagena, Vera Cruz, and Havana. An attempt to establish defence by galley forces from 1578 broke down because of the huge operational costs of galleys in a period of rising food prices. Fortification of towns was expensive and slow.[44] Not all towns wanted fortification. Some preferred illegal trade. It was certainly better than turning out to face a night assault by an English landing party led by someone like Drake, who supplemented his pikemen, musketeers, and archers with 'firepikes' to illumine his attack and drums and trumpets to exaggerate its size.[45] It was this sort of hit-and-run raid by swarms of ships around the 100-ton mark with pinnaces of 10 tons and upward which admirals like Menendez just could not handle. A fixed settlement, by comparison, was easy meat, as the unfortunate Frenchmen he butchered in Florida in 1565 found.

That fact explains both the nature and the failure of Raleigh's attempts to establish a settlement on Roanoke Island between Pamlico and Albemarle Sounds behind the Outer Banks, that chain of dangerous sand spits off the shore of what is now North Carolina. The site was deliberately obscure to make it difficult for Spaniards to find it. At the same time, it was near enough to the West Indies to serve as a base for activity in the Caribbean. Sir Richard Grenville, who transported the first party of settlers out in 1585, indulged in lucrative privateering on the return voyage. The original settlers were almost all young males with a military background, wholly incapable of establishing a self-sufficient agricultural colony. But then that was not what they had come out to America to do.[46] Ralph Lane, who was military governor after Grenville departed, was a violent opportunist under whom relations with the local Indians were likely to become strained, as they did. The queen had given the incipient colony little beyond the use of her name in the allusive form of Virginia. By the summer of 1586, the remaining settlers insisted on being taken off by Drake as he returned from a Caribbean cruise and anchored as near as he could to their hopelessly shallow harbour to offer them assistance, in the first instance to maintain their settlement. Grenville, who arrived just too late with a supply ship, left a tiny holding force, which vanished before Raleigh's third group of colonists arrived in 1587. Sent to establish the city of Raleigh in Virginia under the governorship of the artist John White, they sent him home to appeal for additional help before they themselves disappeared into the mists of history. When he did eventually return in 1590, White could find some of his and their goods and equipment, but no colonists. From start to finish the voyages connected with the colony involved privateering. It was a colony only in the sense that it was an incipient nest of privateers, though men like White and the younger Hakluyt dreamed it might be more. To see it as the foundation stone of the British Empire is nonsense. It had no connection with such a thing. Even to incorporate it into the saga of 'England's Sea Empire' in the period 1550–1642 is to construct non-existent continuities as well as a non-existent empire.

Historians have endlessly reiterated, edited, and rephrased under the guise of their own narratives the strident but often, indeed usually, wildly unrealistic propaganda of a tiny minority of publicists and self-publicists. Richard Hakluyt the younger published in 1589 the first edition of his *The Principall Navigations, Voiages and Discoveries of the English Nation* in a stately foolscap volume. A revised enlarged version in three volumes was to appear in 1598, 1599, and 1600. Hakluyt, whose expectations of the Virginia colony were rooted in a basic misunderstanding of its climate, could not understand what had happened, let alone why the settlers had in 1586 abandoned 'this paradise of the world'. He opined that perhaps it was the result of the wrath of God due to their violent misuse of the native inhabitants. The reasons for that violence were obvious enough. Incapable of feeding themselves, the colonists were forever plundering Indian fish weirs or their stores of maize corn. At short range their armour, firearms, and steel-edged weapons made them much more lethal than the Indian bowmen they faced, as the local chief Pemisapan must have reflected when, in Lane's words, he was 'shot thwart the buttocks by mine Irish boy with my Petronell'. A petronell was a heavy cavalry pistol, and Lane had men from Kerry with him. Yet there was nothing worth stealing except food. Lane was quite clear that only 'the discoverie of a good mine, . . . or a passage to the Southsea [i.e. Pacific] or some way to it, can bring this country in request to be inhabited by our nation'.[47]

Only gold or the prospect of access to lucrative Asian trade would have persuaded the collection of pressed men and adventurers he led to stay. What had kept very similar gangster bands going in the first Spanish Empire in the Greater Antilles was the discovery of placer gold in the streams of Hispaniola, Puerto Rico, and Cuba. Placer gold was what sustained Spanish interest in the Isthmus of Panama (known to the Spaniards as Castilla del Oro, Castile of the Gold) as the brutal exploitation of the island populations led effectively to genocide and the limited gold deposits there ran out.[48] Since there was no gold in Virginia, sensible men like George Abbot, master of University College, Oxford, were clear by 1599 that the experiment of settlement there by Englishmen was simply a failure and the land secure to its ancient inhabitants. He thought, correctly, that the lack of serious state support for an enterprise charged on the inadequate fortunes of private individuals like Raleigh was fatal.[49] If a few men who valued geographical knowledge for its own sake be excepted, the overall impact of the experiment on English national consciousness of any kind was probably minimal. The younger Hakluyt's contemporary reputation was not immense. His influence on government policy was neither continuous nor profound. He left no great continental reputation behind him, despite his contacts with Flemish and French cartographers. His deification, literally as a sort of permanent secretary to the Grand Geographical Council in Elysium, was a phenomenon of the nineteenth and twentieth centuries.[50] There is even some difficulty in showing any close links between his works and the writing surrounding the renewal of English voyaging to America in the early seventeenth century. In the preface to his first edition of 1589, Hakluyt stressed that he did not write about 'any action perfourmed neere home, nor in any part of Europe commonly frequented by our shipping'. That included the foiling of the Armada, 'that victorious exploit not long since atchieved in our narrow seas under the valiant and provident conduct of the right honourable the lord Charles Howard high Admirall of England'.[51] Yet home waters and European power-politics were infinitely more important than the exotic episodes which Hakluyt chronicled. Even the privateering war, successful as the bulk of its more modest enterprises were, was not a major theatre from the Spanish point of view, because it could not seriously disrupt the bullion flows. Under the pressure of war and of the ruthless predatory practices of some of Hakluyt's closest associates, English society was demonstrably fracturing and not just along the Old English fault line.

Legislation of a Westminster parliament in 1581 introduced enormously more severe penalties for Roman Catholic practices, including potentially crippling fines. A group of Catholic gentry, in association with politicians like Sir Philip Sidney who were Anglican but sympathetic to the Catholics, had started to negotiate with Sir Humphrey Gilbert with a view to setting themselves up in an American colony based on the patents Gilbert held from the Crown. They were to have freedom of conscience and the rents of their home estates in exchange for guarantees of loyalty. The government seems to have given a tacit blessing to the scheme, which appalled the Spanish ambassador Mendoza, who saw it as weakening a fifth column for counter-revolution in England, as well as challenging Spain in the New World. He assiduously threatened potential participants with having their throats cut by the Spaniards, as the French had been served in Florida. After that he assured them they risked roasting for ever in the searing fires of hell for defying the papal will. Lack of finance seems to have been the real key to the abandonment of a plan which is a startling early demonstration of the fact that the overseas expansion of England was not a simple result of the growth of a wonderful new English Protestant national consciousness and assurance.[52] That was the line peddled by Hakluyt. In fact, overseas settlement was to be more a reflection of the profound tensions which were tearing the late-Elizabethan English community apart. War pressures did help consolidate many groups behind government, but the side-effects of the same pressures did at least as much to alienate large and important groups from that government. Conflict on colonial frontiers was no exception to these generalisations.

Notes and references

1. Ciaran Brady, 'Conservative Subversives: The community of the Pale and the Dublin administration, 1556–86' in P.J. Corish (ed.), *Radicals, Rebels and Establishments*, Historical Studies, 15 (Appletree Press, Belfast, 1985), pp. 11–32.

2. 'James Fitzmaurice's Proclamation 1579', printed as document 17 in Grenfell Morton, *Elizabethan Ireland* (Longman, London, 1971), p. 126.

3. Michael Maccarthy-Morrogh, *The Munster Plantation: English migration to southern Ireland 1583–1641* (Clarendon Press, Oxford, 1986), Chap. 1.

4. Lord Justice Pelham and the Council of Ireland to the Privy Council: Dublin, 26 November 1579, printed in James Hogan and N. McNeill O'Farrell (eds.), *The Walsingham Letter-Book or Register of Ireland May, 1578 to December, 1579* (Irish Manuscripts Commission, Dublin, 1959), p. 238.

5. Niall Fallon, *The Armada in Ireland* (Stanford Maritime, London, 1978), pp. 30–32 and 53–56.

6. A.L. Rowse, *Raleigh and the Throckmortons* (Macmillan, London, 1962), p. 134.

7   Quoted in David B. Quinn, *Raleigh and the British Empire* (English Universities Press, London, 1947), p. 148.

8. Signet letter to Sir John Perrot for Ralph Lane, 8 February 1585, and editorial notes, printed in David B. Quinn (ed.), *The Roanoke Voyages 1584–1590. Vol. 1* (Hakluyt Society, 2nd series, No. 104, London, 1952), pp. 149–50.

9. A.L. Rowse, *Sir Richard Grenville of the 'Revenge'* (Jonathan Cape, London, 1937).

10. Peter Earle, *The Last Fight of the Revenge* (Collins and Brown, London, 1952), pp. 34–35.

11. *Ibid.*, Chap. 15, 'An Heroical Fable'.

12. Excerpts from Edmund Campion, *A History of Ireland* are conveniently available in James P. Myers Jr (ed.), *Elizabethan Ireland: A selection of writings by Elizabethan writers on Ireland* (Shoe-String Press, Hamden, CT, 1983), pp. 22–35.

13. Felipe Fernandez-Armesto, *The Spanish Armada: The experience of war in 1588* (Oxford University Press, Oxford, 1988), pp. 48–49.

14. CSP Ireland, Elizabeth, 1574–85, Wallop to Walsingham, 14 March 1581, p. 292.

15. Queen to Sir Henry Sidney, 6 July 1567, printed in Tomas O Laidhin (ed.), *Sidney State Papers 1565–70* (Irish Manuscripts Commission, Dublin, 1962), p. 71.

16. Sean O'Domhnall, 'Warfare in sixteenth-century Ireland', *Irish Historical Studies*, 5 (1946–47), p. 43.

17. CSP Ireland, 1574–85, p. 146.

18. Kenneth R. Andrews, *Elizabethan Privateering: English privateering during the Spanish War, 1585–1603* (Cambridge University Press, Cambridge, 1964), remains the basic authority on all aspects of this subject.

19. Kenneth R. Andrews, *Trade, Plunder and Settlement* (Cambridge University Press, Cambridge, pbk edn, 1984), pp. 128–29.

20. Charles Wilson, *Queen Elizabeth and the Revolt of the Netherlands* (Macmillan, London, 1970).

21. Simon Adams, 'The Outbreak of the Elizabethan Naval War Against the Spanish Empire: The embargo of May 1585 and Sir Francis Drake's West Indies voyage' in M.J. Rodriguez-Salgado and Simon Adams (eds.), *Spain and the Gran Armada 1585–1604* (John Donald, Edinburgh, 1991), pp. 45–69.

22. G.C. Williamson, *George, Third Earl of Cumberland (1558–1605): His life and his voyages* (Cambridge University Press, Cambridge, 1920), pp. 63–64 and 67–69.

23. Robert W. Kenny, *Elizabeth's Admiral: The political career of Charles Howard, Earl of Nottingham 1536–1624* (Johns Hopkins Press, Baltimore, 1970), Chap. 3: 'The Fruits of the Sea'.

24. Richard Hakluyt the younger (ed.), *Voyages* (8 vols., Everyman edn, Dent, London, 1962 reprint), Vol. 8, p. 51.

25. *Ibid.*, Vol. 7, pp. 68–71.

26. *Ibid.*, pp. 148–53.

27. *Ibid.*, Vol. 5, pp. 57–68.

28. Cavendish's extraordinary final MS is printed in facsimile in David B. Quinn (ed.), *The Last Voyage of Thomas Cavendish 1591–1592* (University of Chicago Press for the Newberry Library, Chicago, IL, 1975). The quotation is found on p. 111.

29. Andrew Roberts, *Eminent Churchillians* (Weidenfeld and Nicolson, London, 1994), Chap. 2.

30. G.D. Ramsay (ed.), *The Politics of a Tudor Merchant Adventurer: A letter to the earls of East Friesland* (Manchester University Press, Manchester, 1979), pp. 66–69.

31. David Beers Quinn (ed.), *The Voyages and Colonising Enterprises of Sir Humphrey Gilbert*, Hakluyt Society, 2nd Series, No. 83 (London, 1940), Vol. 1, pp. 176–80.

32. *The Oxford English Dictionary* (2nd edn, Clarendon Press, Oxford, 1989), p. 602.

33. D.B. Quinn and A.N. Ryan, *England's Sea Empire, 1550–1642* (Allen and Unwin, London, 1983), pp. 150–51.

34. 'Edward Hayes' Narrative of Sir Humphrey Gilbert's Last Expedition', in Quinn (ed.), *Voyages of Gilbert*, Vol. 2, p. 404.

35. *Ibid.*, Vol. 1, pp. 88–89.

36. Louis B. Wright, *Religion and Empire: The alliance between piety and commerce in English expansion 1558–1625* (Octagon Books reprint, New York, 1973).

37. Ramon Iglesia, *Columbus, Cortes, and Other Essays*, trans. and ed. Lesley Byrd Simpson (University of California Press, Berkeley, CA, 1969), pp. 30–33.

38. E.G.R. Taylor, *Tudor Geography 1485–1583* (Methuen, London, 1930), pp. 75–78.

39. Peter J. French, *John Dee: The world of an Elizabethan magus* (Routledge and Kegan Paul, London, 1972), pp. 192–99; Gwyn A. Williams, *Madoc: The making of a myth* (Methuen, London, 1979), pp. 38–39.

40. *Vide* the two letters of 1577–78 from Parkhurst printed in E.G.R. Taylor (ed.), *The Original Writings and Correspondence of the Two Richard Hakluyts Vol. 1*, The Hakluyt Society, 2nd Series, No. 71 (London, 1935), pp. 123–34.

41. Richard Hakluyt the younger, 'A Discourse of the Commodity of the Taking of the Straight of Magellan', pamphlet of 1579–80, printed in *ibid.*, pp. 139–46.

42. *Idem*, 'Ye Commodity of Taking Ye Straightes of Magellanus', note of 1580, printed in *ibid.*, pp. 163–64.

43. *Idem*, 'Discourse of Western Planting by Richard Hakluyt, 1584', *ibid.*, Vol. 2, pp. 252–54.

44. Kenneth R. Andrews, *The Spanish Caribbean: Trade and plunder 1530–1630* (Yale University Press, New Haven, CT, 1978), Chaps. 4, 6, 8, and 10.

45. There is a convenient version of the account of Drake's night assault on Nombre de Dios in 1572, eventually published only in 1626, in Janet and John Hampden (eds.), *Sir Francis Drake's Raid on the Treasure Trains Being the Memorable Relation of His Voyage to the West Indies in 1572 Faithfully Taken from Eye-Witness Reports by Members of the Expedition, and Enlarged by Drake's Own Hand* (The Folio Society, Westminster, 1954), pp. 26–32.

46. Karen Ordahl Kupperman, *Roanoke: The abandoned colony* (Rowman and Allanhead, Towota, NJ, 1984), pp. 13–14.

47. Ralph Lane's narrative of the 1585–86 settlement on Roanoke Island is conveniently reprinted with other relevant documents and helpful notes in David B. Quinn and Alison M. Quinn (eds.), *The First Colonists: Documents on the planting of the first English settlements in North America 1584–1590* (North Carolina Department of Cultural Resources, Division of Archives and History, Raleigh, NC, 1982), pp. 24–45.

48. Carl Ortwin Sauer, *The Early Spanish Main* (University of California Press, Berkeley, CA, Centennial pbk, 1992).

49. H.C. Porter, *The Inconstant Savage: England and the North American Indian 1500–1660* (Duckworth, London, 1979), pp. 254 and 259.

50. David B. Quinn, 'Hakluyt's Reputation', in David B. Quinn (ed.), *The Hakluyt Handbook*, The Hakluyt Society, 2nd Series, No. 10 (London, 1974), pp. 133–52.

51. Richard Hakluyt the younger, *The Principal Navigations Voyages Traffiques and Discoveries of the English Nation* (James MacLehose, Glasgow, 1903), Vol. 1, Preface xxiv.

52. Quinn (ed.), *Voyages of Gilbert*, Vol. 1, pp. 71–76.

CHAPTER FOUR

Nadir of statesmanship: the origins of the last Elizabethan colonial war

In the years immediately before the Armada of 1588 Ireland was ruled by Lord Deputy Sir John Perrot. Reputedly a bastard of Henry VIII, he certainly looked like him and had the same temper. His rule was marked by the usual competition between the Gaelic, Old English, and New English lords. What is interesting is the way his policies gradually shifted towards a more pragmatic line, eventually accepting the idea that change was only feasible if the traditional ruling classes were allowed to benefit by it. What they objected to was not so much change as change which they could not control and which was used by others to rob and humiliate them. Perrot's quite spectacular failure to drive the Crown's high-handed and authoritarian legislative programme through the Irish parliament in 1585–86 was significant. The Crown's own nominee for the post of speaker, Nicholas Walsh, though an Anglican, summed up the views of his increasingly Roman Catholic fellow Old Englishmen when he said in his closing speech that Ireland was a constitutional polity in which the function of government was to defend loyal subjects without discrimination between them. Basically, this was a repudiation of attempts to ram through anti-Catholic legislation comparable to the tougher statutes which the English parliament had been passing under the stress of war with Spain. It also defied government attempts to secure an arbitrarily higher revenue by a process known as composition, whereby landowners had to abandon the practice of retaining armed men – 'coign and livery'. They were to be relieved of the burdens of military service and billeting of troops, and the obligation to render supplies to the government at artificially low rates under the system known as purveyance, but in exchange they would pay a fixed money rent. Above all, Walsh and his fellows gave the lie to the self-serving rhetoric of New English lawyers who waxed eloquent on the arbitrary power of the royal prerogative over an allegedly dependent Ireland, mainly because they could manipulate that prerogative to usurp the property of others. The rage of the executive at a parliament which failed to act as a mere tool of government was shown in the 27-year gap before another one was summoned in Ireland, but Perrot, despite his notorious irascibility, seems to have learned his lesson.

The composition of Connaught which he carried through by executive action was successful, because he began to distance himself from the predatory practices of the New English faction, carrying through the regional settlement by local negotiation through commissioners. These, though headed by an English soldier, Sir Richard Bingham, were otherwise mainly local Gaelic and Old English lords, like the earls of Thomond and Clanricarde, the Baron of Atherny, Sir Turlough O'Brien, Sir Richard Burke, the O'Connor Don, the O'Rourke, and the O'Flaherty. The deal was immensely complex, involving areas which were granted as 'freedoms' exempt from composition rent, and compensation to landlords for their new rent to the Crown in the shape of the right to monetary rents from their dependants. Bingham himself might have tried to persist in earlier attempts to use the process of composition to undermine the position of the major chiefs and landlords, but Perrot disliked him and leaned on Old English reformers such as Nicholas White and Chief Justice Thomas Dillon of Connaught. The Crown gained a revenue of £4000 per annum. Local landowners were secured. The New English could enter the province by purchase, which they did to a modest degree and to nobody's great distress in so underpopulated an area.[1]

The lord deputy's own eccentricities were such that doubts have been expressed about his balance of mind, but there is little doubt that his latter years in office were marked by a distinct outbreak of sanity in Crown policy in Ireland. Bingham supplied the iron fist which ensured that a reasonable deal was accepted. His administration of justice was ruthless, and he dealt decisively with an irruption of Scottish mercenaries moving down from the Innishowen peninsula to support a rising of the Mayo Burkes. Though they slipped past him at first with perhaps 1400 men plus a train of camp followers, he caught them with their backs to the River Moy, the boundary between Sligo and Mayo, in September 1586. What was impressive about the action which followed was that Bingham with no more than 500 foot and 80 horse completely shattered the hastily formed Scots battle line with a surprise attack in which cavalry charges, supported in the opening stages by musketry fire from skirmishers, were decisive. The grim massacre of the trapped, beaten, fleeing force underlined the fact that these were not armoured gallowglasses but redshanks whose lack of body armour made them vulnerable not only to houghing or hamstringing from behind but also to paunching or disembowelling by frontal assault with blade weapon. Among their leaders, two nephews of Sorley Boy, sons of James MacDonald of the Isles, fell.[2] With this action the composition was recognised as the best available compromise, giving a stable, largely self-funding Connaught until it was sucked into a wider war in the 1590s. By then Perrot was long gone, and the war cruelly revealed the limitations of Bingham's generalship. Nevertheless, the principles of the composition of Connaught were successfully applied as late as 1591 in Monaghan, where the Crown settled with the MacMahons of Monaghan in a way which preserved the income and position of local landowners.

Nor was Connaught the only province to benefit from Perrot's utterly unexpected capacity to learn from his mistakes. In Ulster in 1584 he had decided to ignore instructions from Elizabeth merely to hold the line and 'look through his fingers at Ulster'. He was worried by the arrival in Ulster of a wave of MacLean redshanks from the southern Hebrides, and persuaded himself that it was imperative that he use his limited forces to smash Clan Donald South in Antrim before it made common cause with its fellow Highlanders and the Ulster Gaels. In September with a modest £11,500 from Elizabeth to fund his army and an accompanying naval squadron, Perrot caught Sorley Boy MacDonald, by now the recognised chief of his clan, unprepared. Perrot captured Sorley's stronghold of Dunluce from its 40-man garrison and set up small garrison posts in north Antrim. Sorley wisely chose to disappear westwards. After ten days Perrot returned to Dublin, leaving local command to others. Sir Henry Bagenal was not perhaps in the first flight of commanders, but Elizabeth had despatched one of her best soldiers, Sir William Stanley, to help hold north Antrim. It availed her not. When Sorley Boy made his inevitable come-back, with massive support from Scotland and all the tactical mobility which a galley fleet able to land men on any reasonable beach conveyed, Perrot's garrisons proved easy meat and his field commanders were soon seeking shelter in Carrickfergus. At this point a triumphant Sorley offered to hold the Route and the northern third of the Glynnes as a peaceable vassal of Elizabeth. The southern two-thirds of the Glynnes were to be held by his nephew Donnell Gorme on similar terms.

Instead of accepting this reasonable offer, which Sorley had every reason to honour, for it would give him the legal title he craved to his lands in north Antrim, Perrot hazarded war again in 1585 when fortune, that fickle jade, seemed to smile on him. By the spring of that year the Antrim MacDonnells had all retired to Scotland, leaving only an observation force of 120 light infantry commanded by Sorley's son Alexander. Turlough Luineach O'Neill had lined the Bann with his troops in support of the lord deputy's forces, blocking any withdrawal by the Scots into western or central Ulster, and as Sorley had the sense not to want to stand and fight, Scotland was a good place to be. By August he was back in Antrim. Even the English had grasped that the king of Scots did not have the power, if indeed he had the will, to stop Clan Donald South from pursuing its activities in Ulster. In November Sorley Boy recaptured Dunluce Castle, hanging its constable and putting its garrison to the sword. By the winter of 1585–86 he had reduced the queen's troops in Antrim to desperate straits. He still wanted peace. His wife, a daughter of Con Bacagh O'Neill, was long dead, as were many of his immediate family. The death of his eldest son Alexander MacSorley in action and his own advanced age seem to have impelled him to seek a final settlement which his military prowess had made Perrot grumblingly willing to concede. In exchange for a pantomimic 'submission' to Perrot in Dublin, he secured a pardon, a patent of denization (which was not quite naturalisation but had the same effect for most purposes), and a grant of all his territorial holdings, including the constableship of Dunluce. His eldest nephew, Angus MacJames MacDonnell, had already been given a formal grant of territories in the Glynnes in exchange for rent and military service to Elizabeth, but with the interesting proviso that his obligations to her were to be suspended if England went to war with Scotland. The only unhappy party was Rory MacQuillan, who protested loudly that the MacDonnells were being bribed with lands they had usurped from the MacQuillans. Indeed they were. However, it was the only sane course. The key to the success of the Highland Scots had throughout been their avoidance of set-piece battle and their ability literally to vanish back to the southern Hebrides and return at will. The exception which proved the rule was that ill-fated expedition commanded by Angus MacDonnell's two brothers Donnell Gorme and Alexander Carragh, which set off to aid the MacWilliam Burkes in September 1586; it was caught with no escape route by Sir Richard Bingham, governor of Connaught, and was wiped out in formal battle.[3]

The effects of Perrot's deputyship were in the end positive and important. Both Munster and Connaught had been stabilised, the latter in a fashion which secured the position and cooperation of local elites. The queen had as much control in those two provinces as she needed. That was why Armada galleons and their crews had such an appalling welcome on the western shore of Ireland. When not massacred by Crown forces, the unfortunate Spaniards were often robbed and murdered by locals. They were easy prey. Edward Whyte, a member of the council of Connaught whose brother was an alderman of Limerick, reported that 'they were so miserably distressed coming to land that one man, named Melaghlin M'Cabbe killed 80 with his galloglass axe'. Only in Ulster did they generally receive kindness and refuge.

The crews of two Spanish ships which had ended up in Blacksod Bay in north-west Connaught packed themselves into the more seaworthy ship and struggled back to Lougherris in Tyrconnell, where they ran ashore in a gale. The local MacSweeneys welcomed them warmly and arranged for them to move down to a safe harbour, Killybegs, on the north side of Donegal Bay, where several Armada ships were sheltering. Joining the *Girona*, one of the four big galeasses (ships using both oars and sail power) of the squadron of Naples, they added the crews of two more small ships before they tried to run along the north coast of Ulster to what they knew would be a friendly welcome in James VI's Scotland. Despite heavy wastage there were perhaps 1300 men on the galeass when it went down in a storm near the Giant's Causeway in Antrim, close to Dunluce where James MacDonnell gave the handful of survivors shelter. He also picked the pockets of the dead on the shore and did some salvage work, with professional help from Scotland, but that was only sensible, and helped fund embellishing the castle with Scottish baronial features. Scotland's record of hospitality to Armada survivors was matched only by Ulster's.[4] Even in that most independent of Irish regions, the Crown after 1586 was no longer wasting its miserably inadequate resources in endless, unwinnable, and unnecessary campaigns against the MacDonalds of Antrim. Apart from Bingham's lucky battlefield success, all of this had been achieved mainly by late, reluctant but in the end profitable decisions to abandon attempts to cut against the grain of local power-structures. What happened to Perrot on his return to England was therefore deeply subversive of the long-term viability of the Elizabethan system of governance. He was destroyed by a factional conspiracy which used trumped-up charges so preposterous in nature that the choleric Perrot, who died in the Tower of London in 1592, dismissed the most serious ones as beneath the dignity of an answer.

Perrot had been elected member of parliament for Haverfordwest in his native county of Pembrokeshire. He was admitted to the privy council early in 1589, and became active both as a government manager of business in the House of Commons and as an authority on Irish policy whom Irish peers used as their natural line of communication with the court. He correctly concluded that his successor as lord deputy, Sir William Fitzwilliam, was corrupt. Fitzwilliam was connected by marriage with the queen's most important councillor, Lord Burghley, and the two men mounted a counter-offensive against Perrot, drawing heavily on material generated by the violent quarrels which had marked the relationship between Perrot and his hawkish governor of Connaught, Bingham. Dubious witnesses swore that Perrot, an early patron of Protestant preachers, was crypto-papist. Perrot was alleged to have patronised Gaelic bards to write satire against the queen. He appears in fact to have stopped a local English commander from using poems in an Irish language which Perrot knew the commander did not understand as an excuse for barefaced robbery of a group of O'Clerys who had moved down from Tyrconnell to Connaught, with Perrot's permission, to escape from a local power struggle. A letter in which Perrot offered the crowns of England and Ireland to Philip II of Spain appears to have been what Perrot said it was – an unconvincing and impudent forgery. Perrot had undoubtedly expressed coarse and unflattering views of Elizabeth, but then most of her servants had good reason to think what Perrot made the mistake of saying.[5] With the deaths of Leicester and Walsingham, the regime was increasingly dominated by Burghley. Only much later in the 1590s did the Earl of Essex consciously mount a challenge to that hegemony which had already done a great deal of harm by narrowing access to the Crown to the point where provincial elites could not make their voices heard, and where able men, natural counsellors of the queen (in the case of Perrot possibly her half-brother), were struck down unscrupulously to cement the ascendancy of the Cecil connection. It was a classic recipe for failure of early-modern monarchy.

In a sense, the failure of the *Felicissima Armada*, though not really a decisive event in naval history, had, as its most perceptive historian said, punctured the triumphalist Counter-Reformation juggernaut deliberately built up by a Spanish monarch. Like modern Protestant and Catholic factions in Northern Ireland, Philip II knew where God was – on his side. Military victory in 1588 would have made this a self-fulfilling theological insight as destructive of continued resistance as the memory of the astonishing feats of the *conquistadores* in the Americas. There were further crises in the Anglo–Spanish war, but never again quite the sense of impending Armageddon.[6] Yet the Elizabethan regime became more paranoid as its base relentlessly narrowed. Suspicious, secretive, authoritarian, the 'second reign of Elizabeth' from the 1590s was increasingly a *regimen cecilianum*, dominated by the Cecils, father Burghley and son Robert. It was interested in hegemony, not consensus, driving the central state structure to the limits of its autonomous power in a way reminiscent of its modern successors, and inventing politically incorrect opponents such as a largely non-existent 'Puritan movement' which it then demonised.[7]

In Ireland the regime had become increasingly unenthusiastic about spending money on unnecessary military objectives. One reason why Perrot had adopted a much more modest Ulster policy was that the queen's government refused to underwrite plans which he advanced for the creation of a network of forts in the province, on the reasonable grounds that they had seen too many schemes which promised quick results and yielded only expense. By 1586 Perrot was being told in so many words that the cost of the war with Spain ruled out any further commitment in Ireland. In the short term the results of this situation were not at all unsatisfactory, as the events of 1588 proved. There was still a frontier on which low-level colonial warfare sputtered in Ulster and parts of Connaught. The garrison of Carrickfergus, so often ambushed as it marched north bent on conquest, actually developed an effective hit-and-run technique depending on good intelligence, local allies, and a cavalry force. In March 1588, for example, one of its columns managed to cross the Bann to take out Fordorough O'Cahan. He had local enemies like Manus O'Cahan, who accompanied the force as an ally of the Crown, and Dublin merchants, who complained about his extortionate levies on the commercial fisheries on the Bann. The striking force brought little back except Fordorough's head, but it was vital to get out as fast as they had moved in and the operation encouraged a somewhat more respectful attitude to the Crown as the principal victim of the raid had been 'blasphemous against Her Majesty in all his speeches, and as rank a traitor and maintainer of Scots, as any traitor living'.[8]

There was, however, a whole series of potential timebombs under the fragile balance of interstitial pressures which made the situation relatively stable at tolerable cost in 1588. Memoranda, almost certainly by the Welshman Sir William Herbert, were submitted to Burghley in 1588 warning him of the deeply unstable situation in Munster, where the writer identified the New English with a military background as potentially disruptive because they were 'frustrated of their expectation, to have the land divided amongst them, and fearing the prosperous success of this colony'. The writer could see no hope of altering their predatory outlook. He therefore deemed it essential 'to lessen their power to do evil' before they drove the 'natural inhabitants' into rebellion. He urged demilitarisation of the province. As it stood, it was devoid of capacity for defence against a serious Spanish invasion:

> The strongest place in this province is Limerick; Her Majesty hath therein some munition, four demi-cannons, one culverin, and a demi-culverin, a minion and a falcon all out of reparation, lying upon the ground, the carriages broken and rotted. Moreover two or three hudred calivers all in decay and unservicable, sundry sheaves of arrows, the feathers gone through the moisture that hath spoiled them; some other weapons and armour there are, but all in very evil case.

What was needed was a small professional garrison truly under Crown control; the razing of castles which were almost bound to be rapidly seized by Desmond sympathisers in the event of a rebellion; and the stripping of the New English of their military commands, which they abused to provoke rather than contain rebellion, for 'great is the gain, to be paid by Her Majesty and to prowl for ourselves'. The result might be that the bulk of the lesser local landowners would feel as secure in their property rights as the Welsh gentry, and be as willing to cooperate in operating the polity as they.[9]

The prescription was sensible and perceptive, the practice quite different because of the way the court functioned or rather malfunctioned. There was dissatisfaction at the highest levels of the Irish administration with the continuing heavy-handed ruthlessness of Sir Richard Bingham in Connaught. Perrot had seriously tried to have him removed and transferred to service against the Spaniards in the Netherlands. Fitzwilliam openly regarded him as an example of all that was most counter-productive in the New English style. With the Armada out of the way, it would have been sensible to overlook the fact that a very few Gaelic leaders in the province had offered succour to distressed Spanish ships and crews. Among them were Richard MacRickard Burke, Murrough na Doe O'Flaherty, and Brian O'Rourke, a very influential man in the recently formed County Leitrim. Instead, Bingham virtually licensed an Englishman, John Browne, recently settled in as sheriff of Mayo, to raise levies for a *conquistador*-type *entrada* or plundering speculative land raid on the Burkes. Very understandably, the Burkes killed him, and they then rose in rebellion with their allies, though with a singularly reasonable set of demands which Fitzwilliam thought negotiable and on which he did negotiate with them. The Crown was asked to name a Macwilliam, the traditional head of these Burkes. The sheer tyranny of Bingham's administration of Connaught was denounced and his removal demanded. It was a demand wholly acceptable to both the ruling lord deputy and his predecessor, both of whom thought Bingham a murderous and self-seeking bastard who should go. He nearly went, in the sense that a legal inquiry was set up into his record, but he was protected by the patronage of Walsingham, still a power at court and in council. Bingham survived and his brother crushed the rising with rather less indiscriminate slaughter than was the Bingham norm. The precedent was simply appalling. The issue had been very finely balanced, and the removal of Sir Richard would have been a massive step towards a *de facto* political system in which Gaelic, Old English, and the saner New English administrators could have sketched a consensus on at least the outer limits to a sustainable polity.

A form of English identity was undoubtedly being created by the experience of the reign of Elizabeth, building on the achievements of the English Reformation, but it was extremely narrow and metropolitan. It is true that the Crown in England had to cooperate with provincial elites. Perhaps ten powerful families really ran Lancashire, and a dozen Cheshire, for example. Yet there was enough coherence in the Anglican aristocracy and gentry, and they had enough local power, to ensure Crown control and the indispensable parliamentary supplements to Crown revenues for the waging of war. Elizabeth has been lauded by a writer in the 'Gloriana'-worshipping tradition of historians like Sir John Neale, on the grounds that 'She had brought unity and strength to a divided England.'[10] This is a singularly optimistic view of where her regime was by the 1590s. It was an exclusive, not an inclusive regime. In Ireland it had fractured English identity, not to the point of destruction in the case of the Old English, but beyond easy repair. The 'imperial' kingship Elizabeth inherited from Henry VIII was based on the precedent of the Roman Emperor Constantine, which meant that the monarch was head of the church. Elizabeth used a slightly different title from her father to express this, but more because of her sex than because of a difference in interpretation. The seventeenth century was to show that Scots Protestants had fundamental problems with this concept.[11] Instead of negotiating within a political framework with subjects who had different political priorities, the late-Elizabethan regime preferred to draw enough strength from the acquiescent parts of the queen's dominions to reject compromise, whilst exploiting bogies such as the Puritans to keep the acquiescent cooperative for fear of worse. Hence the lethal problem of the marginal courtier groups who were or lay behind the New English in Ireland. They could not be contained within a framework of functioning political compromise, and they could always exploit the *damnosa hereditas* of the 1541 declaration which committed the Crown to ruling every nook and cranny of the island. Many, though of course not all, of the colonial wars in sixteenth-century Ireland were not a sign of the strength of the English state but rather evidence of its weakness, political failure, and inability to control anarchical elements amongst its subjects. This was pre-eminently the case with the last and greatest of these wars.

The 1590s were not a time when Queen Elizabeth needed any more wars. She had been giving the Dutch military assistance since she signed the Treaty of Nonsuch with them in August 1585. That had brought upon her head the 1588 Armada. No sooner was that crisis passed than another visceral one raised its head in France, where Philip II of Spain had since the secret Treaty of Joinville of 1584 been the paymaster and manipulator of the formidable Catholic League. In 1588–89 King Henry III of France united with his Huguenot heir Henry of Navarre to fight the Catholic League, which had developed into a major threat to French kingship. Just when the two Henrys had virtually smashed the league, the assassination of Henry III made a Huguenot the rightful king of France. Philip II had to intervene directly to support a revitalised league. His army of Flanders saved Paris from Henry IV in 1590 and Rouen in 1592. He mounted a drive to make his daughter, the Infanta Clara Eugenia – whom he had in 1588 suggested for the English throne – queen of France. Elizabeth had no choice but to send troops and money to assist Henry IV. The failure of Drake and Norris in the 'counter-Armada' of 1589 to destroy the remnants of Spanish naval power meant that a protracted sea war raged from the Baltic to the Caribbean. In 1586, Dr Bartholomew Clark wrote that 'Never any King of this land was able to continue wars beyond seas above one year'. By 1593 the cost of even Elizabeth's strictly limited over-seas commitments was causing major internal tensions in England.[12] Her chances of avoiding a major war in Ulster hinged by then almost entirely on the calculations of the immensely able, English-educated Hugh O'Neill, Baron of Dungannon and from 1587 second Earl of Tyrone, a man she was foolish enough to dismiss as 'a creature of our own'. He was certainly originally built up by the Crown as a counter to Turlough Luineach. He was also court connected; his third wife was a daughter of old Marshal Nicholas Bagenal. Henry Bagenal, son and successor to Nicholas, violently disapproved of the match – with total justice, for Hugh's various wives (there was another to come) usually found the hot competition from his mistresses too much and Henry's sister Mabel eventually proved no exception. Disreputable, ambiguous, and devious Tyrone might be. Subservient he was not.

He had to play along with the Dublin administration as long as the political situation in Ulster remained fluid. His own rise was at the expense of Turlough Luineach. At stake in the first instance was the control of the Lordship of Tyrone. Its core was to become County Tyrone, but it also included the southern parts of the County Londonderry invented in the seventeenth century, and most of what was to be County Armagh. To the north-west the Sperrin Mountains and Slieve Gullion, to the south the River Blackwater, provided its natural boundaries. Though there were lucrative fishings on the Foyle and the Bann, the bulk of the revenue of a lordship which was as unurbanised as its Scottish equivalents (and it much more resembled a unit like the Regality of Argyll than anything surviving elsewhere in Ireland) came from the land. By 1585 Hugh was clearly winning a perfectly normal succession struggle, since he controlled two-thirds of the Lordship – partly due to support from the equivalent regional prince to his west, Hugh O'Donnell, at one point his father-in-law. However, Turlough was only finally pensioned off in the 1590s, and at one stage there were still other factions in play. The O'Donnell was more important to Hugh O'Neill than the Crown, though Hugh did want the Crown recognition that went with the title of earl of Tyrone. That largely accounts for his phase of cooperation, including military cooperation with the Crown, and his presence in the Irish House of Lords in the 1585–86 parliament. Brought up in the household of the Earl of Leicester, Hugh had court patrons. Nevertheless, he and everyone else in Ulster knew that it was the Gaelic structures of the Lordship which generated real power, and that was the political and social order which he was determined, if possible, to sustain.[13]

The relatively sophisticated forms of surrender and regrant which had been developed in Connaught under Perrot were creeping towards or even into south Ulster. Though they empowered the sept leaders by turning them into landed proprietors, and in the more sensible compositions such as that with the O'Reillys of east Breifne, later County Cavan, compensated the traditional leader for the abolition of the local warlordship – in this case the O'Reillyship, with a larger share of the landed cake – they all had distinctly rough edges. Just how they were finally implemented was something over which the locals tended to have minimal control. More generally, one can argue that whereas in England peers were exchanging local power for court influence, in Ireland even as powerful a man as the Earl of Ormonde, on whom the Crown was to lean heavily in its crisis years in the 1590s, was never rewarded with high office in a Dublin administration dominated by mediocrities and nobodys on the make. There was always resistance to new arrangements and Dublin developed the habit of kidnapping and detaining potential leaders of conservative recalcitrants. The composition of Connaught automatically destroyed long-standing claims to overlordship over its northern parts from the O'Donnell. Sir John O'Reilly, who had surrendered the O'Reillyship for secure tenure, had also abandoned the military system which might have helped him keep at bay his old-style swordsman rival Pilib O'Reilly. Perrot seized the latter, holding him in prison in Dublin for seven years. Similarly, young Hugh Roe O'Donnell, a potential rallying point for conservative opponents of surrender and regrant policies in Tyrconnell – and all the more dangerous because his formidable and ruthless mother, the Ulster Scot Ineen Dubh MacDonnell, had easy access to flows of Scottish mercenaries – was kidnapped from a wine ship in Loch Swilly in 1587. By the time he escaped from Dublin Castle at Christmas 1591, he was a bitter man.

Though the Monaghan composition seems to have been welcomed by many sept leaders as an escape from the tyranny of the MacMahon, it too was accompanied by violence; by the imposition of a system of primogeniture which did not sit easily with the elite's customs, let alone their mating habits; and by grants, especially on former church lands, to incomers such as New English army officers and the odd Newry merchant. The Earl of Tyrone would have been a fool indeed had he not seen that a fundamental threat to his regional power was now inching forward on the outer frontiers of Gaelic Ulster. He was far from being a fool. He had actively cooperated with the Crown. Finding Fitzwilliam corrupt as well as tired and disillusioned, he had successfully bribed him. That was a form of political control and participation through the back door, or pocket, but it did not work over major policy issues. The time was approaching when force would have to be added to the game, but this third phase of Tyrone's twisted relationship with Elizabeth was dangerous, and in the early stages Tyrone was still wise enough to see this and to fight first through surrogates. There was no difficulty in finding them.

Hugh Roe O'Donnell had celebrated his return to his native Tyrconnell by driving out the newly appointed sheriff, Captain Humphrey Willis, and confirming his seizure of power on the old Gaelic basis by having himself inaugurated as the O'Donnell. By the spring of 1593 he was communicating through the Catholic archbishop of Tuam with exiled Irish lords in Spain, arguing for the formation of a Catholic confederacy backed by Philip II and the papacy to fight the English Crown. Hugh Roe was one of the sons-in-law of Tyrone. Another was Hugh Maguire, whose own Lordship had recently been shired by the Crown as County Fermanagh. The threat to his ascendancy was embodied in the local activities of the same Humphrey Willis whom Hugh Roe had expelled and also George Bingham, a brother of the much loathed Sir Richard Bingham. What had happened in Monaghan, and perhaps more particularly the fact that there had been a good deal of support for it among local heads of septs, left Hugh Maguire in little doubt that the dismantling of his power would be the next item on the political agenda. In the spring of 1593 he crossed the Erne into Sligo and Roscommon on a series of raids which enabled him to accumulate resources in the shape of cattle, but brought him into battle with Sir Richard Bingham. In the course of the campaign, the Catholic archbishop of Armagh, another strong spokesman for a Catholic confederacy, was killed while accompanying Maguire. The Ulster Catholic hierarchy were traditional supporters of the Gaelic social order as well as naturally hostile to a heretical sovereign. Tyrone was much less a prisoner of any given religious or social order. The only unambiguous commitment in his life was the one to Hugh O'Neill, second Earl of Tyrone. He might have accepted a measure of Anglicisation in Ulster, had he been sure it could be manipulated to enhance his power but, as he himself said, his contacts at court – like the Earl of Leicester, Sir Christopher Hatton, and Sir Francis Walsingham – were dead. Unenthusiastically, he helped his brother-in-law Marshal Sir Henry Bagenal to defeat Maguire's invasion of Monaghan at a ford on the Erne near Belleek. Maguire's men had been badly positioned and were exposed to musket fire from three sides to a point where they had lost heart before the loyalist forces, English infantry in the centre, Tyrone's horse on the flanks, swept across the ford. Routed and pursued by cavalry, the defeated force suffered as heavily as might be expected. Tyrone was resentful at the lack of appreciation shown for his services by Bagenal. Wounded in the thigh, he retired to Dungannon, never to serve Elizabeth again. Hugh Maguire's castle of Enniskillen fell in February 1594 to a combined force of English troops and Maguires led by Hugh's rival Connor Roe Maguire, known as 'the Queen's Maguire'. It was no mean feat, for the besiegers did not have heavy enough guns available to breach the walls of the water-girt castle. Eventually, they seized the gate tower by *coup de main*, forcing the garrison of fewer than 40 soldiers to surrender. It was to prove one victory too many, for it meant a Crown garrison had to be left exposed there in a hostile countryside.

Given the small numbers usually involved in Irish warfare, an exposed garrison was more than usually dangerous. Garrisons were small. Even a major seat of regional power like Dunluce Castle would normally be held by not more than fifty men. Larger numbers would be impossibly expensive on a long-term basis. Enniskillen Castle could therefore be relatively easily masked against a sally by its garrison of 40 towards the end of the period when supply shortages might force surrender. A government relieving army, trying to avert the loss of face involved in the surrender, was therefore likely to face the bulk of any local insurgent force if the latter chose to fight, which it might do if it could choose its ground against opponents whose approach was by definition highly predictable. Tyrone had for some time been secretly or not so secretly backing his two insurgent sons-in-law. By June 1594 Hugh Roe O'Donnell and Hugh Maguire were jointly besieging Enniskillen Castle. As befitted the son of a Scottish mother, Hugh Roe had imported thousands of Scots mercenaries before the start of the campaign. Though he controlled far less fertile land than the O'Neill, the O'Donnell did control some, and he had considerable revenue from his offshore fisheries – to the point of being known to foreign merchants as 'the king of fish'. He could afford traditional warfare.

Fitzwilliam's period in office closed with a major catastrophe when the relief column of about 650 men, less than 50 of them horse, which he sent with a substantial supply train was ambushed by O'Donnell and Tyrone's brother Cormac MacBaron at a ford a few miles south of Enniskillen. A high proportion of the 1000 ambushers were Scottish, but Cormac O'Neill had brought a force of musketeers as well as some horse. Fitzwilliam's column suffered casualties to the tune of about a quarter of its numbers and losses of equipment and food so heavy that the action was known as the Battle of the Ford of the Biscuits. Tyrone had submitted to the Crown a long list of complaints which historians have tended to find a bizarre mixture of the grave and the petty; but in fact they constitute a clear argument that with the death of his court patrons, the loss of the favour of the hitherto supportive Fitzwilliam, and the presence of such hostile predators as Sir Richard Bingham and Sir Henry Bagenal, there was little point in his playing a government game set up to ensure that he could only lose. The point was so obvious that even Elizabeth was prepared to offer concessions.

Hitherto Tyrone had acted through surrogates like the O'Donnells, the Maguires, or close henchmen of his own Lordship such as the O'Hagans and his brother Cormac, whose actions he could repudiate. Just as Elizabeth moved to promise the replacement of Fitzwilliam (in any case weary and anxious to go) and a ban on Bingham acting against Tyrone – as part of an indefinite truce – the defeat of the relief column before Enniskillen revealed the hollowness of the Crown's military position in Ireland. The brute force which underpinned the New English policy of aggressive land-hunting was more bluff than reality. Apart from garrisons pinned down in Connaught and Munster, the new lord deputy, Sir William Russell, son of the Earl of Bedford, could dispose of a field army of no more than 1100 men. That force was hopelessly outnumbered by the standing army of Tyrone's Lordship. When Tyrone boldly went to meet Russell in Dublin, what he offered was eminently logical. There had to be an end to the idea of shiring Tyrone and Armagh. He had to be given in effect a commission to rule Ulster under the Crown but autonomously, and in exchange he would reverse preparations for large-scale war such as the importation of Scottish mercenaries. Since raids from the Wicklow hills were ravaging the suburbs of Dublin, it must have seemed to Tyrone that Elizabeth and her representatives had to see that they would do well to save face, protect the lands of the old Lordship of Ireland, stabilise the Munster plantation, and try to work out a less provocative regime in order to stabilise Connaught; rather than adding to their list of problems an expensive and probably unwinnable Ulster war. Like other northern chiefs before him, he under-estimated the obstinate stupidity of which the queen was capable. After he returned from his parley in Dublin, she raged at her administrators for not kidnapping him when they had the chance. In her preferred game, he could indeed only lose.

Tyrone still avoided open rebellion to the point of allowing Russell to relieve and provision Enniskillen Castle. However, the military force at Tyrone's disposal was by now so impressive that it spelled out a determination to recover control of developments in the north of Ireland by threat or use of force. Food production in Tyrone's Lordship had been built up deliberately. Cattle could not only feed the troops of the army of Ulster but also, like the more cereal-oriented demesne farming which Tyrone had developed vigorously, yield cash income from sales of surpluses when markets could be found in Ireland or Scotland. Tyrone's total income from his Lordship was probably of the order of £80,000 a year. His professional army had a core, licensed by Elizabeth, of a regiment of 600 trained by 6 English officers. It was used as a basic training camp, its soldiers being automatically replaced by recruits when they had completed their induction. Mass hostings of freemen in Ulster were becoming as obsolete as they had in the Pale. Tyrone hired professionals, many of them Scots, but more Ulstermen, known as bonaghts – they were hired in the spring by the thousand, on agreed terms which always included their keep. By 1601 they were also receiving threepence a day and a bonus of four shillings twice a year. They were grouped in what even on the Crown side tended to be the largest normal administrative unit: companies of 100 men under a captain. In 1594 Tyrone hired 2000 bonaghts. As the war intensified, that figure doubled and then grew again. With real administrative talent and foresight, Tyrone had established magazines deep in inaccessible sites beyond the military frontier on the Blackwater. Stocking them was less difficult than might be imagined, since Ulster was deeply enmeshed not only with the Scots Gaidhealtachd but also with the western trading burghs of the Scottish Lowlands. They in turn were intimately linked with the great emporium of the Netherlands where goods from the Baltic were as easily bought as goods from the Mediterranean. Powder, shot, firearms, body armour, edged weapons, and indeed every warlike necessity below the level of heavy artillery flowed in to Tyrone across waters so narrow that they were a virtual highway, but were also so complex that English naval squadrons had little hope of establishing a tight blockade – least of all in the face of shallow-draught west Highland galleys which need only run for a few hours with favourable wind and current, and which could use any beach as a debarkation point.

In 1595, against Russell's field force of 1100, Tyrone could set 1000 pikemen (replacing the traditional gallowglass) and 4000 musketeers (replacing the outmoded kerne with their bows and javelins), as well as a thousand cavalry whose spirit was to impress English observers. The handguns were operated by the matchlock mechanism, and were a mixed collection described by contemporaries as arquebuses, calivers, and muskets. The first two terms were interchangeable, since the English word came from the French phrase *arquebuse du calibre de Monsieur le Prince*. Basically, they all fired a roughly $\frac{1}{2}$-ounce lead ball, with limited accuracy beyond about 50 yards and very little beyond 75 yards, in terms of ability to hit individual targets. They also lost a lot of their penetrating power by the 100-yard mark. Muskets, always fired from forked rests, were much heavier pieces in the sixteenth century, firing a heavy 2-ounce lead ball with lethal force at much longer ranges and the ability to smash through body armour at 100 yards. A good archer was more accurate at longer ranges with a much higher rate of fire. Some of the victories of the Antrim MacDonnells had been achieved by hanging on to the flanks and rear of Perrot's punitive columns and inflicting unendurable losses over time with harassing arrow fire, but members of Clan MacDonald had access to those west Highland archers who were still being recruited by Charles I well into the seventeenth century. Elsewhere, good archers were increasingly difficult to find and needed many years of training. Firearms were weapons which a man could be taught to use comparatively quickly, despite the unavoidably complicated process of loading and firing. None of this meant that shock tactics were dead. Ammunition did not last for ever and rates of fire were not great, so a final rush with cold steel was common towards the close of actions. When one side sensed that the other was losing heart, this was the normal way to move in for the kill. Bullets were lethal, but from 80 yards out from a firing line good armour did protect men against their increasingly spent force, especially if they were from an arquebus or caliver, which were the most transportable of firearms. Only at very close range when in close ranks could infantry sweep a killing zone with massed fire. Broken and in flight, musketeers (to use the generic term) were easy meat for the blade weapons of pursuing cavalry and could be virtually massacred under the right conditions.[14]

Set-piece battle was often fast moving, always risky and unpredictable. Tyrone was not one of the few contemporary commanders with a flair for that sort of thing. He only fought two set battles, Carricklea in 1588 and Kinsale in 1601, and lost both. He was normally far too sensible to risk his expensive forces, which he himself said could cost upwards of £500 a day, at so unpredictable a game. Up to 1596 he was not so much rolling the dice of war as trying to get through to a hostile queen the simple message that she could not win against him and ought to compromise. His dynastic alliances in Ulster meant that the Crown could not follow a divide-and-rule policy there. Nor did he lose much by them in real terms, for O'Donnell was a junior partner whose role was exaggerated by annalists writing within his Lordship. Even in Fermanagh, where the O'Donnell had had traditional aspirations to overlordship over the Maguires, it was Tyrone who called the shots. O'Donnell had to be content with re-establishing his traditional ascendancy over the O'Dohertys of Innishowen, and his ambitions were very much channelled into other claims he held over areas of north Connaught. Initially, even these did not cut across Tyrone's basic strategy of seizing the fortified positions which closed the southern approaches to Ulster. Cormac MacBaron O'Neill captured the Crown fort on the Blackwater which protected a major potential invasion route into the Lordship of Tyrone in February 1595. Enniskillen Castle fell to the Maguires in May. Tyrone besieged Monaghan Castle. Marshal Bagenal managed to reprovision it in June but on the return journey was exposed to a running ambush at Clontibert. Decimated by musketry fire from the flanks and harassed by well-handled cavalry, he suffered a major defeat. In the same month in Sligo, Captain George Bingham was murdered by a servant who promptly handed the place, the one strong position in north Connaught, to Hugh Roe O'Donnell. Tyrone might formally be declared a traitor at the end of the month, but as Bagenal's battered army sought refuge in Newry the southern gates to Ulster were effectively closed.

With the reconversion of Henry of Navarre to Catholicism and the subsequent collapse of the Spanish and Catholic League threat in France, it had become possible for Elizabeth to withdraw her troops from France and to try to run down her commitments in the Netherlands. She still had a major war with Spain on her hands, but it was possible for her to move troops into Ireland from the continent as well as commanders like the three soldier brothers Sir John, Sir Henry, and Sir Thomas Norris. Sir John was a former president of Munster. He did not work well with Lord Deputy Russell, though they did combine in the summer of 1595 to secure Armagh against Tyrone and to confirm the Crown grip on the fort on the south side of the Blackwater which dominated the ford essential for any deep penetration of Tyrone's territory. News that heavy cannon had been shipped to Newry to support the expedition moved Tyrone, very shrewdly, to abandon ideas about fortifying himself in depth at Dungannon; instead of that, he slighted his existing defences there. September saw Sir John, with a commission as general of Her Majesty's forces in Ulster which gave him political as well as military prerogatives, easily revictual Armagh. He had been further reinforced from England and by many Irish recruits. Subsequent skirmishing with Tyrone's forces between Armagh and Newry led him to the same conclusion which other sensible Crown commanders had reached and were to reach again: that this was both a tough and an inherently unprofitable war, since Tyrone had virtually been driven into rebellion by politically inept royal policies. Norris was for negotiation. Off and on, a truce of sorts which held from late 1595 into 1598 was arranged.

Of course, sixteenth-century concepts of war and peace were a great deal less precise than modern ones. Scrapping for position, up to a point, was not true belligerence, and in any case the folly of the man who thought that one could not negotiate with Tyrone was equalled by that of the man who thought it was possible to negotiate with him without having and being prepared to use appropriate force – and exceeded by anyone who did not carefully monitor Tyrone's observance of any bargain struck. In practice, fighting which occurred during the lengthy stand-off or truce tended to have stabilising consequences rather than destabilising ones. The O'Donnell's ambitions in Connaught were far more uncontrollable than the hitherto mainly Ulster objectives of his great ally. O'Donnell raids had swept over Connaught on a scale which finally undermined the military confidence of Sir Richard Bingham, who admitted he could not hope to retake Sligo. It still proved difficult to lever him out of office, but when he left for England in high dudgeon without permission, a better man in the shape of Sir Conyers Clifford replaced him as governor. With heavily local forces, he did turn back the tide, recapturing Sligo with the aid of a man who was arguably its rightful proprietor, Donogh O'Connor Sligo. From abolishing the MacWilliamship, the Crown had moved to the infinitely more sensible policy of trying to sell its own MacWilliam to those particular Burkes. During the brief lord deputyship of Lord Thomas Burgh between May and October 1597 there was an attempt to use Sligo as a springboard to seizing Ballyshannon, one of the strategic keys to Tyrconnell. This was to be coordinated with a march by Burgh over the Blackwater and then deep into the territory of Tyrone and the Maguires. Burgh's own council in Dublin could not see how it could be done, as Tyrone's army was much bigger than Burgh's. The lord deputy did manage to revictual the fort on the Blackwater, but that was all. He retreated, and died. Clifford, whose own penetration close to Ballyshannon became a near-fatal strategic trap as superior forces converged on him, was lucky to extract the bulk of his force to Connaught, where the possession of Sligo meant that a tide of raiders could not easily swarm after him. On the other side of Ulster an extraordinary, unprovoked attack by the garrison of Carrickfergus on a not unfriendly force commanded by James MacSorley MacDonnell was decisively thrashed. A viable *de facto* balance along defensible frontiers was emerging.

It was always fragile, but that was the nature of the beast. On the English side, there were those like the mighty Old English magnate the Earl of Ormonde who was acutely conscious of the dangers of overstretch under a stingy queen, knowing her well from his spells at court – the 'common patria' of the Englishry. Ormonde was to become lieutenant general of Her Majesty's forces during the hiatus which followed the death of Burgh. He was convinced that the Blackwater fort was a fort too far. Tyrone could not make peace with that gateway for invasion hanging over his head. The fort could not supply itself in a hostile environment, so an army had to be sent into danger every time to revictual it. Better to scrap the fort voluntarily and strengthen nearby Armagh, which like Newry and Carrickfergus had to be held if the Crown was to retain any credibility. Yet Ormonde was far from soft. When the truce lapsed in June 1597, Tyrone tested the waters as often before by blockading Cavan Castle himself, sending troops to blockade the Blackwater fort, and lastly sending a force into Leinster to stir up trouble. That was Ormonde's province. He pounced on Tyrone's men, defeating them bloodily, which was probably the only way he could have retained the deep respect which Tyrone felt for him. Obviously, the Old English had a vested interest in keeping the scale of conflict in Ireland down to a minimal level, since the Crown with its incessant cessing had effectively worked out ways of taxing them without their consent to help pay for warfare from whose higher management they had been systematically excluded. Their magnates were denied access to the ear of the monarch in matters of high policy in a way which violated the fundamental feudal principle that the Crown had an obligation, not an option, to seek counsel of them, its cousins and natural counsellors. Nevertheless, the Old English remained deeply entrenched in certain parts of the Dublin administration, notably the higher legal posts, where Eustaces, Dillons, Nugents, and Plunketts abounded. This was equally true at provincial level where in Munster in 1581 the provost-marshal noted that the chief justice, the second justice, the queen's attorney and solicitor, and the sheriffs, were all Irish-born.[15] There was therefore a powerful lobby for a pragmatic and limited approach to a difficult situation. Nor was it confined to the Old English. Sir John Norris, most experienced of New English soldiers, who with his brothers died in Ireland, was emphatically of the same school of thought as Ormonde when he contemplated the Ulster situation: containment and compromise were the objectives, not expensive conquest – least of all under a queen most unlikely to provide adequate means.

There were, of course, other voices. The one that has attracted the most relentless attention since was in fact not heard at all at the time, for his tract was rightly deemed outrageous propaganda for one extremist faction in the government camp and was suppressed. Because Edmund Spenser wrote *The Faerie Queen* – a poem read in virtually every department of English literature, if seldom anywhere else – he has become a screen on which some historians have chosen to project fantasies and violent prejudices of their own with little basis in the historical situation. Literary scholars have been better at accepting the discipline of what Spenser actually wrote, though of course they can accept his prose or poetry as valuable in its own right when a historian must ask what ulterior purpose he was seeking to serve, and whether he succeeded. Spenser was a minor bureaucrat in Ireland, described in 1598 as 'not unskilfull or without experience in the service of the wars'.[16] He had by the time he was supposed to have written his *A View of the Present State of Ireland* in 1596 some sixteen years of service in Ireland behind him, during which he had lived off fees and grants – none of them very generous and culminating in a not very desirable small Munster estate carved out of Desmond land which had escheated to the Crown after the rebellion and death of the Earl of Desmond.

Some historians have a vision of 'Erasmian humanism' which is an embodiment of all that is sweetness and light, and use it as a foil for equally notional constructs like 'Calvinism', as if Erasmus and Calvin, humanists both, do not demonstrate that humanism as a general term has substance only at the level of style rather than content. There are generalisations about humanists which, though far from universal in application, can cover very many of them, including both Erasmus and Spenser. Many, probably most of them, were grasping and importunate opportunists and their principal weapon of self-advancement was the manipulation of power- and wealth-wielders through sycophantic flattery. Spenser had done his best to butter up Elizabeth in his *Faerie Queen*, of which he published a second edition during a visit to England in the course of which modern scholars have fancied him to have written his *View* of Ireland. There is, in fact, no contemporary evidence whatever to link Spenser with the *View*. Revisionist scholarship, obsessed with its own politics and the projection of those politics into the past, found the work quotable and the temptation to vilify Spenser as an archetypal and brutal 'colonialist' irresistible. The argument that the Elizabethan government suppressed the work because 'Spenser' made its own nefarious plans too obvious flatters a government which lacked the ability to silence a subversive publication effectively. The 'Martin Marprelate' scandal in which a pamphlet offensive struck at the Elizabethan episcopate underlined the inability of Elizabethan government to control the presses. Spenser's *Faerie Queen* was banned – but in Scotland, by James VI, who objected to its allegorical attack on his mother in Book V. Elizabeth ignored his demand that the poem be banned in England.[17]

There is no contemporary preface or dedication extant for the *View*. The plethora of variant manuscript versions suggests at best a first draft in 1598, and opens the possibility of later additions. Before James Ware's 1633 edition, which attributed it to Spenser, nobody had suggested he was the author and Ware's motive was probably to add weight to a tendentious point of view which was trying to dominate the discussion of Irish politics shortly after Charles I's great minister Thomas Wentworth, Earl of Strafford, was appointed lord deputy of Ireland. Certainly the manuscripts collected as *A Brief Note of Ireland* and published by Alexander Grossart in his edition of Spenser's works with the suggestion they were 'Spenser's own State Papers' – whatever such might be – should never have been attributed to the poet. Spenser's life in Ireland is difficult to reconstruct, but he appears to have been prepared to rent land to a native Gaelic tenant and the rabidly anti-Gaelic tone of much of this material is probably not at all compatible with Spenser's own views. The whole body of misattributed and probably partially misdated material contains statements which are contrary to views embedded in Spenser's *Faerie Queen*. There is a case for going beyond the already damning objections to making Spenser the subject of endless modern denunciations of a conveniently over-simple kind on the basis of material to which he cannot be positively linked, to saying that there is evidence he could not have been the author of this material.[18]

This work calls for a massive escalation of violence in Ireland with a view to forfeiting vast amounts of land which might then be given, at no capital cost of course, to immigrant adventurers. Much of the justificatory rhetoric takes the form of an attempt to cast Gaelic Ireland into the 'savage' category of the 'civil versus savage' trope which was one of the vast collection of tired platitudes in humanist discourse, though in an Ireland where all cultures overlapped and interpenetrated it was more than usually dishonest. Historians have tended to recite the fact that the author of the *View* compared the Gaelic Irish to ancient Scythians without mentioning that almost invariably what he compares their manners to is 'Scythian, or Scottish manners',[19] for he was heavily dependent on the writings of that eminent Gaelic-speaking scholar George Buchanan, tutor to James VI and a neo-Latin poet of European stature and inherent literary merit fully equal to Spenser. However, the Gaels were a stalking horse for the Old English, whom the author of the *View* hated with deep passion, denouncing them as 'degenerate'. There is little doubt that it is the voice of the author we hear through the character of Eudoxus in the text of the *View*, who tells us that 'all the lands I will give unto Englishmen whom I will have drawn thither'. Forfeiture and escheat to the Crown with regrant to the New English is the obsessive and not very subliminal message of the *View*. For Tyrone it proposed total forfeiture of all his lands, with the usual projector's glib promise that this was the way forward and that it would in the not-too-long run be self-funding, even allowing for a permanent Ulster garrison of 1500 soldiers.[20] The work was that of a mischievous and irresponsible would-be predator. The first version was registered by the Master Stationers in 1598 but never appeared. Thereafter it rusted unpublished for thirty-five years. Modern critics have made of this negative a positive by searching it for thought patterns such as the linkage between contact with the American Indian and attitudes to the Irish. Such comparisons do occur in contemporary literature, but are only impressive when assiduously hunted down and reassembled in concentrated and therefore misleading form. In reality they were scarce.[21] It might be more to the point to look at the obvious contemporary resemblances between the rhetoric of the author of the *View*, a marginal nobody, and Sir Walter Raleigh, who in 1596 did publish a book and who by then in court terms was a marginal somebody.

Raleigh was a friend of Spenser and had been hyped in *The Faerie Queen*. The first illustration of a tobacco plant was published in London in 1570, though the accompanying illustration of a smoker showed that sailors had misinterpreted the Amerindian cigar as a funnel. Spenser praised Raleigh for helping to introduce 'divine tobacco or panacaea' to England both as a real smoke and, as the second name suggests, a medicinal herb.[22] By 1596 Raleigh was still out of favour at court, as he had been since his impregnation of and clandestine marriage to one of Elizabeth's maids of honour, Bess Throckmorton, in late 1591 or early 1592. Trying to redeem himself by venturing, he sailed to Guiana in 1595 and published his *Discoverie of the Large, Rich, and Bewtiful Empyre of Guiana* in 1596. Though like Spenser a

Munster landlord, Raleigh was by 1596 an absentee – whose mind was preoccupied with the central issue haunting those responsible for conducting the war against Spain, which was how it could possibly be brought to a satisfactory conclusion. Philip II had launched a second armada late in 1596, driving it out at a season far too prone to storms for his decision to be defensible. That armada, launched from Ferrol in north-west Spain, had indeed been destroyed by a storm in December with a loss of 30 to 40 ships and 3000 men before it could even approach its proposed objective, which was England. Nevertheless, it was clear that he could try again, and the problem was how to weaken King Philip to the point where he ceased to be a threat. Raleigh's associate the second Earl of Essex, the rising hawk who had been made a privy councillor in 1593, was to propound a scheme for a close blockade of the Spanish and Portuguese coasts to cut both the flow of bullion from the Indies and the equally vital flow of Baltic naval stores without which the navies of Spain could not fight. It depended on taking and holding a major Spanish port and was probably impractical, but compared with Raleigh's proposal in his account of Guiana it was the very embodiment of sobriety.[23]

The Discoverie of Guiana starts with the mandatory dedication to the powerful, in this case Lord Admiral Howard of Effingham and Sir Robert Cecil, Burghley's younger son and eventual successor, already an influential privy councillor. Its substance, however, is a complaint about Raleigh's fall from a position of influence at court, and a promise to provide 'a better Indies for her majestie then the King of Spaine hath any'.[24] This wild promise comes wrapped in deceptively sensible remarks about the difficulty of seriously harming the King of Spain's empire in the Americas when its wealth and strength lie deep inland, making the sacking of any of its few port cities an unimportant and eminently repairable problem for the Spaniards. Raleigh's Guiana was not the coast of the modern Guianas or even their interior. It was the wish fulfilment of the dreams of elderly *conquistadores* like Antonio de Berrio, whom Raleigh captured in a raid on Trinidad in 1595. One of Raleigh's captains had already probably captured in 1594 promotional literature cast in the form of a report by Domingo de Vera, who had travelled up the Orinoco to explore its biggest southern tributary, the Caroni, to enter what he swore was the outer edge of a vastly populous Inca-type empire fabulously rich in gold. Raleigh drew heavily on these Spanish sources and continued to send captains to explore the access routes to El Dorado, the mythical empire named for its ruler, who was allegedly gilded ceremonially with gold dust.[25]

He did not succeed in selling the idea that the conquest of this empire was the way to enable Elizabeth to match Philip II in the fiscal sinews of war, but he in fact hit his own kind of gold by winning his way back into her favour by other means after 1597. El Dorado only became a priority for him again much later when he desperately needed a miracle to help him in the near impossible task of winning the favour of her successor. What, however, is significant is the language he used at the very end of the *Discoverie*, where he said that 'Guiana is a Countrey that hath yet her Maydenhead, never sackt, turned nor wrought.'[26] In itself, the phrase merely tells us about the mind of one unusual man. There are few worse guides to a historical era than the odd phrase torn at random from literature, especially from the literary canon, but the whole point about this phrase is that it conforms entirely with the mentality of a whole class of marginal hangers-on of the court, as shown by deeds rather than words, though it is interesting that the words of the few of them to leave literary remains can be shown to be designed to justify a particular kind of behaviour. They were political rapists hoping to leap from nothing to something by a sudden act of possessive violence. To do that they needed instability and violence to exploit. They were recognised as a menace by the more sober servants of the crown of England, but there was no end to their antics. Though they were kept well away from the power-structures of the south-east heartland of the regime, it was always possible for them to hope to snatch an opening with so centralised and remote a government either by manipulating its always dim comprehension of the periphery of the state, which was anywhere outside the south-east, or by simply creating a *fait accompli* using existing force.

Catastrophically, the marshal of Ireland, Sir Henry Bagenal, was almost designed by nature to maximise these problems. He had persistent aspirations to gain control of land in Ulster. He also had command of considerable Crown forces. That his attempt in August 1598 to reprovision the fort at Portmore on the Blackwater (yet again reduced to desperate straits) culminated in his death when he was shot through the head in action was not in itself any great loss. It removed a troublemaker and cleared the way for a marked improvement in the operational handling of the queen's troops. It was the scale of the military disaster he created and its totally destabilising impact on a delicate balance which was decisive.

Notes and references

1. Steven G. Ellis, *Tudor Ireland: Crown, community and the conflict of cultures 1470–1603* (Longman, London, 1985), pp. 288–91, and Colm Lennon, *Sixteenth-Century Ireland: The incomplete conquest* (Gill and Macmillan, Dublin, pbk edn, 1994), pp. 237–63.

2. Cyril Falls, *Elizabeth's Irish Wars* (Methuen, London, 1950), pp. 158–60.

3. J. Michael Hill, *Fire and Sword: Sorley Boy MacDonnell and the rise of Clan Ian Mor 1538–90* (Athlone Press, London, 1993), Chap. 10.

4. Robert Stenuit, *Treasures of the Armada* (David and Charles, Newton Abbot, 1972).

5. Hiram Morgan, 'The fall of Sir John Perrot', in John Guy (ed.), *The Reign of Elizabeth I: Court and culture in the last decade* (Cambridge University Press, Cambridge, 1995), pp. 109–25.

6. Garrett Mattingly, *The Defeat of the Spanish Armada* (Jonathan Cape, London, 1959).

7. Guy (ed.), *Reign of Elizabeth, passim.*

8. CSP Ireland, 1586–88, pp. 503–05, report by Francis Stafford to Sir Henry Wallop, 25 March 1588.

9. *Ibid.*, pp. 527–47, Tracts, apparently by Sir William Herbert; the extended quotation is on p. 530. There is a modern edition of one of his tracts in Latin: Sir William Herbert, *Croftus sive de Hibernia Liber*, eds. A. Keavanay and J.A. Madden (Irish Manuscripts Commission, 1992).

10. Joel Hurstfield, *Elizabeth I and the Unity of England* (English Universities Press, London, 1960), p. 180.

11. I am extremely grateful to my colleague John Guy for allowing me to read the text of his unpublished paper ' "Imperial" Monarchy and the State in the Sixteenth Century: England, Scotland, France' which he delivered at the conference 'Epochs of British History in a European Context. The sixteenth century' in Munich on 5–6 October 1995. I have also benefited in many conversations from access to his unparalleled knowledge of the labyrinth of the Tudor Crown's self-definitions.

12. R.B. Wernham, *After the Armada: Elizabethan England and the struggle for Western Europe 1588–1595* (Clarendon Press, Oxford, 1984), p. 514.

13. The most recent study both of the Lordship and of the coming of the war which destroyed it is Hiram Morgan, *Tyrone's Rebellion: The outbreak of the Nine Years' War in Tudor Ireland* (Royal Historical Society, Boydell Press, Woodbridge, 1993).

14. One of the best discussions of the capabilities of early-modern infantry firearms is in John Francis Guilmartin Jr, *Gunpowder and Galleys* (Cambridge University Press, Cambridge, 1974), pp. 146–49.

15. W.L. Renwick's 'Commentary' to his edition of Edmund Spenser, *A View of the Present State of Ireland* (Clarendon Press, Oxford, 1970), pp. 174–75.

16. *Ibid.*, p. 172.

17. Janet Claire, *'Art Made Tongue-Tied by Authority': Elizabethan and Jacobean dramatic censorship* (Manchester University Press, Manchester, 1990), pp. 99 and 108.

18. Jean R. Brink, 'Constructing the *View of the Present State of Ireland*', in *Spenser Studies. A Renaissance poetry annual*, eds. Patrick Cullen and Thomas P. Roche, 11 (1994), p. 203. I am deeply grateful to my old friend Dr Brink for taking the time, at a period when she was herself under terrible pressure, to talk to me about her important discoveries and conveying to me the substance of her work on 'Documenting Edmund Spenser: A new life record', in *American Notes and Queries*, and 'Appropriating the Author of *The Faerie Queen*. The attribution of the *View of the Present State of Ireland* to Edmund Spenser', in Peter Medine and Joseph Wittreich (eds.), *Soundings of Things Done: Essays on early modern literature in honor of S.K. Heninger Jr* (University of Delaware Press, forthcoming).

19. *Ibid.*, pp. 40 and 49.

20. *Ibid.*, pp. 124–29.

21. By far the handiest and best guide to the overblown industry which Spenser's *View* has become is Patricia Coughlan (ed.), *Spenser and Ireland: An interdisciplinary perspective* (Cork University Press, Cork, 1989).

22. Rachel Doggett (ed.), *New World of Wonders: European images of the Americas 1492–1700* (Folger Shakespeare Library, Washington, DC, 1992), p. 80.

23. L.W. Hutton, 'The Earl of Essex as Strategist and Military Organizer (1596–7)', *English Historical Review*, 68 (1953), pp. 363–93.

24. *The Discoverie of the Large, Rich, and Bewtiful Empyre of Guiana, with a relation of the great and Golden Citie of Manoa (which the Spanyards call El Dorado) and of the Provinces of Emeria, Arromia, Amapia, and other Countries, with their rivers, adjoyning. Performed in the yeare 1595 by Sir W. Ralegh Knight, Captain of her Maiesties Guard, Lo. Warden of the Stanneries, and her Highnesse Lieutenant generall of the Countie of Cornewall*, imprinted at London by Robert Robinson, 1596 (facsimile edn, Scolar Press, Menston, 1967), sig. Ir.

25. John Hemming, *The Search for El Dorado* (Michael Joseph, London, 1978), pp. 155–73.

26. Raleigh, *Discoverie*, edn cit., sig. N4v.

CHAPTER FIVE

The bankruptcy of Elizabethan imperialism and the fatal fracturing of the Englishry

August 1597 saw two fairly predictable moves on the part of Elizabeth's administration in Ireland. Because of the unstable Ulster situation and well-authenticated reports that Tyrone was actively negotiating for Spanish aid, the queen had made exceptional efforts to send troops and supplies. The troops proved to be of low quality, but there were over 2000 of them and the supplies for 2100 men for 112 days were much more adequate than usual. Ormonde moved back into the disturbed districts of Leinster. That was where his own strength lay, and though he was criticised in retrospect for the decision, it was at the time obvious and right. Far more dangerous was Marshal Bagenal's march to reprovision the Blackwater fort. He marched from Armagh with nearly 4000 foot and 320 horse, but with the absolute certainty that he would meet the full force of the army of Ulster commanded by Tyrone and O'Donnell at a place and time of their own choosing and probably on a battlefield prepared to receive Bagenal. It was a catch-22 situation with a vengeance, and the opinions of experienced soldiers like Sir Henry Brounker that the fort was a strategic trap, opinions shared by Ormonde, were vindicated in the most horrendous fashion. Bagenal moved towards the fort with his army in blocks of two regiments; of these blocks, one was the vanguard, one his centre, and one brought up the rear. They were too widely spaced, unavoidably drawn out in marching order as they moved to a point where the vanguard could be seen by the gallant garrison of the fort, and offered a maximum of flank to the inevitable enveloping tactics of their enemies – who certainly outnumbered them, though perhaps by no more than a thousand. As the vanguard crossed the ford on the Callan brook which gave the battle its name as the Battle of the Yellow Ford, it ran into yet another classic tactic. To block the advance of the enveloped force a trench barrier surmounted by a thorn hedge had been constructed.

Tyrone had repeatedly urged his subordinates only to fight under extremely favourable circumstances, by which he explained he meant in woods, bogs, or defiles. Wood and bog now gave his flanking musketeers the cover he needed and the narrow approach corridor virtually turned the battlefield into a defile. Withering musketry decimated the ranks of the relieving army. Its van suffered heavily in forcing the trench, only to be then broken by charges of horse and foot against its disordered ranks. Against the advice of his subordinates, Bagenal rushed to the front, where he fell dead with a bullet through his head. Sir Thomas Wingfield, the senior officer remaining, contrived with great difficulty to extract the army, but with such heavy loss, compounded by the explosion of a powder wagon, that he eventually had no more than 1500 shaken men back in relative safety in Armagh. Casualties, desertion, or just straight transfer to the enemy by significant numbers of his Irish troops – and indeed of one or two soldiers from England attracted by Tyrone's pay rates – accounted for the rest. It was the most predictable of defeats. There were several recent precedents, but the scale of this disaster altered totally the pattern of the war.

What had been becoming effectively a stand-off, with both sides holding enough of what was essential to them to make increasing the stakes to play for total victory a very dubious option, certainly in the minds of Elizabeth and Tyrone, suddenly became a game in which doubling and redoubling of stakes became compulsive. Tyrone had predictably been playing with fire by negotiating with Spain. In a sense, it was another option. His support tended to wax and wane, even within his own Lordship, and his relations with the nearest Scots clans, though very important to him, were unpredictable, mainly because of his own behaviour. His judicial execution or rather murder of a rival, Hugh Gavelach O'Neill, at the beginning of the 1590s had alienated opinion among the Macleans, to which clan the victim's mother belonged. More recently, his wife Mabel Bagenal had died after running away from him to her brother Sir Henry, and Tyrone celebrated the good news by dumping a MacDonald wife he had on long-term approval to wed formally Catherine Magennis, daughter of Magennis of Iveagh. This did not endear Tyrone to Clan Donald. Given his lively complex of loves and hates, it is understandable that Tyrone normally kept as many options open as possible. There were, however, two snags to the Spanish involvement. First, it was the last thing Elizabeth could afford to overlook. It could easily slide from being a formidable tease to a declaration of war to the death. Second, the rhetoric of manipulation for an appeal to Spain had to be religious. The way had been prepared by various Catholic prelates who had already, if ineffectually, tried to organise a religious crusade against the heretic Elizabeth. It probably did correspond with the instincts of Hugh Roe O'Donnell. Much more important from Tyrone's point of view was the fact that it was the most potent form of emotional blackmail that could be applied to a court which was trying very hard to corner the leadership of the militant Counter-Reformation, and could hardly afford to be seen to act contrary to that central image. In the spring of 1596 an emissary of Spain, Captain Alonso Cobos, was in contact with him. Physically this was no great problem, for there was no way the west coast of Ulster could be effectively blockaded. The theme the two great Ulster warlords stressed was that they were within an ace of an advantageous compromise peace with Elizabeth, but would reject it out of affection for Philip II and an ardent desire to extirpate the satanic forces of heresy utterly, provided of course Philip sent substantial assistance soon.

From Tyrone these were inherently unconvincing notes. He was not in the habit of doing anything much out of affection for anyone but himself, and a religious zealot – as distinct from an instinctive conservative – he was not. He stressed, as he had to to retain crucial local support, a demand for liberty of conscience, but compared with most contemporary European rulers Elizabeth was notably eirenic in spirit. Certainly no Swedish Lutheran king, let alone any prince of the Roman Catholic Counter-Reformation, would have echoed her sincere insistence that she did not want to open windows into men's souls. There was no problem about *de facto* toleration in Ulster. When Tyrone had repeated his demand for toleration to Ormonde in 1597, he had provoked the question, 'My Lord, what have you and I to meddle with matters of religion?' Tyrone then admitted that he had never been harassed over that issue.[1] The victory at the Yellow Ford, however, not only gave new resilience to the conservative opponents of Anglicising compositions on the margins of Ulster, but also made Tyrone the focus of hope for those who had suffered from Crown policy in other provinces. In the strategically crucial plantation area of the midlands of Leinster the O'Mores and O'Connors took key positions like Croghane and Stradbally. No government which could not prevent this could be regarded as effective even in the old Lordship lands. Worse by far from the point of view of the sheer scale of the disaster was the destruction of the settlements of the 4000 or so New English in Munster by a rising in October 1598 which was triggered by Tyrone's despatch of forces under Owen MacRory and Richard Tyrrel into Limerick.

Munster had been quiescent since the Desmond forfeiture, partly because it was weakened by famine in 1583, and partly because it was not until 1586 that it became clear that the bulk of the forfeited lands was being obtained by English newcomers. Continuing legal aggression in the explosive area of land titles kept resentment simmering until the rapid spread of the rising in 1598 confined Crown forces to walled towns and a few castles, often under siege. Tyrone, very much in his capacity as the O'Neill, made himself the champion of the dispossessed, and set up James FitzThomas, a nephew of the deposed earl, as Earl of Desmond. He was christened the *sugane* or straw-rope earl by his enemies, but he was no jest to a government whose grip on the province continued to deteriorate through 1599 and only began to recover with the arrival of Sir George Carew as the new provincial president in March 1600. It was predictable that as part of the general collapse Hugh Roe O'Donnell was able to invade north Connaught, set up his own MacWilliam Burke in Mayo and raid down into Clare where the Earl of Thomond, the loyalist product of the successful composition of Connaught, was challenged by a brother calling himself the O'Brien.

With Armagh lost, Elizabeth could hardly be said effectively to rule much more of Ireland than Henry VII had.[2] Nor did she deserve to, for on top of the political mismanagement which had conjured a general Gaelic confederacy into existence, her military position in Ireland was much weaker than it looked to a casual observer of the muster rolls of the royal armies. Apart from the fact that those muster rolls were often deeply misleading due to corruption, it is clear that the calibre of the reinforcements she was sending from England, apart from a handful of troops seasoned in France, was abysmal. Sir Ralph Lane said in 1596 that recent drafts from England had shown themselves 'stark cowards against the Irish'. In 1597 it was openly said that the unsoldierly carriage of drafts from England made them contemptible to Irish rebels. Elizabeth's armies in Ireland were full of virtually untrained Welsh and English members of the lower orders. The army of Tyrone had superior training facilities. Bagenal was fighting not just with inferior numbers at the Yellow Ford, but also with inferior troops.[3] There had always been an element of bluff behind the murderous and disruptive politics of the New English adventurers. The torching of Edmund Spenser's Munster seat and the over-running of his estate showed that the bluff had been called.

Whether the queen would have made the military effort needed to redress the situation if Tyrone had not relentlessly burned his political bridges behind him after his dizzying triumphs of 1597 and 1598 is an interesting question. There had always been an element of religious crusade in resistance to Elizabeth in Ireland after the pope had formally excommunicated her in 1570. When James Fitzmaurice had returned from the continent in 1579, complete with a bull of indulgence and a determination to start a holy war against the queen, he had called on his cousin the Earl of Desmond to stand and fight for 'the health of our country and the restoring of the Catholic faith again'. Tyrone had tried to play this card in the period before 1597 when his links with Gaelic dissidents in the Wicklow hills or Munster were still essentially designed to do little more than create diversions which would sap the already grossly inadequate forces which the lord deputy could deploy against him in Ulster. In July 1596, for example, he had issued a circular demanding that the lords of Munster ally with him for the sake of 'Christ's Catholic religion'. The appeal was no great success, but by 1599 the situation was totally different in that Crown forces were in such disarray that the defection of the Old English, especially in the key area of the Pale, would undoubtedly have brought the Elizabethan regime in Ireland down. On the other hand, Tyrone was by preference the O'Neill, a Gaelic prince whose culture was not that of the Old English, and they still were deeply involved with the administration of an Irish state structure from which they had derived their wealth and identity. Nor did most of them see any threat to their property from Elizabeth. Religion was therefore the lever with which Tyrone tried to force them into his camp. In November 1599 he issued a proclamation which in effect demanded that the Old English join him.

He threatened those who failed to come over with spoliation, but also with damnation for failure to embrace the cause of true religion in their native land. He had, of course, the enthusiastic support of some, though not all, of the Catholic clergy, both domestic and expatriate, for this thesis and tried very hard to persuade the pope to excommunicate Old English supporters of Elizabeth. The pope was advised, almost certainly correctly, that though this would place that community in a cruel dilemma, it would be counter-productive. Tyrone's own conduct as late as a triumphal march through the south of Ireland in 1600 was regal. He created noble honours, for example. Yet he knew well enough that any bid for a throne by him would merely alienate vital allies, besides leaving him with no carrot to offer the Habsburgs in exchange for military assistance. He was in fact playing with the idea of a transfer of sovereignty over Ireland by papal donative to perhaps the Archduke Albert, erstwhile viceroy of Portugal and future joint ruler of the Spanish Netherlands. What a Spanish Habsburg would have made of a kingdom where he would certainly not have been allowed to exercise meaningful authority over perhaps more than half of it remains a hypothetical question.[4] What is clear, as Sir Robert Cecil saw when he glossed a copy of Tyrone's demands for a virtually autonomous Ireland with a right to communicate with Spain and the papacy even during a war as 'Ewtopia', was that this was a recipe for swift political and military suicide for Elizabeth.

By 1598 the queen seems to have accepted that the plans for winning the war by breaking Spain's imperial communications and interdicting its bullion flows were impractical. Raleigh's ideas about creating a rival empire of plunder in South America were always a chimera. The plans which Essex had propounded for seizing and holding a major Spanish port as the base for a close blockade of the peninsula would almost certainly merely have given Spain an occasion for focusing its still formidable military tradition on an attainable target: the expulsion of a nest of heretics. In any case, the queen could see that an annual obligation to send an army to relieve such a base, very much a Blackwater fort writ large, would be cripplingly expensive and 'altogether absurd and inutile'. In 1597 Essex and Raleigh (restored to favour, partly by the pleas of Essex) had been sent with a substantial striking force to destroy a new Spanish armada, almost as big as the 1588 one, which was assembling at Ferrol. This they failed to do, and when they then moved west to the Azores to try to intercept the bullion *flota*, which they also failed to do, they opened the way for the last of the great armadas to sail to seize its objective, which was Falmouth. October storms saved England from invasion, but it was clear that the whole idea of a challenge to Spain's imperial power-base was simply impractical. For the rest of the war, and especially after the Peace of Vervins of 1598 between France and Spain left the Dutch and English alone belligerent against Habsburg power, very modest military expectations were the only sane ones.[5] Elizabeth had never entertained serious imperial ambitions.

The rest of the war at sea was to be fought out mainly by private enterprise, with occasional stiffening from the Navy Royal. Its aim was to wear down a tired antagonist, to secure better compromises in the final settlement. Privateering paid and the mercantile marine from which its ships were drawn had started to grow significantly from 1572, when a survey showed a total tonnage of 50,000, to 1582, when another survey gave a figure of 67,000 tons. The next survey did not come until forty-seven years later in 1629. It showed a total tonnage of 115,000, but even more significant was the much higher proportion of what were for the times comparatively big ships. In 1582 only 18 ships of 200 tons or more were recorded, whereas in 1629 there were no fewer than 145 ships in that category. The signs are that between 1582 and 1604–05, when there was a significant check, the rate of growth was steady.[6] There was a particularly strong growth in large ships for the Levantine and African trades. In the Mediterranean, with the permanent threat of Algerian corsairs – not to mention Christian predators, of whom there were plenty – there was a commercial advantage in the use of big ships capable of carrying a heavy armament. On the West African or Guinea coast, the Portuguese jealously tried to enforce a monopoly by attacking any other Europeans who dared show their faces. So notorious was this that French and English merchants would agree to sail together to maximise their firepower in the face of any Portuguese squadron. Here was a school of naval war in which tactics such as the stand-off artillery battle at sea and the use of line abreast formations in action were pioneered as early as 1557 – mostly by the Portuguese.[7]

However, their opponents proved apt pupils. The English not only had increasing numbers of bigger ships capable of bearing heavy broadside guns, but were blessed with an iron industry in the Weald of Sussex which specialised in the production of cast-iron cannon. Though technically inferior to bronze cannon and heavier for a given weight of shot, these iron guns cost only a third or even a quarter of the price of comparable bronze ordnance. In 1573 there were eight furnaces in Sussex and one in Kent casting cannon and shot to a total annual output of 500–600 tons. By 1600 that figure had reached 800–1000 tons. Much of this was exported, but not all.[8] Mounted on ships over 200 tons, these guns could make the Portuguese attempt to monopolise vast areas of oceanic commerce impractical. The Guinea coast was the first testing ground for this, but the most interesting development dependent on this particular way of internalising security costs by carrying them on the gun deck came when Queen Elizabeth finally chartered the English East India Company late in 1600. Funded by London merchants, it knew full well that it faced a Portuguese claim to monopoly rights in eastern waters. That was why the first voyage of the company, commanded by the experienced James Lancaster and leaving the Thames in February 1601, was composed of 'foure tall shippes': the *Red Dragon* of 600 tons, the *Hector* of 300 tons, the *Ascention* of 260 tons, and a smaller victualler, the *Guift*. It was no accident that the biggest ship, the *Red Dragon*, which was Lancaster's flagship as 'general' of the fleet, was more privateer than merchant ship. She carried 40 guns and 200 men. She had been built in 1595 as the *Malice Scourge* by that greatest of noble privateer entrepreneurs, the Earl of Cumberland. As Portugal had been united with Spain since 1580, it was perfectly legitimate for Lancaster, a man with a privateering background, to capture and loot just north of the equator a Portuguese vessel, a victualler which had gone out with a fleet of 2 carracks and 3 galleons bound for India, but had become separated from them by storms. Ironically, the 'three gallions were ships of warre and were to keep the coast of the East-India from being traded with'. Lancaster was lucky in that he never had to fight a Portuguese force, but when he needed Indian textiles to trade for spices in Sumatra and at Bantam in Java, he obtained them by a lucky capture of a Portuguese carrack of nearly 1000 tons off Malacca. The English needed five or six days to unload her of, among other goods, 950 packets of the light highly coloured cotton cloths known as calicoes and pintados which were highly prized in the Spice Islands. Interestingly, the capture was effected by dismasting the Portuguese ship, after which the English were very careful not to discharge their main battery guns again, for fear that 'some unfortunate shot might light betweene wind and water and so sinke her'. With the return of all Lancaster's ships with good cargoes in the course of 1603, it was clear that, whatever hard fighting lay ahead, the English were capable of breaching the Portuguese claim to a monopoly of European trade in African and Asian waters.[9]

The vitality of some English commercial interests was not reflected in the state of the monarchy. The Crown of England was increasingly stressed, fiscally as well as politically. The sheer viciousness of the competition for Crown patronage and the desperation of losers in that game were to some extent a measure of the thinness of the pickings to be fought over. Whereas under Henry VIII the Crown had been the leading patron of carto-graphers, as well as the heaviest user of maps, by the death of Elizabeth the Crown lacked the means to sustain such patronage. It was a private merchant, William Sanderson, who in the 1580s made possible the accurate mapping of the Carolina Outer Banks by means of his support for Raleigh's colonis-ing schemes. By the death of Elizabeth, the Crown was still a heavy user of maps, but they were mostly produced by others for their own purposes, with at most informal assistance from royal authority in specific cases. There was nothing like the official sponsorship of cartography which was standard in Spain and Portugal and was to become standard in the revived French monarchy of the seventeenth century. William Cecil, Lord Burghley, was a notable collector, annotater, and user of maps. His collections reflect the spectacular improvement in cartographic work in Ireland in the second half of the sixteenth century. If even the Dublin administrators were ill informed about large parts of Ireland in 1550, by 1600 Elizabeth's ministers were as well informed about the detailed geography of most of Ireland as they were of that of England. Here state sponsorship did play a significant role, though English estate surveyors were working to their usual standards in Ireland for private patrons as early as the 1580s, and the extant 1598 plan of Sir Walter Raleigh's estate at Mogeely in County Cork is as fine as anything being done on the other side of the Irish Sea.[10] In general, one can argue that the struggle between the English and Spanish Crowns was by the later 1590s a race between two desperately tired runners, and that the only advantage which Elizabeth held was the fact that parts of the metropolitan economy of England were inherently more buoyant than anything to be found in the deeply troubled economies of the Iberian peninsula.

The weaknesses in Elizabeth's position were underlined by the fate of the Irish campaign of the Earl of Essex in 1599. Robert Devereux, the second earl, had a very different career from his father, who had wasted his sub-stance in futile attempts to seize land in eastern Ulster. The younger man was a major court figure. The Irish episode was embarked on with an eye to further enhancing his position as the leader of the hawks on the royal council and the incipiently dominant rival of the Cecils – hence his prestigi-ous title of lord lieutenant of Ireland. In his entourage were to be found young adherents of his faction such as Shakespeare's patron, the Earl of

Southampton. Essex knew that to profit from his charge, to which he had insisted on being appointed, he had to beat Tyrone in the field and return from Ireland like a conquering Caesar, as Shakespeare loyally said in the fourth act of *Henry V*, 'Bringing rebellion broached on his sword'. Even Shakespeare had doubts, as his text shows, whether this fantasy embedded in a fiction was likely. Despite his unprecedented troop totals of, at least nominally, 16,000 foot and 1500 horse, Essex did not achieve the decisive blow against Tyrone which so many expected. In theory, he was to strike at Ulster, starting by establishing a base on Loch Foyle which would enable the enemy's heartlands to be caught between two armies. Unlike the Blackwater fort of disastrous memory, the new fort was to be sustained from the sea. His Cecilian enemies on the queen's council were perhaps not too distressed that neither the carriage horses nor the sea transports necessary for this strategy of converging attack were made available. The Dublin council, quite reasonably, pointed out the extreme fragility of the royal position in the other three provinces, so Essex embarked on a series of marches, starting with one into Leinster where he linked up with Ormonde, confirmed the submissions of Lords Cahir and Mountgarret, and took or revictualled some castles. Turning into Munster, he captured the very important Cahir Castle, possession of which was imperative for operations west of the Suir; and then progressed by Clonmel, Limerick, and Waterford, confirming the traditional loyalty of the towns. His own tactical sense on the battlefield was throughout very professional. No disaster occurred to his command, and the very real official fear of a Spanish invasion of Munster has to be taken into account in assessing the wisdom of his stress on sustaining loyalist opinion in that province.

Disaster did strike two of his subordinates, with whom he had had to leave a very large proportion of his troops, both for defence of loyal areas and for offensives designed to enhance the strategic starting line for a future offensive. While he was besieging Cahir Castle, Sir Henry Harrington with a force of 500 was totally routed by the O'Byrnes in the Wicklow glens. Worse was the defeat and death of the gallant Sir Conyers Clifford in the Culieu hills as he marched to relieve the loyalist Sir Donogh O'Connor, the O'Connor Sligo, who was besieged by the O'Donnell and on the verge of surrender. Clifford had nearly 2000 men when he clashed with the O'Donnell's masking force under Brian Oge O'Rourke, but a long harassing fire fight exhausted his musket ammunition and he had too few pikemen to hold off charges with cold steel. Essex staggered back to Dublin to find that nobody thought he had enough strength left for offensive operations. When he moved north in September with fewer than 4000 men, he found himself facing Tyrone at the head of an army at least twice the size of his own. This did not mean that Essex was powerless. A council of war in his camp was confident that even at these odds, any attack by Tyrone could be repulsed. Effectively, Essex was covering the Pale against the possibility of invasion. Already the harvest was in around Dublin and the seed was planted without fear of interruption. That was no small matter. What he could not safely do was attack. That would raise a high chance of disaster. Essex must have known by this point that his inability to produce spectacular results was bound to undermine his position at court. It is to his great credit that he took the tactically correct decision to stand on the defensive and treat for a truce. The way he did it in personal conference alone with Tyrone at the ford of Bellaclinthe on the Lagan was less well advised, though the substance of the truce (for six weeks but extensible) was pure logic. The parties were to hold what they held. Commissioners were to be appointed to rule on border zones. Any of the confederated allies of Tyrone who refused to observe the terms might be dealt with by the lord lieutenant, who himself undertook to plant no new garrisons. It was a realistic recognition of a *de facto* military balance.

As early as June 1599, in the course of his southern marches, Essex had drawn up a memorandum for the queen which shows that he knew roughly what he was doing. It started by arguing that between their mobility and their high quality and morale, his opponents were extremely difficult to catch and beat. He also noted the crucial alienation of the Old English nobility through religious differences, which deprived the Crown of their wholehearted assistance. The war was, he said, bound to be long and expensive. That the queen could win it he did not doubt. The loyal towns were crucially important bases which the Gaelic confederacy was incapable of storming. Though bogs and woods abounded, so did good open, ridable champaign country which the government's superior cavalry would enable it to dominate. Naval superiority would always allow Elizabeth to feed her forces while they destroyed the food supplies of the enemy. The question was whether such a game was worth the candle. Though the Earl of Southampton was supposed to keep people out of earshot while Tyrone and Essex conferred, it was alleged that they were overheard discussing what would happen when the queen died. Rather than fight an unprofitable colonial war, it might make more sense to use military clout from the periphery to compel a reconstruction of the court elite, breaking the ever-tightening Cecil and conservative Anglican stranglehold on power, and admitting or readmitting into the ruling elite the increasingly desperate 'out' groups – from evangelical Puritan Protestants, to Roman Catholics, to frustrated marginal courtiers and swordsmen adhering to non-Cecilian political factions. In such an incoherent but hungry alliance, there was surely a place for Tyrone. The queen was well aware of the danger that Essex might turn back from the barren frontiers of Ulster to the rich pickings of the Home Counties. He in fact chose to try to redeem his collapsing court position by an unauthorised departure from Ireland for the court, where his bullying tactics were designed to force the royal will to accept his political programme and preponderance, but which, on top of his perceived failure in Ireland, proved counter-productive and led to his political and financial eclipse. By 1601 Essex was so desperate that he tried to pull off an armed coup in London. It failed. He was executed.

Elizabeth's original choice for lord deputy when Essex insisted on going out as lord lieutenant had been Charles Blount, Lord Mountjoy, one of the two leaders of the second rank in the Essex faction, the other being the Earl of Southampton. Mountjoy succeeded Essex as lord deputy and commander-in-chief in Ireland, where he was greatly to distinguish himself. However, he was very much an Essex partisan, informally in touch with James VI of Scotland on behalf of the faction, and spurred to extremes in support of Essex by his mistress Penelope, Lady Rich, who was a sister of Essex. There is enough evidence, much of it generated by the subsequent trial of Essex for treason, to leave little doubt that the possibility of a military coup against the ascendancy of Sir Robert Cecil, who had succeeded to his deceased father Lord Burghley's position, was seriously discussed between Mountjoy and agents of Essex. The idea was that the lord deputy bring five thousand or so troops over to Wales, where Essex had estates and a large following among the gentry. Keeping close to King James, the conspirators would have hoped to destroy the Cecilian ascendancy, possibly in the name of the heir to the throne whom Elizabeth stubbornly refused to recognise. Two emissaries from Essex, Sir Charles Danvers and Lord Southampton, crossed to Ireland to discuss such a coup with Mountjoy. The danger to Elizabeth if Mountjoy had been willing to risk his hand would have been grave. This was precisely the threat from the military frontier which the Tudors had always feared, and for which the narrowing basis of the regime gave both motive and justification. Despite a tongue lashing from his lover, Mountjoy drew back from overt treason.[11] He was not personally desperate. He held high office with every prospect that he would be further advanced as the result of successful military service. Even the queen had grudgingly accepted the idea that the truce Essex had negotiated was too valuable not to be extended if possible, and extended it was to the very end of 1599. It was Tyrone who chose to break it early in 1600, just as Mountjoy arrived in Ireland with his indispensable subordinate Sir George Carew, destined for the presidency of Munster. Everyone knew that the confederate chiefs headed by Tyrone were hoping for a Spanish descent on Ireland.

From the Spanish archives we can reconstruct the military arguments which Tyrone put forward to encourage the Spaniards to send a force to Ireland. Philip II had died in 1598, but his successor Philip III still thought there might be a chance of imposing a Spanish Infanta on the English throne after the death of Elizabeth, but only after a decisive military success. Tyrone expounded how this success might be achieved. He was clear that a force of 6000 Spanish troops would be enough to operate independently and destroy the lord deputy's field army, which would of course be reduced by the continuing threat from the army of Ulster and the local risings in other provinces. Tyrone did not want the Spaniards to land in the north. He was emphatic that they must land in Munster, where alone it was possible to seize quickly a harbour of appropriate size and accessibility for a substantial expeditionary force. A Spanish siege train could move relatively easily over the open ground of the province, where it would blast the towns into submission. The Spaniards could feed off the rich farmlands of the south, rather than adding to the logistical problems of the north. Above all, they could then move triumphantly into Leinster to seize the all-important eastern ports for the invasion of England. It was all a shade too glib in that it ensured that the Spaniards would do work for the Gaelic confederacy without actually entering the domains of the O'Neill and the O'Donnell. The Spaniards were indeed obsessed with the east coast ports and the opportunity to invade England but feared, wisely, that there would be far less support for them from the lords and gentlemen of Munster than Tyrone promised, and could see themselves isolated and besieged by superior forces. The commander of the Spanish force which did eventually land, Don Juan del Aguila, would have preferred to land in Donegal Bay. Pressure from Tyrone's spokesmen in the Spanish counsels forced him to aim at Munster. What was more important than the tactical details was the broader context: to tempt the Spaniards into intervention in Ireland, Tyrone had to slot his own war into a broader picture in which his survival threatened the survival of Elizabeth even in her core territory, and also indirectly enabled Philip III to revive the dream of Philip II that the Dutch rebels might be compelled to return to obedience by breaking their English ally.[12] War to the death was the logical corollary. That it would involve heavy battle losses and systematic destruction of fragile economies; and eventually heavy mortality among non-combatants had to be the fun of it for those who chose to play a potentially zero-sum game. There was no point in complaining about the price, and turning back appeared impossible. For Mountjoy, the follower and successor of a man who had been prepared to put the war in Ulster on indefinite hold, victory in the north was now essential for the security of that court on which he had chosen to focus all his ambition.

In an ironic way, both sides had altered their original objectives beyond recognition. The O'Neill had after 1565 always leaned on the indirect but powerful support of the Earl of Argyll, chief of Clan Campbell, lord of the redshank trade. The Campbells, once potential allies of the English

Crown in Ulster, had become alienated from Elizabeth and helped sustain an autonomous Gaelic society there until the end of the sixteenth century. Hugh O'Neill had started his nine years of conflict with a view to sustaining a virtually independent Ulster. By 1600 he was trying to mount a religious war in all Ireland, looking to Spain, not to the Protestant Campbells, for external support. The Gaidhealtachd was beginning to split into separate Scottish and Irish branches.[13] Equally, the Crown's objectives had changed. Mountjoy's very successful lieutenant in Munster, the Devon man Sir George Carew, was a cousin of the land-grabbing Sir Peter Carew who had provoked the first Desmond rebellion. Yet Sir George was able to re-establish control over Munster by the end of 1600 as much by attracting local support (not least by exploiting local rivalries) as by his skilled use of artillery to capture strategic castles. Like Mountjoy, his objectives were political. He was not primarily a speculator in real estate like his cousin.

He was lucky in the sense that Tyrone's southern progress in early 1600 had not been a great success and during it his son-in-law and vital border ally Hugh Maguire had been killed in a skirmish. Florence MacCarthy, whom Tyrone left behind to head the southern rising, was not a resolute leader, while Carew contrived to defeat the *sugane* Earl of Desmond. The cost of the professional bonaghts who constituted the fighting edge of the Gaelic confederacy had to be offloaded onto the area where they operated, which did not endear them to Munster landlords, so Munster rapidly ceased to be a source of strength to Tyrone, while Carew came to be able to send 1000 men to assist in the rolling up of the O'Donnell's extensive informal empire in Connaught. In the north Mountjoy applied strategies worked out under Lord Deputy Sidney in the 1560s, but at last backed by adequate resources. He had made a slowish start, plagued by accidents such as the kidnapping of the Earl of Ormonde (he was later released) and complicated by the need to secure the strategically vital old midland plantation area of Leinster by crippling the power of the Kavanaghs and O'Moores. That done, he was in a position to turn on the heart of Tyrone's power. In the spring of 1600 he had already forced Tyrone back to the Blackwater by a thrust with troops which had to be brought from Dublin by sea to Carrickfergus because of the difficulty of any southern approach by land. What the campaign achieved was a diversion which allowed Sir Henry Docwra to enter Lough Foyle and set up forts at Culmore and Derry. When he gained the allegiance of Niall Garve O'Donnell, a bitter rival of Hugh O'Donnell, as well as cooperation and supplies from the O'Dohertys of Inishowen, he became a serious menace to the O'Neill as much as to the O'Donnell.

When Mountjoy in October 1600 successfully, if expensively, drove Tyrone's troops out of the trench systems they occupied in the Moyry Pass which controlled the invasion route between Newry and Dundalk, the immunity of central Ulster was at an end, even though Mountjoy left it to the following year to reoccupy and fortify Armagh and re-establish a fort at the classic invasion ford on the Blackwater. Already from Carrickfergus Sir Arthur Chichester, brother of the Sir John killed by the Antrim Scots, had established naval supremacy on Lough Neagh and was raiding east Tyrone with destructive amphibious strikes which could be held off only by the construction of extensive defensive works by Tyrone on the lough's west shore. By the summer of 1601 Tyrone had been defeated by Mountjoy at Benburb. Spanish intervention was now his only hope of sustaining the wildly ambitious programme he had embarked on from 1597. It came too late, in October of that year, and in inadequate strength. Spain was exhausted. Mounting the expedition she did was an effort. Losing part of it to gales was absolutely predictable at that time of year. Indeed, losses that way were relatively light. Aguila landed at Kinsale with 4800 men, soon dramatically reduced by disease, desertion, and casualties to 2500 effectives. Carew and Mountjoy had been expecting the intervention and Carew had built up supplies for the campaign to cope with it. Aguila soon found himself living his nightmare of close siege by Mountjoy. English naval supremacy enabled the lord deputy, a student of siege technique, to move in his heavy guns and to seal off the Spaniards.

Additional Spanish forces under Don Pedro de Zubiaur did reach Castlehaven in west Cork, inspiring a considerable rally of the lords of south-west Munster to their cause, but Zubiaur was obsessed with the invasion of England and insisted on holding harbours rather than joining the northern chiefs in their inevitable but extremely dangerous attempt to lift the siege of Kinsale. Aguila was in a dire situation despite a gallant defence, so though the two Hughs, O'Neill and O'Donnell, besieged the besiegers with superior numbers for a period after a slow plundering march south from Ulster, their lack of naval power more or less compelled them to risk a battle. Bad weather would not close the harbour to Mountjoy's victuallers for ever. Mountjoy was himself under extreme pressure, but the logic of attrition was marginally in his favour and he had always been confident of victory in a set battle. Tyrone's supreme tactical talent had hitherto lain in avoiding one. In the event, the Battle of Kinsale in late December 1601 was a rout, as Mountjoy's superior cavalry caught a quarrelling O'Neill and O'Donnell in disarray as they moved in to coordinate their attack with a Spanish sally which failed to come. Once their outmatched cavalry broke, the northern lords simply did not have an infantry capable of sustaining a line of battle in open country under attack by shock tactics. By 2 January 1602 Aguila had done his professional job by signing a capitulation. He had opened his campaign by a proclamation saying that Pope Clement VIII commanded all Irish Catholics to join him in a religious crusade. It was not true, for the pope was chary of the embrace of the Habsburgs, but it was worth trying and had partially succeeded as long as the Spaniards looked like winning. Now Spanish forces were to evacuate Kinsale, Castlehaven, Baltimore, and Berehaven, and were to be transported to Spain. Subsequent inquiries in Spain exonerated Aguila of all charges of dereliction of duty, and rightly so. The O'Donnell left with the Spaniards to make a personal appeal to Philip III. He died in Spain in September 1602, becoming the Red Hugh of legend but having shown by his last effort that he did not understand royal courts or international realities. Tyrone staggered back to Ulster, fighting off those he had plundered on his way south, but returning with a fraction of the force he had led out.

The military decision was now just a question of time since Mountjoy was able to march into the heart of the O'Neill Lordship in 1602, establishing new forts to secure his route. He took Dungannon; he devastated the inaugural site of the O'Neills at Tullahogue, destroying the stone of inauguration comparable to the Scots one at Scone; above all, he drove cattle and destroyed crops to the point where famine stalked central Ulster in 1602–03. Tyrone was quite good at watching his men die of starvation, as he had shown at Kinsale, but this time starvation was a measure of the collapse of the economy he needed to sustain him in his last redoubt in the bogs and woods of Glenconkein north-west of Lough Neagh, where he was being harassed by Docwra from the north and Chichester coming in from the east over Tyrone's destroyed defence line. Elizabeth, so mean so often to her servants in Ireland, had at last bitten on the bullet and was funding adequate troop strengths, even up to by previous standards staggering, if purely nominal, figures of around the 17,000 mark. Tyrone had left her little choice. In March 1603 he came to terms and surrendered to Mountjoy at Mellifont. Mountjoy by then knew the queen was recently deceased. He revealed this to Tyrone only after the Treaty of Mellifont was settled.

Tyrone in no way suffered from this. On the contrary, he gained immensely. The war had become almost entirely an end game over the future of the Tudor inheritance. That was the issue, and Tyrone's ability totally to destabilise that inheritance, with incalculable consequences, had been rendered obsolete by force of arms. Colonial war of the old land-grabbing kind still appealed, of course, to some Dublin administrators and some New English, but the lord deputy had not fought over the heart of Ulster for that. Tyrone's faith and fatherland line had a future, though necessarily a divisive one, but it had run out of impetus. Mountjoy was in fact desperate to get back to the court, where all the relevant action lay. A new monarch, James VI of Scotland, was about to become James I of England and Ireland. Sir Robert Cecil had won him over up to a point, because only Cecil could stage-manage a smooth succession, but with James, an Essex sympathiser, the old Essex faction could hope to come in from the cold, as indeed men like Mountjoy and Southampton did. What Mountjoy needed was peace and cost reduction in Ireland, where the army was soon to be reduced to a mere 1100 men, and a quick return to court, preferably with Tyrone (an old diplomatic associate of the reigning King of Scots) by his side. The actual terms of Mellifont were extraordinarily favourable to Tyrone and Rory O'Donnell, Hugh's successor. Of course, the old militarised Gaelic principalities had to go. They survived in Scotland because men like the Earl of Argyll ran at most an unofficial and purely private foreign policy, never threatening the survival of the monarchy. The titles of the O'Neill and the O'Donnell were finally renounced, to be replaced under surrender and regrant by the Earls of Tyrone and Tyrconnell. As such, both peers accompanied Mountjoy to meet King James. So anxious was Mountjoy to close that he sold most of the Ulster Gaelic loyalists down the river. In the case of someone like Niall Garve O'Donnell, who had fought for the queen in the hope of benefiting from at least a partition of the O'Donnell's lands, the betrayal was particularly bitter, but a similar fate befell many of the septs on the margins of Ulster – like the O'Cahans as well as loyalist faction leaders among the O'Neills like Sir Arthur O'Neill. Because it is easy to talk about a Nine Years' War costing £2,000,000 sterling and tens of thousands of lives, it is easy also to impose a wholly bogus unity on the period of belligerence.

There were at least three different wars in the period, messily overlapping but quite different. The first Tyrone won. He fought to a standstill the genuinely colonial enterprise of subjecting Ulster to an unconditional Anglicisation designed to cast land titles into instability for the benefit of predatory incomers. He would have been the chief loser. The second war was one he was on balance always likely to lose because he tried to create and exploit an international religious crusade which if successful would destroy Elizabeth. It has been pointed out that the captains who commanded Crown garrisons and detached units as well as companies in the field, and who often had served in a mediatory role between the government and Gaelic Ireland, moved to a hard-line demand for total war after 1598. This has been seen as proof of the shallowness of their commitment to milder policies such as surrender and regrant. It surely demonstrates primarily the fact that any soldier could see that to defeat a general as powerful and evasive as Tyrone you had to destroy the economic base for his army.[14] Captains did not determine high policy about the terms for peace. The third war was about final terms after Tyrone's international role had ceased to be viable. The queen only very reluctantly at the end agreed he should be offered life, liberty, and pardon, but she was incapable of accepting that he could not be radically diminished if a settlement was to come soon. Her death solved that problem. It created another.

Tyrone was in fact greatly enhanced by the peace, once he swallowed the end of princely independence. Like Tyrconnell he became the absolute hereditary proprietor of much more land in Ulster than he had ever really had a right to control before.[15] He won his last war. Partly, this was due to considerations which Mountjoy had spelled out for the benefit of the English council in early 1602. The lord deputy was clear that Tyrone's 'combination is broken'. Without the confederacy which he had once headed, Tyrone lacked the means 'to subsist in any power', but that was not the end of the story, for he could hang on as a guerrilla fighter long enough. Experience had shown that he was too well guarded by his people to be removed by assassination. Europe was full of groups like 'the banditti of Italy' who survived indefinitely in arms in the interstices 'between the power of the King of Spain and the Pope'. Mountjoy argued that this was not an acceptable position when the greatest O'Neill that ever was could blow the embers of a defeated Gaelic Ireland's natural desire to regain its lost liberties, and when a wider Ireland was unsettled by genuine fears and resentments. There was a haunting fear of famine, already rampant in the north. Debasement of the coinage to fund the war had caused an inflation which Mountjoy thought an intolerable grievance. There was fear of 'a persecution for religion'.[16] Mountjoy was uneasily aware that the heritage of his own military victory was a twisted one. Himself a theologically sophisticated Anglican from a Roman Catholic family, he knew that religious differences posed enormous problems for civil governance in the former Tudor dominions, but he could only say that however bad the situation, persecution would make it worse. He wanted a quick and liberal settlement with 'the Irish lords of countries, or such as are now of great reputation among them'. So Mountjoy had been in favour of an early and generous settlement since at least 1602, but the granting to the culturally ambiguous Tyrone of an ascendancy in an Anglicised Ulster which he would probably have accepted in 1594 owed everything to Mountjoy's urgent need to reach the court fast. There he was able to sell to the new king the extraordinary terms he had granted. Tyrone and Tyrconnell had in him a genuine friend at court. The new Scots king had no bias against the earls: quite the reverse. He had dealt with similar creatures in his ancient realm, and social ambiguity was almost a requirement for success with him. Nevertheless, Mountjoy's early death in 1606 was a disaster for the Ulster earls.

As an expansive force Elizabethan imperialism died in 1597 with defeat at the Battle of the Yellow Ford and failure of the naval counter-offensive off Ferrol and the Azores. Thereafter the regime fought to survive on the best obtainable terms, not always helped by the queen's attitudes. The triumphalist iconography of Elizabeth is totally misleading in these later years. For example, the remarkable 'rainbow' portrait at Hatfield House which shows her holding a rainbow, with a jewelled serpent symbolising wisdom on her left sleeve, also shows her draped in what is probably meant as an Irish mantle decorated with eyes and ears to show her as all-seeing and all-knowing in that context.[17] The loving analysis of this arcane iconography appears to appeal to the usual strange modern combination of English Gloriana worshippers and Irish Catholic nationalists, but the whole point is that the iconography here is and always was grotesquely misleading. The queen's Irish policies were remarkable for their stubborn refusal to face reality. They were an appalling failure rooted in ignorance and folly. She ended up having to fight expensively for her life, when there was no need originally to provoke any violence above the scale of the interstitial abrasions which were the necessary price for a partially devolved polity. King James did not inherit an England within striking distance of imperial greatness. He inherited a financially and politically stressed monarchy whose peoples were dangerously divided and which had contrived deeply to fracture the central core of Englishry on which its coherence depended. The queen had been an obstacle to ending an increasingly pointless belligerence with Tyrone, and had not negotiated an end to an Anglo–Spanish war which both combatants knew they could not win. The Tudor court had become much too narrow based and had also shown an alarming tendency to generate instability on the peripheries of the royal dominions. So far from expanding, this government needed reconstruction if it was to be able to carry on. There was no imperial achievement. Elizabeth survived, mainly because her great enemy, Spain, was an extreme example of strategic overstretch. It was under what Sir George Carew, the president of Munster and historian of its final three years of war under Elizabeth, called the 'triumphant monarchy'[18] of King James VI and I that English, Scottish, and Irish overseas colonial ambitions and conflicts became a significant factor in politics.

Notes and references

1. W.L. Renwick's 'Commentary' in his edition of Edmund Spenser, *A View of the Present State of Ireland* (Clarendon Press, Oxford, 1970), p. 180.

2. Michael Maccarthy-Morrogh, *The Munster Plantation: English migration to southern Ireland 1583–1641* (Clarendon Press, Oxford, 1986), pp. 130–40.

3. *Vide* the excellent review of C.G. Cruikshank's *Elizabeth's Army*, by G.A. Hayes-McCoy in *Irish Historical Studies*, 5 (1946–47), pp. 258–60.

4. Hiram Morgan, 'Hugh O'Neill and the Nine Years' War in Tudor Ireland', *Historical Journal*, 36 (1993), pp. 21–37, is the best introduction, though the substance of the paper belies the unitary concept of the war implicit in the title.

5. R.B. Wernham, *The Return of the Armadas: The last years of the Elizabethan war against Spain 1595–1603* (Clarendon Press, Oxford, 1994), Chaps. 10–15.

6. Ralph Davis, *The Rise of the English Shipping Interest in the Seventeenth and Eighteenth Centuries* (David and Charles, Newton Abbot, 2nd impression 1972), pp. 7–11.

7. John Francis Guilmartin, *Gunpowder and Galleys* (Cambridge University Press, Cambridge, 1974), pp. 88–93.

8. Carlo M. Cipolla, *European Culture and Overseas Expansion* (Penguin Books, Harmondsworth, Pelican edn, 1972), pp. 44–49.

9. Sir William Foster (ed.), *The Voyages of Sir James Lancaster to Brazil and the East Indies 1591–1603*, The Hakluyt Society, 2nd Series, No. 85 (London, 1943), pp. 78 and 106–08.

10. *Vide* the excellent contribution by Peter Barber on English cartography in David Buisseret (ed.), *Monarchs, Ministers and Maps: The emergence of cartography as a tool of government in early modern Europe* (University of Chicago Press, Chicago, IL, 1992), Chaps. 2 and 3.

11. Cyril Falls, *Mountjoy Elizabethan General* (Odhams Press, London, 1955), p. 43; and A.L. Rowse, *Shakespeare's Southampton Patron of Virginia* (Macmillan, London, 1965), p. 154.

12. The best study based on Spanish sources is John J. Silke, *Kinsale: The Spanish intervention in Ireland at the end of the Elizabethan wars* (Liverpool University Press, Liverpool, 1970).

13. Jane E.A. Dawson, 'Two Kingdoms or Three?: Ireland in Anglo-Scottish relations in the middle of the sixteenth century', in Roger A. Mason (ed.), *Scotland and England 1286–1815* (John Donald, Edinburgh, 1987), pp. 113–38.

14. Ciaran Brady, 'The Captains' Games: Army and society in Elizabethan Ireland', in Thomas Bartlett and Keith Jeffrey (eds.), *A Military History of Ireland* (Cambridge University Press, Cambridge, 1996), pp. 136–59.

15. Steven G. Ellis, *Tudor Ireland: Crown, community and the conflict of cultures 1470–1603* (Longman, London, 1985), pp. 311–12.

16. Sir George Carew, *Pacata Hibernia or a History of the Wars in Ireland during the Reign of Queen Elizabeth Especially within the Province of Munster*, ed. Standish O'Grady (2 vols., Downey and Company, London, 1896), Vol. 2, pp. 302–13, where Carew cites a letter from Mountjoy to the council in England dated from Dublin Castle, 26 February 1602.

17. There is a convenient reproduction of the portrait in colour in Diana Scarisbrick, *Tudor and Jacobean Jewellery* (Tate Publishing, London, 1995), p. 65.

18. Carew, *op. cit.*, Vol. 2, p. 314.

PART TWO

Three-Kingdom Monarchy and Empire 1603–1688

Reluctant warriors: James I, Charles I, appeasement and the aborting of a three-kingdom overseas empire

The shaping of a triple monarchy after 1603

The accession of James Stuart, King of Scots, to the English and Irish thrones in 1603 was to open a reign in which some of his subjects succeeded, where those of Elizabeth had failed, in setting up enduring overseas plantations. To describe 1603 as the start of 'imperial' kingship is to use language anachronistically. Early-modern European usage still thought of the Holy Roman Emperor when it used imperial phraseology, and most European kings had been closing their crowns with arches and vociferously claiming that they were 'imperial' since the later Middle Ages. In a hierarchical social world where everyone was supposed to be subject to somebody, it was basically a claim to be subject to nobody except God. King James was quite clear that his kingship was of this kind. He was unusual among English kings in being an articulate intellectual who wrote books. In 1598, he had published *The True Law of Free Monarchies*, and he republished it after he reached England. It argued that the monarch's sovereign power derived from God alone, and that theories of rights of resistance to royal authority, cultivated by both radical Roman Catholics and radical Protestants, were profoundly misguided. Similar views had been expounded by Elizabethan clerics in the authoritarian 1590s, notably by Hadrian Saravia, who was to survive to be one of the translators of the Authorised Version of the Bible in the reign of James. Saravia's *De Imperandi Authoritate*, which derived Elizabeth's power from God and denied the right of subjects to limit it, was an official view.[1]

Elizabeth's father, Henry VIII, had been entirely clear that his realm of England was an empire. By this he wished primarily to repudiate external claims to jurisdiction within it, such as the pope's. James, an inherently less belligerent man than Henry, could wax hysterical over papal claims, which were real, that the Supreme Pontiff had the power to depose errant rulers, especially heretical ones. Nevertheless, imperial kingship for the early Stuarts was primarily about denying that their subjects had any inherent right to resist them, though the Stuarts were happy to give somewhat unconvincing guarantees that they would almost always govern according to custom and law. King James did not have imperial ambitions in the sense that a Victorian Englishman living through, say, the late-nineteenth-century partition of Africa would understand them. His obsession was with his own version of sacred monarchy, which had status and territorial implications, but mainly with respect to Anglo-Scottish union. In the early-modern era the European concept of 'empire' did not have a primarily territorial focus. It was more a matter of political authority than lands.

Since James interpreted his accession in 1603 as part of the working of Divine Providence through him, he regarded a 'perfect union' to integrate the Scots and the English as the obvious next step in God's design. Between 1604 and 1607, the integration of Scottish and English political and legal institutions emerged clearly as the supreme objective which the king hoped to achieve through his first English parliament. By 1607, it was clear that stolid conservative opposition in the legislature at Westminster had destroyed the impetus of the project, for which even James admitted there was no wild enthusiasm in Scotland.[2] The king persisted fitfully, but by the time he dissolved this first parliament late in 1610, he was bitter about what he saw as their mindless obstruction of God's will and his dearest wish. They may have been more sensible than he and subsequent historians have believed. Anyone willing to trust James Stuart with the initiative in totally recasting the frameworks of politics and law in the two realms was a risk-taker. As it was, the very important and necessary attempt to restructure the admittedly unsatisfactory fiscal basis of the English monarchy by the so-called 'Great Contract' foundered in 1610 at least partially because of distrust of James. He offered a bargain, in the sense that he was prepared to surrender traditional rights in exchange for more realistic parliamentary funding, but he kept stating that in the last analysis his prerogative could not be restricted. This implied that his prerogative was not under the law, so in theory he could resume the rights he surrendered, in case of necessity.[3]

Part of the large-scale royal propaganda for an integrating union with Scotland was devoted to deprecating past and existing multiple kingships on the grounds that they were transitory, unstable structures. Given good lordship by the ruling dynasty, this was not really so. Both the Spanish and Austrian Habsburgs held imperial powers together for centuries through multiple kingship. Interestingly, the rare reference to what modern people would think of as a colonial empire in this literature can be hostile. For example, in 'A Treatise about the Union of England and Scotland' which survives only in manuscript, the Portuguese 'conquesto in the East Indies of Malaca, Calecut, Cambar, Canoar and other kingdoms there' are cited 'whereof they reteine homage, oath of fidelitie and tribut without any further alteration of their estats'. However, the author, who appears to have been a pro-union Scot, dismisses this sort of arrangement (which in fact laid the basis of a relationship which lasted from the seizure of Goa in 1509 to its capture by the forces of the Indian Union in 1961) as 'no wayes sure or durable'.[4] Oceanic empire was not exactly high priority for the extremely Eurocentric James. His accession was marked by the ratification of the agreement which had been reached between O'Neill and Mountjoy at Mellifont in County Louth in 1603 to end the Nine Years' War. By 1604, the long Anglo–Spanish War was wound up by the Treaty of London. Consolidation of his three kingdoms and a restoration of amicable relations with Roman Catholic Europe were the king's priorities.

Predatory violence between civilised states he detested. During the war with Spain privateering had become a significant English industry, especially in the south-west.[5] James issued a proclamation in 1603 suppressing privateer activity, which was now plainly piratical, but the continuation of war between Spain and the Dutch until a truce was arranged in 1609 left a loophole which allowed Englishmen to fund, equip, and serve with Dutch privateers until some of these ships were effectively English. Another proclamation of 1605 failed to suppress this practice which was condoned by local vice-admirals. Commissioners were sent to investigate piratical activity in 1608 and 1610. The truce between Spain and the Dutch in 1609 helped. By the latter part of the reign, piracy was coming under control with strong Royal Navy patrols operating as far afield as the waters off Newfoundland. In fact, the English had never been 'a nation of pirates', though that was the warped vision which many continental Europeans had of them. During the Anglo–Spanish War, licensed privateering, especially in the Caribbean, was a rational, profitable way to employ ships and seamen denied access to honest trade by Habsburg embargoes. In peace, the English were liable to lose alarming numbers of ships and surprising numbers of people to such freebooters as the Barbary pirates of North Africa. Peace and Anglo–Spanish cooperation against Barbary pirates made eminent good sense.[6] Hard-liners like Sir Walter Raleigh who tried to persuade James to keep the war with Spain going after his accession were flying in the face of reality. He fell out of favour, was deprived of honours and revenues, and ended up being accused and convicted of high treason – more by association than active participation – with Lord Cobham, an unstable nobleman who was in negotiation with Count Aremberg, ambassador of the Archduke Albert, the Habsburg ruler of the southern Netherlands. Raleigh admitted he had been offered a large bribe by Cobham to facilitate an Anglo–Spanish peace. He insisted he had ignored the offer.[7]

That peace was duly negotiated and given final form by the Treaty of London of 1604. English claims to trade with the East and West Indies were at the heart of the protracted haggling in Somerset House which preceded the final settlement. Henry Howard, Earl of Northampton, who was the principal English spokesman on this aspect of the negotiation, was a pro-Spanish politician from a Roman Catholic background, so he could cope with the politico-theological arguments which the Spaniards wheeled out in order to uphold their claim to monopoly rights in both Indies by papal donative. Northampton was further fortified by memoranda prepared by the antiquary Sir Robert Cotton. Cotton was a great searcher for convenient precedent, but also a man with a realistic grasp of how weak and fraudulent was the Spanish claim to control much of the Americas. He wrote:

> And for the Spanish Territories . . . wherever you shall view not the 20th part of them possessed, and interruptions sometimes of a 1000 and 1500 leagues between the ports or places of any their just interests, and how basely they are inforced to attend the devotion of barbarian lords, making their safety by continual purchase.

There was no desire on the English side to exploit this situation by attacking established Spanish colonies. However, when the Spanish negotiators proved obdurate, the treaty nearly fell through. Spain had too many wars. She needed peace with England more than England needed peace with her. Her team drew back. The final terms bowed to Northampton's aggressive stance on the Indies trade. It was agreed to insert a general article on trade in the treaty, based on one in a recent Franco–Spanish treaty. Its ambiguity was deliberate and adequate for English purposes.[8]

Effective occupancy was the wholly reasonable yardstick by which King James measured the territorial claims of other Christian princes in the Indies. Where such princes had effectively controlled dominions, James had no desire to challenge them; but he stoutly defended the right of his subjects to trade with and settle in areas where no Christian prince held effective sway, and to defend themselves if attacked whilst doing so, even by the subjects of another Christian prince. The king seems to have had little or no positive interest in imperial expansion as such. It was all a question of upholding the dignity of his monarchy by insisting that other princes treat it and its subjects with a minimum of respect. The emphasis on Christian princes did not mean that James was a crusader. Between 1615 and

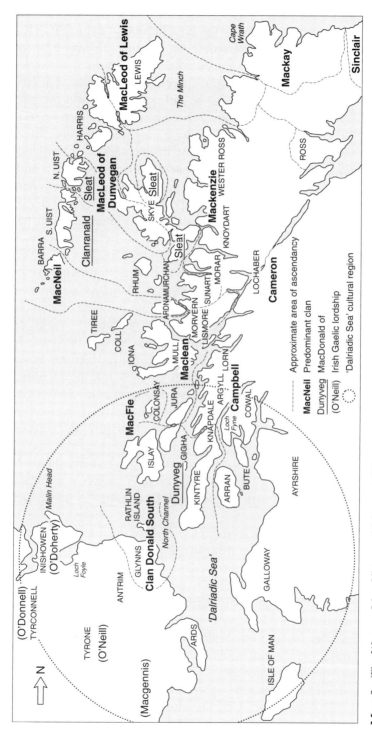

Map 3 The Western Isles, Ulster and Man, *c.* 1600

1619 he had an ambassador resident in Moghul India, Sir Thomas Roe, whose salary was actually paid by the East India Company (EIC). Roe had been a member of the Royal Council for Virginia. He was a member of Raleigh's circle, to the point where Raleigh had sponsored an exploratory voyage which Roe made to the vast delta of the River Amazon in 1610–11. Roe's sole objective in India, which he did not achieve, was the obtaining of a firm treaty with the Emperor Jahangir, a treaty which would guarantee free access to Moghul ports under reasonable terms for EIC ships. Naval victories over the Portuguese by EIC squadrons commanded by Captain Thomas Best and Captain Nicholas Downton in 1613 and 1615 did inspire more respect for the English and Roe left with a general imperial *firman* or decree from Jahangir expressing his wish for better Anglo–Indian relations. He also patched up relations with Jahangir's heir, who was governor of Surat.[9]

Nobody doubted that the Great Moghul was a mighty and civilised, if infidel, sovereign. The peoples who were in danger from King James were those within his claims to jurisdiction whom he labelled barbarous or uncivilised, or whom he could be manipulated into thinking of as such. This particular syndrome, though rooted in humanist platitude, seems to have taken a very specific shape during James' reign as king of Scots. Around 1595, James seems to have received an official report which much exaggerated both the wealth of the western isles of Scotland, the Hebrides, and their potential as a source of revenue for an impecunious and extravagant crown. Normally, James was averse to forfeiture as a mechanism of government. In his book *Basilicon Doron*, he noted that forfeiture was to be avoided and the nobility should not be thus repressed, as they had been by his grandfather James V.[10] Cooperation was the key to stability. James VI was reluctant to proceed to extremes against even so turbulent a noble as the Earl of Huntly, chief of Clan Gordon and 'Cock of the North' (strictly the north-east).

However, the 'barbarous inhumanity' of the natives of the Hebrides was deemed to exempt them from this general reluctance to proceed to forfeiture. In 1597, an act of the Scots parliament required all chiefs and land-owners in the Highlands and Islands to produce valid title deeds under pain of forfeiture. Written all over this legislation was the expectation that many would be unable to produce such deeds. The potential field of operation was the Hebrides, apart from Mull (where the Crown may have deemed the Macleans a useful counterpoise to the MacDonalds, who were likely to be in practice the principal victims of this policy), and the western seaboard territories which had belonged to the once-mighty MacDonald Lordship of the Isles, finally forfeited in 1493. The king himself had no military force at his disposal to enforce any forfeitures. He was no general; on the contrary, he was a notorious and craven coward, so any policy of forfeiture had to be enforced by others. For the king, the attraction was the idea of collecting what he deemed long-withheld rents, if necessary by replacing the 'barbarous' withholders by 'civilised' Lowlanders, who would not only pay rents but stimulate the local economy, as envisaged in the 1597 legislation, by the foundation of burghs.

Luckily for some Highlanders, several of the proposed forfeitures fell through. The now Marquess of Huntly, for example, was in 1607 offered the North Iles (i.e. those north of Ardnamurchan other than Skye and Lewis), on the shameful condition that he massacre their entire populations. Huntly jibbed at the level of feudal duty James proposed to levy on him for these lands. The Kirk by Law Established protested violently against enhancing the power of a crypto-papist royal favourite like Huntly. Nothing came of this scheme. In 1613, a royal plan to grant Morvern to Sir John Campbell of Lawers fell through because Lawers and his chief, Argyll, calculated they could not cope with the predictable ferocious opposition of Clan Maclean, which claimed Morvern. In 1615 a royal grant of MacDonald of Clanranald's lands to Lord Ochiltree was hastily withdrawn for fear that it would drive Clanranald to join the rebellion of Sir James MacDonald of Dunyveg.[11]

Not all threatened groups were so lucky, though all fought back with spirit. Clan MacLeod was almost as much a target of royal policy as the various branches of the much divided Clan Donald. The MacLeods were organised in two great groups. One was the Siol Tormod branch, whose main seat was at Dunvegan on the Isle of Skye. Its chief, Ruari Mor of Dunvegan, had failed to produce his land titles, which allowed James to declare his lands of Dunvegan, Harris, and Glenelg to be forfeit and granted to a group known as the 'Fife Adventurers' who were also given the great island of Lewis in the Outer Hebrides. They first tried to seize Lewis, coming so totally to ruin in the process that Ruari MacLeod kept his lands. The other branch of the Clan Leod, the Siol Torquil of Lewis, was less fortunate. Failing to produce title deeds, they were forfeited. Apart from Lewis, the clan held Trotternish in Skye and the island of Raasay, as well as Gairloch and Coigeach in Wester Ross and Assynt in Sutherland. They were a tempting target.

They were also divided by an internal feud over the chieftainship. Most Lewis MacLeods supported Torquil Dubh against the rival claimant recognised by the government, Torquil Connanach. The latter had no male heirs and handed his charters to Lewis to the head of his mother's house, Mackenzie of Kintail. The king granted Lewis, fatuously described as 'the maist fertile and commodious pairt of the haill realme . . . enrichit with a incredible fertilitie of cornes and plentie of fischeis', for a very stiff rent to the Lowlanders who had formed the Fife Adventurers. As the name suggests, they mainly came from the peninsula of Fife across the Forth from Edinburgh. They included leading members of local society such as the Learmonths of Dairsie, the virtually hereditary provosts of St Andrews, but they had no significant military edge over the societies they were proposing to expropriate. Because of the strong maritime traditions of the east coast burghs of Scotland, they could find the shipping to convey themselves, their stores, and their followers to Lewis. Once there, they faced stout opposition from the Siol Torquil, as well as systematic obstruction from two Highland chiefs gratuitously offended by King James. Ruari MacLeod of Dunvegan was alienated by the grant of his estates to the Adventurers. Donald Gorm MacDonald of Sleat, another powerful Skye chief, was enraged by James' grant of Trotternish to the Adventurers, for he had just leased it from the Siol Torquil; and to cap it all, Mackenzie of Kintail harboured his own ambitions and covertly did his best to stoke the fires of opposition to the Fife lairds and merchants.

The upshot was defeat and insolvency for the Adventurers, who then sold out their rights to the devious Kenneth Mackenzie, Lord Kintail. Torquil Connanach had already conveyed the barony of Lewis to Kintail, who invaded Lewis in 1611 on his own account. The military power of Clan Mackenzie was a much more serious threat to the MacLeods than the Adventurers. On the broad mountain pastures of their heartland around Glen Shiel, Clan Mackenzie nurtured a race of warrior herdsmen capable of sustained military effort across the waters of the Minch in Lewis. Not until 1616 was Mackenzie hegemony riveted on the island, mainly by the efforts of Kenneth's brother, Roderick Mackenzie, tutor (i.e. guardian and regent to the heir) of Kintail. When James in 1623 made the new Mackenzie chief, Colin, Earl of Seaforth, he formally endorsed Mackenzie imperialism.[12]

At least the beneficiary of this whole disreputable sequence of events had been a Gaelic power. The Mackenzies joined the Campbells and Gordons as the three great imperialist clans of the seventeenth century. King James' categorisation of Hebrideans and some western seaboard Gaels as irredeemable 'barbarians' could have unleashed a vicious general colonial war if the Lowlanders whom he cajoled and bullied into his proposed pattern of privatised aggression and confiscation had had the capacity to use force with profitable efficiency. It would then have paid their leaders to invest in propaganda reinforcing the king's wildly oversimplified and misleading vision. As it was, resistance stifled the possibility of such developments. The fact that the successful predator became Lord Seaforth gave James a sense of integration and familiarity in the north-west. Threatened Gaelic groups were well aware of the advantages of closeness of their leadership to the

Crown. The Gordons' westward expansion had helped create a clan confederacy of their potential victims, known as Clan Chattan. Its chief, Lachlan Mackintosh of Dunnachton, was a courtier, a companion of the future Charles I, and an influential voice in the ear of King James, who knighted Mackintosh before the last named died in 1622.[13]

The odd group within Gaelic society, like the MacLeods of Lewis, could lose out heavily in these politics, but even the MacGregors were not effectively subjected to the genocidal fantasies which occasionally took over the irascible royal mind. The MacGregors were a special case. Long battered by eastward Campbell expansion, their clan structure had disintegrated and they did not possess the unifying feudal authority which along with tribal leadership was the classic formula for an effective chieftainship. The Campbells of Glenorchy were able to evict the chief of Clan Gregor from his barony of Glenstrae. Violent resistance by MacGregors in the central Highlands to a systematic Campbell attempt to take over their allegiance was compounded by the actions of a branch of the MacGregors – Clan Dougal Ciar – which had settled in glens on the east side of Loch Lomond. It all came together in 1603 when the young chief, Alasdair MacGregor, moved into the Lennox, the territory east of Loch Lomond, and clashed with the Colquhouns of Luss on the other shore of the loch. King James authorised Colquhoun of Luss to launch punitive strikes against Clan Gregor, but when he had led a mixed force of Colquhouns, Buchanans, and burgesses of Dumbarton across the loch in February 1603, he was met by Alasdair and a MacGregor force which routed him with heavy loss of life in Glen Fruin.

James demanded that 'That unhappie and detestable race' be 'extirpat and ruttit out'. He made it an offence punishable by death to use their name. Alasdair fell into the hands of Argyll and was hanged at the Mercat Cross of Edinburgh in 1604. In practice, MacGregors were 're-sett' or sheltered by friendly clans. Campbells compensated them for eviction and before long were seeking to enlist their services. Royal influence secured more and more grotesquely barbarous penal laws. It was by 1621 theoretically death for a former MacGregor to own a weapon other than a pointless knife. Female MacGregors who did not drop the name were to be branded in the face and transported.[14] What all this confirmed was the destruction of MacGregor leadership. It is doubtful if persecution and penal laws decreased criminal violence by clan members. They were by definition masterless men on the margins of a richer Lowland society. They stole to live, on occasion. Nothing would be more misleading than to take the draconian statutes which reflected the royal will as a reflection of reality. James, fortunately, lacked the means to enforce his will. Clan Gregor was driven under cover but never 'extirpat'.

It was only when local power-brokers placed their forces behind Crown policy that enough military force could be mobilised to produce significant change. The MacDonalds of Dunyveg in Islay were to experience this reality. Long involved in Ulster through marriage links to the lords of the Glens of Antrim, the Dunyveg MacDonalds had suffered heavily because of loss of manpower through service in the sixteenth-century Irish wars. In Islay they found Campbell of Calder trying to take advantage of their lack of feudal charter, and in Kintyre their resistance to Crown control led the Crown to transfer its claims to Argyll. Both Calder and Argyll were given naval and artillery support against these MacDonalds. In his final campaign which crushed the revolt of the Kintyre MacDonalds, Argyll had, in addition to his clansmen, 400 mercenary infantry, an artillery siege train, and ships of the Navy Royal at his disposal.[15] Sir James MacDonald of Dunyveg fled to Ireland, then Spain. Yet Argyll, despite bringing some Lowlanders into Kintyre, displaced neither MacDonald tenants nor lairds.[16] King James, for all his rhetoric of order, was himself the single most anarchic influence in the Highlands in his reign. It was just as well that instead of race war, his wilder projects were manipulated by others to secure only shifts in the Gaelic balance of power.

In Ireland, the king originally never contemplated policies akin to the plans for widespread expropriation which he devised but could not execute in the Hebrides and western Highlands. He had no need of them. The Treaty of Mellifont might be generous to the two great Ulster warlords who had fought for nine years against Queen Elizabeth, and it certainly sold out some of the Crown's Gaelic allies as the price of an early peace, but it marked the end of quasi-independent Gaelic warlords in Ireland. They had to become landlords and noblemen if they wanted to survive. The policy of surrender and regrant was at last totally triumphant. For the first time ever, Ireland was, at horrendous cost, a single political unit. James was the first monarch whose writ ran over the entire kingdom. That kingdom was recognisably the descendant of the Anglo-Norman marcher Lordship of Ireland, as modified by the invention of a distinct kingdom of Ireland, at the time largely notional, in the early sixteenth century.

The O'Neill, now primarily the Earl of Tyrone, was familiar with the royal court, but Lord Deputy Mountjoy brought him across to meet the new Scots king immediately after the signing of the treaty. On this occasion James issued 'A Proclamation commanding that no man abuse the Earl of Tyrone', on 8 June 1603. It is a revealing document which starts by admitting that Tyrone had rebelled against Elizabeth, and then proceeds with heavy didacticism typical of James to say that such dreadful behaviour should never be encouraged by foreign princes because of the shocking precedent it established for their own subjects. King James' faith in the solidarity of the kings' trade union was always naive, especially across the confessional divide. The proclamation then continued to say that Tyrone had shown appropriate contrition, and implicitly argued that there was no reason why the new reign should not see the slate wiped clean of the north of Ireland, and a fresh start made with Tyrone a loyal subject.[17] To James, Tyrone was inherently no more disturbing than Huntly, the chief of Clan Gordon and as 'Cock of the North' predominant regional magnate in a north-east Scotland which was at least as distinctive geographically as Ulster. Huntly had rebelled and had been forgiven. In both religion and politics, Huntly was as ambiguous as Tyrone, but James had always correctly believed that he could build a constructive relationship with a chastened Huntly.

By August of 1606 it was common knowledge among English elites that Tyrone was disturbed and remonstrating to the king about proposals to send a president and council to Ulster.[18] The idea of establishing a presidency in Ulster was widely discussed in the early years of James I, though there is no evidence that the royal government intended to take any steps to execute such a policy. Rumours were rampant partly because such presidencies had a long history in other Irish provinces, and partly because it represented wish-fulfilment for some important Irish administrators. Even Lord Deputy Arthur Chichester thought an Ulster presidency so certain and imminent that he was anxious to exempt his own grant of the governance of Carrickfergus from the new jurisdiction, though he also rather fancied the idea of being president of Ulster after his retirement from being lord deputy of Ireland. The prospect appalled Tyrone, who hated and distrusted Chichester. A rumour that another man he distrusted, Sir Henry Docwra, was about to be created president of Ulster had led him to declare that 'rather than be governed by anyother than His Majesty and his deputy-general of that realm, he would chose to dwell in England in His Highness's presence'.[19] At least the remark showed that what Tyrone feared were the sharks of the Dublin Castle administration, not the king, in whose good will he rightly trusted.[20]

The situation was further complicated by the fact that Tyrone had always been a considerable shark in his own right. As well as defending himself against Dublin, he had to fend off the often well-justified complaints of the leaders of Ulster septs, often his own kinsmen, who complained that Tyrone was using the surrender and regrant provisions of the Treaty of Mellifont to steal land over which he had never had traditional rights. During an Ulster tour by the lord deputy in 1605, many 'gentlemen of the O'Neills and other septs' presented petitions claiming 'a right in freehold to several parcels of land possessed by them and their ancestors; which the earl withstood, alleging the whole country to be his own and in his own

disposition'.[21] It was a genuinely difficult situation in which the king ultimately would have to act as umpire between several quarrelling and self-
interested parties, but it was all cut short by the quite unexpected flight
abroad of the earls of Tyrone and Tyrconnell in September 1607, when
they took ship from Rathmullin on Lough Swilly in Donegal, never to
return to Ireland.

There was no outburst of rebellion in Ulster, a fact which came as a
relief to the genuinely baffled and confused King James, who nevertheless
tried to strengthen his military hand in the province where the end of the
war had seen a rapid run-down in his forces. In October 1607, the king
wrote to the archbishop of Canterbury saying that the earls had fled despite
his pardon and were trying unsuccessfully to raise trouble in foreign parts.
Nevertheless, 100 horsemen were to be levied to ensure that all was quiet in
Ulster, and the archbishop was to have the unwelcome privilege of levying
the cost of twenty of them from the clergy of the province of Canterbury.[22]
One hundred horsemen was a posse, no different in substance from the
posse which James formed to police the traditionally disturbed Borders
regions between Scotland and England which the king in his propaganda
insisted he would turn into wholly pacified 'Middle Shires'. At the time of
his flight, Tyrone offered as an explanation for his decision to accompany
Tyrconnell the argument that everyone would assume that he had been
left behind as a 'sleeper' who would help to raise a rebellion when and if
Tyrconnell managed to return with foreign money, troops, and supplies, so
he would almost certainly have been apprehended.

That was true, but arrest and lodging in the Tower of London was not
necessarily a disaster. The Tower could be, for great men and women, the
equivalent of an expensive hotel. Noblemen were forever being warded
there or in Edinburgh Castle, and if there turned out to be no substance to
the accusations against them, they would be released, none the worse.
Tyrone probably would have been the worse for the experience because of
the mire of legal disputes which surrounded him, some due to the greed of
others, some due to his own greed. Nevertheless, it has been always assumed that the initiative in the flight of the two earls came from Tyrconnell
and his close ally Cuconaught Maguire. Until recently it was thought that
their principal motive was financial distress and a desire to seek profitable
employment with the rulers of the Spanish southern Netherlands. It now
seems that the situation was, in fact, much more complex, and Tyrone
cannot have been panicked into the flight because he had something
approaching a month's notice of the ship's arrival.

Both men had concluded a treasonable pact with Spain. Negotiations
had begun in London as early as 1604. First payment of their handsome
annuities of 4000 ducats apiece was made in 1607. The deal was overtly

treasonable in that they promised to raise a rebellion if Spain went to war with James. As late as the summer of 1607, James was showing positive favour towards Tyrone. Apart from anything else, the inability of the earl's enemies to erect a presidency in Ulster owed a great deal to the effectiveness of Tyrone's petitions to the king, who had vetoed the project. There were rumours of treasonable activity by Tyrone, but they were vague. The king was still anxious to humour a man who had in fact encouraged Tyrconnell's intrigues with Old English Roman Catholic recusants in Ireland who were deeply discontented due to the Jacobean regime's early religious policy.

There had been a serious threat of rebellion by elements of the Old English in 1603, to back pressure for religious toleration. Many Old English were convinced that James, son of the Catholic Mary, Queen of Scots, would grant them toleration. Instead, Lord Deputy Chichester had embarked on a drastic campaign, known as the 'Mandates' policy, to harass and fine the Old English elite into conformity with the established Protestant Church of Ireland. Tyrone had probably adopted a faith and fatherland policy in the 1590s out of expediency, but as he grew older his commitment to the Counter-Reformation appears to have deepened. Besides, there were still personal reasons why he might regard rebellion by a Roman Catholic league of Gaelic Ulster lords and the Old English as a fallback option. The royal tone towards him changed dramatically in June 1607, and a key proprietorial dispute with O'Cahan looked as if it might be swung against him by his loss of favour. The explanation for the change in official attitudes from appeasement to suspicion was the emergence of a highly placed, if erratic, informer, Lord Louth. While serving in Spanish Flanders, he had picked up hints about the formation of a Catholic league in Ireland and about Tyrone and Tyrconnell's involvement. There was, however, no concrete case. James performed a U-turn on the 'Mandates' policy in the latter part of 1607 when he realised the depth of Old English resentment.

The odds are overwhelmingly that the king, a vacillating coward by nature, would have in due course reverted to appeasing Tyrone, just as he appeased the Old English. James was apprehensive of what Tyrone might do if desperate. It seems that the key to Tyrone's flight was misleading information which he received in August 1607, just possibly originating with James' crypto-Catholic minister Lord Northampton but certainly reaching him in a letter from the Archduke Albert of the Spanish Netherlands. In it, Tyrone was advised he would be arrested in the course of an imminent visit to England and detained, possibly in Ireland. The general tone of the communication was clearly much gloomier than circumstances warranted. It had the desired effect of manipulating Tyrone into joining Tyrconnell in his planned departure. Tyrone probably saw his move as a tactical one in the vigorous and effective political game which he had been playing between 1603 and 1607. As with the treasonable deal which he and Tyrconnell had cut shortly after the not-ungenerous Treaty of Mellifont, it was a move too clever by half – indeed, both irresponsible in a regional prince with moral obligations to his people and ill-advised in a practising Jacobean politician. Even in stable kingdoms, great nobles were by definition part of the system of governance and all monarchs demanded that they ask formal permission to leave the realm. James spoke the truth when he said he had no idea what was going on, but the mere departure of the earls was technically treasonable, and modern scholarship suggests that, though it could not be proved at the time, both were up to their necks in overtly treasonable intrigues.[23]

It was all the more galling to James that the earls were received by other sovereign princes, and not returned to him as the contumacious subjects they were. The Archduke Albert was, appropriately, the arch-offender here, but Henry IV of France proved embarrassingly reluctant to allow the earls to be extradited to the dominions of King James. The embarrassment was mutual, because Henry, assuming the earls had gone straight to Flanders, had expressed sympathy for James to the English ambassador and said how offended he would be if any neighbouring prince harboured his rebels.[24] Then the earls turned up in France on their way to the Netherlands. No prince trying to use the local version of the Counter-Reformation to build up his power and authority could afford to deny these refugees safe transit. The Archduke Albert was in reality embarrassed by their arrival, and shuffled them off his territory as fast as he could. They eventually settled in Rome. Both archduke and king explained that religion and justice demanded that the earls be received.

After the earls had been charged with treason in Dublin on 9 November, James issued 'A Proclamation touching the Earles of Tyrone and Tyrconnell' at Westminster on 15 November. He had it published in Latin as well as English, to reach a European audience. Mostly, it is a furious self-justification by the king, replete with denunciation of his pet hate, the Jesuits, whom he regarded as stirrers-up of rebellion.[25] However, in the text King James denounces the fugitives as 'monsters of nature', not only for rebelling against their legitimate sovereign, but also because they had been 'content to sell over their Native Countrey to those that stood at that time in the highest termes of Hostilitie with the two Crownes of England and Ireland'. To James, patriotism and identity were a function of allegiance. It was a very Scottish attitude, for it was allegiance to the Stuart dynasty – not religion, language, or social order – which defined Scottishness. His own accession to the English and Irish thrones was to him a case of God speaking to three kingdoms through the Stuarts' royal genes. The idea, which Tyrone had played with, of transferring the sovereignty of Ireland by papal donative, would have struck James as blasphemy. To him the union of the Crowns in his person in 1603 had set up a new political order whose unfolding had an intimate connection with the process of human redemption in its last stages.

When not in overtly apocalyptic mode in the years after 1603, James was wont to re-emphasise his mission, of which he had spoken in his *Basilikon Doron* written just before the turn of the century, to see to 'the rooting out of all barbaritie'. Of this, the king was convinced there was a lot in Scotland 'especiallie in the bordouris and Heylandis'. Though James deemed many Gaels barbarians, his reference to his own Borderers underlines the point that James did not think all barbarians were Gaels, let alone that all Gaels were barbarians. Civilisation, as rightly understood and expounded by King James, involved above all the development among subjects of an appropriate sense of civic responsibility and obligation, quite unlike what the king in 1597 had described as the naked pursuit of self-interest by the 'beastlie' Indians of America.[26] Like the good northern European renaissance scholar he was, James had been aware long before 1603 of the fascinating discoveries and knotty intellectual problems thrown up by European penetration and conquest in the New World. It is also clear that he placed the native Indian peoples of the Americas relatively low in the great chain of being, more akin at their worst to beasts than to man.

Ireland was by definition radically different from a New World, being rather an old one in terms of contact with Latin Christendom. The complexity of its several cultural worlds in the sixteenth century was a puzzle to many contemporary outside observers, and has never been to the taste of radical over-simplifiers since. American historians in particular, however competent their technical performance, have a tendency to fall back on a 'four hundred year war', at times of 'genocidal magnitude', to give palatable moral cohesion to the fractured vision created by their own work.[27] In fact, there was little overall continuity. There were many different wars, just as there were many shifting identities in Ireland. By 1603 it was clear that the inhabitants of the newly united, or perhaps created (as distinct from invented) kingdom of Ireland were subjects of the Crown. As the scope of the Common Law expanded in the aftermath of the Nine Years' War to take in the last northern bastions of traditional Gaelic society, it was appropriate that a proclamation be issued in March 1605 enfranchising the inhabitants of Ulster as subjects of King James.

With the flight of Rory O'Donnell, Earl of Tyrconnell; Cuconaught Maguire, Lord of Fermanagh; and Hugh O'Neill, Earl of Tyrone; vast tracts of Ulster were forfeit to the Crown, as they were bound to be under the circumstances. Two relatively minor Gaelic lords then rose in rebellion in 1608. Sir Cahir O'Dougherty, the lord of the Inishowen peninsula, was fearful that the government intended to back-pedal on its promises to recognise his ownership of the peninsula and of the Isle of Inch in Loch Swilly. Rising in arms, he seized the fort at Culmore and rapidly devastated most of the settlement of Derry. More than one despairing former Gaelic chief responded to his example, but the only one of consequence was Shane Carragh O'Cahan, whose sept lands lay around modern Coleraine. Both were rapidly crushed by a still adequate royal army commanded by Marshal Sir Richard Wingfield. Trying to refight the Nine Years' War without serious allies was suicidal. Forfeiture followed, as was inevitable. This huge, quite unexpected windfall of land falling to the Crown provided the basis for the ambitious plans which culminated in the plantation of Ulster. Legislation confirming the forfeiture of the earls was eventually secured, with no difficulty, from an Irish parliament in 1614. By then the recusant Old English had in the Irish parliament fought James to a standstill over his drive for a radical Protestantising of the elites of the old Lordship of Ireland. However, their own original Anglo-Norman identity had as one of its core characteristics territorial expansion at the expense of Gaelic warlords. They combined with the New English to confirm this, the strangest of all transfers of Gaelic territory.

Sir John Davies, the English lawyer who was appointed by King James solicitor general for Ireland in 1603 and attorney general and sergeant-at-law in Ireland in 1606, was beside himself with joy at the unexpected departure of the earls, comparing James to St Patrick on the grounds that the mere countenance of both had abolished poisonous reptiles from Ireland. Davies had been an aggressive exponent of the expansion of Common Law as an instrument of royal control. If he had not done this someone else would have, since the expansion of Common Law to Gaelic areas had been an objective from the day the concept of a kingdom of Ireland had been invented. No such kingdom could function over all Ireland without a law common to all its subjects. After 1603, with the early-sixteenth-century concept of the kingdom achieved by force, there was no alternative, and Davies' career was much less remarkable than some have suggested.[28] His main achievement was to get the jobs after his quite scandalous previous career, culminating in a lengthy disbarring after seriously assaulting a fellow lawyer. Predictably, the first Irish appointment appears to have been achieved by a mixture of undeviating sycophancy towards King James, who knew of Davies as a man of letters before 1603, and the patronage of Queen Elizabeth's last and James' first dominant minister, Robert Cecil, Earl of Salisbury. At the death of Elizabeth, Davies had shot up to Scotland, brazenly soliciting preferment from the new sun.

Warming in its rays, Davies offered parliamentary experience and the necessary bag of legal tricks required by a law officer of the Crown, including a very fair grasp of the potential of Civil Law concepts as they had evolved recently on the continent. Insular Davies was not. Insecure he was, especially when his patron, Cecil, died in May 1612 when Davies was in England busy trying to prepare the way for a permanent and profitable return there. The upshot was the publication of his *Discovery of the True Causes Why Ireland Was Never Entirely Subdued.* It was much less of a military analysis than its title suggested, though the fact that the author's personal ambitions were not of a martial nature enabled him to talk quite sensibly about the facts, apart from his persistent obsession with the concept of a 'perfect conquest' of the whole island. He could see that this had never been a priority for the Crown, which had left the Lordship largely to fend for itself, never sending adequate armed forces to Ireland. Davies could see that even Henry VII would not have bothered to send the limited forces he did had not the Yorkists of the Lordship actively supported two serious pretenders to his throne.[29] He could also see that though 'the particular insurrections of the Viscount Baltinglass and Sir Edmund Butler, the Mores, the Kavanaghs, the Byrnes and the Burkes of Connaught were all suppressed by the standing forces here [*viz* Ireland]', what had made Elizabeth's reign decisively different was the great rebellions of Shane O'Neill, Desmond, and Tyrone which 'drew several armies out of England'.[30]

With large-scale immigration of men and capital, expanding overseas commerce and a growing urban sector, Davies saw James' Irish kingdom as set for a future of peace and prosperity. The underlying reason why Davies claimed so confidently that this was so was that he saw the full extension of the Common Law over the whole of Ireland as the key to the contentment and cultural assimilation of all Irishmen, from the Old English with their traditions of feudal anarchy to the Gaels of recently conquered Ulster. He harped on the theme that it was the failure of previous monarchs to offer many Irishmen the privilege of equal access to the Common Law which accounted for that land's discontent. Even Davies admitted that the string ecclesiastic on the Irish harp was not in tune, but he ended with a rousing assertion of the loyal gratitude which Irishmen would show to the Crown 'so as they may have the protection and benefit of the law when upon just cause they do desire it'.[31] It was a totally misleading rhetoric, with almost no contact with reality, and its final bankruptcy came with the Ulster rising of 1641, which by 1642 had broadened out into something suspiciously like a major war of religion in Ireland.

But then, Davies' book was never a good guide to anything other than its author's ambition and self-promotion. It was primarily a means to secure for him a return to a lucrative legal position in England, which ambition, after a long delay, he duly achieved. The publication belonged to the world of projectors: glib conmen trying to secure what they wanted by telling the Crown what it wanted to hear, regardless of veracity or indeed commonsense. Historians have tended to be as gullible as Queen Elizabeth or King James, placing far too much weight on such flawed materials as the *View* Spencer did not write, or the *Discovery* which Davies undoubtedly penned. The *Discovery* was a recital of services like the one which Sir Arthur Chichester wrote when he wanted further reward from the Crown. Chichester's hyperbole was such that he said 'that I had rather labour with my hands in the plantation of Ulster, than dance or play in that of Virginia'. He did admit that the native inhabitants of Ulster were still numerous and warlike, but he referred to the stabilising effect of those he termed, with great political correctness, the new British settlers. King James was still obsessively and unsuccessfully trying to talk the English and Scots into thinking of themselves as his British subjects. Less welcome to the royal ears probably was Chichester's admission that the failure of his lord deputyship to effect 'the extirpation of Popery' more or less guaranteed the continuation of treachery in 'this land' as well as 'in the rest of your dominions'.[32]

Very little of the plan for the plantation of the six counties of Ulster escheated after the flight of the earls and the minor rebellions went as it was meant to go. Devised between 1608 and 1610, it called for the main responsibility for the settlement of English and Lowland Scots settlers to rest with grantees called undertakers, who were supposed to transplant native Gaels from their estates to other areas. The counties of Antrim and Down were never part of the official plantation, and in north-east Antrim there was a Scottish Gaelic mini-conquest empire in the hands of a chief of Clan Donald South. Ironically, King James was on good terms with him. Elsewhere in the escheated parts of Ulster even the original plans for plantation allowed a lesser category of grantees called servitors to retain Irish tenants. Servitors were often English and were drawn from the civil and military officials of the Crown. From the start, they were to be allowed to have native Irish servants. Pre-plantation grants to a few prominent Gaelic Irish landowners were confirmed, and some Irish landholders in the forfeited areas were restored to a proportion of their former holdings, to be established in the same areas as the estates of servitors. Between these gaps a coach and horses was soon driven through the general provision that undertakers remove all Gaelic Irish from their property.

Settlers were difficult to find and expensive to establish. They had to be tempted by favourable leases. Estates devoid of tenants were useless to prospective landlords. The Gaels were there, willing to accept less generous terms than settlers, and yielding profit to owners faster. Scots undertakers in particular just did not have the money to cope with the always heavy, at times astronomical, cost of implementing official plans. Of Scots under-takers, only the Earl of Abercorn had anything approaching 100 settlers on his estate by 1611 and many of them may have been in Ulster already, as part of the normal circulation of people.[33] By the time the Crown faced up to the facts of Ulster life and in 1628 agreed, as part of a series of political compromises known as the Graces, that native Irish tenants might be al-lowed on a quarter of each undertaker's estate, very many estates had not approached so low a proportion. Evasion of the provisions for removal had been widespread. Some of the new landowners were opportunistic chancers – such as Sir Ralph Bingley, an English soldier who had served with Drake and Hawkins in their voyage to attack the Spanish Caribbean in 1595–96. Bingley had secured employment in Ulster under Elizabeth but no place in the radically reduced Irish military establishment after 1611, and by the 1620s, despite his Donegal servitor's landholdings, he was in financial trouble. From 1625 he tried to take advantage of Charles I's wars with Spain and then France by offering to lead regiments into wars overseas recruited from 'swarms of idle men' who threatened disturbance in Ireland. He died at the head of a regiment of these troops in the Duke of Buckingham's unsuccessful expedition to the Isle de Rhé in France in 1627. Needless to say, there is no reason to think that the proportion of native Irish on his estates was ever reduced to a quarter.

Ralph Bingley was not unique. His brother, Richard, was involved in 1609–10 in taking surplus Ulster swordsmen, out of work after the defeat of the Gaelic warlords, to Sweden for military service. He later secured servitor's land grants in north-west Ulster, but sold out after securing a surveyorship in the Navy Royal. He was suspended from his post as surveyor of the navy in 1618 on corruption charges. Yet another brother, John, was forced out of a position in the English treasury during a major scandal in 1619. They all had a knack of finding get-rich-quick schemes anywhere in the Jacobean world except Scotland (where there was little flesh on the bones available for picking) and of ending up poorer than they started. All three were predictably involved in that guaranteed loss-maker, the Virginia Company. All three were knighted, all three were thieves, though in different ways.[34] They were broad-minded in the sense that they stole indiscriminately from Spaniards, Englishmen, or Irishmen.

In the unstable Ulster of the period 1640–41, with economic conditions deteriorating and Gaelic tenants being marginalised whilst Gaelic land-owners grappled with adversity often on a fraction of their pre-plantation holdings, it is hardly surprising that there was conspiracy among the Gaelic elite for a rebellion 'for regaining their ancestors' estates'. The defeat of King Charles in his two Bishops' Wars with his Scottish subjects seemed to offer a good opportunity to attack the Crown. It is therefore doubly significant that when the rising came in October 1641 it explicitly, and not entirely insincerely, repudiated any programme of this kind. It was ostensibly ultra-royalist. The great Earl of Tyrone had died in exile, but his nephew and surrogate Owen Roe O'Neill indignantly insisted 'we are in no rebellion ourselves, but do really fight for our prince, in defence of his crown and royal prerogatives'. The leaders of the rising were men of substance and position. Originally they only attacked English settlers, leaving Scots untouched. Irish septs took the field in Ulster, but the whole point of the rising lay in its alliance with the Old English.[35] That alliance presupposed a recognition of the authority of Charles I. The leaders of the Ulster rising even claimed to have a signed commission from him which authorised their attacks on the English, bade them not to meddle with the Scots, and generally licensed them to rise on his behalf. The commission was, of course, bogus but the programme was not even aimed at the total elimination of the Ulster plantation. Rather it was designed to use the authority of Charles, king of Ireland, as a shield against an ultra-Protestant clique which was bidding to use the Westminster parliament as a means of usurping royal authority, with the corollary of a likely change for the worse in Crown policy towards Roman Catholics. A Catholic confederacy soon linked the Ulster rising with the Old English world to the south, but the stress its leaders laid on the autonomous sovereignty of the Irish state was no more extreme than views articulated by leading bureaucrats in the Dublin administration.

If the claim to have a direct commission from the king was false, the claim of the confederate Catholics to be executing the royal will was at least partially true. Charles I certainly regarded the availability of a loyal Irish Catholic army as a card he would like to have the option of playing against his English opponents. Though in theory he had to disband the force assembled by his loyal servant and lord deputy the Earl of Strafford, in practice he had tried to keep much of it on foot under guise of recruiting for Spanish service. The War of the Three Kingdoms which was in train by the latter part of 1642 was not in Ireland an attempt to restore the lost world of the Gaelic lordships. That particular colonial war had been fought and won, for good or ill, and probably in its latter stages mostly for ill. The war, or rather wars, in Ireland in the 1640s and 1650s were primarily about control of the Anglo-Norman state of Ireland, with the Old English acting as leaders of a Catholic proto-nationalist alliance which saw its future depend on gaining effective control over that state. The trouble was that the Old English, like their monarch Charles I, lost their war. A second conquest ensued in which, with massive assistance from English armies, the Anglican New English element seized control of the Irish state. By the eighteenth century, they were even articulating their own version of Protestant Irish nationalism. The broken Old English interest by then was submerged into a Catholic nationalist community.

Anglicanism was not, however, the only form of Protestant Irish nationalism. From 1641 proto-nationalist tendencies can in retrospect be seen evolving in the settler areas of Ulster, and especially the Scots ones. Intermingling of peoples there had long preceded the early-seventeenth-century plantation. The immunity of the Scots from attack did not survive by 1642. Many fled back to Scotland. Most did not, and Presbyterian ministers exiled by the aggressively Anglican Strafford regime actually started to return to Ireland in 1642. Those who stayed or returned opted for Ireland and for Ulster, and laid the foundations of a unique identity which from an early stage was also a uniquely irritating one for other peoples. Heavily defeated by the Ulster Irish at Benburb in 1646 – despite the support of a Scottish expeditionary army – these extraordinary people hung on, fighting at different times both for and against Charles I and driving both Oliver Cromwell and his Latin secretary, the poet John Milton, to paroxysms of rage over their obduracy and apparent perversity.[36]

These Ulstermen were to evolve full-blown theories of self-reliant nationalism only in the latter part of the twentieth century, characteristically as the result of their experiences of the attitudes of other Irish and British peoples towards them during the long period when their normal self-referential term was 'unionist'. In the seventeenth century, their partial repudiation in practice of the general rule that Irish politics after 1641 became what most Irish politics has remained – an argument as to who should hold power in a unitary state in Ireland – was largely unselfconscious. In this it differed sharply from the one great exception to the acceptance of the end of the world of the Gaelic warlords, which also emerged from an Ulster Scot background, albeit the Gaelic and Catholic one of Clan Donald South in Antrim. Their leaders had never accepted the defeat and expulsion of MacDonald chiefs from the Mull of Kintyre and parts of the southern Inner Hebrides by Clan Campbell. Through the agency of sponsorship of missionary Franciscans they were softening up the areas of their intended future re-expansion before the 1640s, by ideological means.[37]

In Randal MacDonnell, second Earl and later first Marquis of Antrim, Clan Donald South had a chief linked to the highest court circles by his marriage with the widow of King James VI and I's great favourite, the Duke of Buckingham. Mentally, however, Antrim had the very Scottish Gaelic knack of living in two quite different worlds. In 1644 he unleashed his kinsman Alasdair MacColla MacDonald on Scotland with some 2000 infantry. Linking up with the royalist Marquis of Montrose, MacColla was the military muscle behind the six spectacular victories which seemed to lay

Scotland at Montrose's feet in 1644–45; but he then went off to cut Campbell throats in western Argyll, avoiding thereby participation in the rout of Montrose at Philiphaugh in the southern Lowlands by regular Scottish regiments withdrawn from service in England to cope with the Montrose menace. The same regulars drove MacColla out of his last positions in Kintyre in 1647. He retreated to Ireland where there had been a brief rebirth of the redshank trade from the quasi-autonomous Gaelic Lordships of western Scotland. Important Highlanders like MacDonald of Glengarry and a son of the captain of Clanranald were commanding troops in the service of the confederated Catholics. Like MacColla, most of them died in battle in 1647–48.[38]

All of this was hidden in the future in 1608–10 when the plantation of Ulster was being planned but, with the benefit of hindsight, it is clear that the reign of James VI and I marks the end of the classic colonial wars on the frontiers of the Irish Gaidhealtachd. MacColla practised the particularist imperialism of an independent warlord, but he was a throwback to times past. After 1610, the Irish and Scottish states became the foci of ambition and conflict for Gaelic and non-Gaelic elites alike. In Scotland this proved a mixed blessing for in the terrible century between 1645 and 1745 there were repeated, horrendously violent, Highland interventions in Lowland politics.[39]

The aborting of the overseas dimension of triple kingship

To give him his due, King James hoped to give his Scots and Irish subjects a distinctive role in the overseas expansion and colonisation which was one of the characteristic features of the major early-modern Western European sovereignties. This did mean challenging Luso-Hispanic claims to exclusive rights in both the East and West Indies, though it did not mean that James was anti-Spanish. Indeed, with his accession a historian has rightly said that 'the history of English anti-Hispanism entered a new and less virulent phase'.[40] Exponents and developers of the 'Black Legend' of Spanish imperial atrocities during his reign, like the clergyman Thomas Scott, tended to be critics of their monarch's pro-Spanish foreign policy. For James, the right of his subjects to colonise in those vast stretches of both North and South America where the subjects of Philip III had no serious presence was axiomatic, and he correctly regarded the response of the Spanish Crown to the exercise of that right as a test of its real, as distinct from its professed, respect for the Stuart monarchy.

The great privateering offensive by Englishmen into the Caribbean in the late sixteenth century was by definition over after the Peace of London, but it had left an extensive deposit of knowledge about the wealth of the Guiana Caribs and Spanish exploration of the River Orinoco. From 1595, Sir Walter Raleigh was active in the area of Trinidad and the Orinoco delta. It was understandable that in the face of a likely blockade of the Orinoco by Spanish forces drawn from the kingdom of New Granada (modern Colombia), he turned to the River Amazon as an alternative unblocked way of accessing, via one of the Amazon's tributaries, the central area of Guiana, where he was convinced there lay the last great unconquered wealthy Amerindian civilisation.[41] By 1607, Sir Walter Raleigh was a prisoner in the Tower of London, desperately trying to persuade James' leading minister, the Earl of Salisbury, to free him to lead an expedition in the course of which he swore 'We will break no peace; invade none of the Spanish towns.'[42] In exchange he averred: 'Secondly, if I bring them not to a mountain, near a navigable river, covered with gold and silver ore, let the commander have commission to cut off my head there.'[43] Raleigh's alleged samples of the ore were a matter of dispute. This mountain of gold and silver existed only as the wilful self-deception of a desperate projector, but the interest which Raleigh had shown in the Amazon had passed to other Englishmen. In any case, the main north channel of its enormous delta, north of the Ilha Joannes, had by the early seventeenth century become a thriving locus of trade for many different Europeans: French, Dutch, and English among them.

Some of the English were marginal would-be courtiers of Raleigh's stamp. The classic case is Robert Dudley, illegitimate son of the Earl of Leicester, who was enraged by his failure to be recognised as the legitimate heir and who, whilst keeping in contact with the English maritime community, had entered the naval service of the Grand Duke of Tuscany. Predictably, Dudley saw the Amazon primarily as a means of access to the realm of El Dorado, the gilded Indian 'emperor'. After 1609, even Salisbury was becoming worried about the increasingly aggressive, bullying tone of a Spain free of the burden of its endless Dutch war thanks to the signing of a 12-year truce in 1609, and he was interested in possible armed intervention in Guiana – which is why he was involved in the Amazon reconnaissance conducted by Sir Thomas Roe, the future diplomat and friend of Henry, Prince of Wales, in 1610–11. Salisbury warned Roe that he had to find gold mines to justify and finance a clash with Spain before King James could possibly be persuaded to abandon his policy of appeasement. If there were no gold mines and a clash, more appeasement and a conviction for piracy was the likely outcome for Roe. Roe penetrated 300 miles up the river, finding neither mines nor Spaniards. Gold there was for the making in the Amazon delta, but it was in the form of tobacco leaf.

It was an Irish tobacco trader working out of Dartmouth, Philip Purcell, who led the way. Whilst trading with Trinidad for tobacco in 1609, at the peak of the English contraband trade there, Purcell learned enough about the opportunities on the Amazon to involve himself with it for the next twenty years. He was probably from Munster, and may have had Dublin connections. Certainly other Irish merchants involved in trade and colonisation on the Amazon operated out of Dublin. Starting under the aegis of Roe, Purcell established a group of Irish settlers at the 'Tauregue River' on his second Amazon voyage. It was emphatically an Irish colony, and always referred to as such by contemporaries. It coexisted happily enough with similar small English colonies. A pattern was emerging whereby each of the three Jacobean realms had its distinct overseas plantations, all owing allegiance to King James.

The Amazon delta was particularly attractive because neither Spain nor Portugal had established any meaningful occupation in it, and it was well suited for rapid development of tobacco exports to feed the infinitely elastic European market. English traders migrated down the Guiana coast towards the Amazon to avoid direct confrontation with Spaniards. Quite a few of them joined settlements established by Zealanders who wanted to underline their own quite different attitude, which was one of hostility to the truce between the Dutch Republic and Spain. By 1619, there was an English Amazon Company, established specifically to advance trade and settlement in the Amazon. Its moving force was Roger North, a younger son of Lord North. Roger had been with Raleigh in his last expedition to the Orinoco in 1617. By 1620, King James had effectively repudiated his own charter in the face of a furious diplomatic offensive by the Spanish ambassador, Diego Sarmiento de Acuña, Conde de Gondomar.

The Spanish Crown did not have any economic or military presence on the Amazon, which was in fact an extreme case of the absence of effective occupation that often lay behind its aggressive posture in the Americas. It had no choice but to call in its Portuguese subjects from Brazil to attack other Europeans. The Spaniards themselves were scarcely capable of maintaining minimal settlements in Trinidad and on the Orinoco. The first Portuguese strike, by combined metropolitan and colonial forces, was against a French colony on the Bay of Maranhão south-east of the Amazon delta. The fighting in 1614–15 between the French and their Indian allies and the Portuguese and theirs was furious and protracted. It ended in complete Portuguese victory. For the local Tupinambá Indians, who had hoped for French protection, the outcome was a disaster. Many had migrated hundreds of miles to Maranhão to escape from the horrors of the Portuguese conquest of Pernambuco. Now they were at the mercy of their old enemies and even the influential Jesuits of the Portuguese colonial establishment could not save them. In 1616 a Portuguese force sailed 400 miles further along the coast to establish a fort at Belém on the eastern side of the delta, at the mouth of the Pará River.[44]

For about seven years the Belém fort was no threat to the English, Irish, and Dutch on the Amazon. It was preoccupied with Indian wars. The Portuguese were the crudest of cultural imperialists. Unlike the French, who studied to understand the Indians, the Portuguese were quite capable of waging obliterative punitive war against 'heathens' (i.e. unconquered Indians), without bothering to record the names of the peoples they slaughtered. Maranhão was soon ablaze with rebellion against its new overlords' abuse of their powers. The Indians of the Pará joined in. They were crushed with extreme savagery by the Portuguese commander Bento Maciel Parente who, one contemporary said, killed 30,000 Indians between 1619 and 1621. Ultimately, 'it was disease that annihilated the Indians',[45] reducing them to a viciously exploited margin of a European colonial society. However, physical violence should not be understated.

After 1623 the new Portuguese Empire of terror on the eastern side of the Amazon delta struck out at the other Europeans elsewhere in the delta. Because it was possible for local Indians to incorporate tobacco as a cash crop in their traditional agriculture, the Irish, Dutch, and English colonists were by 1623 employing some 12 to 15 ships to export 800,000 pounds of tobacco per annum. Irish colonists were still moving in, often in association with the Dutch. There is no doubt at all that English opinion had much resented James I's early retreat over the Amazon Company. Gondomar had recorded the anger in the current English parliament:

In Parliament it was proposed that the discovery and settlement of that part of the River Amazon belonged to this crown, and that on the representations of the Spanish ambassador the king had broken the patent and dissolved the company. Thus it was certain that, if this should be permitted, the ambassador would claim that the king should revoke the patents of the rest of the ancient companies that were in London, and that thus Parliament ought to attend to the remedy of it. The king tells me that he will set about punishing such great effrontery, since it is principally his concern . . .[46]

James was correct in believing that foreign policy was within his prerogative, but the security of chartered rights was within the Common Law's procedures, and even the traditional royal control of foreign policy was based on the assumption that, broadly, the Crown would reflect the prejudices and aspirations of the community of the realm. In Ireland the religious divide between the Crown and the Old English had created virtually insoluble political problems, but on the subject of the right to explore, trade, and settle in the Americas, the Old English were still basically of one mind with the influential classes of England proper – despite frantic attempts by Spanish diplomats and their priestly allies to insinuate that any Roman Catholic subject of King James who headed for America was doubly a traitor to his faith, since he was violating the absolute rights of the Catholic king and running away from his or her duty to fight Protestantism to the death at home. It was a most convenient theory – for Spain. To the Old English, fighting against both the predatory land-grabbing of the New English and an Irish crown bent on breaking their natural dominance of Irish parliaments, the prospect of new frontiers in the Americas could be attractive.

Viscount Falkland, an Englishman with a Scottish peerage named after the hunting palace of the royal Stuarts in Fife, became in 1622 lord deputy of Ireland. He had already an established interest in attempts to colonise Newfoundland, and he set about recruiting support in Ireland. That year saw the publication in Dublin of one of the few pieces of colonial promotion literature published outside London, *A Short Discourse of the New-Found Land*. It made much of 'The generall profite which may acccrue hereby to Ireland', which it saw as a mixture of export stimulation from the establishment of a new market, plus a share in the lucrative Newfoundland fishery profits, based on a huge market for cod in southern Europe. Even Falkland was aware that the facile optimism of the promotion literature, which was full of 'The facilitie and Easiness of this plantation', depicted as 'not above twelve or fourteene dayes sayle from the West of Ireland',[47] was somewhat overdone. He and Sir George Calvert, the future first Baron Baltimore, were mutually acquainted and were both trying to recruit in Ireland for Newfoundland plantations in the 1620s. Both were keen to secure support from men of substance. The odd Old English landowner did go out – like Sir Robert Talbot, who went to the Calvert grant of Ferryland in 1628 – but not many others seem to have followed. As in Nova Scotia, only the local Indians, here the Beothuks, had a culture capable of efficiently exploiting the land and rivers of the region. Even when Calvert transferred his attention to his Caroline grant of Maryland on the Chesapeake, it was not Old English aristocrats who came to this Catholic haven from Ireland, but peasants as indentured servants. The fact that, by 1660, 150 or so 'English' families were established on parts of the Newfoundland coast was remarkable in view of the failure of so many projects to persuade or con men of capital into participation.[48]

Though the outbreak of war with Spain and later France did further handicap the struggling English Newfoundland settlers, nearly all in the Avalon peninsula, by interrupting their sketchy sea communications with every impediment from ship requisitioning to impressment of seamen for the Navy Royal, to enemy privateers on the Atlantic; it cannot be said that war, even in the late 1620s, was a major determinant of their fate. Far different was the situation on the Amazon. There war was the sole determinant of the fate of English and Irish settlements which were otherwise economically viable and neither destructive of, nor unwelcome to, the local Indian peoples. They were simply assaulted by Portuguese forces from Belém led by ruthless and experienced Indian fighters like Pedro de Teixeira. Undefended settlements were overwhelmed or abandoned. Blockhouses could not usually hold out for long. There were no truly secure forts, and one Irish garrison of 70 men which, in the words of an official report on a Teixeira expedition, 'surrendered their fort and all the country without fighting', seemed to have made a smart decision until Teixeira, to the horror of a friar who was present, cold-bloodedly massacred 54 of them.

It was a war in which forces moved in canoes, in which both sides had vital Indian allies, and in which European troops used the normal contemporary accoutrements of European infantry war. Reinforcements from friendly sources were all important to morale and success. Despite the fact that the breakdown in Anglo–Spanish relations after the collapse of proposals for a Spanish match – not to mention the death of King James in 1625 – enabled lobbyists to secure a charter in early 1626 for the new English Guiana Company, the English and Irish on the Amazon rightly felt abandoned by their crowns. The new company was hopelessly undercapitalised and the Old English who controlled the Irish interest in the Amazon were extremely unhappy about its claim that all their settlements lay within the jurisdiction of its charter. Since 1625, the Portuguese had established a second major fort within the Amazon delta from which, to the distress of the Capuchin friars who accompanied them, they had established sway over neighbouring Indians by the most brutal forms of physical terror. In 1629, representatives of the old Irish interest had returned to the Amazon under the aegis of the Dutch West India Company and established a substantial stockaded fort at Tauregue on the north channel of the Amazon. They beat off a Portuguese attack in May, helped by the arrival of reinforcements. September saw a massive Portuguese attack led by Teixeira. At much the same time, a Dutch supply ship and ships of the new English Guiana Company with 400 men, but also with a missive demanding that the Irish accept the company's authority, were coming up the river. The commander of the Tauregue fort knew he was hopelessly outnumbered. He tried to play for time. When the Portuguese intercepted his attempt to communicate with the incoming English and Dutch, and threatened an assault which would certainly have ended in a massacre, Tauregue surrendered.

The commander then took advantage of the ambiguities of multiple identity. He explained that he had realised that if the Irish defenders 'joined with the 400 English and the reinforcements from Zeeland, the Irish and Catholics would lose command to the heretics and the Indians would be heretics not Catholics'.[49] This was predictably the prelude to a request for service under the King of Spain. What is clear is that King James' policy of systematic appeasement of imperial Spain in Guiana and the Amazon delta had two major disadvantages. It did not work as a means of extracting from Spain what he wanted, which was a less generally belligerent Spanish inter-national policy, an infanta as bride for his heir, and acceptance of the need to restore to his son-in-law Frederick, the Elector Palatine, territories on the Rhine which had been occupied by the Spanish army of Flanders. Secondly, appeasement of Spain produced deep divisions between himself and both the Protestant English of England proper and the Old English of Ireland. The former saw him as surrendering English interests to Catholic aggression. The latter had their hopes unrealistically raised by the closeness of James to Spain and in particular by the Spanish match, whose utter impracticality only became apparent to the Stuarts after an abortive visit to Madrid in 1623 by Prince Charles and James' greatest favourite, the Duke of Buckingham.

James was not the tool of Gondomar. His policy of peace with Spain in 1603–04 was profoundly sensible, as was his desire for better relations with the Spanish Crown thereafter. However, his inability to see the disadvantages of allowing a truce with the Dutch to free the Spaniards from a burden which checked their capacity to implement their ambitious policies was dis-concerting. Overweening intellectual conceit allied to chronic fiscal incontin-ence made James passionately anxious for a Spanish match which might enable him to pose as the reasonable mediator between the religious extremes of contemporary Europe, as well as collect a large dowry which would plug some of the holes in his financial system whilst reducing his dependence on his subjects. After 1618, with the Spanish Habsburgs funding warfare by their Austrian relatives which rapidly turned into a Counter-Reformation crusade, whilst the Spaniards themselves manoeuvred for position in the Dutch war they had obviously decided to renew in 1621, there was no case for pretending that Spain was other than an aggressive and triumphalist power. Nor were the bleatings of James Stuart likely to alter this reality.

Yet in no well-ordered court would Gondomar have been allowed to enjoy so much closeness to and freedom of expression before the king. The man was the ambassador of a foreign power whose exclusionary claims in the Americas were repudiated by all other European dynasties. In com-plaining of Raleigh, he once entered the royal presence literally shouting abuse. His ability to dictate the vocabulary of his dealings with King James was absurd and crucial. It turned negotiation into a tainted ongoing peace process which by 1623 was in terminal decay, but which before that was expressed in terms which ensured that the only possible outcome was unconditional surrender to Spain, whose idea of concession was a grudging willingness to accept that surrender in stages rather than instantly. Gondomar dinned it into James' ears that Philip III's rights to the Amazon were identical to those of James to England or Scotland, or Philip's to Portugal or Galicia.[50] James did not necessarily take it all at face value, but in private he cringed and wheedled when he needed to repudiate firmly indefensible assertions by a presumptuous ambassador. The king's appeasement of Gondomar, absolutely predictably, led to more and more extreme attitudes. In writing to Philip III in 1621, purring about the fact that there had been 'a very good example of the imprisonment of Captain Norte [North], who is in the Tower here, his goods and the ship in which he went to the river Amazon embargoed', Gondomar never contemplated even nominal reciprocity of any kind. His rhetoric about any Europeans in the Americas other than subjects of the Spanish Habsburgs was deliberately obliterative. He ended the same letter: 'And the English thieves' dens in Virginia and Bermuda constitute a matter which requires a very considered and effective remedy. May God keep the catholic person of your Majesty as christianity has need.'[51] Philip III died shortly afterwards.

The deep distrust which Gondomar's successful sabotage campaign against the Amazon Company roused among members of the 1621 English parliament has tended to drop out of recent revisionist versions of Jacobean politics, as indeed has Gondomar – despite clear evidence of his status as a major bogey figure, not just at the time of his two embassies of 1613–18 and 1620–22, but also in retrospect to members of the English parliament of 1626.[52] It mattered that Englishmen and Irishmen had learned to suspect that an active foreign policy by the Stuart dynasty was liable to become active betrayal of their subjects' overseas interests. Nor were Englishmen and Irishmen the only Stuart subjects to be exposed to this trait.

Sir William Alexander was the man who tried to extend the incipient Jacobean pattern of a 'three kingdoms' pattern of overseas colonisation to his native Scotland. A substantial laird patronised by magnates such as the Earl of Argyll and the Earl of Mar, he made his way into the affections of James VI as a fellow poet; followed him to London when he became James I; was appointed master of requests for Scotland in 1614, with effective power as its secretary of state (a position formalised by Charles I in 1626); and reached the peerage as Earl of Stirling in 1633. He was first interested in Newfoundland, securing a title from the Newfoundland Company to a large southern coastal area there, but then was seized by 'my designes for *New Scotland*'. In 1621, he was granted under the great seal of Scotland a vast area from the St Lawrence to the St Croix River, in modern times roughly Canada's Maritime Provinces plus the Gaspée peninsula. In 1624 he boasted 'that mine be the first National Patent that ever was clearly bounded within *America* by particular limits upon the Earth'. Passionately patriotic, he told English promoters of overseas colonisation that 'my countrimen would never adventure in such an Enterprize, unless it were as there was a *New France*, a *New Spaine*, and a *New England*, that they might likewise have a *New Scotland* . . .'.

His first bid to plant a colony of people from south-west Scotland in Nova Scotia in 1622–23 was an expensive fiasco. Many of them deserted to the Newfoundland fishing industry. Funds were boosted by a characteristic James VI and I device of creating an order of baronets of Nova Scotia in 1624. They paid Alexander for the privilege of the baronetcy, which carried notional Nova Scotian land grants, and the option of paying more to duck the obligation to send out settlers. Even so, Alexander had to commit his personal fortune heavily for the 1627–28 expedition which sailed from Dumbarton and tried to establish a small colony. It failed, but in 1629 an Anglo–Scots expedition finally succeeded. One group which was led by Lord Ochiltree settled on Cape Breton Island, where they were promptly attacked, captured, and shipped back to Europe by the French. The rest, led by Sir William Alexander, younger, went to Port Royal in peninsular Nova Scotia, where they maintained for three years a Scottish colony. In April 1629, a truce terminated two years of war between Charles I and the Crown of France. In the negotiations which followed it was clear that French Canada, seized by a New England expedition led by the Kirkes in July 1629, would have to be returned because seized after the truce. New Scotland, to the French Acadia, was different.

There were long arguments. Alexander pointed out that Scottish colonisation had been peaceful; was secured to him by charters of 1621 and 1625; and that if the French had ever been in the area of his settlement, they had long ago abandoned it. The French chose to make it a point of honour, threatening to break negotiations. Desperate for the unpaid portion of his French queen's dowry, as well as for the end of a botched war, Charles I settled by the final Treaty of Saint-Germain-en-Laye on a bogus compromise. Alexander retained his rights, evacuated Port Royal, and was to have the right to resite the colony nearby. The truth was that his title and a £10,000 sterling grant to compensate for his losses 'by giveing ordour for removeing of his Colony at our express command' were a cover for surrender. He never received the money. No attempt was made to resite the colony before 1710.

Alexander had hyped his schemes in a 1624 tract *An Encouragement to Colonies*, which held out Nova Scotia as a constructive national alternative to service as mercenary soldiers in Europe, or migration to Ireland, for Scotland's surplus population. It has been convincingly argued that European seventeenth-century colonisation in the area he chose was misguided. Neither climate nor soil was a rational choice for farmers who could remain in Europe. Only the native Indian peoples of the region, principally the Abenaki, had a culture capable of exploiting the potential of the area – as the disastrous history of the English colony of Maine, French Acadia, and Nova Scotia showed by 1690. By that date 'it was the Indian peoples of the north-eastern maritime region who held sway in 1690, and not the European colonies',[53] not least because of the destructive innate mutual intolerance and violence of the rival European cultures. By 1690 Maine, Acadia, and Nova Scotia were such that it has been said 'All three colonies, in short, existed as shells.'[54]

The Earl of Stirling's efforts were those of an undercapitalised court projector whose ignorance led to disaster. His death in 1640 was a shrewd career move, as the disruption of his funeral at Stirling by frustrated and enraged creditors showed. Yet in the last analysis the fate of his colony in Nova Scotia was settled by colonial war between Charles I and Louis XIII. It has been rightly pointed out that 'While it lasted, the Scottish settlement at Port Royal was just as successful as any other new colony in North America up until 1629, and more so than most.'[55] In 1632 it was a lot healthier than Acadia in 1690, where the governor was a fugitive guerrilla leader, the population chronically disturbed by enemy incursions, and the link between governor and governed minimal. Charles I chose to back down in the face of Richelieu's will-power, itself explained by the need to maximise the Bourbon dynasty's image as the protector of Catholic Frenchmen from foreign heretics. The French held a very poor hand in North America. Port Royal was a willed issue. By failing to call their bluff, Charles paid the reverse of the coin in which Richelieu dealt. His surrender completed the pattern of sell-out of the English and Irish colonies on the Amazon by his father, depriving his dynasty of an important potential propaganda prop as protectors of the three kingdoms' outward thrust. The French had threatened 'une petite guerre' against the Scottish expedition of 1623 as soon as they knew of it.[56] The irony is that they were able to destroy a potentially enduring Scottish colony in Nova Scotia without firing as much as a shot against it. Like King James, King Charles chose unsuccessful war in Europe and appeasement in the Americas. The potentially unifying effect for their complex of subjects of selective but vigorous colonial warfare against a Spain and France which they ended up fighting anyway was not to the taste of the first two Stuart rulers of England and Ireland. The colonial future lay in North America south of the St Lawrence and north of the most northerly Spanish garrison, at San Augustín in Florida, not least because that stretch of eastern seaboard was remote from the reach of French or Spanish power.

Self-help was to be the key to initial survival and success for Englishmen overseas who faced a situation in which force played a key role in their relations with other peoples, European or non-European. The English settlements in North America faced danger only from the nature of their relations with the indigenous peoples, at least in the first decades. In the competing empires of trade and protection in eastern waters in the seventeenth century, other Englishmen – indeed on occasion Englishmen who had already seen service in North America – faced dangers from rival European monopolists or would-be monopolists. Organised under the aegis of the English East India Company, these men were to discover what Englishmen on the Chesapeake or Amazon discovered, that under the early Stuarts the only truly reliable form of security available to them was the musket in their hands, or in Asia more realistically the cannon on their gundecks. So far from being able to count on the Crown to act as a shield, they were lucky if it did not fine or repudiate them after they defended themselves.

Notes and references

1. J.P. Sommerville, *Politics and Ideology in England 1603–1640* (Longman, London, pbk edn, 1986), pp. 11–12 and 115–16.

2. Bruce Galloway, *The Union of England and Scotland 1603–1608* (John Donald, Edinburgh, 1986).

3. John R. Cramsie, 'Crown Finance and Governance under James I: Projects and fiscal policy 1603–1625' (University of St Andrews unpublished PhD thesis, 1997), Chap. 5.

4. Bruce R. Galloway and Brian P. Levack (eds.), *The Jacobean Union: Six tracts of 1604*, Scottish History Society, 4th Series, Vol. 21 (Edinburgh, 1986), p. 39.

5. Clive Senior, *A Nation of Pirates: English piracy in its heyday* (Davis and Charles, Newton Abbot, 1976).

6. David Delison Hebb, *Piracy and the English Government 1616–42* (Scolar Press, Aldershot, 1994).

7. Willard M. Wallace, *Sir Walter Raleigh* (Princeton University Press, Princeton, NJ, 1959), pp. 189–201.

8. Linda Levy Peck, *Northampton: Patronage and policy at the court of James I* (Allen and Unwin, London, 1982), pp. 106–08.

9. Michael Strachan, *Sir Thomas Roe 1581–1644: A life* (Michael Russell, Wilton, 1989), Chaps. 6 and 7.

10. Gordon Donaldson, *Scotland: James V to James VII* (Oliver and Boyd, Edinburgh, 1971), p. 216.

11. W.R. Kermack, *The Scottish Highlands. A short history (c. 300–1746)* (Johnston and Bacon, Edinburgh, 1957), Chap. 10.

12. Allan I. Macinnes, *Clanship, Commerce and the House of Stuart, 1603–1788* (Tuchwell, Phantassie, East Lothian, 1996), pp. 60–61.

13. *Ibid.*, p. 59.

14. W.R. Kermack, *The Clan MacGregor* (Johnston and Bacon, Edinburgh, 1953), pp. 12–24.

15. Kermack, *Highlands*, pp. 85–87.

16. Andrew McKerral, *Kintyre in the Seventeenth Century* (Oliver and Boyd, Edinburgh, 1948).

17. Text in James F. Larkin and Paul L. Hughes (eds.), *Stuart Royal Proclamations. Vol I: Royal Proclamations of King James I 1603–1625* (Clarendon Press, Oxford, 1973), pp. 27–28.

18. CSP Domestic, 1603–10, p. 329, citing Dudley Carleton to John Chamberlain, 20 August 1606.

19. CSP Ireland, James I, 1608–10, Preface, p. xxii.

20. *Ibid.*

21. *Ibid.*, p. xxxi.

22. CSP Domestic, 1603–10, p. 373, King to Archbishop of Canterbury, 5 October 1607.

23. John McCavitt, 'The Flight of the Earls, 1607', *Irish Historical Studies*, 29 (1994), pp. 159–73.

24. Maurice J. Lee Jr, *James I and Henri IV* (University of Illinois Press, Urbana, IL, 1970), p. 92.

25. 'A Proclamation touching the Earles of Tyrone and Tyrconnell', Westminster, 15 November 1607, in Larkin and Hughes (eds.), *Stuart Royal Proclamations. Vol. I*, pp. 176–79.

26. Arthur H. Williamson, *Scottish National Consciousness in the Age of James VI* (John Donald, Edinburgh, 1979), pp. 132–33.

27. Sir John Davis, *A Discovery of the True Causes Why Ireland Was Never Entirely Subdued*, ed. James P. Myers Jr (Catholic University of America, Washington DC, 1988), Introduction, p. 56.

28. Hans S. Pawlisch, *Sir John Davies and the Conquest of Ireland: A study in legal imperialism* (Cambridge University Press, Cambridge, 1985).

29. Davies, *Discovery*, ed. Myers, p. 102.

30. *Ibid.*, p. 107.

31. *Ibid.*, pp. 223–24.

32. Sir Arthur Chichester's recital of services to the King, CSP Ireland, James I, 1608–10, pp. 519–21.

33. M. Perceval-Maxwell, *The Scottish Migration to Ulster in the Reign of James I* (Routledge and Kegan Paul, London, 1973), pp. 135–37.

34. R.J. Hunter, 'Sir Ralph Bingley, *c.* 1570–1627: Ulster Planter', in Peter Roebuck (ed.), *Plantation to Partition: Essays in Ulster history in honour of J.L. McCracken* (Blackstaff Press, Belfast, 1981), pp. 14–28.

35. A. Clarke, 'The Genesis of the Ulster Rising of 1641', *ibid.*, pp. 29–45.

36. A.T.Q. Stewart, *The Narrow Ground: Aspects of Ulster 1609–1969* (Faber and Faber, London, 1977), pp. 85–90.

37. David Stevenson, *Scottish Covenanters and Irish Confederates* (Ulster Historical Foundation, Belfast, 1981), pp. 6–7.

38. *Ibid.*, Chap. 4, and Jane H. Ohlmeyer, *Civil War and Restoration in the Three Stuart Kingdoms: The career of Randal MacDonnell, Marquis of Antrim, 1609–1683* (Cambridge University Press, Cambridge, 1993), Introduction and Chap. 1.

39. David Stevenson, *Alasdair MacColla and the Highland Problem in the Seventeenth Century* (John Donald, Edinburgh, 1980).

40. William S. Maltby, *The Black Legend in England: The development of anti-Spanish sentiment* (Duke University Press, Durham, NC, 1971).

41. Joyce Lorimer (ed.), *English and Irish Settlement on the River Amazon 1550–1646*, Hakluyt Society, 2nd Series, No. 171 (London, 1989), p. 67.

42. Sir Walter Raleigh to the Earl of Salisbury [1607], Historical Manuscripts Commission, Salisbury, XIX (HMSO, London, 1965), p. 455.

43. Sir Walter Raleigh to Viscount Haddington [?1610], *ibid.*, XXI (HMSO, London, 1970), p. 283.

44. John Hemming, *Red Gold: The conquest of the Brazilian Indians, 1500–1760* (Harvard University Press, Cambridge, MA, 1978), pp. 210–12.

45. *Ibid.*, p. xv.

46. Gondomar to Philip IV, 2 May 1621, printed in Lorimer (ed.), *English and Irish Settlement on the Amazon*, pp. 222–23.

47. G.T. Cell (ed.), *Newfoundland Discovered: English attempts at colonisation, 1610–1630*, Hakluyt Society, 2nd Series, No. 160 (London, 1982), reprints *A Short Discourse of the New-Found Land*, on pp. 227–37. The quotes are on pp. 229–30 and p. 231 respectively.

48. *Ibid.*, p. 57.

49. Lorimer (ed.), *English and Irish Settlement on the Amazon*, p. 92.

50. Gondomar to Philip III, 30 May 1620, *ibid.*, p. 205.

51. Gondomar to Philip III, 16 February 1621, *ibid.*, pp. 218–19.

52. Conrad Russell, *Parliaments and English Politics 1621–1629* (Clarendon Press, Oxford, 1979), p. 302.

53. John G. Reid, *Acadia, Maine and New Scotland: Marginal colonies in the seventeenth century* (University of Toronto Press, Toronto, 1981), p. 185.

54. *Ibid.*, p. 189.

55. John G. Reid, *Sir William Alexander and North American Colonization: A reappraisal*, lecture delivered at the University of Edinburgh, 1 May 1990 (Centre for Canadian Studies, University of Edinburgh, 1990).

56. Memorial of the comte de Tillières, printed in George P. Insh, *Scottish Colonial Schemes 1620–1686* (Maclehose, Glasgow, 1922), Appendix A, pp. 212–13.

CHAPTER SEVEN

No enthusiasts for empire: the English East India Company and the struggle for maritime trade in seventeenth-century Asia to 1689

Breaking in or the East India Company as the trader armed before 1660

An important key to the erection of the English East India Company was the very marked success of the Dutch *voorcompagniën*, nine joint-stock companies formed by Dutch merchants in the 1590s for the purpose of trading with Asia by the oceanic route. These proved to be the precursors of the mighty United Dutch East India Company formed by their union in 1602 and usually referred to for convenience by its Dutch acronym as the VOC. The *voorcompagniën* were formidable in their own right. Their total capitalisation was not far, if at all, short of that of the VOC, and they carried much smaller overheads than that body was to elect to carry so they were very profitable once they had overcome their teething problems. There was therefore always an element of rivalry with the Dutch in the pressure which a group of wealthy London merchants placed upon the government of Queen Elizabeth to charter the English East India Company, usually referred to by historians for convenience as the EIC. If such a body had not been set up, Elizabeth's subjects would have ended up buying Asian imports from the Dutch. They were not likely to buy these goods openly from the pioneers of European oceanic trade with Asia, the Portuguese, for Elizabeth had been at war with Philip II of Spain since 1585, and he had been the ruler of Portugal since 1580. To surrender the oceanic routes to Asia to the Dutch was to pay them the middleman's profit, which was not going to be modest.

On the other hand, the Anglo–Dutch relationship was supposed to be intimate and friendly. Elizabeth was allied to the United Netherlands by the Treaty of Nonsuch of 1585, which had been the occasion of the outbreak of

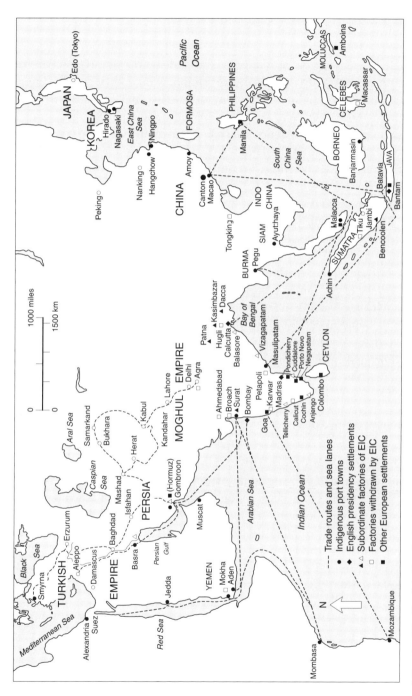

Map 4 The English East India Company in the trading world of seventeenth-century Asia

the Anglo–Spanish War. The two regimes were linked by a common Protestantism, as well as by ancient social and economic ties between eastern
England and the Netherlands. Yet Elizabeth had little real sympathy for
the Dutch, whom she saw as rebels and vulgar republicans. She was also
desperate to escape from her dangerous struggle with Philip II, so chartering
an east India company which, by definition, would defy the Portuguese
claim to monopoly rights all the way down the African coast as well as
throughout the seas of Asia, was not something she regarded as desirable if
it would complicate an Anglo–Spanish peace settlement. To the London
merchants, the news that the Dutch were proposing to hire English ships to
expand their Asian enterprise was the last straw. In July 1599 they petitioned the queen to charter a company to trade in Asian waters, and they
did so in the strongest terms, stressing that the national interest was at
stake.[1] The queen still stalled for over a year. Only when Anglo–Spanish
talks broke down yet again did she invite a new petition and charter the 218
petitioners as the EIC on the last day of 1600.

The linkages between the EIC and the Netherlands are well illustrated
by the career of Sir James Lancaster, who was general of the first fleet sent
by the EIC to Asia. It sailed in April 1601, returning to anchor in the
Downs in September 1603, by which time Elizabeth was dead and King
James had succeeded her. Lancaster had been an English merchant resident in Portugal until the Spanish take-over of 1580. After commanding a
ship against the Armada in 1588, he led a filibustering expedition into the
Indian Ocean in 1591–92, but was shipwrecked in the Caribbean on his
return voyage. He recouped by leading an Anglo–Huguenot privateering
raid in 1595 on the Portuguese Brazilian harbour of Recife, where valuable
Asian goods from a big carrack were stored. At the mouth of the harbour
were three large ships described as 'Hollanders' in Hakluyt's narrative of
the episode. These had been summoned from Europe to carry the carrack's
goods to Portugal. These ships thoughtfully cleared out of the way to allow
the raiders to land and rout an unsteady militia which failed to use brass
cannon well placed to inflict the sort of casualties which the attackers subsequently suffered when they ran into regular troops as they moved inland.
Nevertheless, the raiders escaped with their loot, much of it carried by the
'Hollanders' after they renegotiated their original contracts. Business was
business, especially for ships needing a return cargo.

These ships were not Dutch, as Henry Roberts' contemporary pamphlet
Lancaster His Allarums shows. Roberts called them Flemings, which is inherently more likely, for to the Luso-Hispanic authorities ships from the northern Netherlands would have been rebels from 'the disobedient provinces'.
The confusion in the sources reminds us that it was in fact difficult to tell
the difference between peoples who before 1579 had been part of a single

ethnic and cultural community, one which might have been held together with better luck or more effective and prompt foreign assistance to the originally widespread resistance among the Netherlands provinces to the centralising policies of their Spanish overlords. It needed a huge military and religious effort to create a Counter-Reformation culture in the southern Netherlands, which sharply separated their communal identity from that of the rebel republic evolving under heretical leadership to the north.[2]

Lancaster's EIC fleet of the 1601–03 voyage went out literally in the tracks of Dutch predecessors, reading on rocks in a Madagascar anchorage messages from five ships of a *voorcompagniën* fleet of 13 vessels which had left Holland in April 1601 under Jacob van Heemskerk and Wolpert Harmenszoon. Lancaster himself had at least one Dutch pilot in his fleet. When he reached Achin to trade for spices he found two resident Dutch factors left behind by another Dutch expedition which had recently been in Achin, to collect next year's cargo. A Dutch pinnace which had been separated from Joris van Spielberg's squadron came in later to anchor alongside the English ships. At this time there is no suggestion of animosity between the Dutch and the English. It was the establishment of the VOC in 1602 which radically altered the situation. It was an autonomous structure with quasi-state powers and was designed to assault Luso-Hispanic positions and trade in Asia, securing its victories – some very hard earned – by the construction of forts and the maintenance of expensive garrisons. To pay for the staggering cost of its aggressive policies, the VOC hoped to secure privilege and monopoly. In its first eight or so decades it was driven everywhere by a passionate, ingrained mercantilist lust for the chance to screw profits into super-profits by buying only from those it could coerce into selling well below market price, and selling in a market where its monopoly position meant that it had its customers over a barrel. The VOC was far larger than the EIC from the start. To launch it 6,500,000 florins of capital were quickly subscribed, and this was in real terms more than the annual revenue of the English state. The EIC had started with a modest £30,000 of capital, later augmented to £72,000, by which time several Dutch capitalists who had not found a niche in the capital structure of the VOC had moved money into its English rival. One Amsterdammer alone, for example, contributed £4000 to the EIC. As a result there were always more big Dutch ships, and therefore more Dutch seaboard cannon, in Asian waters in the seventeenth century than there were English. The VOC sent out fifty-five great ships in its opening seven years, the EIC twelve in nine. It was the Dutch who broke the Portuguese monopoly of access to the Maldive Islands, the pre-eminent spice islands, but of course they then went on to enforce against both the inhabitants and other Europeans a ruthless monopoly of their own.[3]

The Portuguese *Estado da India* was a system for controlling Asian maritime commerce through a series of fortified bases from which the Portuguese exercised a wide though shallow maritime supremacy based on a few ocean-going ships and superior naval gunpower. Portuguese naval guns were neither numerous nor very efficient, but they normally were trying to terrorise a few big Asian ships which had no battery guns, ships which indeed were constructed in a way that meant their hulls could sustain neither attack from cannon fire, nor the stresses created by trying to mount and fire shipboard cannon.[4] It was always rather a different story when the Portuguese had to deal with the Chinese junk in the Far East. The junk was a stoutly constructed vessel and under the Ming dynasty it was normal for junks of the imperial Chinese navy to carry artillery. Portuguese tactics based simply on ruthless use of violence at the first opportunity did not work against such a naval power. In 1522 the Chinese defeated a Portuguese flotilla off Tunmen. Elsewhere in Asian waters the locals inevitably responded to the Portuguese threat, and some worked out ways of at least partially countering it by the end of the sixteenth century. Muslim states like Aceh in Sumatra began to build bigger, more heavily planked ships on which artillery could be mounted. Though they by no means always won their battles with the Portuguese, they did raise the price for preying on them to prohibitive levels. The inhabitants of the south-western coast of India, the Malabar Coast, went one better by developing small ships which were known as grabs, powered by both oars and sail. They operated in packs, using heavy guns mounted on the centre line and firing forward to harass to death big European ships caught at a disadvantage in the maze of coastal lagoons and channels – dominated by offshore and onshore breezes rather than by the major wind patterns – which was their natural habitat. In the eighteenth century they were to capture a British Eastindiaman in the heyday of the EIC's naval service, and in the seventeenth century they were so effective against the Portuguese that they were hired by the great Moghul port of Surat in Gujerat to protect its commerce from the persistent aggression it suffered from the Portuguese strongholds of Diu and Daman which sat on either side of the approach to Surat through the Gulf of Cambay. Thus the Portuguese were already being pushed on the defensive at sea. Their swing towards territorial conquest in Sri Lanka and East Africa was to some extent compensatory, though it did probably prove a handicap when the waves of English and Dutch shipping started to beat against what was left of their naval ascendancy, and the Portuguese missionary establishment furiously opposed any reduction in territorial commitment to free resources for the defence of the underlying maritime structures.[5]

The Portuguese nevertheless persisted in their policy of trying to drive all other Europeans out of Asian waters into the seventeenth century. The three great Islamic empires of the Ottoman Turks, the Safavids of Iran, and the Moghuls of India were each in their own way capable of handling the problem of European naval aggression, basically by using their control over resident European merchants as leverage to discipline and if necessary punish the excesses of pirates, whose takings were always a small fraction in value of what could be made from legitimate access to the land-based economies of these imperial states. The Japanese were to operate a similar system to protect their unarmed merchant ships until they opted to for-swear overseas trade on their own account entirely. The Portuguese tried to uphold by force in India the sort of monopoly of overseas trade which the Dutch were granted by the Tokugawa military dictatorship in Japan after 1640. In December 1612 the EIC's Captain Thomas Best, lying off Surat with two ships, had to fight off with cannon fire an attack by four Portuguese galleons. Even so, their continuing and threatening presence made him leave early without full cargoes. In trying to pressure the Em-peror Jahangir into banning the Dutch and English from his realm, the Portuguese over-reached themselves, as the events of the first voyage sent out by the EIC after it had terminated its original system of separate fund-ing for individual voyages showed. This was in 1614–15, the general of the fleet being the experienced Nicholas Downton who had been second in command to Sir Henry Middleton in the sixth voyage. Downton had to fight the Portuguese to trade at Surat, but he could afford to fight them with no holds barred, for they were already at war with a Jahangir tired of their endless presumption. In a battle with a viceregal fleet from Goa, the capital of the *Estado da India*, at Swally Hole (the anchorage for Surat), Downton's men bloodily repulsed Portuguese boarders whom Downton admitted fought with desperate bravery. The main part of the action saw the English make excellent use of their main battery guns to pound the viceroy's ships until the Portuguese broke off the fighting, thereby admit-ting a decisive defeat. That was in January 1615, and it was a victory over traditional Catholic enemies.

By January of that year Downton's fleet was in Bantam, trading for the spices that could be bought much more profitably by merchants who car-ried Indian wares – such as cottons – which were in strong demand in what was to become in the twentieth century the Indonesian archipelago. Downton loaded mace, a valuable spice, as well as silks and porcelain, the latter being brought to Bantam by Chinese merchants. Then alarming reports of Dutch behaviour began to come in: 'there came newes by a juncke from the Moluccas of the *Thomasine* [an EIC ship] being there, and of twelve sile of Hollanders at Ternate, which hindered all men they could from trade'. That sums up the tone of virtually all the reports which reached Downton about Dutch behaviour in eastern waters. There were reports of the Dutch violently repelling the EIC's *Concord*, commanded by George Ball and sent to trade at Amboina and in the Bandas for spices.[6] At Bantam the representatives of the VOC were hostile and bullying in their attitudes towards the English, using force to deny EIC factors access to the spice market. Like the Portuguese, the Dutch aimed at monopolising the contacts between indigenous regimes and European markets. Force was part of their market strategy. Exchanges between EIC and VOC ships became notably guarded. Edward Dodsworth, an EIC factor who wrote an important account of Downton's voyage, referred to the 'inbred bowrishe dispossitione'[7] of the Dutch. Boorishness was less a national characteristic and more a business option which only confrontation by equal or superior force was likely to modify. Matters were far more polarised than they had been in the days of Edmund Scott, EIC factor at Bantam from 1603 until he returned with the second fleet in 1605. Scott reported that the local people could not distinguish between the English and Dutch, though even at this stage the confusion could be an embarrassment to the English when the Dutch roughed up the locals, intimidating them with the power of their naval gunnery.[8]

It is perhaps too easy to see the EIC and VOC as manifestations of their respective national imperialisms. There is a case for the view that the VOC in particular was by no means exclusively Dutch in personnel. Its labour pool was drawn from a wide area of northern Europe and included many Germans, Scandinavians, and Scots. In its relationship with the authorities of the United Netherlands who had chartered it, it was aggressively independent minded. It established few territorial colonies, being more emporialist than imperialist in the sense that it tried to establish control of markets – emporia – on a monopolistic basis, but normally not of territory. The VOC of the seventeenth and eighteenth centuries was not at all like European territorial imperialists of the nineteenth century. It did not even bear any resemblance to the Spanish *conquistadores* who went out looking for territories full of exploitable peasants, just as the great Islamic conquerors like the Moghuls did.[9] On the other hand, the VOC did have a basic relationship with the emerging Dutch nation which was real in ethnic terms, because only a sense of nationality would enable the United Netherlands to cohere sufficiently to survive without accepting the uncivilised option of creating a centralised state like other powerful Europeans. The EIC was a London company, dominated by wealthy City magnates. It was the overseas trading company most successful at keeping control of its organisation in purely mercantile hands by resisting the attempts by gentry, nobles, and leading court figures to take over the direction of its policies. Coups by such elements were a regular feature of many colonial chartered companies. The EIC exploited King James' need for loans to force him to confirm and strengthen its original charter in 1609.

The main link which the EIC had with the body politic was through its head, the king. They supplied him with money through gifts and customs duties. It was to him they looked to uphold their privileges and to protect them against foreign aggression. Their central privilege was that of a monopoly of English trade east of the Cape of Good Hope. To give the EIC its due, it was not so foolish as to try to exclude any other Europeans from trading east of the Cape. In India it was anxious to secure firm trading rights and privileges from the Moghul Empire, secured by treaty, but ran into the problem that the Moghuls regarded diplomatic dealings with mere merchants as beneath the imperial dignity – especially when the Portuguese Jesuits resident at the Moghul court kept stressing that the English sent by the EIC to treat were just hucksters, unlike the Portuguese, whose mercantile and missionary endeavours had always operated within a firm framework of royal authority. As a result the EIC paid for the sending of a royal ambassador, Sir Thomas Roe, who attended the Moghul court between 1615 and his return in 1619. All he achieved in the way of commercial agreement was a few firmans, or imperial rescripts, which were valid only for the life of the reigning emperor, but which did place English trade on a defensible legal basis in Surat and throughout the empire. Enforcing them was always a struggle, but Roe was crucial in persuading the Emperor Jahangir that behind the EIC stood a sovereignty he could understand and of which he could with dignity take cognisance.

Just how far that sovereignty was truly behind the EIC elsewhere in Asia was an interesting question. By 1619 the English and Dutch had been at war for some time in the spice archipelago. Jan Pieterszoon Coen, the hardest of Dutch hard-liners in Asia, had argued to the home authorities in 1614 that 'trade in Asia must be driven and maintained under the protection and favour of Your Honours' own weapons, and that the weapons must be paid for by the profits from the trade; so that we cannot carry on trade without war nor war without trade'.[10] It was not a view which commanded universal support within the VOC in the archipelago. Men like Laurens Real and Steven van der Hagen had grave doubts about the exclusive contracts and blockades which the Dutch imposed on the Moluccas in exchange for 'protecting' the locals from Spanish and Portuguese intrusions which, while bad enough in their own way, were nothing like as sustained a tyranny as the Dutch one. These men also argued that the VOC would do better to make moderate profits from a large volume of trade in free markets, rather than aim at excessive profit on small turnovers in monopolistically controlled markets, where the overheads for the coercion needed to sustain the monopoly would burden the company with debt. They had a point. Coen's policy received a heavy boost in 1619 with his successful seizure of the port of Jakarta, in defiance of orders from the

Heeren XVII (the lords seventeen), who ruled the VOC from the distant Netherlands. Yet his critics were right: his way imposed appalling overheads on the company. It was by no means a foregone conclusion that the VOC would persist in its bully-boy tactics. The Moluccas were tempting because their rulers were devoid of naval strength. There was no comeback. It was an ideal scenario to encourage violence.

The way to discuss the matter with the likes of Coen was to fight him. By 1618, the EIC had decided to do so. Its court of directors resolved 'to send a good strength both to the Mollocoes and Banda . . . to trye what the Hollanders will doe if a man of couradge may be had that will not endure their wrongs'. Fighting was not going to convert the pathologically anti-English Coen, but if hard pounding looked like seriously undermining any possible profitability for the VOC, he might lose out in its internal debate over policy, a debate which was active both in the Netherlands and in the archipelago. The brave man who led out the fleet in the spring of 1618 was none other than that old warhorse Sir Thomas Dale, the former martial governor of Virginia. With his six ships added to the 1617 fleet under Martin Pring which was still at Bantam, where there was street fighting between the English and Dutch, Dale had the edge on Coen in terms of ship numbers and forced him to withdraw to the Moluccas, though the Dutch garrison in the fort Coen had built in Jakarta in defiance of the local ruler held out heroically against a combined English and Jacartan siege. On the point of surrender, the Dutch, who had defiantly re-christened the fort Batavia, were saved by the insistence of the local ruler that the English withdraw. Coen returned, raised the siege, and with superior forces inflicted heavy damage on the English. Dale died of disease. His right-hand man, John Jourdain, former factor at Bantam, was killed in action. The surviving English commander, Martin Pring, brought reinforcements to Sumatra in 1619. In the spring of 1620, reinforced by three more ships from Surat, he was heading for Bantam in April, fully expecting bloody combat, when news reached him via the ship *Bull* that an accord had been reached between the two companies in Europe in July 1619. The Dutch were coming to the end of their 12-year truce with Spain which expired in 1621, so they agreed that the English should have one third of the spice trade of the Moluccas, Bandas, and Amboina, as well as half of the pepper trade of Java. On their part, the English were to pay a third of the costs of a station at Pulicat on the south-eastern or Coromandel Coast of India, and were to contribute ten ships for a common defence force. It was an agreement which Coen loathed, and over the next four years he systematically undermined it.[11]

About the only instance of Anglo–Dutch cooperation in Asia after 1620 came in 1621 when they combined to defeat a Portuguese viceregal fleet. Coen's ruthless conquest of the Bandas and Amboina in the early 1620s placed him in a position to exclude the English, which he did. In 1622 the EIC, which had developed an interest in the Persian silk trade, had cooperated with the forces of the shah of Persia to eliminate the fortified positions from which the *Estado da India* dominated and exploited the trade of the Persian Gulf. This was the town and citadel on the island of Hormuz, still in the twentieth century a major strategic pivot. First the Anglo–Persian force took out the covering fortress of Qishm on the mainland opposite Hormuz. Its garrison surrendered in a few days when exposed to bombardment from the sea by the EIC ships. Those ships then transported the Persian army to the island, where the town fell at once and the citadel after a stubborn defence. The town was transferred to the mainland because of the Persian lack of seapower to defend it. The citadel was garrisoned. On balance, the world was a slightly better place with the removal of a major impediment to honest commerce. Portugal was passionately resentful, but by 1624 had given up hope of recovering Hormuz.

What was really significant for Anglo–Dutch relations in this Anglo–Persian episode was the treatment the EIC received at the hands of the English Crown. Lord High Admiral the Duke of Buckingham, acting through his able chief commissioner for the navy, Sir John Coke, reckoned that the EIC had gained goods worth £100,000 in the Hormuz campaign, and blandly demanded his tenth of £10,000, under threat that he would indict the company for piracy in his court if it did not pay. A civil lawyer consulted by the company pointed out that the tenth was a usage, not a statutory right, and usually only levied on those to whom the admiral had granted letters of marque. The learned doctor added most significantly that all this was hypothetical and that he would never plead against the all-powerful favourite Buckingham. Despite the legal facts and the endless murderous attacks by the Portuguese on EIC ships, the company had to buy off the duke. It was then shamelessly fleeced for another £10,000 by King James, for himself. The precious pair of monarch and favourite then went on to tell the EIC that it would have the honour of largely funding a scheme for state trade in Persian silks sold to them by Robert Sherley, the sort of ambiguous scamp whom the Stuarts too often found irresistible, especially when he promised £500,000 per annum in customs revenue from a plan which the EIC knew to be radically unsound and from which they were only saved by the death of King James in 1625. This monarch was hardly a reliable supporter of the interests of the EIC.

And it needed support in March 1623 when Gabriel Towerson, the EIC chief factor on Amboina – along with nine other Englishmen, ten Japanese mercenaries, and a Portuguese overseer – were all beheaded after torture. The Dutch governor, Van Speult, may have made a tragic mistake in believing inherently implausible stories about a plot against the Dutch, but it was the sort of mistake Dutch governors were liable to go on making until Coen's policies were discountenanced. The English had in fact shifted the emphasis of their trade away from the Moluccas to Bantam and Macassar, but even there they were being aggressively hustled by the VOC.[12] The Dutch only had complete control over the Moluccas, with their invaluable nutmeg, clove, and mace crops, after the Spaniards finally withdrew from Ternate in 1663, but the implications of their drive for monopoly through-out the archipelago were clear long before then, especially in 1656 when they overdid deliberate lowering of clove production to raise prices and created absolute shortages in both the European and Asian markets. Al-though the ships and men of the EIC had fought stoutly, they faced an acute problem in the shape of the vastly superior VOC shipping presence in Asian waters, which of course meant superiority in broadside cannon. In the period 1621–30 the Dutch sent 148 ships to Asia compared with 53 English, and in 1631–40 the respective figures were 151 to 52.[13] The EIC needed support from the Crown, support which could most easily be given in the narrow seas around the British Isles, over which the Stuart dynasty was wont to assert very extensive jurisdictional rights. The problem was that the collapse of the Spanish match and the impending war with Spain had turned the Dutch into desirable allies.

The year 1624 saw almost endless correspondence and discussion between the ministers of King James, the Dutch, and the EIC. The last named even embarked on a literary campaign to draw attention to its wrongs. It sponsored the publication of *A True Relation of the Late Cruel and Barbarous Tortures and Execution Done Upon the English at Amboyna*. Of this it eventually resolved to print 2000 copies in English, 1000 in Dutch, 'and then to have the press broken'. James approved the printing but only if the publication did not display bitterness towards the government of the Dutch Republic. From start to finish he dragged his feet over any action which might involve further complications in his already complex foreign policy.[14] In fact allies – whether of comparable stature such as the Dutch in the seventeenth century, or disproportionately powerful like the United States in the twentieth century – are often almost as big a problem as declared enemies, for they presume on their special status. There is nothing inher-ently wrong with resisting an ally's unreasonable pressure, especially if it is exerted by a body which is not technically the government or which can be distanced from the government if that government so chooses, and force is often the only form of discourse capable of commanding attention. So when Dutch East India fleets were allowed to sail through the Channel in 1625 in full view of the English Navy Royal and without any molestation, after it had become obvious that the Dutch had no intention of making serious reparation for the Amboina episode, the implications for the EIC were clear. Many of its stockholders concluded that Sir Morris Abbott, deputy governor and from March 1624 governor of the company, had been excessively gullible in dealing with the king and his council, accepting pompous assurances at face value and acting as a government stooge in playing down the agitation and pressure which was the only way the company was likely to secure state support. The EIC was well aware that 'the French and Danes trade freely in the Indies because wrongs done to them are revenged at home, if His Majesty will do the like the Dutch will soon give over molesting the King's subjects'.[15] The king's evasive and alarming response to the effect that he would show his commitment by becoming a member of the company was a suggestion that the company was fortunately able to decline. Similar proposals were to be made on behalf of his heir, the future Charles I. The EIC knew full well that neither man would pay a penny for the large slab of stock they would assume to be their due and that they and their court cronies would loot a company they had hitherto only intermittently fleeced.

Threats by the EIC to cease trading were not implemented in the 1620s, though in practice that was what happened in the 1640s. In November 1616, when ambassador to the Emperor Jahangir, Sir Thomas Roe had written to the directors of the EIC in London a famous and much quoted admonition to the effect that it was an error to seek for garrisons and land wars in India. Roe argued that the Portuguese wasted their profits on defence, and that the Dutch 'who seeks plantation heere by the swoord' were going down the same road. If the English could not avoid fighting, Roe counselled 'engage yourself but at sea, where yow are like to gayne as often as to loose'. As ambassador to the Sublime Porte at Constantinople in 1624 he reiterated his view that the English in Asia 'are mere merchants there'.[16] There was nothing imperial about the early struggles of the EIC. It fought not for 'an empire of trade', but for survival. The biggest threat to that survival was the Stuart dynasty. James was bad enough, but Charles I was worse. His word, the sacredness of which was one of his constant themes, was singularly worthless. He continually licensed interlopers to trade in Asian waters in violation of the EIC charter. Of these the most notorious were the two William Courteens, father and son, whose Courteen Association was at one stage a serious rival of the EIC. The skippers of the association's ships were notorious for attacks on Asian shipping, unpaid debts, and in one case for passing counterfeit coin. For these episodes, the EIC tended to be blamed. The elder Courteen was a heavy lender to the king, which meant that he was likely to obtain what he wanted by way of permission to trade east of the Cape. He was not the only one so favoured and, with that profound deviousness which seems to have been ingrained in his character, Charles had worked out a rationale for violating the EIC's rights. Typically, it was through the crypto-Catholic, pro-Spanish Secretary Windebank that he operated his second level of Asian policy, just as he operated through the same man an alternative and secret European foreign policy often at odds with the publicly acknowledged one run through Secretary Cotton. One argument used to justify trading by Courteen, Endymion Porter, or other royal favourites was that they only traded where the EIC was not active (the EIC predictably then being forbidden to trade near these new establishments). Another was much more alarming: that by failing to establish territorial possessions and build forts the EIC had both failed its sovereign and brought the English 'into contempt and left them at the mercy of the natives'.[17] As Roe had many times pointed out, it was a recipe for disaster. Charles really was obsessed with aping the regal style of the great Catholic monarchies he so admired, and his paranoid Protestant subjects may have misunderstood his theology, but not at all the drift of his court culture.

The irony was that Courteen was of Flemish extraction and half his company was based in the Netherlands, though the second generation saw a bitter split between the English and Dutch sides over his estate. The seizure of two Courteen ships by the Dutch in the East Indies in 1641 finally drove the younger William Courteen into a bankruptcy which aggressive mismanagement of the association had done much to set up.[18] By 1641 the EIC itself was having trouble raising capital. It had been helped by an Anglo–Portuguese truce negotiated in Goa in 1635 and confirmed by the Treaty of York of 1642. It was the principal supplier of saltpetre, the main constituent of gunpowder, which it alone imported in bulk to England. This implied a close relationship with the Crown, which had a monopoly of gunpowder-making that it leased out. In practice, it became just another source of grief, for the king plundered the EIC's warehouse holdings by compulsory sales linked to compulsory loans as he moved towards the crisis of civil war. In June 1641 it was said flatly at a meeting of the central committees of the EIC that they still needed assurances against abuse by the Dutch and that 'the encouragement must come from the King and State, in which case there would be a new Stock'.[19] In practice the English survived as traders in the archipelago, though under continual harassment, by moving to areas peripheral to the main Dutch interests and by shifting their emphasis more and more to India. Even there, they had to fight to hold off predation by local ships such as the nine Malabar vessels which overwhelmed the EIC vessel *Comfort* and captured another 60-ton vessel in 1638, after a desperate fight at the end of which the English blew up the *Comfort* rather than yield her.[20]

Willingness to fight was essential. The Dutch, like the Portuguese, used as much force as they thought they could get away with without paying too heavy a price. In 1649–50 they crushed an incipient Genoese east India company by seizing, in the face of no resistance, its ships. Nor did they need to worry about retaliation in Europe: Genoa could not hurt them.[21] Like Englishmen in the Americas, the EIC and its servants discovered the basic truth that the Crown was an unreliable source of support, and the best solution to a security problem was to generate power to control it them-selves. Compared with the Chesapeake militias, adequate only for control of native tribes, the gundecks of East Indiamen constituted formidable fighting power. They could handle the Portuguese. The VOC was a different story, though even there the EIC could give the enemy a good run for his money and was pushed off and aside rather than destroyed. They did not go in for settlement and fortification. The apparent exception of Fort St George, Madras, where they slowly built a simple castle with corner bastions be-tween 1640 and 1654, was the result of a mistake. The men on the spot claimed that the local ruler who furnished the ground on which the future fort and city were to rise had also agreed to pay for the fort. The London authorities were enraged when they discovered, too late to pull out, that that was not how the local *naik* understood his grant. The main defence system for the EIC remained shipboard guns.

They worked. Even during the chaos of the collapse of Stuart monarchy in the War of the Three Kingdoms, English trade with Asia kept going. The EIC was in bad shape, and the problem of interlopers demanding free trade in Asia, and petitioning the parliamentary authorities for it, was chronic. In 1650 an agreement between the EIC and the leading interlopers to form and trade under a united joint stock was signed. At that point, matters were complicated by the passing of the first Navigation Act in 1651 and the Anglo–Dutch War of 1652–54. The two events were not automatically linked. Nor is there any reason to think that the Rump Parliament, which launched the war, was a mere puppet of mercantile interests, though it was well aware of them. It was the only one of the first three Anglo–Dutch wars, all fought in the Narrow Seas between England and the continent, which the English can be said to have won.[22] The Amboina episode was cited as one of the justifications for the war, but in practice the conflict had no true Asian dimension. It was just an embarrassment to the EIC and the VOC. At the end the Dutch company had to pay £85,000 to the English one to settle past claims, and in theory the EIC was ceded the island of Pulo Run in the Bandas to settle. In practice, with an economy and population devastated by the VOC's disciplinary and production control measures, it was not worth having. Protector Cromwell, when he replaced the Rump, could never persuade the EIC to establish itself there.

In other respects, the lord protector and the EIC rubbed along together. The heyday of independent English traders in Asia proved to be the period 1654–57. However, the EIC was an important creditor of the protector's treasury. Of the £85,000 compensation obtained from the Dutch, £60,000 had promptly been borrowed by the Commonwealth of England, Ireland and Scotland. When the EIC threatened to auction off its extensive fixed capital in India, but added that a new charter would enable it to continue and forget some commonwealth debt outstanding, Cromwell promptly issued a new charter confirming the EIC's traditional rights.[23] More generally, it has been argued that the interlopers in the Asian trade represented one aspect of a profound social change which enabled a new breed of aggressively capitalist and imperialist colonial merchants eventually to achieve political power and shape the policies of the English state to their own imperialist–capitalist agenda, brushing aside the 'feudal' structures of the old privileged compan-ies. As the nomenclature shows, this is a variation on the stubborn Marxist or neo-Marxist defence of the idea that the politics of mid-seventeenth-century England somehow just has to be subservient to the social history in which historians of Marxist inspiration have invested so much.[24] There is simply no reason to accept the basic contention. In the East Indies by the 1640s English merchants of any kind were interested only in making money. So far from being imperialists, their long struggles with the Dutch and Portuguese did not even turn them into emporialists like the Dutch. There was no profit without power for them, but that power was defensive on their ships. In a minor way what comes out clearly from EIC records is just how bad the lordship which James I and Charles I offered them was. Loyalty did not come from lordship, but from good lordship. Like most conservative men at all times and in all places, the EIC leadership was unenthusiastic about an open challenge to established authority in 1642, but his dealings with them – as with so many others – explain why the sheer badness and ineptitude of the kingship of Charles Stuart is a far more convincing prime factor in any explanation of the political crisis of the early 1640s than intricately unconvincing arguments about social change. Social factors may have shaped responses to the crisis. They did not cause it. Nor were Englishmen in Asia hammering out a new capitalist–imperialist iden-tity in the first half of the seventeenth century. They were sharing in the mounting identity crisis afflicting an English king-worshipping nation when a large proportion of its leaders discovered that their idol had feet of clay.

The rise and fall of Stuart imperialism in Asia after 1660

Although the republican Commonwealth of England, Scotland and Ireland was by definition an attempt to solve the problems posed by a radically

unsatisfactory dynasty's failure to manage a three-kingdom composite monarchy, it did not prove a stable or acceptable solution in the long run. It was
an archipelagic structure and the protector looked more and more like a
king, but the Scots and Irish resented the fact that the commonwealth was
dominated by England and, above all, by a standing English army. By 1660,
the English civilian elites had agreed to restore the Stuarts as the only way
to re-create a legitimate monarchy, seen as a bastion against anarchy and
social upheaval. General Monck and the troops of the garrison in Scotland
provided the military power necessary to neutralise republican holdouts
among the army leaders. With the return of Charles II in 1660, a commonwealth identity ceased to be a possibility before it had ever become a
reality. Ironically, it was to be the restoration regime which was to embark
on an ambitious bid to reshape English identity in a very specific direction,
in which imperialism of a particular kind was meant to be a central component. In this at least there was consistency. Navalist imperialism came
easy to the former senior servants of the commonwealth who had formed a
coalition with the royalists to restore the monarchy. By 1669, the architects
of the Restoration were passing from the scene to be replaced by 'new men,
the émigrés whose outlook was not English at all, men whose model in this
was the King himself',[25] but even they wanted to stress the imperial theme,
especially with an anti-Dutch slant.

The essential background to the militant anti-Dutch imperialism of a
crucial part of the Restoration elite, including the two royal brothers, was the
perceived success of the Rump Parliament's war against the Netherlands.
From the English point of view, some aspects of that war had indeed
been very successful, due to England's extremely favourable strategic position athwart the main sea approaches to the Netherlands and due to
the clear English superiority in numbers of the larger warships of the day
mounting 40–50 guns or more – not to mention the superior calibre of
the heavier English ordnance. Line-ahead as the standard battle formation
was a concept which was only evolving during this first Anglo–Dutch War,
so engagements were vast, confused events based on ship fighting ship in a
thundering, flame-shot murk in the North Sea. The two great English naval
victories in the summer of 1653, off Harwich in June and off Scheveningen
in August, underlined the desperate nature of the Dutch position. In Western European waters the Dutch also suffered huge losses of merchant
shipping. The English had been seizing significant numbers of Dutch
ships on the western approaches in the years before the outbreak of the
war, but they probably lost in excess of 1200 more ships during the war.
Yet this was only one part of the story, for elsewhere the Dutch were able to
hit back very hard. With Danish assistance they chased the English out of
the Baltic. In the Mediterranean they achieved just about as absolute a ban

on English shipping, massively damaging England's lucrative Levant trade. In eastern waters the Dutch swept the English and their Portuguese allies out of the Persian Gulf. Over 400 English ships of high average value were lost to Dutch warships and privateers, and even the Rump was anxious to end an expensive war, despite the ravings of a tiny ultra-radical Protestant faction which saw the war as a necessary scourge for a Dutch nation which had abandoned God for the temptations of material greed. Cromwell's decision to wind up an unwinnable war whilst he still looked ahead in it was astute.[26]

Much of the reality of the final stages of the first Anglo–Dutch War was as lost on the more rampant of the royalist court factions after 1660 as it had been in 1654 on the Protestant ultra-radicals those factions so loathed. The nature of the restored monarchy of Charles II encouraged factionalism. His first great minister, the Earl of Clarendon, believed in minimal government by departments, so he made no attempt to monopolise initiatives within government, which would have mattered less had he not served the most evasive and devious of kings. Charles was quite capable of enunciating a policy and then encouraging an associate to set up an entirely contradictory one. The Duke of York and Albany, the first fully adult royal brother to be active in politics for a very long time, was lord high admiral, from which base he rapidly built up a powerful faction of younger courtiers, sea officers, and colonial merchants hungry for advancement and profit. It was from this circle that the first pressures came for renewed confrontation with the Dutch, though other interests such as that headed by the former Cromwellian general and architect of the return of Charles, George Monck, Duke of Albemarle, rapidly jumped on the bandwagon. They all assumed victory was a foregone conclusion. They valued the political advantages which victory would give them. Charles Berkeley, Earl of Falmouth, was well on the way to a spectacular career as the favourite who could handle and reconcile both Charles and James when he lost his life in the war he did so much to provoke. Merchants were used and manipulated by this group of upper-class hawks in the sense that men like Sir Thomas Clifford contrived to secure anti-Dutch mercantile testimony before vital House of Commons committee meetings, but merchants no more caused the second Anglo–Dutch War than they did the third, which broke out in 1672.[27]

There was an ideological element to the wars only in the sense that despite their links by marriage with the House of Orange and the fact they had spent a significant amount of their time in exile in the Netherlands, the Stuart dynasts genuinely detested the Dutch, though for reasons which they had to wrap up in fancy garb for more general consumption. Both Charles and James, and especially James, despised the Dutch regime as a kingless republic of non-episcopal Protestants, ripe for plunder and possible partition.

The extremely over-simplified private ideology of the royal circle – which regarded unconditional obedience to an anointed sovereign as the only basis of a stable political and social order, and High Anglicanism or preferably Roman Catholicism as the only acceptable religion, on the ground that they alone taught subjects they were damned if they resisted their kings – was inherently aggressive. It had to stamp on and destroy rival systems which belied its own shaky premises. To Charles and James, as to Louis XIV, the mere existence of a stable, prosperous United Netherlands was a piece of intolerable presumption. There was an Anglican royalist pro-war propaganda which depicted the Dutch as reaching out greedily for a universal empire of trade supremacy. It denied their claim to be genuine Protestants, because their state's origins lay in ungodly rebellion against a legitimate king (the ultimate horror to a paranoid conservative Anglican after 1660). Above all, because it was not ruled by a king, their state was a political obscenity.[28] It was a convenient creed for those bent on war anyway, but there was large-scale sales resistance to it in England. Many, including many good Anglicans, could not see why a refusal to accept the extirpation of their religion at the hands of the Roman Catholic Philip II in the late sixteenth century made Dutch Protestants non-Protestants.

Many merchants who complained, justly, of Dutch bully-boy tactics did not want a full-scale war. The Levant Company knew from experience that war would close the Mediterranean trade to it. The EIC was desperately unhappy about the prospect of a second Dutch war. Sir George Oxenden, the leading EIC figure in Surat, was as stout-hearted a merchant as could be found. In 1664 he defended the English factory in Surat against the marauding forces of the great Maratha warrior Sivaji and repulsed them so decisively that he was awarded thanks and honours by the Moghul Emperor Auragzeb, to whom Sivaji was both a bandit and a symbol of a resurgent and insurgent Hinduism chafing all too successfully against the tyranny of an Islamic ascendancy. Yet Oxenden remembered only too well the damage suffered by the EIC in the first Dutch war. He had no desire for another. He feared that Bombay, ceded to Charles II in 1661 by Portugal as part of the dowry of Catherine of Braganza and subsequently transferred by Charles to the EIC at a nominal rent, would inevitably be lost. Informed analysts, even those who supported the war as state policy, could not see how the EIC could gain from the conflict.[29] The VOC was approaching the zenith of its power in Asia and was systematically assaulting Portuguese footholds in Sri Lanka and south India. By the late 1650s the Dutch were acutely aware that the Portuguese were anxious to place some of their more exposed posts on the Malabar Coast, like Cochin, under English protection. VOC leaders were in fact determined to take these places as soon as possible to pre-empt any such tactics.[30]

Under the outstanding leadership of Rijkloff van Goens, the VOC had conquered the former Portuguese strongholds of Cochin and Cannanore on the Malabar Coast in 1662–63. After 1664 the EIC was able to trade under the auspices of the anti-Dutch Zamorin of Calicut, and from there and from a post at Tellicherry they contrived to continue in the Malabar trade, despite Dutch hostility and naval patrols designed to knock out rivals. By seizing the lowlands of Sri Lanka, the Dutch had secured monopoly access to the main world source of cinnamon and they sought similar monopoly over the pepper trade of the Malabar Coast. When news of the outbreak of the second Anglo–Dutch conflict reached Dutch officials in Sri Lanka they were worried that the English might make common cause with the king of Kandy, to whom the Dutch were technically allied but against whom they committed as much aggression as they thought current circumstances would allow. In fact, Edward Winter, the president of the EIC council in Madras, sent emissaries to Raja Sinha, the monarch in Kandy, proposing a mutual alliance in exchange for acknowledgement of the English right to trade freely in the island. This was the last thing the VOC would tolerate, and when its agents heard of Winter's plans it stepped up its seizure of key ports from its nominal ally Raja Sinha in order to tighten the noose of its monopoly round Sri Lanka.[31]

The war had started with a piratical strike against the Dutch West India Company stations in West Africa, before any formal declaration of war. It was executed on behalf of the Royal African Company by Sir Robert Holmes, a commander who had come up as a member of Prince Rupert's circle but who rapidly became a favourite of the Duke of York, a dominant figure in the Africa Company. Admiral Michiel de Ruyter led the inevitable and devastating Dutch reprisal raid on English posts and shipping in West Africa. The EIC, naturally enough, had an interest in West Africa, where it maintained trading posts with factors. There was even an element of secondment from the EIC personnel on the coast to the Royal Africa Company service, but it is significant that relations between the seconded EIC men and their new colleagues were often appallingly bad.[32] The EIC was very much of a mind with Sir George Downing, Charles II's ambassador to The Hague, who is often and wrongly blamed for the outbreak of the war. He believed that appeasement had merely encouraged more aggression by the Dutch. What was needed to curb this aggression and improve Anglo–Dutch relations, he argued, was a mixture of hard pounding very precisely aimed to counteract such Dutch policies as hindering English trade in Indian waters under specious pretexts, and relentless diplomatic pressure on the States General of the United Netherlands. The aim, as Downing explained to Clarendon, was to 'set their subjects a crying as well as his Majesty's', at which point the States General might deem the risk of war not worth taking and might curb its over-mighty corporate subjects, 'for they love nor honour none but them that they think both can and dare bite them'.[33] The hawks, ideologues, and chancers around the Duke of York actually wanted war for its own sake. They had their fill of it by the end.

From the English point of view, the war started well when James, commanding in person with great courage as lord high admiral, won a smashing victory off Lowestoft. Thereafter, it was downhill all the way. The victory was not followed up as it might have been. An attempt to capture a large Dutch fleet, including valuable VOC vessels, sheltering at Bergen failed. Holmes did pick up some VOC ships in a characteristically piratical sweep across the North Sea, but the return of the victorious De Ruyter from Africa was the prelude to heavy sea fighting in 1666, in which the English were not always successful. Plague began to ravage London. The France of Louis XIV was reluctantly forced to honour its alliance with the Dutch and enter the war. Since Louis was desperately anxious to safeguard his new fleet, which represented a huge investment but was not seasoned for war, his intervention was half-hearted, but it underlined the unwinnability of a war in which the Dutch were blessed with the truly inspirational leadership of Johan de Witt, pensionary of Holland. By 1667 political discontent was rife in England.

The war had been launched with a barrage of propaganda from a war-mongering court. Thomas Mun had written a tract in the reign of James VI and I which that canny monarch would not allow to be published for fear it excoriated Anglo–Dutch relations. We now know its genesis lay in four memoranda submitted by Mun to the commission for trade set up to probe the reasons for the sharp recession of 1622–23. Mun died in 1641, and we cannot tell how far the text published in 1664 had been doctored for contemporary consumption, though the marginalia – with their stress on the perfidious nature of the Dutch and the enormous value of the East India Trade – as well as textual references to the Dutch having 'gotten divers places of great Strength and Wealth in the East Indies' all smack of the 1660s.[34]

When London was devastated in September 1666 by a great fire, the Stuart regime had to field its most shameless sycophant in the shape of the poet John Dryden, if only because the combination of war, plague, and fire did not suggest to an age which still more than half-believed in the direct intervention of Divine Providence in human affairs that God was overly fond of the English government. Dryden opened his poem *Annus Mirabilis* with an address to the City of London, including a firm statement of his belief in Providence. He also depicted the relationship between Charles and his people as that of the mystic unity of two once-separated lovers. After that improbability, the suggestion in his poem that a pacific Charles had tried to counterbalance a 'martial people' hell-bent on war with the Dutch was no more misleading than the prophesies with which the poem ended. These suggested that the hard part of the war was clearly over and that what lay ahead was unimaginable success and prosperity ladled out by a generous God suitably impressed by the devotion of the English to their monarch, a devotion which the Almighty had of course been merely testing in a mean sort of way by inflicting all these disasters on them. Dryden ended with the unctuous lines:

> *Already we have conquer'd half the War,*
> *And the less dang'rous part is left behind:*
> *Our trouble now is but to make them dare,*
> *And not so great to vanquish as to find.*
>
> *Thus to the Eastern wealth through storms we go;*
> *But now, the Cape once doubled, fear no more:*
> *A constant Trade-wind will securely blow,*
> *And gently lay us on the Spicy shore.*[35]

The appalling debacles which marked the English war effort in 1667 must have been a slight embarrassment to Dryden, though he lived it down: a week is a long time in poetical politics and memories are short. Financial mismanagement and mistaken confidence led to the laying up of the bulk of the English fleet in the summer of 1667, which in turn made possible the spectacular Dutch victory when De Ruyter's fleet raided the Medway, sinking, burning, and towing away the battleships which were the supreme symbols of Stuart imperialism. Dryden went on to further feats of legerdemain in the service of the Crown, depicting the royal brothers in 'Absalom and Achitophel' as benignly patriarchal moderates and those who opposed their very extreme and wildly destabilising policies as extremists. In *The Hind and the Panther* the church of the militant Counter-Reformation in the age of Louis XIV becomes a shy, retiring beast, much too gentle for her own good. As with much late Stuart propaganda, the trouble was not the packaging but the inherently unconvincing nature of the message.

The poet Andrew Marvell, once Cromwell's Latin secretary, served as MP for Hull after the Restoration. He was a supporter of religious tolera-tion, and indeed of the second Dutch war at its inception. By the time it was nearing its end he was deeply disillusioned by the corruption and incompetence of the court which had so mismanaged it. It has been argued, with prodigious learning and great persuasiveness, that the courses of the first two Anglo–Dutch wars were ideologically driven. From this point of view, the first was motivated by frustrated republican idealism after the

English republicans had contrived to persuade themselves that the Dutch were neither good republicans nor good Christians, and the second could not be fought through to success because English opinion had swung round to demonising Louis XIV rather than the Dutch. That this is a convincing analysis of articulate opinion in certain key groups in England is beyond question. It underplays economic factors somewhat, and it has to be said that it also underestimates the role of the fortunes of war.[36] Charles II and James, Duke of York, were hoping in both their wars against the United Netherlands that smashing early victories of a profitable kind would create a wave of supportive opinion for their policies. They knew they did not have the fiscal structure for a war of attrition. Failure allowed negative attitudes in the English political nation to take over, and negative attitudes were there in spades, mainly because few trusted the royal Stuarts.

After the Peace of Breda of 1667, Charles II embarked on a public policy of alliance with Sweden and the Netherlands against the rising menace of France, not least to distract attention from the reality of his secret negotiations with France for an alliance against the Dutch. As usual, the royal Stuarts combined deviousness with an inability wholly to conceal their ulterior policy drift. Leading figures in the EIC were part of an alert, lettered community in London which shared its scepticism about the government's competence and honesty by correspondence. Thus, Marvell wrote in August 1671 to Thomas Rolt, later to be a senior office holder of the EIC, who was then in Persia. Marvell had sent one of his letters to Persia by means of an Armenian merchant, part of a global network of Armenian wheelers and dealers whose tentacles reached deep into Indian banking. In the August 1671 letter he made clear his distrust of the financial corruption of the royal government, and of the motives behind Charles II's latest demands for vast additional grants of money. He added, 'We truckle to France in all things, to the Prejudice of our Alliance and Honour.' It was a fair comment.[37]

Marvell by 1677 was expressing profound concern over the commercial and maritime expansion of France, backed as it was by great military power and a brutally protectionist tariff system.[38] The EIC had its ongoing troubles with the VOC, but the French were also emerging as aggressive rivals in Asian waters. Louis XIV's minister Jean-Baptiste Colbert was determined to relaunch French activity in Asia after several earlier corporate ventures had foundered. In 1664 he established the *Compagnie Royale des Indes Orientales* with a nominal capitalisation of 15,000,000 livres. By 1670 he was despatching the most powerful European royal battle squadron ever sent to Asia in the seventeenth century to entrench the aspirations of the French company firmly in Asian reality. The EIC was simply appalled by the prospect of more competition driving Asian commodity prices up. Since the French hoped to make alliances with enemies of the VOC in Asia, and there were plenty of them, it was logical for Colbert to hope for an alliance with the English and the Portuguese, but both of these proposed allies had doubts about the ability of Colbert's five men o'war, a frigate, and three store ships to tip the balance against the VOC decisively. The EIC was hostile to any such alliance, and its lobbying may have helped Charles II to decide to evade the French proposal. In the event the French proved reluctant to attack Dutch fleets off India. They did eventually try to seize and hold a Coromandel port, but were defeated by a combination of the VOC and the sultan of Golconda. When Louis XIV invaded the United Netherlands in 1672 he lost interest in non-European theatres of war and his Asian squadron withered on the vine.[39] By 1672 the covert alliance between Charles II and Louis XIV had become a partially open one when they jointly attacked the Dutch Republic and at one stage came close to wiping it off the map, which was indeed their intention.

The Stuart brothers, and particularly James, were anxious to remake the preponderant sense of English identity of their day into a format which would ultimately be much more acquiescent towards the creation of an absolutist monarchy whose chief glory would be its freedom from dependence on its subjects. Abraham Woodhead, the recluse who was James' favourite Roman Catholic apologist and whose influence in court circles outlived his death in 1678, was anxious to replace the old-fashioned Protestant perception of the pope as Antichrist by a national obsession with Islam as the true Antichrist. His technique was a mixture of studied meekness towards Protestant adversaries and passionate, crude denunciation of Mahommed and Islam.[40] As king, James was much given to stressing the crusading imperative against the Turk. It suited his policies well to have such an over-riding emotion available; the trouble was that there was no way the Turk could be sold to most Englishmen as the most urgent threat to their way of life. That was Louis XIV, and by 1672 not even the Dutch could be used to distract attention from that fact. In any case, England had enjoyed good relations with the Ottoman Empire since the Elizabethan era. Parochial Englishmen in general might be, like the bulk of most contemporary populations, but their literary culture included travel accounts like Sir Paul Rycaut's *Present State of the Ottoman Empire* (1668) and Launcelot Addison's *West Barbary* (1671), books which, to their credit, tried to dispel irrational prejudice against Muslims as 'barbarous'.[41]

In vain did Dryden churn out in 1673 a catchpenny production of a play entitled 'Amboyna, or the Cruelties of the Dutch to the English Merchants'. Raking over those old coals on behalf of the court could not conceal that the trade issues advanced to justify the third Anglo–Dutch War of 1672–74 were specious excuses. The real aim of the Crown and its ministers, aims which they ineffectively tried to conceal, was to use the war, conceived as a massive smash-and-grab raid, to increase their own irresponsible power. They intended to eliminate the Crown's need for cooperation from its English subjects, especially in the shape of the Westminster parliament and the county militias. An enriched crown equipped with a military force built up nominally to deal with the Dutch 'threat' would brook no defiance from subjects. When after ten months Charles II had to ask for parliamentary aid, it meant his plans had become totally derailed.

His alliance with France was desperately unpopular, and in 1674 he proved an unconvincing liar when he told parliament that there were no secret agreements with France aimed at the liberties and religion of England. Dutch propaganda skilfully exploited English scepticism about Crown motives. In any case, the war had become a disaster as swarms of Dutch privateers inflicted insupportable losses on English merchant shipping. There was some slight consolation in 1673 when an English squadron not only recaptured the EIC's island staging point of St Helena from a Dutch force sent from the Cape, but also captured three out of six returning VOC ships in a naval ambush there. A fourth was captured later off the Texel. However, by 1674 the prize war was so clearly lost that Charles II was forced to sign a separate peace to escape from what was essentially a botched war. The fact that his navy subsequently devoted a very high proportion of its time and resources to supplying convoy services to protect English shipping in the Mediterranean from Barbary pirates in order to keep open the lucrative Levant trades may be related to the bitter experience of mercantile marine loss in 1673–74. Mediterranean convoys or squadrons in that sea designed to discourage European rulers from discriminating against English ships were much higher naval priorities between 1674 and 1688 than operations in the Americas or Asia, of which there were very few.[42]

The EIC had been apprehensive of serious losses in India on the eve of the second Dutch war in 1665. The protracted business of transferring Bombay from Portuguese jurisdiction to that of Charles II and then transferring responsibility for it to an unenthusiastic EIC was not completed before 1667, and the Surat council of the EIC told its London superiors in January that it feared the loss of Bombay was almost inevitable in any Dutch war, for the VOC had its eye on it.[43] When to this is added the fact that writings sponsored by Colbert showing the aggressive ambitions of the French East India Company were being translated into English at about the same time expressly to warn the EIC of this new danger, it is clear that swaggering confidence was not likely among the EIC leadership.[44] They were in fact very lucky to escape from the two Anglo–Dutch wars of the Restoration with no basic structural damage to their position in Asia. Partly this was due to the fact that the Dutch had their work cut out for them nearer home. Even the VOC was likely to curb further plans for aggression in Asia when it was having a great deal of difficulty in running its return fleets past English warships in the sea approaches to the Netherlands. However, it was clear that the Stuart court had little real interest in the grievances of the EIC against the VOC. The objectives of Charles II's war policy by the 1670s were blatantly domestic. Most Englishmen were not just paranoid about a Franco–Roman Catholic threat to their way of life and their political liberties, but also broadly correct in thinking that such a threat existed and was much the most serious threat they faced after 1670. Louis XIV was aggressive; his anxiety to emerge, especially after 1679, as the new Charlemagne of the Counter-Reformation made him militantly anti-Protestant at home and abroad; and there was a conspiracy to bring in French-style absolutism and embark on a radical Catholicisation of England. The Popish Plot scare was exploited by rogues, and innocent Roman Catholics were cruelly persecuted, but there was indeed such a plot, with the king at its heart.[45] The Stuart attempt to restructure English identity by building the Protestant, republican Dutch into public consciousness as a national bogey, with the help of much raking over old Asian coals as distinct from effective action there, failed because it deserved to: its insincerity was transparent.

Even in Asia, the French threat to English interests continued to grow after 1674. In Siam the Dutch had ousted the Portuguese as the main European traders, and by the 1660s they were employing their usual tactics of enforcing naval blockades on Siamese trade to extract exclusive trading privileges. King Narai of Siam was understandably anxious to find a European counterbalance to endless Dutch bullying. This could have been the EIC, but it never managed to make its Siamese trade pay. By 1680 it was clear to King Narai that the EIC was not willing to commit itself, so he turned to the French, who had been involved in Siam through missionary activity since the 1660s. The king's agents in executing this policy included former EIC servants who had entered his service – such as the brothers George and Samuel White and the extraordinary Greek adventurer Constantine Phaulkon, who rose to be first minister of state. By 1686 he had established an ambiguous relationship with France which made Louis XIV jump to the conclusion that Siam was ripe for religious, military, and commercial conquest. By 1687 Louis had inserted a significant French expeditionary force into Siam. This did not mean that the Dutch had ceased to pursue aggressive policies elsewhere. They attacked the EIC's access to the pepper trade in Sumatra by military intervention which reduced the once independent sultan of Bantam to a mere stooge of the VOC. By 1685 the Dutch were building a fortress in his capital to enforce their supremacy and exclusive privileges. About the same time the VOC set about establishing a general stranglehold on the trade of the west coast of Sumatra. On the Malabar Coast of India they put the new EIC settlement at Tellicherry under naval and psychological siege. In a letter to their colleagues in Madras in 1687 the EIC leadership at Tellicherry said they did not know 'how long we may be able to keep our station . . . on the coast of Malabar if the Dutch resolve to pursue their long laid design of engrossing all the pepper trade of India by armes which our duty to our king and country obligeth us to prevent to the utmost of our power'.[46] Sir Josiah Child, the tough ex-Cromwellian magnate who was rising to a position of dominance within the EIC, was convinced by the early 1680s that the Dutch would have to be fought in Asia, and that the EIC needed Crown support to do it. Child had by then bought his way back into the good graces of Charles, who originally distrusted him as an ex-republican but who then warmed to him as a conveyor of EIC cash presents and an MP who showed no enthusiasm for either the Church of England or the exclusion of the Duke of York from the succession. Nevertheless, an increasingly lethargic Charles was not keen on serious trouble with the Dutch.

The accession of James II in 1685 put together an instinctively imperialistic English monarch and an English EIC temporarily controlled by one of its few members who thought like a hard-line VOC governor general. Child and James were a marriage made in heaven. There had been a drift towards endowing the EIC with quasi-governmental powers in Asia ever since 1660. Its 1661 charter gave it the right to make war and peace with Asian powers and to exercise martial law within its settlements, but none of this was meant to be other than reactive. These were powers to enable the EIC to cope with local problems and misfortunes not of their own making. The company's policy remained resolutely pacific. Under James a note of aggressive assertion at once began to creep into the company's style. Thus in November 1685 the EIC petitioned James, from whom a positive response was forthcoming at once, for permission to coin in their settlements in India any species of currency current in the subcontinent. The EIC had always done this, but only after asking for a licence from the appropriate Indian prince. Now they explained that 'having been at great charge to make their fortifications more considerable and more independent of those princes, they pray the King's permission without seeking any other license'.[47] The EIC also sought power to exercise, at the royal discretion, martial law on its ships east of the Cape of Good Hope as well as in its settlements 'when they are at war with some other nation'.[48]

This was the language of Sir Josiah Child's ascendancy, which became marked in the early 1680s, but long before then an intimate relationship had developed between the Restoration regime and the EIC. It was based on the facts that the company was an important source of loans for Charles II's perpetually needy government, and that it was the only large supplier of saltpetre for his gunpowder-hungry fleet. Moderate business magnates such as Sir John Banks (no friend of Child) mediated between the court and the EIC.[49] The political storms of the period 1679–81, when there was a serious bid by the first Whig party to challenge the power of the monarchy, were reflected in a struggle within the EIC between Sir Josiah Child, who stood for close alliance with the Stuart court, and a Whiggish group led by Thomas Papillon, who had already in the 1670s distinguished himself as a member of a mercantile pressure group in the City of London – many of them like him of French Protestant origin – which had pressured Charles II for a much tougher line against hostile French tariffs.[50] In 1681 Sir Josiah finally defeated the Papillon group in EIC elections and drove them from the counsels of that body until his own death in 1699. Sir Josiah was to make one John Child (not in fact a relative) his agent in India, securing for him the presidency of the EIC council in Surat, a baronetcy, and then the preposterous title of captain general in north India. At first the two Childs pursued a cheese-paring policy which provoked a well-justified mutiny (against them, not the Crown) amongst the small garrison which the EIC's lease obliged them to keep in Bombay. Given the level of local violence endemic in Bombay, where Portuguese power remained close and unfriendly and where the Moghul admiral, the Sidi, habitually anchored his ill-disciplined fleet before attacking the nearby shores controlled by the resurgent Hindu Marathas, the garrison was essential. Under the leader of the mutiny, Captain Richard Keigwin, firm military action worked wonders in ensuring decent respect for English interests. Charles II sent a small naval and military force out under Sir Thomas Grantham, who very sensibly negotiated a surrender and pardon which allowed Keigwin subsequently to command a king's ship in the West Indies, where he died gallantly leading an assault on St Christopher's in 1690. Like Sir Thomas Dale's earlier in the century, Keigwin's career and death occurred on a global stage.[51]

Back in the East Indies after 1685, the two Childs experienced a Pauline conversion to an extreme version of the Dutch style of marrying trade with the aggressive use of force. It is no accident that the policies which they started to follow, with the staunch support of James II, were very close to those being advocated simultaneously by the hawks within the French circles who were anxious to make space in Asia for their own chartered company, and who proposed to start by a dramatic religious, commercial, and military take-over of Siam. The French missionary and diplomat François de Choisy, for example, was clear in 1686 that the French company could only succeed by ruining the Dutch, and that the way to ruin them was to copy their methods. In Bengal the Moghul authorities had welcomed European companies and the increase in trade and customs revenue which they brought. Bengal prices were still low compared with other parts of India. By the early 1700s the region was supplying nearly 40 per cent of all Asian goods sent by the VOC to the Netherlands, and over half of the Asian textiles it imported.[52] By 1686 the EIC's tough local agent in this commercially vital area, Job Charnock, had progressed from quarrelling with the local Moghul authorities to fighting them. The two Childs then actually declared war on the Moghul Empire, hoping to seize and fortify a port in Bengal, such as Dacca or Chittagong, and compel the Emperor Aurangzeb to exempt them from customs dues as well as to accept their extra-territorial jurisdiction within what they seized. Driven out of Surat, Sir John Child was soon having difficulty holding out in the EIC fort in Bombay in the face of an invasion of that settlement by the Sidi at the head of the Moghul fleet. In Bengal, despite military and naval assistance from James II which enabled the EIC to deploy larger forces than Clive had at his disposal during his successful coup in Bengal in 1757, the English were just defeated by an able Moghul viceroy. They could not cope with his swarms of light horse. They did not have quick-firing light artillery. A third of their infantry were pikemen, necessary to protect the slow-firing matchlock-equipped musketeers. Arguably, Europeans did not have any decisive military edge over Asian powers, except at sea, in the late seventeenth century. Military technology was easily transferable. By 1688 it was clear that the EIC was losing its war.

It was in fact losing two, for it had become involved in a naval war with Siam over the activities of men it regarded as 'interlopers', but who would have insisted that they were just ex-EIC employees legitimately active in local trade and politics. Phaulkon, the extraordinary Greek first minister of King Narai of Siam, had come to Asia as a servant of the EIC. He contrived to have two other former EIC men raised to office in what was then still the Siamese port of Mergui on the Bay of Bengal (it was later annexed by Burma). Richard Burnaby became governor of Mergui, and Samuel White its port officer. The latter two, who recruited English seamen for their ships freely, were deep into trade in the Bay of Bengal, in the course of which they fell foul of the Indian sultanate of Golconda. Seizures and reprisals soon led to open naval war, and since the EIC was already resentful of the treatment of its representatives by Phaulkon, it was easily roused to belligerence when White and his associates inevitably seized ships and goods in which the EIC had an interest in the course of their harassment of Golconda's trade and its main port of Masulipatam. Sir Josiah Child demanded a warlike response. James II issued a typically haughty order that his subjects immediately abandon the service of foreign princes, especially the king of Siam, and the Madras council of the EIC optimistically wrote to White and Burnaby suggesting that 'a quiett surrender of Mergen, which being now under your Government, is in your power'. It was the least they could do when an EIC expeditionary force hove in sight.[53] In fact that expedition came to grief in 1687 with the loss of one of its ships and many of its men in a massacre following a sudden attack when they were ashore.

Despite its high tone towards White and Burnaby, the Madras council of the EIC was extremely unhappy about the aggressive policies being mandated from London. Council did despatch Captain Richard Cook in command of the *Royal James* into the Bay of Bengal in August 1687 with orders to seize any Moghul or Siamese ships he could find,[54] but they were acutely aware of the fact that they were not safe from Moghul power as they sat in Fort St George. The Madras council was presided over by Elihu Yale when it issued its orders to Richard Cook. Elihu's brother Thomas was also in EIC service at Madras. These were sophisticated men with a wide geographical vision. The Yales were New Englanders originally. Thomas had served as ambassador to Siam, and their relative and fellow New Englander Francis Davenport was one of the English adventurers in Siam and was currently serving as White's secretary in Mergui.[55] The men in Fort St George knew that the Emperor Aurangzeb was on the verge of a final conquest of Golconda, which would bring his power very close to them at a time when the EIC was at war with him.[56] They were frantically stockpiling arms and munitions, even at the cost of taking them from their own naval force on the eve of its departure to try to seize Mergui, just in case they found themselves besieged.[57] Elihu Yale and his colleagues knew by September 1687 that EIC forces in Bengal were 'so few, and weak' that they 'were not able to continue the War much longer'.[58] It was obviously a matter of enormous satisfaction to them that terms for peace were agreed in that month.[59] It was a humiliating peace, involving a large sum in reparations, but any peace was better than none. Equally, the naval war with Siam was an obvious disaster which any sane man was glad to see halted. It merely damaged trade. After Samuel White contrived to escape to England, it became meaningless. Phaulkon had not wanted it, though his support had been crucial for White. By early 1688 Phaulkon himself was heading for disaster as part of a violent Siamese reaction to the crudely obvious French attempt to establish a stranglehold on Siamese commerce and government and to undermine the Theravada Buddhism which was the core of Siamese culture and identity. Phaulkon was overthrown and executed. The French General Desfarges, though a far better soldier than Sir John Child, was forced to withdraw his forces from Siam. Ironically, James II had for once achieved his ambition of matching the policies and performance of Louis XIV.

The attempt by Sir Josiah Child and James II to create in Asia an aggressive imperial identity for an increasingly absolutist Stuart England was a total fiasco, not least because only a handful of men seem ever to have believed in the concept. The whole policy of using force on behalf of a monopolistic company allied to an autocratic court was denounced root and branch by critics who naturally had a field day after the fall of James II in the Glorious Revolution of 1688. To the more militant critics, the only two posts used by the EIC which could not with advantage be disposed of were St Helena and Bombay, and that was because both were technically Crown property. There was heavy pressure for freer access to an Asian trade based purely on commercial competitiveness, and against the odd manifestation of domineering cultural arrogance there can usually be set equally strong statements of the opposite nature, such as:

> As for the Barbarity of the Indians, the contrary thereof is so well known, that it will not pass for any Argument, there being no people in the World more civilized: Our late Carriage towards them, has indeed given them too much occasion to account us Barbarous; but they have not by their Behaviour ever given us any cause to esteem them so.[60]

Of course, extreme hostility to any form of fortification was as unreal as Sir Josiah's declared ambition to create a permanent English dominion in India. Violence was a fact of Indian life. What saved the company was its insignificance. In the contemptuous imperial firman or decree in which Aurangzeb admitted the EIC back into Indian commerce, after a grovelling apology from it as well as a fine of 150,000 rupees (about £15,000 sterling), he made it clear that he thought of the company as little more than an irritating flea on the back of his imperial elephant.[61]

Yet Aurangzeb, because he was an extreme example of imperial over-reach, could not guarantee security for the EIC against the Marathas or indeed his own undisciplined sailors. Limited insurance by modest self-help in the form of appropriate fortifications and predominantly local mercenary or volunteer forces to man them was the only way forward in several places in India. There had always been a case for the use of massive persuasive force, though perhaps not primarily in India, to curb the general bloody-mindedness of the VOC. That body hastened to insinuate to anyone in Asia who would listen that the Glorious Revolution was a Dutch conquest of England. Certainly the EIC suffered greatly both from the terrible effects of Dutch William's European war on its shipping between 1688 and 1697, and also from challenges to its monopoly which produced a rival company and a brief era of ruinous competition. However, in the longer run it was really the VOC which lost out when the same man was king of England and stadholder of the United Netherlands between 1688 and 1702. Anglo–Dutch relations in Asia remained bad, but William usually came down on the English side of specific quarrels because he knew how bitterly unpopular he already was on account of his reckless use of English economic assets to defend the Dutch Republic from the sustained assault of Louis XIV. Reason of state forbade William III incurring more odium in England.[62] It has been said that 'The world outside Europe had only a shadowy existence for him.' He could not conduct an informed discussion of the Spanish overseas empire and admitted to the Earl of Portland that he was 'not very well informed about the Indies'.[63] He had no emotional commitment to reversing the commercial decline of the VOC in Asia by force. As a result, the eighteenth century was to usher in nearly forty years of peace and prosperity for the EIC in Asia, a phenomenon which, as it demonstrates nothing which can easily be praised or denounced with any kind of fervour, has been singularly neglected by historians of the English abroad.

Notes and references

1. John Keay, *The Honourable Company: A history of the English East India Company* (HarperCollins, London, 1991), pp. 13–14.

2. Charles Wilson, *Queen Elizabeth and the Revolt of the Netherlands* (Macmillan, London, 1970).

3. K.H.D. Haley, *The British and the Dutch* (George Philip, London, 1988), p. 58.

4. Sanjay Subrahmanyam, *The Portuguese Empire in Asia 1500–1700* (Longman, London, 1993), pp. 75–78.

5. Geoffrey Parker, *The Military Revolution: Military innovation and the rise of the West, 1500–1800* (Cambridge University Press, Cambridge, 1988), pp. 83 and 104–06.

6. Sir William Foster (ed.), *The Voyage of Nicholas Downton to the East Indies 1614–15 as Recorded in Contemporary Narratives and Letters*, Hakluyt Society, 2nd Series, No. 82 (London, 1939), pp. 41–44 and 49–50.

7. *Ibid.*, p. 129.

8. Sir William Foster (ed.), *The Voyage of Sir Henry Middleton to the Moluccas 1604–1606*, Hakluyt Society, 2nd series, Vol. 88 (London, 1943), pp. 99–102.

9. George D. Winius and Marcus P.M. Vink, *The Merchant Warrior Pacified: The VOC (the Dutch East India Co.) and its changing political economy in India* (Oxford University Press, Delhi, 1991), pp. 4–5.

10. Cited in Charles R. Boxer, *The Dutch Seaborne Empire 1600–1800* (Hutchinson, London, 1965), p. 96.

11. Holden Furber, *Rival Empires of Trade in the Orient 1600–1800* (University of Minnesota Press, Minneapolis, 1976), pp. 38–50.

12. M.A.P. Meilink-Roelofsz, *Asian Trade and European Influence in the Indonesian Archipelago between 1500 and about 1630* (Martinus Nijhoff, The Hague, 1962), pp. 191–203.

13. Niels Steensgard, 'The Growth and Composition of the Long-Distance Trade of England and the Dutch Republic before 1750', in James D. Tracy (ed.), *The Rise of Merchant Empires* (Cambridge University Press, Cambridge, pbk edn, 1993), p. 109.

14. CSP Colonial, East Indies, 1622–24, conveniently calendars and extensively indexes much of this large volume of material.

15. Lord President Mandeville to Secretary Conway, 16 July 1624, *ibid.*, item 511, pp. 324–25.

16. Sir Thomas Roe to Sir Dudley Carleton, 27 November 1624, *ibid.*, item 692, p. 453.

17. Secretary Windebank to the Governor of the EIC, 15 March 1638, and draft memo on 'Mr Courteen's factory at Batacola [Bhatkal on the Malabar Coast]', probably March 1638, both in Ethel Bruce Sainsbury (ed.), *A Calendar of the Court Minutes etc. of the East India Company 1635–1639* (Clarendon Press, Oxford, 1907), pp. 294–95.

18. *Dictionary of National Biography* (hereafter *DNB*), Vol. 12, pp. 333–35.

19. 'A Meeting of the Court of Committees with the Mixt Committee', 9 June 1641, in Ethel Bruce Sainsbury (ed.), *op. cit.*, pp. 170–71.

20. EIC court minutes, 30 October 1640, *ibid.*, p. 107.

21. S. Subrahmanyam, 'On the Significance of Gadflies: the Genoese East India Company of the 1640s', *Journal of European Economic History*, 17 (1988), pp. 559–81.

22. Charles Wilson, *England's Apprenticeship 1603–1763* (Longman, London, 1965), pp. 63–64.

23. Maurice Ashley, *Financial and Commercial Policy under the Cromwellian Protectorate* (Frank Cass reprint, London, 1972), pp. 112–15.

24. Robert Brenner, *Merchants and Revolution: Commercial change, political conflict and London's overseas traders 1550–1653* (Cambridge University Press, Cambridge, 1993).

25. Archibald P. Thornton, *West-Indian Policy under the Restoration* (Clarendon Press, Oxford, 1956), p. 15.

26. Jonathan I. Israel, *Dutch Primacy in World Trade 1585–1740* (Clarendon Press, Oxford, 1989), pp. 207–13.

27. The best analysis of this question by far is now J.R. Jones, *The Anglo–Dutch Wars of the Seventeenth Century* (Longman, London, 1996), Chap. 5.

28. Steven C.A. Pincus, 'Popery, Trade and Universal Monarchy: The ideological context of the outbreak of the Second Anglo-Dutch War', *English Historical Review*, 422 (1992), pp. 1–29.

29. *Ibid.*, correspondence cited, pp. 8–9.

30. Letter from the commissary Rijkloff van Goens to Governor General Maetsuyker and the council for India, 6 July 1658, printed in P.E. Pieris, *Some Documents Relating to the Rise of the Dutch Power in Ceylon, 1602–1670* (Curzon Press, London, 1973), p. 255.

31. Governor General to Directors, 30 January 1666, *ibid.*, p. 283.

32. Richard Ollard, *Man of War: Sir Robert Holmes and the Restoration navy* (Hodder and Stoughton, London, 1969), pp. 109 and 115.

33. Downing to Clarendon, 18 September 1663, cited in John Beresford, *The Godfather of Downing Street* (Houghton Mifflin, Boston, MA, 1925), p. 170.

34. B.E. Supple, 'Thomas Mun and the Commercial Crisis, 1623', *Bulletin of the Institute of Historical Research* (hereafter *BIHR*), 27 (1954), pp. 91–94; Thomas Mun, *England's Treasure by Forraign Trade* (reprinted from the 1664 edn for the Economic History Society, Basil Blackwell, Oxford, 1928).

35. *Annus Mirabilis*, vv. 303–04, James Kinsley (ed.), *The Poems and Fables of John Dryden* (Oxford University Press, London, pbk edn, 1970), p. 105.

36. In Steven Pincus, *Protestantism and Patriotism: Ideologies and the making of English foreign policy 1650–68* (Cambridge University Press, Cambridge, 1996).

37. Marvell to Rolt, 9 August 1671, printed in H.M. Margoliouth (ed.), *The Poems and Letters of Andrew Marvell* (Clarendon Press, Oxford, 3rd edn 1971), Vol. 2, pp. 323–26.

38. Pierre Legouis, *Andrew Marvell* (Clarendon Press, Oxford, 2nd edn 1968), pp. 155–56.

39. Glen Joseph Ames, 'Colbert's Grand Indian Ocean Fleet of 1670', *The Mariner's Mirror*, 76 (1990), pp. 227–40.

40. Anne Barbeau Gardiner, 'Islam as Antichrist in the Writings of Abraham Woodhead, Spokesman for Restoration Catholics', *Restoration*, Fall 1991 issue, pp. 89–98.

41. Charles L. Batten Jr, 'Literary Responses to the Eighteenth Century Voyages', in Derek Howse (ed.), *Background to Discovery* (University of California Press, Berkeley, 1990), p. 153.

42. Sari R. Hornstein, *The Restoration Navy and English Foreign Trade 1674–1688* (Scolar Press, Aldershot, 1991).

43. Surat Council to Court of EIC, 2 January 1665, printed in William Foster (ed.), *The English Factories in India 1661–64* (Clarendon Press, Oxford, 1923), pp. 340–41.

44. *Vide* F. Charpentier, *A Discourse Written by a Faithful Subject to his Christian Majesty, Concerning the Establishment of a French Company for the Commerce of the East Indies*, translated by R. L'Estrange (London, 1664), printed in Geoffrey Symcox (ed.), *War, Diplomacy, and Imperialism, 1618–1763* (Macmillan, London, 1974), pp. 257–67.

45. J.F. Bosher, 'The Franco-Catholic Danger, 1660–1715', *History*, 79 (1994), pp. 5–30.

46. Quoted in K.N. Chaudhuri and Jonathan I. Israel, 'The East India Companies and the Revolution of 1688–89', in Jonathan I. Israel (ed.), *The Anglo-Dutch Moment* (Cambridge University Press, Cambridge, 1991), p. 416.

47. CSP Domestic, February–December 1685, item 1956, p. 394.

48. *Ibid.*, item 1957, p. 394.

49. D.C. Coleman, *Sir John Banks Baronet and Businessman* (Greenwood Press reprint edn, Westport, CT, 1975), Chap. 5.

50. Margaret Priestly, 'London Merchants and Opposition Politics in Charles II's reign', *BIHR*, 29 (1956), pp. 205–19.

51. Ray and Oliver Strachey, *Keigwin's Rebellion (1683–4): An episode in the history of Bombay* (Clarendon Press, Oxford, 1916).

52. Om Prakash, *The Dutch East India Company and the Economy of Bengal 1630–1720* (Princeton University Press, Princeton, NJ, 1985).

53. Council to Richard Burnaby and Samuel White, 27 August 1687 (copy), printed in *Records of Fort St George Diary and Consultation Book of 1687* (Government Press, Madras, 1916), pp. 133–34.

54. *Ibid.*, Consultation, August 1687, pp. 124–25.

55. The best overview of these events is to be found in Maurice Collis, *Siamese White* (Faber and Faber, London, 1936) and E.W. Hutchinson, *Adventurers in Siam in the Seventeenth Century* (Royal Asiatic Society, London, 1940).

56. Consultation Extraordinary, February 1687, printed in *Records of Fort St George 1687*, p. 29.

57. *Ibid.*, Consultation, March 1687, p. 51.

58. *Ibid.*, Consultation, September 1687, pp. 144–45.

59. *Ibid.*, Consultation, September 1687, p. 152.

60. Anon., *A Discourse Concerning the East India Trade Wherein is shewn – that the said Trade may be carried on by a Regulated Company, to much greater Advantage of the*

Publick, than by a Company with a Joint-Stock (London, printed for Richard Baldwin, 1693).

61. Bruce P. Lenman, 'The East India Company and the Emperor Aurangzeb', *History Today*, 37 (1987), pp. 23–29.

62. Charles Boxer, 'William and Mary and the World of Maritime Asia', *History Today*, 38 (1988), pp. 52–58.

63. Andrew Lossky, 'Political Ideas of William III', in *Political Ideas and Institutions in the Dutch Republic: Papers presented at a Clark Library seminar, 27 May 1982* (William Andrews Clark Memorial Library, Los Angeles, CA, 1985), pp. 35–57.

CHAPTER EIGHT

War in the New English marchlands in North America 1607–1676

The violent genesis of plantation society on the Chesapeake 1607–1644

When Elizabethan Englishmen interested in settlement in North America wrote about the dangers which might face any infant English settlement from 'the enemy', they naturally assumed that such an enemy would be European, almost certainly Spanish, and that the attack would come from seawards. In notes which he probably wrote in 1578 for Sir Humphrey Gilbert, who was contemplating a colonising voyage, the elder Richard Hakluyt, cousin of the preacher and future compiler of voyages of the same name, demonstrated this mentality. He urged:

> That the first seat be chosen on the sea side, so as (if it may be) you may
> have your own navy within the bay, river, or lake within your seat safe
> from the enemy; And so as the enemy shall be forced to lie in open road
> without, to be dispersed with all winds and tempests that shall arise. Thus
> seated, you shall be least subject to annoy of the enemy; so may you by
> your navy pass out to all parts of the world; and so may the ships of
> England have access to you to supply all wants; so may your commodities
> be carried away also.[1]

Hakluyt was absolutely and correctly convinced that the only way an English settlement in the Americas could hope to flourish was by 'sea traffic'. Wealth was power and without it the English settlers would simply be consumed 'by the Spaniards, by the French, or by the natural inhabitants of the country'. He does seem very much to have envisaged a two-way

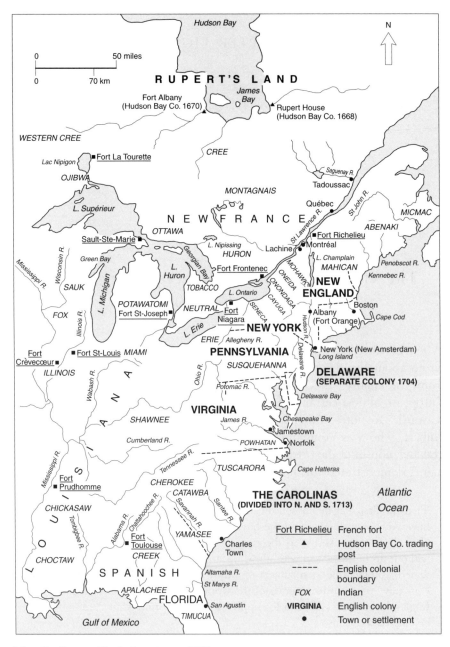

Map 5   Eastern North America, *c.* 1680

traffic, with the settlement importing European goods for the local inhabitants as well as exporting the local commodities for which there was a demand in Europe. Because that local market was seen as potentially vital, it followed that 'all humanity and courtesy and much forbearing of revenge to the inland people be used'. At the same time:

> Nothing is more to be endeavored with the inland people than familiarity. For so may you best discover all the natural commodities of their country, and also all their wants, all their strengths, all their weakness, and with whom they are in war and with whom confederate in peace and amity, etc., which known, you may work many great effects of greatest consequence.

All European elites were well aware of the astonishing military feats of the Spanish *conquistadores* in Mexico in the early sixteenth century, and most of them envied the way Hernán Cortés had so suddenly conquered the Aztec Empire between 1519 and 1521. Few indeed understood how it had been possible to achieve so much in so short a space of time. Contemporary Spanish propaganda tended to stress divine sponsorship. Equally dubious is the modern argument that Aztec theology bestowed a divine aura on the invading Spaniards, paralysing Aztec responses until the Spaniards were deep into the Aztec heartland and in a position to take advantage of the superior weaponry of a gunpowder-, steel- and cavalry-using civilisation against the doomed armies of the last great Stone Age culture. More recently, it has become clear that gunpowder played a very minor role, and that steel swords and armour and even horses did not place the Spaniards beyond the capabilities of the much larger and very adaptable Aztec armies. It was local allies who played the decisive role. The Aztecs ran a tributary empire which spared them the costs of direct administration and widespread garrisons, at the acceptable price of regular seasonal campaigning to hold their tributaries in awe. It was a system which worked well as long as there was no rival power around which disgruntled tributaries might rally. The Spaniards filled the gap.

Viral massacres on a staggering scale then devastated all the native peoples, probably reducing their numbers within a century from over 20 million to under 2 million, and leaving what is now central Mexico vulnerable to a new alien military and ideological hegemon.[2] What is extremely interesting is that Hakluyt, admittedly an exceptionally well-informed observer, seems to have grasped that the key to political effectiveness in a sixteenth-century native American context was an ability to see and take advantage of the lines of political and military cleavage between indigenous peoples. His stress on this underlines the opportunism which lay at the heart of early English settlement schemes in North America. There was, despite the arguments of some modern historians, no set programme for dealings with native Americans, soon to be usually called Indians. Settlers would go to America and then see what was possible, though Hakluyt's primary hope was clearly for an emporium, not a territorial empire.

The elder Hakluyt was consistent in his views about the desirability of peaceful and prosperous trade rather than conquest. When he wrote a piece on the reasons for colonisation in 1585, though he said the three principal objectives were the spread of Christianity, the pursuit of trade, and making conquests, he made it clear that he regarded trade as the first option. This essay was to be printed by John Brereton in his *Discovery of the North Part of Virginia* (1602), and was apparently adapted from its original format to suit Brereton's interest in more northerly latitudes. It was originally intended to offer advice to Sir Walter Raleigh and his associates, who were on the verge of trying to establish England's first North American settlement, originally intended for the Chesapeake, but eventually set up on Roanoke Island in Pamlico Sound in present-day North Carolina. Hakluyt admitted that 'What is to be done is the question.' He was clear that 'Traffic without conquest seemeth possible and not uneasy.' Like most geographical experts contemporary with him, the elder Hakluyt suffered from the illusion that regions within similar latitudes must have similar climates, so he expected the Chesapeake area to produce Mediterranean commodities high in demand in world trade and much imported into England. More realistic was his assessment of the likely high price of policies which led to avoidable conflict with the local peoples. He warned:

> But if, seeking revenge on every injury of the savages, we seek blood and raise war, our vines, our olives, our fig trees, our sugar canes, our oranges and lemons, corn, cattle etc., will be destroyed and trade of merchandise in all things overthrown; and so the English nation there planted and to be planted shall be rooted out with sword and hunger.[3]

As it happened, the first attempt to establish an English settlement in North America was sponsored by a man deeply involved in the privateering war against Spain. Sir Walter Raleigh denied that he stooped to 'picorie' or petty theft, defined as seizing ordinary Spanish merchantmen. He insisted that 'It became not the fortune in which I once lived to goe journeys of picorie, it had sorted ill with the offices of Honour which by her Majesties grace I hold this day in England, to run from Cape to Cape, and from place to place, for the pillage of ordinarie prizes.'[4] But of course Raleigh was a heavy investor in the privateering voyages of other men who were not at all averse to picorie or pickory and, like other grandees such as Lord

Thomas Howard and the Earl of Cumberland, he was into the game of owning and operating – though not in his case personally commanding – a private man-o'-war, whose function it was to return a tidy profit on its operations. After a reconnaissance voyage in 1584, Raleigh's kinsman Sir Richard Grenville established the first settlement, under Ralph Lane as governor, on Roanoke Island in 1585. It was based on a fort, but Lane himself subsequently made it clear that he was only interested in precious metals or the discovery of a passage into the Pacific from Pamlico Sound (the very idea shows the profundity of contemporary European ignorance about North American geography). As he put it: 'the discovery of a good mine, by the goodnesse of God, or a passage to the Southsea, or someway to it, and nothing else can bring this country in request to be inhabited by our nation'.[5] So Lane was no farmer settler, yet he still contrived to come to blows with local Indians, feeling obliged to launch a pre-emptive strike against one of their villages to avert an alleged plan to attack him. It has been argued that the general effect of the overseas expansion of early-modern Europe was to intensify and spread attitudes of intolerance, absolutism, and racism among Europeans.[6] There is obviously truth in this, but the argument can be overdone in the sense that Europeans were already a very violent, ethnocentric collection of cultures whose rulers were often reaching out for forms of absolutism within the unavoidable limits imposed by the social order and the constraints of contemporary communications systems. The exception to this qualification is the progressively stronger identification of slave status with negro ancestry as plantation agriculture developed in the Americas, but Englishmen certainly did not go to Virginia – as Raleigh's vast grants were named in 1585 in honour of his monarch – to set up slave-based agriculture. The chances of casual violence between such different cultures as that of the English and that of the native peoples they met in Virginia were very high indeed, just on the basis of misunderstanding. The Atlantic world was a very violent one in the late sixteenth century. John White, the artist who was with Lane and subsequently became governor when the colony was reimplanted in 1587 after the original settlers had seized the chance to abandon it offered by an unexpected visit from Sir Francis Drake in 1586, was prevented from returning to his charge from England in 1588 because his ship was overwhelmed and looted off Madeira. All the more maddening was the fact that the attackers were French ships from La Rochelle, whom White had hoped might be friendly. So they might have been had not a close reconnaissance convinced them that the English were weak and vulnerable, and therefore an opportunity rather than a potential ally. 'Woe to the weak' was a creed which Europeans applied with a commendable absence of ethnic bias.

The charters and other grants from European rulers which were the basis of the operations of European intruders in the Americas invariably assumed that the European ruler in question had an absolute right to assert authority over the lands and native inhabitants of all or part of the hemisphere. The complex issues and complicated arguments about titles to rule and claims of jurisdiction in the Americas which soon began to occupy much of the time of European legal experts and diplomats were primarily arguments between Europeans. More specifically, they were arguments between those early in the field, the Spaniards and Portuguese, and those European monarchies and republics which later challenged their claim to exclusive rights in the Americas. The papal donations on which the Luso-Hispanic camp would have preferred to base their exclusive claims were simply not accepted by anyone else, least of all the great Catholic monarchy of France, because they were so obviously designed to serve Spanish and Portuguese ends. Therefore, a range of other arguments was developed and propagated, as much for the purpose of stiffening the resolve of a given monarch's subjects to uphold his or her claims in the American hemisphere as for the purpose of convincing opponents, which in fact no argument of any kind ever did. These intricate ideological minuets, which drew on a wide conspectus of ideas from crusading theology, to Roman or civil law, to feudal law, and which endlessly moved round the closed circle of exclusive or pre-emptive claims versus demands for effective occupation and meaningful possession, were deeply ethnocentric in the sense that nobody – not the Spaniards, Portuguese, French, English, Dutch, or any other European power – doubted for a moment that they could and should take control over Amerindian peoples and American land, by one means or another, if it suited them so to do.[7]

Raleigh was no different from others, except in his profound comprehension of the element of the bizarre in all of this. Not all Europeans were incapable of seeing the intellectual problems involved in establishing claims on the New World. Twentieth-century activists have raved about the presumption of early-modern Europeans in claiming to 'discover' things well known to the locals, but it is doubtful if between 1500 and 1700 by 'discovery' was meant much more than reaching an area not yet frequented by Europeans. No major state put forward mere visual apprehension alone as establishing valid title to territory. It was remarked that on that basis all an Asian prince would have to do to annex Europe was to send a ship to cruise off a few European coasts. Where Raleigh's penetrating intelligence made him unusual was in his grasp of the fact that there was really no satisfactory answer, least of all from the theologians, to the endless conundrums which contemporary reality generated – because the 'great charter whereby God bestowed the whole earth upon Adam and confirmed it unto the sons of

Noah, being as brief in words, as large in effect, hath bred much quarrel of interpretation'.[8] Nevertheless, his colonists had no active territorial ambitions. They wanted supplies from the local Amerindians, whose guests they were meantime happy to be until something better turned up.

On the other hand, they formed the conclusion, in the course of their casually violent episodes, that if serious conflict did break out between them and the Indians, they would win and win easily. Lane asserted that 'ten of us with our arms prepared, were a terrour to a hundred of the best sort of them'. There was in his remark a tacit admission of the vulnerability of the English to surprise attack,[9] but when another of Raleigh's colonists, Thomas Harriot, wrote his account of the 'new found land of Virginia' as a hyping exercise to encourage further interest, especially financial interest, in the project, he missed out even a hint of vulnerability, saying that:

> If there fall out any warres between us and them, what their fight is likely to bee, we having advantages against them so many manner of wayes, as by our discipline, our strange weapons and devises els, especially ordinance great and smal, it may easily be imagined, by the experience we had in some places, the turning up of their heeles against us in running away was their best defence.[10]

When, therefore, the Virginia Company sent a fleet into the Chesapeake in 1607 and established at Jamestown what was to be the first enduring English settlement in North America, they must have regarded Spain, and not the local Indian peoples, as the power which could conceivably destroy the new settlement at a blow. Indian weapons were a combination of bows and arrows and clubbing weapons for use at short range. They seemed outclassed by swords, pikes, and, above all, muskets. In any case the settlement did not initially face any hostility from the most important ruler in the area. Indian hit-and-run tactics had not impressed the Roanoke settlers. The Chesapeake Indians did also occasionally employ mass assault tactics, either in square formation or in a crescent formation designed to surround their opponents progressively, but the vulnerability of these formations to European firepower was demonstrated in September 1607 when an English party which had landed at Kecoughtan was attacked by sixty or seventy warriors in square formation. They were easily dispersed by a splutter of musketry.[11] The Spaniards were a different proposition.

Philip III of Spain and Portugal was the heir to traditions which viewed obliteration by massacre as the most effective response to other Europeans' attempts to establish footholds in the Americas. That was how the problem of French penetration into Brazil had been handled in the end. An 'Anarctique Gaul' had been set up on an island in what was to be the harbour of Rio de Janeiro in 1555 by an expedition from Le Havre. It virtually disintegrated due to sectarian disputes between its members, and the remnant were slaughtered by the Portuguese in 1560. The Spaniards used the term 'Florida' to cover a vast extent of eastern North America, but it was in the northern parts of the modern state of Florida that they had a bitter confrontation with French Huguenot attempts to establish a settlement. In 1564 Laudonnière successfully set up a base at Fort Caroline on the St John's River on the east coast, but by 1565 it had been overwhelmed by the formidable Pedro Menendez de Aviles, who cold-bloodedly massacred its captured garrison. His explanation that he did it because they were heretics was unconvincing. No doubt the fact added zest to the decision, but no colony of Frenchmen was likely to be tolerated so close to the track of the Spanish gold fleets as they swung northwards on the Gulf Stream after emerging between Cuba and the Florida Keys. Only the fact that the site of Raleigh's Roanoke colony was so obscure prevented a serious attempt to serve it the same way. Ironically, the site which gave security was also an insuperable barrier to future development because of its poor access to the open sea. Ideally, the Spanish monarchy would have wished by 1607 to have at least a skeletal presence on the east coast as far north as modern Chesapeake Bay, and such had been the intention of Menendez after 1565. He established what turned out to be the permanent garrison at St Augustine and from there two major thrusts northwards were launched. About 1570 a Jesuit mission was established in Chesapeake Bay, and a few years later Asturian settlers were sent to the fortified site of Santa Elena, which is now Port Royal Sound in South Carolina. Neither enterprise flourished. Long experience of Spanish forays, brutality, habitual treachery, and cultural intolerance had made most of the Indian peoples of south-eastern North America their confirmed enemies. Missionaries and settlers faded away under Indian attack, whilst the metropolitan government lacked the resources to subsidise failure.[12]

None of this altered the underlying Spanish conviction that all other Europeans should be excluded from North America. The Treaty of London of 1604 had not mentioned the American issue, because it became clear that the negotiations would break down if Spain continued to demand that King James undertake to ban his own subjects from any dealings with the western hemisphere, but the diplomatic good will which James was so anxious to cultivate with Spain was entirely on his side. The Spanish ambassador, Pedro de Zuñiga, intrigued with Roman Catholic dissidents and insisted that the whole purpose of the Virginia Company's settlement was piratical. It was not, but any other European, apart from a Portuguese in Brazil, was in Spanish terms a pirate in America. The Virginia Company deployed the formidable financial resources available to a joint stock company funded out of the City of London, so the ambassador sensed at an early stage that theirs was an operation far larger than anything Raleigh's pocket had been able to sustain. His response was to say to Philip III that 'Your majesty will appreciate How important this is for your royal interests, and so I hope you will quickly command the extirpation of these insolents.' Zuñiga envisaged breaking the peace treaty if James declared himself sovereign of Virginia (which by the second charter he issued to the Virginia Company James did), but by the time the Spanish ambassador was writing so belligerently to Philip III in the spring of 1609, it was too late. Spain had needed the peace of 1604 more than the English Crown did, and it even contrived in 1609 to agree a 12-year truce with the rebellious Netherlands. Spanish policy was not in a phase where a conscious choice to reopen a war was likely.[13] Nevertheless, it was common prudence for the instructions issued to Sir Thomas Gates in May 1609, when he was about to leave for Virginia where he served as governor of the colony under the second charter, to stress that he was potentially as much at risk there from 'strangers', by whom was clearly meant Europeans, as from 'natives'. Stress was laid on the importance of seaboard fortification to hold off any European attack. Even Zuñiga admitted that Gates was a formidable soldier. However, Gates never had to cross swords with Spaniards in Virginia, as he had done in his campaigning in the Netherlands. When a Spanish ship commanded by a veteran of the murderous Menendez offensive against the French settlement in Florida in 1565 reached the mouth of the Chesapeake in 1609, it was spotted, the English settlers were alerted by smoke signals from warning bonfires, and the ship itself was persuaded to depart by the sort of language a Menendez man understood – in the form of Captain Samuel Argall in a larger, stronger English ship visibly spoiling for a fight.[14] Nobody could be sure that the Spaniards would not come back, least of all the Society of Martin's Hundred which in exchange for investing in the financially hard-pressed Virginia Company established a secondary patent over 20,000 acres situated about halfway between Jamestown and the modern city of Williamsburg. In 1618 its ship the *Guift of God* left England with 220 settlers aboard. They had instructions to erect a settlement to be called Wolstenholme Towne after their most important shareholder Sir John Wolstenholme, who had already sunk money in the ultimately futile searches by Henry Hudson and William Baffin for a north-west passage to China in northern latitudes. By the time the *Guift of God* sailed, Spain had decided to renew its war with the Dutch in 1621 when the current truce ran out and soon was funding and assisting its Austrian cousins in campaigns against central European Protestants. The main aim of Spanish policy was necessarily to try to keep England neutral. That was the best Spain could hope for. All this was less than clear to English settlers in

America. Significantly, the artillery defences of the fort which the new settlers established at what is now known as Martin's Hundred seem to have been designed to deal primarily with a threat from European ships on its James River waterfront.[15]

Ironically, it was not the Spaniards, against whose ships the English mounted ordnance in their forts and whose landing parties were in mind when the field of fire for musketeers on the firing steps of the forts were designed, that proved the near-mortal threat to the colony. It was the local Algonquian-speaking Indians. Their paramount chief, Powhatan, whose name is also applied to his people, held an extensive imperial ascendancy over a large number of tribal communities speaking related dialects, along the waterways of the Chesapeake and across the coastal plain of what was to become the Virginia tidewater. The English talked about the Indian peoples as 'nations' from the start, and tended to assume that a ruler like Powhatan had the same sort of powers as an 'absolute' king in Europe. This was not so. Powhatan was primarily a military overlord, under whom there were regional chiefs and township chiefs, both called werowances, who enjoyed substantial day-to-day autonomy. Chiefs had draconian powers, extending to life and death, over those within their jurisdictions, but apparently within the framework of immensely strong customary laws, whose details we can now never hope to recover. Powhatan was a very active imperialist whose techniques of rule included forcible movement of whole tribal populations after he had conquered them. That was how he served the Kecoughtan Indians, who contrived to remain independent of him until as late as 1596-97. After conquest, their survivors were transported across the York River to be resettled among reliable supporters of Powhatan. The latter's ascendancy was surrounded by areas of permanent tension. There was in 1607 a very uneasy peace between the Powhatan Indians and their neighbours to the south, the Algonquian-speaking Chowanocs and the Nottoways and Meherrins who spoke an Iroquoian language. Two decades later, the Chowanocs were exchanging occasional raids with the Powhatans. This was nothing compared with the permanent state of war which existed between Powhatan and the Siouan-speaking tribes to the west, the Monacans of the upper James River valley, and the Mannahoacs of the upper Rappahannock. They launched annual offensives down the rivers. We know little about Powhatan's northern frontier, which was complex as it included the northern marches of the eastern peninsula, except that distant but much feared enemies intermittently came down the Potomac River and the Susquehanna River in canoes and devastated Powhatan Indian villages. War was therefore endemic. Its impact was limited by the rarity of 'clean' kills in actions which were typically ambushes or running skirmishes in covered country. Disabled by arrows, an Indian warrior would have his skull smashed by a war-club, if he were not reserved for ritual torture. Enemy men were killed when possible, but women and children, the genetic bank from which future warriors could be drawn, were captured and, very sensibly, integrated into the social and biological systems of the Powhatans.[16]

Like the English, the Powhatans were a complex and cosmopolitan people. They were great travellers and traders, with a knowledge of 'foreign' peoples ranging from just south of the Great Lakes in North America to Western Europe. In 'Don Luis' they had produced a man of local rank who had been kidnapped and educated by the Spaniards, and whom Menendez hoped to use as an ideological and political fifth column to prepare the way for Spanish ascendancy on the Chesapeake. He reverted to a local identity and went along with the wiping out of a Jesuit mission in 1571, but then he had seen a Cuba where the native peoples were being exterminated as well as a colonial Mexico in which they were a subject race. From the days of the Roanoke settlement of 1585–86, English relations with the Chesapeake tribes were poisoned by importunate English demands for corn, often at times of the year when – in the local mixed farming, fishing, and hunting economy – stored maize was a scarce resource. The agendas of natives and settlers were never truly compatible. Initially Powhatan saw the English both as potential allies and as a threat. The English offered, as part of a deal, to join him in attacking his Monacan foes in what Europeans were to christen the piedmont area between the falls in the great rivers and the Blue Ridge mountains. Significantly, by 1611 the English had become aware that by planting forts and settlements close to the falls they had forced the two Indian groups into alliance in the face of the common threat from seaborne invaders. There was never any great likelihood of indefinite coexistence between two such aggressive, ethnocentric, and culturally incompatible peoples as the English and the Powhatan Indians.

By 1610 the first Anglo–Powhatan war had broken out, though in a form the English found confusing to the point where they may not have realised that it was a 'real' war. The core of the problem lay in the chronic English shortage of food. In exchange for corn Powhatan expected what he probably saw as a new and odd tribe to offer him loyalty and military support. As the English food crisis worsened, he began to demand muskets, which English renegades were teaching the Indians to use. When the English allied with his enemies in 1608, he decided to starve them out by cutting off the corn trade. It was at this point that the acting governor, Captain John Smith, an old soldier with Eastern European campaign experience, launched a series of ruthless raids against local Indian settlements to force their werowances to give up corn. Powhatan sensibilities were outraged when an English punitive strike at a settlement at Paspahegh involved killing Indian women and children. This violated local 'rules' about the usage of war. Then the settlers started to spread out in the lower James River valley, seizing land to do so. Local Indian chiefs hit back with guerrilla tactics. At one point Powhatan had driven in the English raiders and so starved their Jamestown redoubt that there was a consensus there that the colony ought to be abandoned. Its history would then have closely resembled that of many attempted Spanish settlements in what is now Florida. After unsuccessful forays over wide areas of southern North America by Juan Ponce de Leon in 1513, Panfilo de Narvaez in 1528, and Hernando de Soto in 1539, the Spaniards sent a large expedition under Tristan de Luna in 1539 to establish a settlement specifically at Ochuse, roughly modern Pensacola. Natural disaster, threatened famine, and Indian hostility simply wore it down. Despite church support for the idea of a permanent base for 'pacifying' Florida, four relief expeditions, and a change of governor later, the survivors went back to Mexico.[17] Jamestown was different only because the unexpected arrival of reinforcements enabled the English to go back on the offensive in 1610 in a series of 'feed fights' for control of the fields of squashes, beans, and corn which were vital to the Indian subsistence economy. Powhatan's paramount chiefdom was not capable of a coherent response to the situation. Peripheral parts of his ascendancy continued to trade with the English for the metal tools which had become immensely desirable because of their labour-saving potential, and may not have regretted the weakening of the central ruler by the crisis in his core territories. This apparent lack of consistency lies at the root of the endless English complaints about the 'inconstancy' of the 'savages'. There was no decisive outcome to this first war. Only when Powhatan's daughter Pocahontas was captured and held as a hostage did hostilities peter out.[18]

There was never the slightest possibility that the English, or any other Europeans, would not deem the Chesapeake Indians to be savages. Any other terminology was unthinkable. Even the French – who in their settlement of the lower St Lawrence valley in the seventeenth century were in the unusual position of not threatening existing Indian land use, and who were extremely anxious for tactical reasons to ingratiate themselves with the tribes in the vast fur-bearing regions around the Great Lakes – never doubted that these were peoples without law, faith, or king whose destiny was to be 'civilised' by French royal and ecclesiastical authority. The occasional doubts of extremely sophisticated observers, like some Jesuit missionaries, as to whether this was an adequate approach had no practical impact at all. Indeed, as the French position became more secure towards the end of the seventeenth century, French willingness to accommodate to native culture notably decreased and French authorities could be terrifyingly ruthless with Indian tribes which crossed their will.[19] The concept of 'Wild

Irish', ultimately of Old English origin, implied quite clearly that many inhabitants of Ireland (notably the Anglo-Norman Old English) were not at all wild. It was traditional Gaelic society which was being attacked by that trope. By everyone's standards in Old England in 1607, North American Indians were all savages. That they led highly structured lives was as invisible to English observers as their reasons for resisting instant conversion to Christianity. Yet, none of this ruled out respect for the Indians, of which in the early stages there was a good deal. Intelligent Englishmen could see that these were handsome, vigorous people with lively minds. They learned English much faster than Englishmen learned their language. Their ruling elites met the classic European criteria for nobility. Powhatan was impressive. Accusations of congenital idleness and profligacy were just as likely to be levelled by English writers against the lower orders among the colonists, some of whom had been kidnapped and brought to America against their will, as against the average Indian. A mixture of guilt and fear eventually was to lead to the stereotyping of the Indian as the unspeakable 'other', but those who sneer at the condescension of colonist John Rolfe's stress on his desire to elevate Pocahontas and save her soul through marriage and conversion to Christianity need to remember two things. One is that he more or less had to say that, and it was probably sincere enough. If he had been from a Counter-Reformation culture he would have had to say it at even greater length. The other is that what is touchingly personal in his statement is his repeated emphasis on the fact that he had fallen deeply in love with her.[20]

The English colony had teetered on the brink of extinction due to a fearful mortality rate, aversion to work, and the general improvidence of its inhabitants. Under Governor Sir Thomas Dale, from the spring of 1611 onwards, it was subjected to the stern discipline of his 'Lawes Divine, Morall, and Martiall', whilst its health was improved by a policy of spreading settlement away from the unhealthy Jamestown site. Though the Virginia Company management in London had an oversimplified vision in which another punitive invasion of Indian territory would solve all problems, Dale's march on the Pamunkey people in 1614 with 150 men, the largest English force hitherto assembled in Virginia, was followed by a realisation by both sides that escalation was to nobody's advantage. Negotiated peace was confirmed by the marriage of Rolfe and Pocahontas. The latter went to England with Rolfe and their son, becoming a celebrity at the royal court but dying prematurely. Already, Rolfe had set the stage for the final Anglo–Powhatan confrontation, unwittingly but lethally, by introducing into Virginia a strain of tobacco known as Orinoco from Trinidad, which suited English tastes better than the native Virginian variety. As a mild narcotic, tobacco had become familiar in England as an import from the Caribbean or South

American mainland. In 1614 Rolfe shipped the initial four barrels of cured leaf to England. Within three years the colonists were shipping 50,000 pounds annually. As prices rose in the 1620s, there was a tobacco bonanza, despite the deep disapproval of King James in his anonymous but virulent *Counterblast to Tobacco*. At last, the settlers had a compelling motive to spread up the rivers which provided such a convenient transportation network and to seize the lands of the native inhabitants, for profit.[21] The windy rhetoric of the promotion literature produced in England for decades – with its call to rival the heroes of antiquity, convert the heathen, drive out the bounds of England, and recognise the peculiar moral sanction on Englishmen to do so – was a mass of contradictions and misconceptions, of which the idea that England was overpopulated and needed to dump its surplus somewhere was only one.[22] Such propaganda would not have produced permanently expanding English settlement in America. Tobacco did.

The first charter issued by King James to the Virginia Company in 1606 had been vague as to the precise nature of the royal claims in North America. It was a classic speculative feudal licence to a marcher lord, in this case a corporate one, granting him what he could take, if he could take it. The second charter of 1609 was far more sweeping, making grants of lands from sea to sea (nobody had of course any idea of just how far away the Pacific was), though it hedged the royal bets on the possibility of other Europeans having already established themselves in the relevant parts of North America. After 1620 James I and Charles I simply claimed possession of most of North America by pre-emptive right, and they and their subjects who were colonial promoters assumed they could dispose of it by charter. Despite protests from James I in 1621, the Dutch ignored this in their penetration and settlement of the Hudson valley.[23] Reality on the ground was what counted. By 1620 the real ruler of the Powhatan Indians was beginning to conclude that on the Chesapeake that reality was becoming unendurable.

When the power of Powhatan began to wane, as it did after the capture of his daughter Pocahontas, real authority shifted towards the most astute politician in the chiefly house, his second-younger brother Opechancanough. By 1614, he was the real ruler of the Powhatan Indians, ruling through the last years of the ageing Powhatan and effectively through the paramount chieftainship of his elder brother Otiotan before he finally became paramount chief in his own right. Between 1618 and 1622 the situation in Virginia moved to crisis point for the Indians. From 1618 the Virginia Company began to try to attract settlers by offering each adult family member fifty acres of land in private right. Servants transported to Virginia also rated at fifty acres, while some wealthy backers were given huge grants. The year 1619 saw the establishment of a representative assembly in Jamestown, to ensure settler cooperation and enhance the attractiveness of the colony. Between 1619 and 1622 a thousand new settlers poured into the Chesapeake. Already the Indians had been decimated by imported European diseases. This phenomenon had been noticed among the Carolina Indians in the 1580s. As early as 1608 the Jamestown settlers saw that a 'strange mortality' was slaying 'a great part of the people'.[24] In 1617–19 another terrible epidemic scythed down the Powhatan Indians. Only an act of genocide against the invaders could save the Indians from diseases against which they had no resistance, eviction to make way for tobacco plantations, and total cultural and political destruction. The decision to strike taken by their new unofficial leadership was risky but probably the right decision under their desperate circumstances. Its execution was not faultless, but broadly it was well done. The English were lulled into a false sense of security, by flattery and promises of cooperation on such matters as sending them Indian children to rear, which was obviously a first step towards eliminating Indian culture. George Thorpe, a prominent colonist, had written letters to England in May 1621, letters so optimistic about Indian good will towards all things English that they provided material for what has been described as 'the most ironical sermon in English history',[25] preached to the members of the Virginia Company by Patrick Copland at Bow Church, Cheapside, on 18 April 1622. It praised the 'happy league of peace and amity' established between the English and Indians 'and rejoiced that fears of mutual slaughter had vanished away'. About four weeks earlier, on 22 March, there had been a massive assault on the English plantations along the James River. The news of it only reached London eighteen weeks later.

The attack had originally been planned for 1621, but when the Indians on the eastern shore of the Chesapeake had been asked to join in, they had promptly alerted the English, forcing postponement and underlining the problems of solidarity and security Opechancanough faced. It is not surprising that the English received a few warnings in 1622, but the Indians were still able to attack suddenly from within English settlements in which they had become familiar figures. They had to use close combat techniques, for although some had been taught to use firearms before the Virginia Company tightened up on this practice in 1616, they had no serious firearm capacity. Night attack might have faced the problem of alarms from the fierce mastiffs which the settlers kept and the Indians feared. The onslaught killed nearly 350 colonists, a quarter of their number, and within a year another quarter was to die either from Indian attacks or famine caused by English inability to plant crops, or by the disease encouraged by defensive concentration on the mephitic Jamestown defended site in high summer. The Indians had attacked English trading vessels in the York River basin, and trying to lure trading ships far enough up river for them to be exposed to surprise attack by canoes seems to have been one of the ploys of the Powhatans in the intermittent negotiations with the English which punctuated the untidy struggle that followed. If so, they were more than served back in kind when the English contrived to make Powhatan negotiators drink a toast in poisoned wine, after which the assembled Indians were suddenly fired on. Opechancanough escaped wounded from this occasion. His strategy had clearly failed. By now the Indians needed to be hunting down and killing scattered remnants of the English after the initial assault. Quite a few members of the priestly and chiefly elites of the Powhatans had visited England by 1622. Some spoke reasonably good English. They must have known that the Virginia Company had severe financial problems, and may even have had an inkling of the possibility that total calamity would finish it, without necessarily provoking a massive military backlash from so impecunious a monarch as James I. On the other hand, they could not be sure. The first requirement for any sort of bargaining position was the extermination of the English on the Chesapeake.

But the English survived and fought back, winning the biggest action of the war in a battle at Pamunkey in 1624. There was a truce in 1628 which neither side seems to have entered in good faith and which the English broke in 1629. A war of endless raids and ambushes finally wound down into a peace negotiated separately with the two main Powhatan groups involved, the Chickahominies and the Pamunkeys in 1632. From 1627 the English were beginning to settle the York River. After 1632 there was an explosion of settlement which took the rest of the James valley, all the lower York and much of the eastern shore, and began to invade after 1640 the rich soils of the Rappahannock valley and the south bank of the Potomac. It was hardly surprising that the Powhatan leadership remained privately unreconciled. Opechancanough rebuilt his network of influence and prepared for another round, while lulling the English once again into relative complacency. Though the eastern shore Indians did not cooperate, the solidarity of the mainland groups was impressive and security much tighter. The assault went in on 18 April 1644, with no previous warnings. About the same number of English were killed as in 1622, but with the flood of tobacco farmers this was a mere twelfth of the immigrant population. The backlash was ferocious. Tribes adjacent to English settlements were driven out. The aged Opechancanough was captured and killed. When peace was negotiated in 1646, it marked the end of the paramount chieftainship. Individual Indian groups accepted the status of dependants of the English, paying a tribute of beaver skins annually. There was even the beginnings of a reservation system in the sense that certain lands were guaranteed to the Indians. The guarantees began to be violated almost at once, but it was clear that the English now preferred separation to assimilation for the Indians.[26]

In a famous address recorded by Captain John Smith, Powhatan had in 1609 put to him the question 'What can you get by warre, when we can hide our provisions and fly to the woods?'[27] It was a fair question then and Smith lost his war, but the guerrilla tactics of the Powhatans broke down against a reinforced colony in which every male was a member of a militia, with a musket and, usually, extensive armour. When the English set out to smash Powhatan society after 1622, they could force the Indians to stand and fight for their crops. They could also destroy Indian fishing weirs, and even disrupt their hunting with cavalry patrols, bloodhounds, and mastiffs. It was a feed fight on an unprecedented scale. That the Indians were instantly demonised after the 1622 massacre was unsurprising. Enemies usually are. The Powhatans were known to be vulnerable. Their land was now valuable to the English, who rejoiced that under the usages of war they could seize fields by force instead of negotiating and buying. It was a classic case of profitable entrepreneurial violence. Because the Powhatans seem to have had few stone arrow points due to the alluvial nature of their soils, the armour of the English was effective and even the problem of lethal splinters when arrowheads broke on impact, which plagued Spaniards elsewhere in the Americas, was minimised. The royal government in London contrib- uted little beyond shipments of old armour from the Tower of London,[28] and the stress of war did finish the Virginia Company, whose charter was quite reasonably forfeit after due legal process by writ of *quo warranto*, on the ground that it had ceased to be able to fulfil the terms of its grant. However, none of this helped the Indians, who faced the genocidal drive of what was from 1624 a colony dependent directly on the Crown. The Indians were perceived as a real threat long after 1622. To fear of them the English added a guilty necessity still to deal with them by theft or trading to obtain the corn supplies which military activity and an obsession with tobacco profits prevented the English from growing in adequate quantities them- selves.[29] In the long run, however, the situation righted itself and the in- vading community ceased to be dependent in this paradoxical way. By the 1640s, the Indians were outnumbered and fighting more as an alternative to humiliation than with a reasonable chance of victory as in 1609 or 1622. By the 1660s they had become in tidewater Virginia mere shadows on the land.

What replaced them on the Chesapeake, in Virginia, and in the great palatinate of Maryland – granted by Charles I to Cecilius Calvert, Lord Baltimore, in 1632 (where the Indians were 'persuaded' to fade from the scene in the early settlement areas with much less violence) – was a new cultural province of the English nation, under two different legal jurisdic- tions. The English courtier and poet Michael Drayton celebrated the grant- ing of its first charter to the Virginia Company in 1606 with a poem 'To

the Virginia Voyage' in which he fairly urged 'You brave heroique minds'
to embark for Virginia, leaving 'loyt'ring hinds' to lurk at home with shame.
It was platitudinous poetic hyperbole, and continued:

> *Britans, you stay too long,*
> *Quickly aboard bestow you,*
> *And with a merry gale*
> *With vowes as strong*
> *As the winds that blow you.*[30]

What was unusual here was the reference to Britons, but in the period
1606–10 King James was obsessively trying to push through a complete
union of Scotland and England, in which adopting a new British identity
would be the least gesture his subjects could make to express their gratitude
to God for the inestimable privilege of being ruled by him. Ben Jonson,
greatest of court poets, was very careful at this time to fill his poems with
references to Old England becoming Great Britain.[31] On the Chesapeake
the idea never flew. Virginia and Maryland were dependencies of the English Crown whose white inhabitants were emphatically English.

By the early eighteenth century, this was simply taken for granted. For
example, when in 1709 'Robin, a Pamunky Indian' petitioned the president
and council of Virginia to be exempted from an order which his tribal
elders had obtained from the council 'that all Indians of that nation should
return to their Town', he explained that he did not wish to forsake 'the
company and conversation of the English (among whom he has been bred)',
and who had taught him the craft of shoemaking. In response the council
agreed that 'In Consideration of the Petitioners' having been bred so long
amongst the English, and that his trade will be of no use to him, if he
returns to his own Nation', he be granted leave to remain. Both the Indian
petitioner and the council used the term 'inhabitants' – in the petitioner's
case in the form 'Inhabitants of this Colony' – as synonymous with 'the
English'.[32] Lieutenant Governor Alexander Spotswood of Virginia, writing
to the bishop of London in 1716 about the problems of educating and
converting the Indians of Virginia to Christianity, was confident about the
opportunities for influence which 'the constant intercourse between the
English and Indians' for commercial purposes offered. He had been de-
lighted in 1711 when the 'queen' of Robin's people sent her son and some
other Indian youths 'as hostages', but 'all decently cloathed after the English manner' and with a request that they be educated at the College of
William and Mary's Indian school in Williamsburg. There were plenty of
people of non-English origin around on the Chesapeake by the early eighteenth century, even if black slaves be exempted. Spotswood came from a

distinguished Scottish family, and showed distinct tendencies to stress 'British' interests early in his proconsular career, but latterly – when living as a landowner and ironmaster in the colony he had once ruled, married to a girl of aristocratic Anglo-Norman Irish ancestry – he undoubtedly was absorbed by the predominant English culture of the colony, beginning to talk about the defence of English liberties as befitted a man who had joined that nation late, in Virginia.[33] Seventeenth-century white Virginian society was English. It was different from other provincial English cultures, but then they were all different, and the one on the Chesapeake was by no means the first to live as a marchland engaged in intermittent territorial expansion against another culture. English communities led by Anglo-Norman barons had lived that way for centuries on the marches of Wales or on the external or internal frontiers of the Lordship of Ireland. By the mid-seventeenth century it was a commonplace that communication by ship with England from Virginia was possible at least every second month almost all year round. The time gap was no greater than that involved in travelling from London to the remoter parts of Scotland or Ireland, given the extreme slowness of land travel in those parts. Chesapeake Englishmen had simply moved 'from one of London's provinces to another'.[34] As in previous marcher provinces where the Crown had made no serious commitment of its own resources and the military entrepreneurship was locally generated, the ability of the Crown to control profitable land grabbing was extremely limited, as became clear with the experience of Governor John Harvey, appointed in 1626. On arrival he found that the colonists were just not interested in exploring possibilities of peace with the Indians. When he tried again in 1635 to control the aggressive attitudes of his colonists, they forcibly removed him and sent him back to Old England, with a barrage of self-righteous complaints about his 'arbitrary' government. That was the beginning of a long tradition.[35]

The bankruptcy of integration in New England by 1676

New England was a somewhat different phenomenon, not in the sense that the settlements which started to grow up there from the 1620s were not English – quite the reverse – but because they were established and ruled by people who, at least at first, were anxious to put a distance between themselves and that part of the English nation which was effectively controlled by the Crown and its established Anglican Church. Not for them even the minimalist Anglican establishment which was set up without any difficulty or serious objection in Virginia. There was no permanent English settlement north of the Chesapeake in 1620 when the Crown granted a new charter to a group of associates headed by Sir Ferdinando Gorges, who had explored along the northern seaboard south of the Bay of Fundy and whose hopes of profitable development were encapsulated in the title they received in the charter: the Council for New England. The first permanent English settlement within their area was set up in the same year at Plymouth on the mainland just south of Cape Cod by a group of Separatists who were anxious to set up a community free of what they saw as a hopelessly corrupt Church of England. They had no real legal title in English law for their enterprise, and these Pilgrim Fathers were clearly recalcitrant subjects anxious to escape from the authority of the Anglican church-state, though so weak as not to wish to challenge monarchical authority publicly. For all the fundamentally religious motives which they made sure would dominate their mini-polity, and the initially friendly attitude of the local Wampanoag tribe, they had by 1622 generated conflict with the Indians through the usual European inability to produce food in adequate quantity over the winter, which led them to steal from the vital underground corn stores of the Indians. They were initially spared any very violent response, probably because men like their principal ambassador to the native inhabitants, the English-speaking Patuxet tribe member Massasoit, hoped to use them as allies in inter-tribal warfare. However, when a group of non-Pilgrim immigrants who had settled north of Plymouth ratched up the level of plundering and intimidation against the Massachusetts Indians to intolerable levels, serious fighting occurred. The Pilgrims had come from exile in the Netherlands, the prime school of war in Europe, and had recruited a professional soldier, Miles Standish, who now led a punitive column which killed eight Indians and impaled a sachem's* severed head on the palisade of the fort at Plymouth. To his credit, the Reverend John Robinson, one of their spiritual leaders (who was still in Holland), was shocked when the news reached him and denounced the settlers for behaving like savages.[36] In practice, the problem of violence then faded away for several decades, because the new religiously motivated English settlements in the north were full of people who wished to farm, and they soon learned to grow their own corn.

Much larger-scale immigration of English settlers who established the Massachusetts Bay Colony from 1630 did not immediately provoke any

---

* 'Sachem' is a term which entered American English around 1622. It comes from the Narragansett Algonquian word *sachima* meaning a chief, especially of a confederation of tribes on the north Atlantic coast.

parallel atrocities. The Bay Colony was in religious terms not very different from Plymouth, but it was much more cautious, sustaining an ambiguous posture towards the Anglican Church. Whilst in practice running a congregationalist ecclesiastical system, the rulers of the colony stressed that they did not regard the Church of England, of which they were in their own opinion the best part, as beyond hope of internal reformation. Their use of their royal charter was equally devious. The Crown had awarded it in good faith on the assumption that the company, like any other, would have its directorate and keep its charter in London, where they would be accessible to normal scrutiny and monitoring by the royal government, which was as a rule scarcely intrusive. By moving charter and leadership to America, the Puritan leaders of the enterprise arguably demonstrated bad faith from the start. The New England way in its Massachusetts version consisted of taking advantage of what association with the Crown could offer, whilst refusing, behind a cloud of verbiage, to accept its authority. The English settlements on the Connecticut River, which were pioneered by people from Plymouth in 1632 and then greatly expanded by religious dissenters from the Bay Colony from 1635, also escaped early conflict, despite a complex pattern of interaction with local Indians and the Dutch, who had set up a fur-trading post at Hatford in 1633. John Winthrop Jr, who had moved in from Massachusetts to lay out a settlement at Saybrook at the mouth of the river, was able to negotiate a recognition of his authority from the eight hundred or so English living in the Connecticut valley by 1636, in what had become an autonomous jurisdiction administered by a representative commission. What was remarkable about these settlements was not that eventually they did become involved in war with some Indians, but that war came late and was at first not at all general.

Educated sixteenth- and seventeenth-century Englishmen, who formed a high proportion of the New England leadership (and even of the early Chesapeake leadership), were not naive about patterns of conquest and migration. They knew that Old England was a product of such historical processes. Machiavelli had distinguished between conquests made by princes and those made by migrations of whole peoples, which involved far more destructive life-and-death struggles between human groups for control of land and other resources, in which countries lost their names. The Roman province of Britannia literally vanished when the Anglo-Saxons over-ran it, driving the culture of the ancient Britons into the refuge of the Welsh hills. A Conservative churchman like Bishop Gardiner in the reign of Henry VIII was well acquainted with this body of thought. He also was, like all the rest of the English ruling classes, conscious of the fact that the English political tradition went back to the Norman Conquest of 1066 and that that had been a brutal conquest sweeping away an existing aristocracy in favour of immigrant French speakers and Flemings. That was one reason why he was anxious both to have a Habsburg monarch in the shape of the future Philip II of Spain (as a guarantee of religious conservatism) and to limit his rights to introduce Spanish nobles and troops into England.[37] Most intelligent contemporary observers, despite the mandatory rhetoric of conversion of the Indians as prime motive, would have expected violence when a farming population invaded part of North America, and sooner rather than later. That it came later rather than sooner requires explanation.

Disease goes far to explain the lack of severe competition for access to land which was characteristic of early New England. Pathogens were, everywhere in the Americas, the true shock troops of the European invasion, and they were far more lethal than swords and muskets because of the Indians' lack of resistance to them. In northern parts contact with the vast numbers of European fishermen operating off Newfoundland spread pathogens long before actual European settlement, as did the activities of individual exploring expeditions. By the first decade of the seventeenth century explorers had penetrated deep into the north-eastern region below the St Lawrence River. In 1609, when the Englishman Henry Hudson, who worked for the Dutch, sailed up the river which was to be named for him, he came within seventy-five miles of the furthest penetration in the same year by the French explorer Samuel de Champlain down from the St Lawrence towards Ticonderoga. An unidentified epidemic seems to have raged among the human population of the St Lawrence valley in 1535. Another massacred Indians as far south as New England in the period 1564–70. Typhus struck the same area in 1586. Most significant of all for English settlement was a terrible epidemic which started amongst the eastern Abenaki peoples in 1617, swept down the coast of Maine, and between 1617 and 1619 devastated the Indians of New England, apparently often killing over 75 per cent of tribal populations. The Puritans moved into what has been described as a widowed landscape and a power vacuum, occupying abandoned Indian fields without opposition and achieving peacefully what the Chesapeake settlers had to use force to achieve after 1622.[38] Inevitably, Cotton Mather, clergyman, scientist, and grandson of pioneer Puritans, saw all this in retrospect from the vantage point of the 1690s as a pre-eminent example of the unappreciated providence of God whereby a 'prodigious Pestilence' had swept over the land so that the 'Woods were almost cleared of those pernicious Creatures to make Room for a better Growth'. Cotton Mather was, like so many other Englishmen, well acquainted with the *Decades* of Peter Martyr (Pietro Martire d'Anghiera), the official chronicler of the early Spanish conquests in the Americas and, indeed, a literary competitor, but his prose is less the cant of conquest than an inflated jeremiad designed to shame his fellow New Englanders into a return to religious commitment. He de-emphasises violence to stress the divine favour which had given his people their land without conquest. Even the first serious war, which was with the Pequots on the expanding Connecticut settlement frontier, is hardly stressed in his work, for to him it was 'by the marvellous Providence of God immediately extinguished – by prospering the New English Arms, unto the utter subduing of the Quarrelsome Nation, and affrightening of all the other Natives'.[39] The Pequot War of 1637 was, in fact, infinitely more complex than this bald summary suggests.

The Pequots, often referred to in modern anthropological literature as the Mohegan-Pequots, were an Algonquian people whose pre-European contact heartland was probably what became known as the Thames River valley in Connecticut. Just before contact their population appears to have been about 13,000, but the great mortality of 1616–19 and subsequent epidemics such as that of smallpox in 1633 had reduced them to about 3000 before 1637. Despite a mortality rate of over 75 per cent, they had played the post-contact field very successfully, extending their power over into the Connecticut valley, up to Block Island, and over to the eastern tip of Long Island. Though they were clearly a martial and dominant people, they derived crucial strength from their position between the coastal areas which produced wampum, the prized beads that came in two varieties, white and purple, and were ground and polished from the narrow inner pillars of the shells of marine species particularly common between Cape Cod and New York. The Dutch, whose West Indian Company had established a fur-trading post at the west end of Long Island at Manhattan, appear to have been the pioneers in building wampum into a profitable triangular trade which involved the exchange of European manufactures such as cloth, metal products, and muskets, for wampum (whose manufacture could be much expedited by European tools). The wampum was then used to purchase furs from up-country Indians for export to European markets. Secretary de Rasieres of the Dutch Company seems to have introduced the English into this trade by selling the Plymouth settlers £50 sterling's worth of wampum in 1627. Plymouth, in particular, was burdened by debt, so trade in furs was important to it, and subsequently the Bay colony would also take early profits out of the fur trade. Once it was established, the Massachusetts colony could even sell corn to Indian peoples to the north who were being compelled by the competitive pressures of the trade to specialise more in hunting and move from traditional areas of seasonal cultivation. One of the effects of the Pequot War of 1637 was that by conquering the Pequots and building control of other wampum-producing Indians into the Hartford Agreement of 1638, which concluded the hostilities, the English settlers secured huge tributary payments of wampum amounting between 1634 and 1664 to at least 7,000,000 beads worth some £5000 sterling. This they used to underwrite their colonising activities.[40] However, if the settlement included perhaps the New Englanders' first conscious attempt at self-funding predation, it is clear that the origins of and motives for the war were far murkier and more confused than a simple economic model might suggest.

The events of the war are not in dispute, and it has been studied to death by American scholars who have tended to concentrate on the ultimately opaque question of the settlers' motivation and how this was grounded in their ethnocentric attitudes. At one extreme there is the view that 'the whole story of the Pequot "war" is one long atrocity'.[41] On the other is the work of those scholars who stress the inter-racial nature of the coalition which attacked the Pequots and the important role of Indian manipulation in creating the paranoia which was the trigger mechanism for the decision of the Massachusetts and Connecticut settlers to go to war. So far from being in a strong position, the Pequots were struggling with hostilities with the powerful Narragansett Indians, and were breaking up as the Mohegan bands assumed an independent and hostile position under leaders like the shifty and clever sachem Uncas, who had a real flair for manipulating the immigrant English with 'conspiracy' theories.[42] It was he who depicted to the English as a dangerous plot the futile appeal of the Pequots to the Narragansetts to desist from hostility and unite in the face of the much more serious threat of the European invasion. In fact the Pequots had derived much of their power from an ability to monopolise access to trading posts on the Connecticut River set up by the Dutch, who had established their main base at New Amsterdam on Manhattan Island in 1627. Though the Pequots appear to have obtained comparatively few muskets, Dutch trade goods were crucial in the competition between Indian societies, and by 1636 the Pequots could no longer monopolise them. They had at one point in 1634 invited settlement from the Massachusetts Bay colony to offset their enemies, who included not only Indians but also the Dutch, whom they had attacked as part of their attempt to keep control of the trade patterns. Dutch retaliation had cost them their ablest leader, sachem Tatobem. Roger Williams, the eccentric Puritan who had been too much for the leaders of the Bay colony, whence he departed to become the founder of the equally eccentric colony of Rhode Island, refused to join the incipient coalition of settlers, Mohegans, and Narragansetts which was lining up for a confrontation with the Pequots, as indeed did some individual Narragansett sachems. When John Winthrop Jr, who was both governor of Saybrook and the official negotiator on behalf of the Massachusetts colonists, chose to present the Pequots with an unacceptable ultimatum, he was challenging a deeply troubled group. He demanded the surrender of the murderers of a ruffianly English ship captain who had probably been kid-napping Pequots and also demanded hostages and heavy tribute payments which would confirm the Pequots' subordinate status. War was inevitable.

Military tactics among the aboriginal peoples of North America had already been decisively modified by the arrival of Europeans with their firearms. Originally the European musket was a matchlock fired by the mechanical lowering of a smouldering end of a specially prepared cord or match into a priming pan of powder, which then ignited the main charge in the barrel. For all its weight (it was usually fired from a rest), the susceptibil-ity of the match to rain and the inappropriateness of a weapon with a permanent glow for night ambush, the matchlock rendered the formal battle rituals of the eastern Indians obsolete, as the French explorer Samuel de Champlain had demonstrated in 1609 in a battle where he supported Algonquian allies against the Iroquoian Mohawks in what was to be the Richelieu River valley. The Indians had lined up in mass formation behind arrow-proof wooden shields, some of them wearing cotton and hide armour, and had then moved to within thirty yards of one another to exchange arrow fire, not very lethally, when a single discharge of musketry from a small group of concealed French killed two of the three Mohawk chiefs leading the advance and mortally wounded the other. By 1620 pro-fessional soldiers like Miles Standish of Plymouth Colony had the more advanced snaphance musket which was lighter and used flint striking on steel to produce self-ignition by spark. Though the colonists fought the Pequots with a mixture of matchlocks and snaphances, and as late as 1650 the Connecticut General Court was insisting that towns keep a supply of match, there had been a general transition among the settlers by 1675 to the flintlock muskets which were a superior version of the principle of self-ignition embodied in the snaphance. The Pequots in 1637 had very few muskets, and only a general desire to acquire firearm technology rather than any serious understanding of the problems involved. When in April 1637 they and their Pyquag allies captured two young English girls in an attack on a settlement at Wethersfield, they traded them to the Dutch after they discovered that they did not know how to make gunpowder. Ironically, the fertility of the women in the northern European colonies was at least as dangerous a threat to the survival of the Indians as European pathogens and firearms.

There seems always to have been an intention on the part of the Pequots' enemies to make the war self-funding. Operations started with an expedi-tion against the Pequots' allies on Block Island, accused of murdering a Massachusetts merchant. The idea was to kill the men and fund that effort by selling the women and children as slaves. Captain John Endicott's ar-moured musketeers blundered around in the woods on the island, finding few Indians to kill or capture, and then sailed to the mouth of the Connecticut River. There the Pequots had the wit to refuse formal battle and could besiege the garrison at Saybrook after Endicott and his men had departed, leaving behind them burned Indian villages and cornfields. So far the resort to arms had been self-defeating, as the indignant commander at Saybrook insisted. However, there were serious professional soldiers available to the settlers. Captain John Mason of Connecticut had, like Captain Miles Standish of Plymouth, been bred to arms in the Dutch Netherlands. Exploiting the flexibility of seapower, the Connecticut settlers sent the ninety men they had raised under Mason down river to Saybrook in 'one Pink, one Pinnace and one Shallop', accompanied by Uncas and his Mohegans in canoes. At Saybrook, Captain John Underhill and nineteen of the garrison joined the expedition, being replaced by twenty men from Mason's command. The English sailed 40 miles eastward, landed, picked up no fewer than 500 Narragansett allies, and then marched back overland to completely surprise the Pequots, whose own army was well to the south when the coalition attacked the main fortified village of the principal Pequot sachem, Sassacus, on the Mystic River.

Historians have argued endlessly about what followed, but John Mason's own account has the ring of truth when he records that the original intention was to storm the two entrances and then 'to destroy them by the Sword and save the plunder'. That would have been consistent with the canny awareness of the financial balance of war which had been one of the few rational aspects of the Block Island expedition. As it was, a volley into the palisades proved predictably futile, and the first assault met stout opposition within the village. Rather than take heavy losses in what amounted to hut-to-hut fighting, Mason seems to have taken an impulsive decision to use Indian domestic hearths as the source of a fire which would destroy the whole very inflammable village. There was nothing unusual in this: burning villages by torching their thatch roofs was standard European practice. What was shocking was the massacre of the Pequots as they fled into a double circle of English musketeers with snaphances, backed by Narragansett and Mohegan Indians. All four hundred or so Pequots – men, women, and children – died. The blood lust was extraordinary, for in a subsequent and unsuccessful attempt to surround and destroy Pequot warriors who had taken refuge in a swamp stronghold Mason insisted in retrospect that his forces were 'loth to destroy Women and Children, as also the Indians belonging to that Place'.[43] Captured hostiles were saleable: that was the bottom line.

The Pequot army was deeply demoralised by what it found at Mystic. It could do nothing to avenge its dead, because the English shipped out down river on their flotilla of small vessels, which had come for them. Sassacus lost his political and military credibility, fled to the Mohawks, and was killed by them with all his party. Other Pequots faded into the Mohegan or joined the Narragansett if they could avoid being killed by the Massachusetts allies of the Narragansett. It had been what was later to be known as 'a splendid little war' for the colonists, whose losses had been light. The massacre terrified even their Indian allies. Their use of water transport had been brilliantly successful, and had ruled out effective ambush tactics by an enemy with few firearms. But the war was also deceptive. The Pequots were demographically horribly vulnerable, with their small population and ring of enemies. That the victors trumpeted their divine sanction as an Israel guarded by the hand of God in the wilderness was pretty routine. They now had freedom to expand into former Pequot land. They would have done this anyway, if they could, regardless of which version of a common European Christian ideology of self-justification they professed, if only because there was no point in coming to America if they could not lay their hands on Indian land. As it happened, the pressure of demand was not great outside the unique operational setting of the Connecticut River, and for three decades New England could feel confident that it could easily impose its will on Indian peoples, without any great desire to fight them. It was a view which bred independence of spirit towards the Crown, and near-fatal complacency towards rapidly evolving Indian societies.

By both choice and necessity the Indian peoples of New England continued to absorb and adopt European military techniques. Their general arming with flintlocks was complete by the mid-1670s. They had never had much time for the matchlock, moving almost at once from snaphance to classic flintlock weapons. This was partly because Europeans used them as hunters, both for commercially valuable furs, above all beaver, and to a lesser extent for game, which was initially abundant but more difficult to hit than the average English farmer found convenient. Indians rapidly became expert users of firearms, on which they held clear views, preferring a relatively short-barrelled weapon as most appropriate for woodland conditions. Recent archaeological work has also made it clear that they learned how to service their firearms at an early stage. This evidence confirms the statements of contemporary Puritan leaders like William Bradford who in the 1640s complained that the Indians had bullet moulds (the Indians had learned how to cast brass, lead, and pewter shortly after the arrival of the colonists); possessed screw plates for the making of screw pins; and could repair flintlock mechanisms and restock muskets as competently as the English. Indian blacksmiths could use broken muskets bought from colonists as a source of spare parts. Making gunflints was well within the existing technological competence of the native peoples. The Indians could not make gunpowder, but then neither could the settlers. The first colonial gunpowder mill began operations in Massachusetts Bay Colony only in 1675. It had to import most of the key chemical constituents, and colonials never built up a viable gunpowder industry even faintly capable of meeting their needs.[44] The War of the American Revolution was fought, on both sides, with imported gunpowder.

Aboriginal society always underwent such drastic change after first contact with Europeans that it is right to think of the Indian peoples as living in 'new worlds' in the post-contact era. Some suffered such drastic dislocation of social, geographical, and ideological continuity that it is doubtful if any significant body of European immigrants to North America experienced comparable modification of their ways simply because they moved to America. In military affairs the aboriginal way of war became obsolete, to be replaced by a new weaponry and tactics. If Indians borrowed from Europeans, Europeans from the first borrowed from Indians, and some historians have pushed an argument that because, for example, New England town meetings came to rely as much on consensual decision taking as an Algonquian tribal council, therefore Euro-American society in this and other respects turned its back on the hierarchy and theocracy of Europe so fast as to have created a quite new civilisation more permeated by Indian values than has been appreciated. The implication that American identity was almost always unique and politically correct in structure, if not perhaps in discourse, is just not sensible when carried to these extremes. The fact that settlers in New England grew corn or used snow shoes merely showed that they were not entirely daft, and all early-modern European societies, regardless of theory, rested on a very large measure of customary consensus. French historians trying to justify the establishment of a permanent French presence in the Middle East between the two world wars used to argue that because French crusader barons in the same area took to using soap, taking baths, and wearing more sensible clothing in the mediaeval era therefore the French had an innate genius for creating 'new' civilisations blending French with indigenous culture. In fact all this showed was that crusaders could be sensible. They remained invading overlords dependent on superior force and often as alienated from their non-Latin Christian subjects as from Muslims.[45] Even the unusual New England leaders like Roger Williams of Rhode Island who stressed Indian rights and denounced European brutality were colonists who envisaged no long-term future for indigenous civilisation, other than buying-out, absorption, and therefore destruction by an immigrant and alien one. It was a life-and-death struggle in which dispossession was achieved as often by economics as by violence, but even there superior force was necessary to enforce the European view of contract on indebted Indians. 'Free market' advocates are always anxious to control government and invariably advocates of state coercion for

244

anyone who jibs at their particular definition of a market. The Cherokee Indians were to derive little benefit from assuring white Americans who wished to drive them from their Georgia lands in the 1830s that there was no word in the Cherokee language which corresponded with 'interest'. Ironically, nor did they benefit much from the securing of a ruling from the United States Supreme Court which should have stayed the implementation of the Indian Removal Act of 1830. President Andrew Jackson was the embodiment of white settler expansionism, and he simply refused to enforce judicial rulings which curbed the ebullient imperialism of the newly independent United States of America.

The decades of peace between settlers and Indians in New England after 1637 were a remarkable phenomenon, but beneath the surface tensions relentlessly mounted. The colonies themselves became extremely assertive politically as Old England plunged in 1642 into the internal turmoil generated by the War of the Three Kingdoms, which marked the collapse of the Stuart monarchy and which involved bitter civil wars within all three kingdoms as well as mutual invasions between them. In the years between 1642 and 1649 metropolitan authority was in no position to monitor the activities of English colonies seriously. May 1643 saw Massachusetts, Connecticut, Plymouth, and New Haven form the United Colonies of New England, consciously along the lines of the Dutch union which had defied imperial Spain. Until the Restoration of 1660, the United Colonies functioned as a coordinating body for the militia forces and territorial claims of the New Englanders. In theory, the union was committed to 'fair' purchase of Indian land, but in practice relations with the local Indians had been characterised by endless bullying and chicanery ever since the Pequot War. Obliging upstart chiefs like Uncas were sponsored by the settlers in exchange for willingness to cede 'unoccupied' Indian lands. When the Narragansett chief Miantonomi found himself cheated out of Pequot lands he had been promised in exchange for military support to Massachusetts – and, to add insult to injury, unilaterally declared by the settlers to be within their jurisdiction – he reacted strongly. He spoke intermittently of the need for pan-tribal solidarity to check further expansion by the invading English. They were engrossing the land and their arable farming techniques and their domestic animals were incompatible with the survival of traditional Indian food resources. There was nothing illegal about the expression of such views, so the United Colonies, after deliberation, had him murdered by Uncas, conveniently outside their jurisdiction. Continual sharp practice over small parcels of land always threatened to turn into massive theft by con men exploiting the Indian lack of any concept of absolute property rights and vulnerability to legal chicanery after they were entrapped into or just declared to be in debt to the colonists. From 1659 a particularly disreputable chain of events enabled a powerful group of Massachusetts and Connecticut speculators organised as the Atherton Company to claim, with the help of arbitrary and swingeing fines imposed by the Commissioners of the United Colonies on the resident Indians, that they owned the whole Narragansett country, by foreclosure. Rhode Island was understandably furious, for the Atherton claims threatened its aspirations as well as those of the Narragansetts. Then in a scramble to secure charters from the newly restored Charles II, Connecticut and Rhode Island obtained charters with incompatible territorial provisions, so colonial solidarity was never the same again. In any case, the restored Stuart monarchy rightly denounced as void 'that usurped authority' which was the United Colonies. King Charles regarded his Indian 'subjects' with ineffable condescension. Like his predecessors, he did not regard his claims over them as negotiable with them, though he might negotiate with other European monarchs about those claims. At least his agents tried to enforce minimal equity between these subjects and their white neighbours. Investigating the New England situation in 1665, his commissioners transferred the whole area to Rhode Island jurisdiction pending a final royal decision, and reduced to manageable proportions the absurd burden of debt which had been designed to cheat the Narragansetts out of their land. However, Charles II could not change the mind-set of the colonists, so it is hardly surprising that there were war scares in 1667 and 1669 as the settlers began to sense the mounting desperation of the Indians, or that in 1671 the colonists tried to disarm the Wampanoag Indians whose leader they accused of plotting a rising. All the conditions for spontaneous combustion had been in place for decades, as musket-armed Indians faced overbearing and ever-increasing white settlers.[46]

By the outbreak of war in June 1675 the Indians in southern New England probably numbered about 20,000 all told. They were outnumbered by approximately two to one by the English settler communities in the hundred or so settlements which had been established south of Maine, where there were a few more. On the western fringes of Plymouth Colony the elderly sachem of the Wampanoags, Osamequin, had long kept on friendly terms with the English, but after his death his elder son and successor Wamsutta and Wamsutta's younger brother Metacomet who succeeded after Wamsutta's unexpected death in 1662 were harried by paranoid colonists. Metacomet, whom the English called King Philip, lived on the Mount Hope peninsula and had been mortally offended by the disarmament attempt of 1671. Though the colonists had confiscated the guns taken from him and his entourage at the meeting where they accused him, not for the first time, of plotting a rising, Metacomet had wisely refused to disarm his people after he left the meeting. To disarm was to retire from the political scene. The murder of a Christian Indian who had been close to Metacomet but who had left him to return to Plymouth with tales of a plan for a general Indian rising, and the subsequent arbitrary hanging by the colonists of three Indians accused of the killing, seem to have been the last straw for the Wampanoags. Warriors from several groups began to join Metacomet, whose own people sent their women and children to safety before they began to attack the small settlement of Swansea which was so situated as to be a potential block to their escape from the peninsula, itself vulnerable to the superior naval power that the colonists could muster, especially with assistance from Rhode Island.

Though it became an article of faith with the colonists that Metacomet had been planning a rising for years, and there is little doubt that intelligent Indians had talked extensively about the need for some degree of unity among the tribes if there was to be any chance of a successful rising, the core force available to Metacomet may have been as small as 300 warriors, and they may have been pushing him forward rather than being incited by him. At the end of the war, when Metacomet was dead, Caleb Moore, 'Master of a Vessel newly Arrived from Rhode-Island', published a short newsletter in London which implied that 300 was the maximum number of men Metacomet himself ever commanded.[47] Other Indian peoples entered the war spasmodically, as opportunities for effective action seemed to offer themselves. Metacomet's success in evading the early concentration of English militia against Mount Hope, his escape into Pocasset territory where a female sachem Weetamo ruled, and his successful raids on exposed settlements and towns drew Nippimuck Indians from Massachusetts and River Indians from Connecticut into the war. Even William Harrison – a litigious land-shark from Providence who during the war tried to ingratiate himself with Secretary of State Sir Joseph Williamson in London by writing him newsletters – admitted that the early colonial punitive columns blundered about, giving their enemies every possible warning of their arrival by repeatedly firing into bushes to flush out non-existent Indian ambushers.[48] The vulnerability of the colonists to hit-and-run tactics using the gunpowder technology the Indians had mastered so well must have vastly cheered the long-suffering tribes. Nevertheless, some Indians, like the Mohegans, stood by their English alliance. The surviving Pequots allied with the English, presumably because they did not want to face total genocide. The colonists, even as they reeled under Indian blows, clearly saw the war as a way of seizing even more Indian land, this time under circumstances which would rule out a Crown veto. The Narragansetts were pushed into the war by colonial aggression when only individual Narragansett warriors had joined Metacomet. This led to the Great Swamp Battle in a swamp where the Narragansetts had secretly built a fort, complete with firing steps and what seem to have been European-type bastion defences. This refuge was betrayed to the colonists by an Indian, but did not prove quite the deathtrap which Mystic fort had been in 1637, for after repulsing an assault many of the garrison did break out.

The United Colonies of New England effectively came to life again to organise the fight back from the early English disasters. Suspiciously, the first fruit of this resurrection was the attack on the Narragansetts. Not much wonder the colonists tried through the medium of published newsletters to convince London opinion that this was on their part the justest of wars.[49] New England clergy interpreted the war as a judgement of God on a backsliding generation of colonial Englishmen, executed through the deeds of a diabolical foe.[50] This was a standard response from contemporary Christian culture. Spanish friars saw Mayan resistance to their own cultural imperialism in the Yucatán peninsula in Central America as rooted in diabolic possession of the Amerindians.[51] Nevertheless, New Englanders went on to mobilise Indian allies and utilise local Indian scouts, as well as to copy Indian tactics. Captain Benjamin Church was the outstanding colonial exponent of Indian forest warfare methods, while Governor Andros of New York successfully stirred up the Mohawks to attack the Wampanoags and their allies. Colonial columns destroyed Indian forges and supplies of lead, when they could find them. This was a gunpowder war, though the accuracy and reliability of muskets, especially in the damp setting of swamps where much of the fighting occurred, was limited. Church's own war diary shows both his and an opponent's musket misfiring at point-blank range, after which he resorted to trying to break his enemy's neck by twisting it violently. An Indian ally came to Church's assistance with the preferred Indian method of killing, which was to smash a tomahawk down into the foe's brain.[52] It was a crude and brutal conflict in which the English had in the last analysis numbers, war supplies, and potential reinforcements beyond the wildest dreams of their enemies. Even so, the sudden collapse of an apparently still formidable Indian war effort after the spring of 1676 was dramatic. Early on, Metacomet's success bred support, and at least one Englishman defected to the Indian side. He was captured by a colonial force, which reported that his musket was loaded with several slugs (one way to increase the chance of a hit) before they hanged and quartered this admirably independent-minded fellow countryman.[53] By May 1676 the Indian coalition was disintegrating due to near starvation, shortage of weapons and munitions, and desertion. The economic strength to outlast the English in total war had never been there in the first place. A war of aggressive infantry and cavalry patrols mopped up what was left of the rising. Metacomet was hunted down and shot by a Christian Indian in August 1676. His last outstanding commander, Annawon, was killed in early September. Amerindians were slaughtered or sold into slavery, often to a living death in the West Indies. The rising generation of English, products of the fecundity of the original wave of settlement, could find farms.

Conclusion

But the cost was terrible, to English as well as Indians. Six hundred colonists had been killed, and many more wounded. Of their hundred or so towns, 52 had been attacked and 12 destroyed. Raids had reached to within ten miles of Boston. True, colonists had killed perhaps 3000 Indians; 10,000 colonial militia soldiers supplemented by paid volunteers and Indian allies proved in the end too much for their opponents. However, the cost of the war had been crippling. Plymouth was effectively bankrupt. Food was scarce all over New England, and the frontier of settlement was driven back by twenty to fifty miles in most places. All of this was well known throughout the English Atlantic world. Governor William Berkeley of Virginia, an Anglican royalist with limited sympathy for the closet republican Saints of New England, knew exactly the impact of King Philip's War. As he explained in a letter to Philip Ludwell in April 1676, he and his advisers had been forced to restrict the export of foodstuffs from Virginia because the New Englanders had sent an 'abundance of vessels to buy of us great quantities of all sort as pork beef and corn'. He knew that the northern colonies were in bad shape fiscally; that their frontier had shrunk back; and that their recovery would be slow because 'they have lost all their beaver trade, half at least of their fishing and have nothing to carry to the Barbados with whose commodities they were wont to carry away our tobacco and other provisions'. Paradoxically, Berkeley was himself in the toils of an Indian war.[54] The powerful Susquehannock people lay to the north of Maryland and Virginia. They were related to but often rivals of the Five Nations of the Iroquois, whose homes lay north of them, and they were active fur traders. Access to muskets was not a problem for them. They had been armed by the small colony which the Swedes established on the Delaware in 1638, and when it was overwhelmed by the Dutch in 1655 they turned to a close alliance with Maryland, with which they had sparred inconclusively in the 1640s when they attacked a small tribe allied to that colony. Maryland saw them as a shield against Iroquois raids. These turned into a major Iroquois–Susquehannock war, and when the fortunes of war turned against the latter Maryland helped them to partially relocate on the Potomac, handing over to them the fort at Piscataway which they needed as a refuge. It was meant to defend them against the Iroquois, but in fact their next serious enemies turned out to be Virginia frontier farmers, who lay too close to them and who combined sharp practice towards minor Indian tribes in trading with a general contempt for Indians. A Virginian punitive column attacking Doeg Indians in Maryland in the course of a commercial dispute casually killed Susquehannocks, thus enraging two Indian peoples and Maryland. Angry and violent frontier settlers then attacked Piscataway fort, but were defeated by a spirited defence. Retaliation was quite inevitable and by the spring of 1676, 300 settlers had died. Governor Berkeley quite correctly concluded that his undisciplined and greedy frontiersmen had deserved what had come to them, and advocated a defensive policy of fort building which was meant as much for control of white settlers as of Indians. At this point, fissures opened in Virginian politics.

Both in New England and on the Chesapeake English marcher societies had emerged which were capable of destroying resistance to their seizure of Indian land by force or legal chicanery. Though few New Englanders fully appreciated it in 1676, the local Algonquians were finished as a serious force. Survivors drifted north or west if they were not prepared to join the tamed, settled, 'praying Indian' communities which existed on the margins of the English settlements. These Indians had mainly supported the settlers in the 1675–76 conflict, thus ensuring that it was never a purely racial war, but their distinctive culture was, like their 'praying towns', in long-term decline after 1676. By 1750 the Indian population of New England 'was probably down to a few thousand'.[55] The defeated Indian exiles moving west both maintained their distinctiveness and achieved a measure of vengeance in the bitter resentments they conveyed to new hosts and allies.

Yet New England had been very severely weakened in the medium term. It was vulnerable, not to the Indians it had defeated, but to the Crown it had tried too often to ignore. Virginia's vociferous loyalty had been the shield of its autonomy under the Stuarts, but the combination of a governor who was corrupt and who had been in power much too long and a divisive Indian war was to cause an unprecedented breakdown in constituted authority there, which the Crown could hardly ignore. All marchlands exist in a state of tension between the alien society they war with and the metropolitan authority which validates them but which also monitors them, however intermittently, to see if they constitute a threat, liability, or opportunity. New England was an ideological threat to the restored Stuarts. The disposable wealth of the Chesapeake tobacco economy was an opportunity. Neither was so pressing as to rank high in metropolitan priorities, but weaknesses generated by Indian wars in both societies created favourable circumstances for Crown intervention after 1676.

Notes and references

1. Richard Hakluyt the elder, 'Purposes and Policies to Be Observed in Colonization (1578)', printed in *The Elizabethans' America*, ed. Louis B. Wright (Harvard University Press, Cambridge, MA, 1966), pp. 16–20.

2. Ross Hassig, *Aztec Warfare Imperial Expansion and Political Control* (University of Oklahoma Press, Norman, OK and London, pbk edn, 1995).

3. Richard Hakluyt the elder, 'Reasons for Colonization (1585)', printed in *Elizabethans' America*, ed. Wright, pp. 26–36.

4. Cited in *English Privateering Voyages to the West Indies 1588–1595*, ed. Kenneth R. Andrews, Hakluyt Society, 2nd series, No. 3 (Cambridge University Press, Cambridge, 1959), p. 35.

5. Ralph Lane's narrative of the settlement of Roanoke Island is reprinted in *The First Colonists: Documents on the planting of the first English settlements in North America 1584–1590*, ed. David B. Quinn and Alison M. Quinn (North Carolina Department of Cultural Resources, Division of Archives and History, Raleigh, NC, 1982), p. 33.

6. G.V. Scammell, 'On the Discovery of the Americas and the Spread of Intolerance, Absolutism, and Racism in Early Modern Europe', *The International History Review*, 13 (1991), pp. 441–60.

7. I am very grateful to Professor John Juricek, my good colleague in Emory University, for showing me his important work in progress on this neglected field of intellectual history, and for discussing these matters with me at length. When published, his monograph will be an important and original contribution to the literature.

8. Wilcomb E. Washburn, 'The Moral and Legal Justifications for Dispossessing the Indians', in *Seventeenth Century America: Essays in colonial history*, ed. James Morton Smith (Norton, New York, pbk edn, 1972), pp. 17 and 24.

9. Lane, *op. cit.*, p. 38.

10. Thomas Harriot, 'A Briefe and True Report of the New Found Land of Virginia (1588), as Reprinted by Hakluyt in 1589', in *First Colonists*, ed. Quinn and Quinn, p. 68.

11. Helen C. Rountree, *The Powhatan Indians of Virginia: Their traditional culture* (University of Oklahoma Press, Norman, OK, 1989), p. 122.

12. D.W. Meinig, *The Shaping of America. Vol. I: Atlantic America, 1492–1800* (Yale University Press, New Haven, CT, 1986), pp. 24–28.

13. Pedro de Zuñiga to Philip III, 23 February/15 March; 22 March/1 April; 2/12 April 1609, printed in *The Jamestown Voyages Under the First Charter*

1606–1609, Vol. II, ed. Philip L. Barbour, Hakluyt Society, 2nd series, No. 137 (Cambridge University Press, Cambridge, 1969), pp. 254–60.

14. 'Instructions to Sir Thomas Gates (before 15 May 1609)', printed in *ibid.*, pp. 265–66, and 'Spain Investigates', pp. 291–319.

15. Ivor Noel Hume, *Martin's Hundred. The discovery of a lost colonial Virginia settlement* (Delta, New York, pbk edn, 1983), pp. 65–67, 219–20 and 234.

16. Rountree, *Powhatan Indians*, Chap. 7, 'Law, Politics and War'.

17. Roger C. Smith, 'Ill-fated Galleon', *Archaeology*, January/February 1998, pp. 42–46.

18. *Powhatan Foreign Relations 1500–1722*, ed. Helen C. Rountree (University Press of Virginia, Charlottesville, VA, 1993).

19. Olive Patricia Dickason, *The Myth of the Savage and the Beginnings of French Colonialism in the New World* (University of Alberta Press, Edmonton, 1984).

20. The text of Rolfe's letter to Sir Thomas Dale, the current governor of Virginia, which was printed in Hamor's *A True Discourse in 1615*, is reprinted in *Elizabethans' America*, ed. Wright, pp. 233–37, under the contentious heading 'Rolfe Marries Pocahontas to Convert Her – So He Claims (1614)'.

21. Ronald P. Dufour, *Colonial America* (West Publishing Company, St Paul, MN, 1994), p. 94.

22. Howard Mumford Jones, *Oh Strange New World* (Viking, New York, pbk edn, 1967), Chap. 5, 'The Colonial Idea in England'.

23. John T. Juricek, 'English Territorial Claims in North America under Elizabeth and the Early Stuarts', in *Terrae Incognitae*, 7 (1975), pp. 7–22.

24. James A. Henretta and Gregory H. Nobles, *Evolution and Revolution: American society, 1600–1820* (D.C. Heath, Lexington, MA, 1987), p. 23.

25. H.C. Porter, *The Inconstant Savage: England and the North American Indian 1500–1660* (Duckworth, London, 1979), p. 458.

26. *Powhatan Foreign Relations*, ed. Rountree, pp. 190–95.

27. Printed in *The World Turned Upside Down. Indian voices from early America*, ed. Colin G. Calloway (Bedford Books, Boston, MA, pbk edn, 1994), p. 39.

28. Ian K. Steele, *Warpaths: Invasions of North America* (Oxford University Press, New York, 1994), p. 46.

29. Karen Ordahl Kupperman, *Settling With the Indians: The meeting of English and Indian cultures in America, 1580–1640* (Rowman and Littlefield, Totowa, NJ, 1980), pp. 180–06.

30. 'To the Virginia Voyage' is reprinted in *Early American Writing*, ed. Giles Gunn (Penguin, New York, pbk edn, 1994), pp. 71–73.

31. Martin Butler, ' "Servant but not slave": Ben Jonson at the Jacobean court', *Proceedings of the British Academy*, Vol. 90: *1993 Lectures and Memoirs* (Oxford University Press, for the Academy, 1996), pp. 72–73.

32. The petition of 'Robin, a Pamunky Indian' and the response of the council at its meeting in the Capitol at Williamsburg on 27 October 1709 are printed in *Calendar of Virginia State Papers and Other Manuscripts, 1652–1781*, Vol. I, ed. William P. Palmer (Commonwealth of Virginia, Richmond, 1875, Kraus Reprint edn, New York, 1968), pp. 133–34.

33. Bruce P. Lenman, 'Alexander Spotswood and the Business of Empire', *Colonial Williamsburg. The Journal of the Colonial Williamsburg Foundation*, Autumn 1990, pp. 44–55.

34. Ian K. Steele, *The English Atlantic 1675–1740* (Oxford University Press, New York, 1986), pp. 6 and 10.

35. Gary B. Nash, *Red, White and Black. The peoples of early America* (Prentice-Hall, Englewood Cliffs, NJ, 2nd pbk edn, 1982), p. 63.

36. Dufour, *Colonial America*, p. 110.

37. Peter S. Donaldson, *Machiavelli and Mystery of State* (Cambridge University Press, Cambridge, pbk edn, 1992), pp. 50–60.

38. Colin G. Calloway, *The Western Abenaki of Vermont, 1600–1800. War, migration, and the survival of an Indian people* (University of Oklahoma Press, Norman, OK, 1990), pp. 34–36.

39. Cotton Mather, *Magnalia Christi Americana Books I and II*, ed. Kenneth B. Murdock (Harvard University Press, Cambridge, MA, 1977), pp. 129, 136, and 166.

40. Lynn Ceci, 'Native Wampum as a Peripheral Resource in the Seventeenth-Century World System', in *The Pequots in Southern New England: The fall and rise of an American Indian nation*, eds. Laurence M. Hauptman and James D. Wherry (University of Oklahoma Press, Norman, OK, 1990), pp. 48–63.

41. Francis Jennings, *The Invasion of America: Indians, colonialism and the cant of conquest* (University of North Carolina Press, Chapel Hill, NC, 1975), p. 226.

42. Neal Salisbury, *Manitou and Providence: Indians, Europeans, and the making of New England, 1500–1643* (Oxford University Press, New York, 1982), p. 215.

43. Quotations are from Major John Mason, *A Brief History of the Pequot War Especially of the Memorable Taking of Their Fort at Mistick in Connecticut in 1637* (Readex Microprint Corporation, 1966 reprint of the Boston 1736 edn), pp. 1, 8, and 16. There is a good summary of modern scholarship on the war in Steele, *Warpaths*, pp. 89–94.

44. Patrick M. Malone, *The Skulking Way of War: Technology and tactics among the New England Indians* (Madison Books, Lanham, MD, 1991).

45. Colin G. Calloway, *New Worlds for Old: Indians, Europeans, and the remaking of early America* (Johns Hopkins University Press, Baltimore, MD, 1997), p. 194. For French crusaders *vide* R.C. Smail, *Crusading Warfare* (Cambridge University Press, Cambridge, 2nd pbk edn, 1995), Chap. 3.

46. Douglas E. Leach, *Flintlock and Tomahawk: New England in King Philip's War* (Macmillan, New York, 1958), Chap. 2, 'Gathering Clouds'.

47. *Vide* Caleb Moore, 'The War in New-England Visibly Ended', published originally in London in 1677 and reprinted in *King Philip's War Narratives* (Readex Microprint Corp., USA, 1966), item 5, p. 1.

48. *Idem.* (ed.), *A Rhode Islander Reports on King Philip's War: The second William Harris letter of August, 1676* (Rhode Island Historical Society, Providence, 1963), pp. 28–31.

49. *Vide* the five London news-sheets of 1676–77 published in *King Philip's War Narratives*.

50. *So Dreadful a Judgement: Puritan responses to King Philip's War*, ed. Richard Slotkin and James K. Folsom (Wesleyan University Press, Middletown, CT, 1978).

51. Inga Clendinnen, *Ambivalent Conquests: Maya and Spaniard in Yucatan 1517–1570* (Cambridge University Press, Cambridge, 1987).

52. Colonel Benjamin Church, *Diary of King Philip's War 1675–76*, eds. Alan and Mary Simpson (Pequot Press, Chester, CT, 1975).

53. *Vide* the account from Boston of 8 February 1676, reprinted in *King Philip's War Narratives*, item 2, p. 14.

54. The relevant section of Berkeley's letter to Ludwell is conveniently reprinted in Charles M. Segal and David Stineback, *Puritans, Indians and Manifest Destiny* (G.P. Putnam's Sons, New York, 1977), pp. 198–99.

55. Alden T. Vaughan, *New England Frontier: Puritans and Indians 1620–1675* (University of Oklahoma Press, Norman, OK, 3rd edn, pbk, 1995), pp. 321–22.

CHAPTER NINE

The clash of European states and the rise of the imperial factor in the Caribbean and North America

The Caribbean cockpit 1586–1688

The Caribbean, the central sea of the Americas, had been the site of the first impact of Europeans on the aboriginal cultures of the hemisphere. It was to remain the region where precedents were set in patterns of conflict, but the collapse of Amerindian populations in the larger islands was so dramatic that power games were increasingly played out between rival European groups. Spanish authority was challenged by the French, Dutch, and English, partly because of the comparatively weak and incomplete nature of Spanish colonisation in parts of the Caribbean, especially after Spanish attention began to focus on the great conquests which were achieved in Mexico and in South America. Islands which had experienced comprehensive ecological, political, and demographic disaster, and whose limited resources of precious metals had been exhausted, simply were not worth further massive investments of Spanish state resources, even in the Greater Antilles; while many of the numerous islands in the Lesser Antilles had never been brought under Spanish sway, especially those with a population of fiercely independent Carib Indians. Here was an opportunity for infiltration by other Europeans. In addition, the clockwise flow of shipping through the Caribbean which assembled the precious metals to be despatched to Spain proved fatally attractive to freebooters, as did the thought of the bullion fleets which eventually sailed from Vera Cruz via Havana to round the tip of modern Florida before they swung northwards into the Atlantic. In practice, it was not necessary for a ship to have piratical intentions to be deemed a corsair by the Spaniards. The Spanish *corsario* means no more than 'one who cruises'. Any ship and crew or any individual crew member who sailed in the Spanish Indies without holding a licence from the Casa de

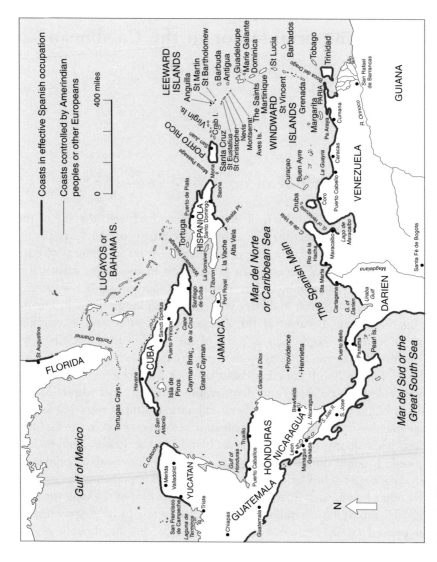

Map 6 The West Indies, *c.* 1680

Contratacion in Seville was in Spanish eyes a corsair. In practice this piece of self-serving political theology was treated with the contempt it merited by other Europeans, and the real question was how far the Spanish monarchy could enforce its will and defend its vital interests in the Indies, with resources which by definition were limited, not least because of the primacy of Spanish commitments in Europe and the Mediterranean.

The option of not involving the Crown but leaving defence to local colonists was never realistic, partly because the Spanish monarchy was a patrimonial structure which felt an obligation to protect its subjects, who were theoretically its children, but more because the empire in the Americas paid profits vital to the Crown's credit structure. The royal *quinto* or fifth of all minerals and precious and semi-precious stones mined in the Indies was based on the legal position that all sub-surface wealth belonged by right to the Crown, which for a price licensed others to exploit that wealth. In the Spanish peninsula proper the levy was as high as two-thirds, but it was reduced in the Indies to 20 per cent to encourage development. The rewards to the monarch of this policy were huge, so the Spanish Crown was the first European state structure drawn into an active role in the Caribbean and, minimally, in the southern fringe of North America. It was always parsimonious, and in the period to 1586 it defended the Indies on terms which were a real bargain. Adopting a basically passive defence policy, it built some fortifications in a few significant areas subject to threat, and it organised escort forces for valuable convoys. Mobile search and destroy units were few, weak, and ineffective. Even in a heavy year, the total expenditures were not as high as those needed to sustain the royal household in Spain, and they were always a mere tenth or so of the cost of the Dutch wars. The whole system hinged on the assumption, which proved correct, that there were no more than thirty to forty corsairs each year, divided about equally between traders and those who were either pure pirates or possessors of letters of marque which entitled the holder to recompense himself for uncompensated damages done by Spanish subjects. Some five million ducats spent on Indies defence between 1535 and 1585 was extraordinarily little for the security rewards earned. What men like Drake did from 1586 was to step up massively the scale of foreign assault, by a factor of 10 at least, and project the Spanish administration into a vastly more expensive situation. Even unsuccessful voyages such as the Drake–Hawkins expedition to the Caribbean in 1595–96 forced the Spanish Crown to maintain levels of commitment unthinkable earlier, and the English threat to the Spanish Caribbean was in many ways less dangerous than that offered by the Dutch.[1]

The Treaty of London of 1604 may have failed to embody the more extreme claims of the Crown of Spain in the Indies, but in the Caribbean it was the prelude to the appeasement of Spain by the government of James VI and I. In December 1604, after the Spanish representatives had reiterated their ferocious hostility to the very idea of an English presence in the Americas, James had hastened to assure the Spanish ambassador that he would punish with death any of his subjects who 'set forth to disturb your majesty's seas'. Even ministers like the Earl of Nottingham – who had started the peace negotiations in no servile mood and had enraged the Spaniards with a spirited outburst against the monstrous nature of the Luso-Hispanic demand that others accept their monopoly of extra-European activity in both the western and eastern hemispheres – had to learn to sing another tune to keep their jobs with a monarch obsessed with drawing unrealistically close to Spain. Nottingham, a crypto-Catholic and a Howard, had been up to his neck with Cecil in privateering enterprise at the end of the Anglo–Spanish War, but he had to accept not only the withdrawal of privateers, but the abandonment of English interloping traders by James to the sort of sadistically cruel deaths which the Spaniards habitually inflicted on those they caught. James' peace offensive towards people who had never altered one iota of their own aggressive rhetoric predictably encouraged the Spaniards to treat the peace as an occasion to wage war ruthlessly. The constable of Castile, who had conducted the peace negotiations in London, had privately stressed the need to pretend to reciprocate James' passionate friendliness whilst gathering force to hit the English hard enough to make them show 'more respect than they have for us now'. The years 1605 and 1606 saw notably ruthless actions against English traders in 'Spanish' waters in the Americas, but those years also marked the limits of the fiscal endurance of the Spanish Crown and its colonists in the Caribbean. By 1607 the Crown was exhausted and its Caribbean colonists were sunk in depression, poverty, and an isolation rendered far more damaging by the policies of their own rulers. Even the Greater Antilles were very sparsely populated. Puerto Rico had only four not very large settlements, and in Jamaica, where the Spanish population may have been just a little over five hundred in 1611, the governor said that the colonists were not strong enough to interfere with the buccaneers who frequented the island with impunity. He was not the only gubernatorial pessimist. His opposite number in Honduras said flatly that the province was completely ruined. By 1611 the pearl fishery on La Margarita off the Venezuelan coast was inoperative, as it still was in 1620. Carib raids on Spanish settlements made the southern part of the Lesser Antilles and nearby coasts hazardous. Penetration of this thinly held Caribbean imperial slum region was only a matter of time.[2]

The first English settlement came within the Leeward Islands. This was hardly surprising, since the clockwise wind patterns made it very difficult for the Spaniards to work back from their settlements to the west to strike at obscure rival European settlements in an archipelago which they had failed either to conquer or settle extensively. In 1624 a small group of settlers sponsored by London merchants and led by the Puritan Thomas Warner landed in St Christopher (or St Kitts). To complete the parallel with the origins of New England, the settlers came mainly from East Anglia. They had to deal with the problem of the resident Caribs, who very wisely tried to throw them back into the sea in 1624, and with the fact that the French were also settling on the same small island. Then there was always in the background the menace of Spain. Common enemies enabled French and English to cooperate. A joint surprise attack broke the back of Carib resistance in 1627. The only case for such a hazardous location had to be profit, and originally the idea was to follow the Virginian example and grow tobacco, using white farmers and indentured servants. Uneasily divided between the French and English, St Kitts had nevertheless contrived to attract some four thousand English people, overwhelmingly young males, by 1635. Merchants made money transporting them to the Caribbean, while the boom in tobacco prices enabled the colonists to more than pay for themselves.

It was a Captain John Powell who in 1625 touched on the currently uninhabited island of Barbados, which lies eastward of all other West Indian islands, and saw the possibilities for English colonisation there. He returned to England by way of St Kitts and once home was able to sell his vision to his wealthy employer, the Anglo–Dutch business magnate Sir William Courteen. By early 1627 eighty settlers had disembarked to establish an English colony. They were vitally dependent on Courteen's financial support, for they were slow to make a success of their original plan to produce tobacco for the European market. In 1630–31 starvation haunted the colony. A group of Arawak Indians had been persuaded by Powell to move to Barbados to grow food crops for the colony whilst the English concentrated on cash crops, but the politics of the court of Charles I rapidly destabilised both the colony and its race relations. By 1629 the impecunious and unscrupulous Scots courtier James Hay, Earl of Carlisle, had secured a royal grant of the Caribee Islands, by which was meant all English settlements in the Lesser Antilles, including Barbados. Mini-civil wars and a general atmosphere of gangsterism culminated in Barbados in the expropriation of the Courteen faction and the enslavement of their Arawak allies. The economy lurched from virtual tobacco monoculture to the rise of cotton production to a level comparable with tobacco. Within ten years of its foundation Barbados was a flourishing colony with significant exports of tobacco, cotton, and indigo (a source of blue dyestuff). The workers were predominantly white males drawn from the large pool of unemployed at the unskilled end of the labour market in England, especially in London.

They were poorly fed, exposed like everyone else to the vicissitudes of a climate which included a regular hurricane season, and exploited by their employers and the succession of quasi-criminal rogues who passed through the governorship. Governor Henry Hawley, for example, imposed a poll tax, ostensibly to finance fortification of the island against possible Spanish attack, but nearly a decade after the end of his reign it was pointed out that 'the Island is not yet fortified, nor gunnes mounted'.[3] Nevertheless, the pattern of English expansion into unclaimed islands in the Lesser Antilles continued apace throughout Barbados' difficult early years. From 1628 Nevis was settled, with roughly half the settlers coming from England and Ireland and half from St Kitts. Early in the next decade surplus population from St Kitts was crucial to the English colonisation of Montserrat and Antigua, as it was to be in the later 1630s to the establishment of settlements on Tobago and St Lucia.

From the start the Crown had been far more actively involved in the politics of these new Caribbean settlements than it had in New England, or even in the Chesapeake colonies. This was partly because of the continuing vulnerability of the islands. In 1639 Sir Thomas Warner, who was at that point governor of the Caribee Islands on behalf of the Earl of Carlisle, warned his patron that the 'about 20,000 planters' within his jurisdiction lived under perpetual threat of attack from the Caribs and hostile European powers. This is as good an estimate as we have of the white free men and bond servants in the English Caribbean at the end of the 1630s, but the numbers went up until they reached a maximum between 1645 and 1647. Outside St Kitts there had not been any significant aboriginal presence on the English islands. Hands to work newly cleared fields were desperately needed, so much so that a large number of Catholic Irish peasant immigrants flowed in from busy Atlantic ports like Cork and Galway. They may even have been a majority of the white population in these colonies in mid-century. In the course of the disastrous war which Charles I embarked on with Spain, a Spanish force attacked St Kitts in 1629, expelling the French and English settlers. It went on to destroy planted crops on Nevis. The Spaniards lacked the ability to maintain a garrison, and the English were in business again in both places by 1630, but they had been reminded of their own dangerous exposure to the forces of the Spanish monarchy. Nor were the Spaniards the only source of insecurity. Unlike the Spaniards, and to an even greater extent the French, the English were not committed to protracted wars of extermination against the Caribs. In the end the French were to win and control large, fertile islands like Guadeloupe and Martinique for their pains. What the English islands suffered from were raids by the Caribs in their seafaring canoes. Antigua was constantly raided, while even St Kitts experienced serious invasions in 1640 and 1654.[4]

Ironically, the development which would decisively sap the capacity of the English Caribbean colonies to defend a substantial degree of autonomy against the Crown was gathering momentum just as those colonies demonstrated their greatest degree of independence from metropolitan control. From the late 1630s experiments in growing sugar were being conducted. The example of the Portuguese in Brazil, where black slaves worked sugar plantations, was close and familiar. So were the Dutch on St Eustatius, the foothold and emporium from which they supplied all the needs of Europeans in the Caribbean, including slaves. Yet in 1638 Barbados, with a population of about six thousand, one third of them servants, had only a couple of hundred black inhabitants. As authority in Old England disintegrated in the early 1640s, Barbados suffered, inevitably, from internal factionalism deriving from metropolitan politics, and there was always the threat of trouble from the often brutalised white indentured servants, who were driven hard during their agreed term of service; but the way these tensions were resolved was to make the island virtually an independent state between 1641 and 1650. Neutrality in the civil wars not only avoided any serious violence between the predominantly royalist settlers and a significant Puritan and anti-royalist minority, but it also offered the best of all worlds: a loyal English identity which was no longer troubled by the unavailing but irritating attempts of Charles I to stop the colonists from taking advantage of the goods, slaves, and cheap shipping services offered by the Dutch. Not much wonder that the other English islands, all grouped together at the southern end of the Antilles in the section known as the Leeward Islands, embraced the Barbadian position with zeal. The problem was that no European metropolitan authority was likely to condone such a free-trade option on the part of a colony, and the new republican regime in the British Isles in 1651, egged on by influential London merchants to which it was notoriously responsive, was no exception. Late in 1651 Sir George Ayscue and two other commissioners arrived off Barbados with a fleet to underline the seriousness of their representations.

Barbadians had felt for some time that the size of the militia which their white population could generate was such that, provided they were not themselves divided, they had considerable capacity for self-defence. Knowing that a fleet was being sent by the Westminster republican legislature, the Barbadians had refurbished their coastal fortifications, raised a small permanent force to deal with any surprise landing, and laid in supplies. The Dutch were an important source for the last, though cannon for the defences were obtained by imposing a levy of 2 pieces on every visiting ship. Ayscue found himself faced by 6000 foot and 400 horse. Despite some brisk cannonading he wisely decided he could not force a landing. A protracted process of blockading and raiding, combined with intrigues splitting the

Barbadians between a moderate majority inclined to accept generous terms and a fanatical royalist minority which would not acknowledge the authority of the new republican regime under any circumstances, ended with a reasonable compromise. The authority of the Commonwealth of England, Ireland, and Scotland – whose legislature called itself a parliament, despite the absence of the monarch who was the most important part of a traditional parliament and its sole source of authority – was acknowledged, but Barbados kept a very large measure of autonomy including, in its own opinion, free trade. Up to 1655 it stubbornly tried to exercise that option.

Ayscue's fleet had seized twenty-four Dutch ships, reputedly worth £100,000 sterling, off Barbados in 1651–52. London merchants such as Maurice Thompson and Martin Noell had between them considerable personal experience of the Chesapeake and the Lesser Antilles, but they preferred to operate out of London and to exercise power by influencing the metropolitan government. Thompson owned plantation land in Barbados. Nevertheless, he was primarily interested in knocking out Dutch competition in what for him was an increasingly lucrative importation of sugar. The Navigation Act of 1651 passed by the so-called 'Rump Parliament' in England had insisted that all colonial goods imported into England be carried by English ships or ships of the country of origin. That left the Dutch free to peddle goods to English Caribbean colonies, but it is clear that Barbados went further, and the first effect of the outbreak of the Anglo–Dutch War of 1652–54 was to ensure that the metropolitan government was too preoccupied to do much about the English Caribbean.

It was the end of the Dutch war and the sudden arrival in the Caribbean of a large Commonwealth force under General Venables and Admiral Penn which ended this, from the Barbadian point of view, ideal situation. The seizure of sixteen Dutch ships at Barbados in 1655 marked the beginning of the triumph of metropolitan power. The Dutch were never completely excluded from the smaller English islands, but by the early 1660s they had little access to Barbados.[5] The Barbadians petitioned the Council of State in London for the restoration of their abbreviated free trade, pointing out that the settlement and soaring sugar-based prosperity of the island had been achieved with 'little or no encouragement or protection from the supremacy of England'. This was true but irrelevant in the presence of Venables' expedition. Some Barbadian politicians had undoubtedly been aiming at the New England option whereby they would, as Governor Searle warned the Council of State, become an effectively free state 'under England's protection, but not to own England's jurisdiction'.[6] The fact that Venables had come to launch an attack on the Spanish colonies in the Greater Antilles was decisive, for it heralded an era of mounting levels of international conflict in the Caribbean.

It is not the case that the newly established Cromwellian protectorate gratuitously attacked Spain under the influence of radical Protestant enthusiasts. Lord Protector Cromwell was undoubtedly looking for employment for the armed forces, and especially for the fleet of over 150 sail which had won the Dutch war. These forces represented an intolerable financial burden on his government. He also needed an active foreign policy to secure the international status of his government, and to ensure that most other European powers competed for his favour and did not simply patronise royalist plotters. Nevertheless, it is clear that he would have settled with Spain for something less than the terms he secured from Portugal, which guaranteed English merchants religious liberty and freedom to trade with the Portuguese colonies in Asia and the Americas. Portugal needed English support to maintain her independence from Spain, and even then the Counter-Reformation culture and monopolistic traditions of Portugal were so deeply embedded that it had needed an English fleet off the mouth of the Tagus under Admiral Blake to concentrate the mind of the Portuguese king sufficiently for him to confirm the settlement.

Cromwell knew full well that Spain would not budge on free trade, but he did want to free English merchants in Spain from the still alarming jurisdiction of an Inquisition with a financial incentive to rule that they had behaved 'scandalously' in their private devotions, and he did want to stop the Spanish habit of automatically attacking any English ship discovered in the Caribbean. Once negotiations broke down, Cromwell was clearly given some very bad advice as to the ease with which the Spanish Empire in the Americas could be profitably dismantled, and he himself had unrealistic hopes that war in the Caribbean need not involve war in Europe. Nevertheless, it will not do to suggest that, due to the weakness of the Spanish Crown in the Caribbean, there was nothing worth fighting for. Spain had benefited mightily from setting the terms of discussion about the Americas with other powers. Her intransigence was absolute. When the exiled Charles II secretly visited Brussels in 1656 to negotiate for what turned out to be modest and very conditional Spanish aid for a Stuart restoration, he had to agree in exchange to hand over Antigua, Montserrat, and Jamaica, and swear never to let his subjects establish another American colony. A paradigm shift on the part of Spain was desirable from all other points of view, and force alone could accelerate it.[7]

It was the incompetent execution of the 'Western Design' against Spain, as well as the grave miscalculations about its potentially self-funding nature, which made the whole episode so embarrassing. In Europe Cromwell had, realistically, auctioned his services between France and Spain, and one reason for the breach with Spain rather than with France was the sensible view that Spain would probably fail to deliver any military subsidies she offered. The loss of English pirate bases in the Caribbean on Providence Island and the Tortugas in 1635 and 1641 had been followed by substantial retaliatory raids on the Spanish mainland sponsored by the Earl of Warwick in 1642–43, but the protectorate marked a sharp break with that tradition of private reprisal. The Commonwealth state moved in, though it seems to have hoped to capture Hispaniola and use it much as Warwick and his associates had used Providence. Critics pointed out at the time that there were problems in taking and holding islands which did not represent the core of Spanish colonial power in the region. Some urged an attack, in alliance with friendly Indians, on the mainland to windward of the Caribbean proper, which Spanish colonial reinforcements would find difficult to reach because of the prevailing north-east trade wind. In the end the attack fell on the city of Santo Domingo in Hispaniola, where rocks prevented disembarkation at the intended point. A divided English force could then never reunite because of the River Ozama lying between the two halves. The Spaniards resisted stoutly. Venables was incompetent. His troops were the sweepings of the home army, with no single regiment of quality included – indeed, no single regiment. Colonial volunteers from the English islands were undisciplined and cowardly. Good troops could not be spared for this side-show and even in Europe it was a consideration that the excellent regiments and good officers sent to Flanders could be quickly withdrawn for home security in the event of a royalist rising. That Penn and Venables could then sail to Jamaica and take it easily against minimal opposition, which mostly ran away when they landed, showed how little Spain valued the sole conquest of the Commonwealth's 1655 campaign in the West Indies.[8]

The regular arrival in Barbados after 1655 of ships from England on their way to Jamaica was another nail in the coffin of hopes for an effectively independent Barbados, but the Barbadian elite was already burying any chance of that option by swamping white workers and farmers with black slaves in order to maximise sugar profits. Jamaica was understandably the last English settlement to go that way. Cromwell himself had hoped that large numbers of the Saints of New England, for whom he entertained a very real respect, might feel it their Christian duty to move down to his new Caribbean outpost to give substance to the long-term hopes behind the Western Design. They did not. The Irish and Scottish prisoners of war whom the republican regime sent to the West Indies in large numbers died out, but English Jamaica was a white man's country for some decades still, albeit not a country with many white men. By 1660 there were 26,200 Europeans and 27,100 black, mostly West African, slaves in Barbados. African slaves were a slight majority in Nevis, and were just in a minority in Antigua, as well as being nearly half the population of St Kitts. In Jamaica, where privateering had a final fling so profitable as to both delay and provide capital for the inevitable sugar revolution, there were only 500 Africans in a population of some 3000 in 1660, but 13 years later there were 9500 black slaves on the island. By 1710 there were 58,000 and they were 90 per cent of the total population. Slavery might be a state unknown to the Common Law in 1607, but by the early eighteenth century slave laws were in place in most of English America, including even New England, where slaves were few and not an increasing proportion of the population.

On the Chesapeake and in more southern colonies established after 1660 there were very large numbers of slaves, but never the overwhelming majorities which built up so fast in the West Indies.[9] The rhetoric of the white colonists in Jamaica after 1660 produced the cry of 'no standing army and the laws of England'. Barbadian planters first asserted that there could be 'no taxation without representation'.[10] Such phrases proved resonant for fellow slaveholders on the Chesapeake, like George Washington in the latter part of the eighteenth century; but the combination of imminent threat from an alien Crown, insular vulnerability to blockade from one's own, and, above all, of fear of an irresistible large-scale servile rising ensured that the Englishness of the West Indian planters – most of whom wanted to retire to Old England, and many of whom as time went on became absentees – did not evolve in the same way as the identities of similar Englishmen on the mainland of North America. The force was not with them. They needed garrisons of regular troops mainly to guard against slave revolts. There were more than seventy aborted or actual slave revolts in the English, later British, islands between 1638 and 1837. Jamaica and Antigua, the first to have regular garrisons, were also the ones most plagued by slave turbulence. The garrisons were never big enough to cope with invasion by the much larger regular forces kept up on nearby Spanish and French islands, though they were a trip-wire against hit-and-run raids. It was the Royal Navy which was the real shield of the islands. Truly significant, however, was the correlation on all the West Indian islands of serious slave rebellions with major withdrawals of European regular troops. The Jamaica assembly was assertive as late as the 1770s, and denied that its funding of garrison costs was other than a voluntary contribution subject to redress of grievance, but in the last analysis the Westminster politicians who controlled the regular army had the planter class over a barrel.[11]

State conflict nevertheless reinforced the message that the island colonies were extremely vulnerable, to the point where all could be, and many were from time to time, over-run by rival Europeans. Permanent conquest of all of them was a practical proposition. It was not Spain which demonstrated this. The Spaniards were only capable of defensive war in the later seventeenth century. They were naive enough to expect Charles II to hand back

Jamaica at the Restoration, and they only reluctantly accepted English claims to all dominions in the West Indies effectively controlled by Charles II when they agreed to the Treaty of Madrid of 1670. In between 1660 and 1670 Charles had confirmed the provisions of the Commonwealth Navigation Act and extended those provisions to insist that in theory all European goods exported to overseas dominions of the Crown must first pass through an English port, and that the key tropical staple crops be deemed enumerated commodities which must be exported from the colonies in the first instance only to Ireland, England, or Berwick-upon-Tweed (a town which still quaintly kept its late mediaeval status as English-occupied Scotland). More significant in terms of Crown commitment was the Act of 1673 which levied a 4 per cent export duty on the enumerated products of the West Indian plantations. Much of the legislation usually described as the Acts of Navigation was difficult to enforce, but bulk commodities largely flowing into London were easy to tax, so plantation duties became an increasingly important source of Crown revenue. Barbados represented a vital cash flow which grew with its sugar industry. In the long run, Jamaica, with its vastly more extensive area of virgin soil, was bound to become a big sugar producer, but for several decades it survived on a very different basis.

It has been argued that it was from the start a military colony subject to 'garrison government'. This was true in the sense that the land forces which had seized it in 1655 were seen as the source of a settled yeomanry which would be capable of defending the new possession, when not growing their own food on small farms. The second Commonwealth military commander on the island, Major General William Brayne, arrived with the first respectable regular units in early 1657, straight from service as commander of the fort at Inverlochy in Lochaber in Scotland – whence the republican government tried to keep control of a sort over the clans at the southern end of the Great Glen, which divides the Highlands with a deep north-east running slash at whose further end sits Inverness. As the Spaniards maintained a guerrilla resistance for some years from camps on the northern shore supplied from Cuba, soldiers were vital to the survival of English Jamaica. The Spanish threat was finally eliminated by Brayne's successor, Colonel Edward D'Oyley. Given the dismal performance of the troops under General Venables during the original Western Design campaign – and the fact that he and Penn appear to have had no idea of the strategic (let alone the economic) potential of Jamaica, attacking it avowedly because it was so soft a target that even their mangy regiments could achieve something there – the combination of aggressive and efficient land and naval patrols and hard-hitting amphibious operations which put an end to the Spanish presence was an astonishing revival of all that was best in the Cromwellian armies.[12] Yet in the last analysis, soldiers rotted away in Jamaica from disease and drink, and there was desertion at an alarming rate. After 1660 Charles II did not have a military colony in Jamaica, nor could he have afforded one. What he had was a centre of irregular trade with the Spanish colonies and a privateers' nest, mostly in the superb natural harbour of Port Royal on the south-west shore of the island.

Jamaica did have, usually, a small royal squadron of ships available, but its defence was privatised, for buccaneers, who were for a period a major industry, were also by definition a free defence force with a vested interest both in keeping the Spaniards off balance and in protecting their own base and market for stolen goods. The buccaneers, who had become a recognised cosmopolitan entrepreneurial group in the Caribbean, had originated on islands like Tortuga off Hispaniola, where their pursuit of wild cattle and habit of smoking their meat over a frame known as a boucan had given them their name. Tortuga oscillated between Spanish, English, and French nominal sovereignty, but had usually a good relationship with Jamaica. Though dictionaries tend to confuse the terms, buccaneers were not strictly pirates.[13] They usually carried letters of marque from some European sovereign, entitling them to attack the possessions of another. If peace broke out between two European monarchs, they could normally find another sovereign body still at war with at least one of them. Pirates were criminals who were liable to save themselves the trouble of guarding and feeding captives by drowning them, and who might well sink or burn a captured ship, to destroy evidence. Letters of marque made it possible to hope for the ransoming of both persons and ships, a fate much preferable to a watery grave for both. The distinction could become vague but Governor Sir Thomas Modyford of Jamaica built the buccaneers and their outstanding leader, the Welshman Henry Morgan, into the prime instrument of force at the disposal, more or less, of his colony. They proved useful in the opening stages of the second Anglo–Dutch War of 1665–67. Admiral de Ruyter had opened the game when he crossed the Atlantic with a Dutch fleet which had just inflicted heavy losses on the English settlements (mainly slaving bases) in West Africa. He arrived off Barbados in April, but could not capture the shipping protected by its harbour fortifications, so he moved up to Martinique to refit with French aid and then departed to attack the Chesapeake. The Jamaica buccaneers hit back, capturing the Dutch Antilles colonies of St Eustatius and Saba. Modyford had a point when he argued that to await the king's orders after sending for instructions after an attack was threatened on Jamaica might well involve nine months' inactivity, which a Jamaica ringed close by foes just could not afford. The Dutch, however, proved a trifling problem compared with the French, and buccaneers were not the answer.

French entry into the war was supposed to be automatic under French treaties for mutual aid with the United Netherlands, but Louis XIV only came in January 1666, mainly for fear that the Dutch and English might patch up a peace. His Antilles colonies had been reorganised under the state-sponsored West India Company from 1664. In St Kitts, where the English occupied the central area between two French portions, the English were confident they could quickly crush their outnumbered opponents, but in fact the French seized the initiative to compensate for their inferior numbers and by a great feat of arms conquered the whole island. The English buccaneer allies proved worse than useless. Elsewhere the French simply had more ships and experienced soldiers. An English fleet under Francis, Lord Willoughby, was destroyed by a hurricane while the French retook Dutch St Eustatius, and captured Antigua and Montserrat. It looked as if the English would be swept from the Lesser Antilles. A small squadron under Captain Berry arrived in 1667 to enable the frightened Barbadians to take the offensive and recapture Antigua and Montserrat. St Kitts proved too much for them. It was a problem even for the powerful fleet under Sir John Harman, which arrived later that year and defeated the French navy in Martinique Roads to gain command of the sea. An opposed landing on a limited coastline in the face of a substantial garrison was no easy matter, but such a garrison was doomed in the long run if the French lost control of the sea, so it was only reasonable that the Treaty of Breda which closed the war in 1667 restored the *status quo ante bellum.*

The French West India Company went bankrupt, but the French Crown picked up where it left off and needed another century to go the same way. English colonists in the Antilles had learned that they needed naval support from their Crown once France was the foe.[14] Both the English colonists in the Caribbean and their Crown had to recognise that their original reliance on buccaneers for defensive and offensive operations in the region had broken down in the face of professional Dutch and French naval forces and of regular French troops. The sequence of disasters – from the loss of St Kitts, to the capture by the Dutch of the English colony established by Lord Willoughby on the mainland of South America in Surinam, and the death of Lord Willoughby in the destruction of his fleet by hurricane in 1666 in the Antilles – enabled William Willoughby, his lordship's brother, who had succeeded him as governor-in-chief in the Leeward Islands, to persuade the London authorities to send an expedition to redeem the situation. Lord High Admiral the Duke of York was heavily involved in the decision to send out a powerful squadron in 1667 under William Willoughby and a regular regiment under the Cromwellian veteran Sir Tobias Bridge. Another squadron of frigates under Sir John Harman followed close on the heels of the first. Essentially, and especially after Harman brought his squadron into action, this effort worked.

However, it was far from easy to sustain the presence of Crown forces in the West Indies owing to the fiscal weakness of Charles II, itself rooted in the pathological distrust between the restored Stuarts and their English subjects. The cash-flow crisis which forced King Charles to lay up most of his fleet had cleared the way for the devastating Dutch naval strike against the Medway, which forced England out of the war. Funding Bridge's regiment, which was still in Barbados at a muster strength of 615 in February 1668,[15] proved a nightmare. There was a dearth of funds not already otherwise assigned. The shipowners who had contracted in 1666 to take the troops out to Barbados, at thirty shillings a head, were still in 1669 petitioning Charles II to fulfil the contract made in his name.[16] Unfortunately, the Crown was simultaneously in receipt of a petition from Major (later Sir Edmund) Andros and Captain James Cotter, on behalf of the men of Bridge's regiment. It was an extremely tactfully phrased petition, as it had to be not to impede Andros' subsequent rapid promotion in the service of the dynasty. It thanked King Charles for assigning half the $4\frac{1}{2}$ per cent export duty to cover their back pay, current subsistence, and clothing needs. The soldiers then added how much they appreciated the fatherly concern with which Charles had referred them to the care of 'the Right honorable Committee for Forraigne Plantations', adding that their sole regret was that all this solicitude had so far had absolutely no effect, and while they were unpaid and in rags, their dependants in England were starving.[17]

There was a third claimant on the duty revenues, in the shape of the local colonial militia, and the shipping interest was itself a complex claimant. On top of the contracts for trooping, at a set rate per head, there had been ships 'impressed and taken up', as their subsequent petition to the Crown said, 'to serve your Majesty against the Enemy in the Leeward Islands'. These were 'hyred upon contract att a monthly freight'. Another condition of service was that if lost, these ships 'should be payd for according to the appraisment'. They, too, had been told that the duty revenue was 'ingaged to them for their security and satisfaction'. That revenue was just inadequate, and the various unpaid claimants were reduced to squabbling about their priority in the list of acknowledged Crown debt-holders, in the remote event that some repayment happened.[18] As an imperial power-projection structure restoration England was less than impressive. By 1671 the government was reduced to obtaining a memorandum to explain to itself what had gone wrong in the Leeward Islands. It made sorry reading, for it had first been intended that the revenue be halved, with one half funding local administration, the other repaying debts.

Originally the militia was to be paid first, followed by shipowners. Then Bridge's regiment was to be 'satisfyed out of the $4\frac{1}{2}$ per cent before any payment whatsoever'. In practice, nobody had been paid.[19]

Charles II was again to wage war on the Dutch in 1672–74, in alliance with France, until the unpopularity of the alliance with his subjects and naval failure compelled him to make peace, but fortunately there was no serious Anglo–Dutch fighting in the West Indies. There it was a Franco–Dutch struggle which went on until the Peace of Nijmegen of 1678/79. After England left the war the Dutch tried seriously to destroy the French position in the Caribbean, but they could not take Martinique and their successes in capturing other islands were reversed by massive French reinforcements carried on a fleet whose admiral destroyed it on reefs by reckless navigation on his way to attack the central Dutch emporium at Curaçao. It was technical stalemate, but the debt-burdened Dutch state was finished as a serious force in the Caribbean. After 1678/79 England faced the mighty monarchy of France there, at extremely close range.[20] Those who had any idea of the situation obtaining in the Leewards knew full well that England was potentially totally outclassed. The privy council's committee for trade and plantations reported to Charles II in 1677 on the defensive state of those islands, after careful consultation with those employed in London as agents for the islands and a thorough perusal of accounts and letters forwarded by Colonel Stapleton, the garrison commander in the Leewards and lieutenant colonel of Bridge's regiment. They pointed out that as early as June 1675 they had made representations about the lamentable state of the two companies of infantry ordered to remain on St Kitts, where the post-war settlement between the French and the English was proving contentious. The companies had both lost between 30 and 40 per cent of their complements to high mortality, were in rags, and had been unpaid for years. In 1675, Charles had agreed to set up a fund for constant payment of these troops, and to the need for reinforcements to bring them up to strength, 'but nothing was effected in reference thereunto'.

Thereafter in January 1676 the committee had pressed on Charles the need for urgent action to resolve the St Kitts situation, where 'the true extent of your Majesty's Sovereignty is there disputed' and 'your aggrieved Subjects are to this day wanting Redress'. Nothing happened. Shortly afterwards the committee came up with a specific series of measures which they thought essential to make an imperial sovereignty meaningful in the Caribbean context. First, and quite rightly, they stressed the weakness of the Church of England, urging the despatch of at least one able Anglican clergyman to each of St Kitts, Nevis, Antigua, and Montserrat, with a prospect of subsequent preferment as a reward for devoted service whereby it might be possible for 'Your Majesty to have the mindes of the People united in their principles and allegiance'. In practice, the Stuart brothers were hostile to the established church, of which they were the successive heads. A better recipe for crippling an early-modern church-state would be difficult to find. The committee reiterated its plaintive plea for reinforcements and back-pay for the regiment, pointing out that 'the French appear in strength and vigour, punctually paid and supplyed from France with cloths and Provisions according to their occasions'. They also outnumbered their ragamuffin, starving English counterparts four to one. The committee clearly grasped the underlying problem of these English slave-powered plantation economies: they did not sustain a large enough body of white men to create loyal local land forces. The committee's suggestion that English criminals be transported to the Leewards was more a sign of desperation than a viable remedy. There was need for a substantial new fort in St Kitts, as well as for a supply of field carriages to give mobility to the guns in the many small forts and redoubts. Predictably, Colonel Stapleton discovered in 1677 that there was virtually no powder and shot, and few infantry weapons, on the islands for which he was responsible. Nor was the occasional naval force despatched from London in time of war at all an adequate answer to the permanent presence of superior French naval units. As the committee said:

> Wee also found a great want of a fifth rate Frigatt to attend the Governors Commands in those parts, which might be relieved from time to time, the French having seldom less than six good Frigatts plying thereabouts giving great Honor, Strength and Encouragement to all their Concernes.[21]

Sycophancy towards Louis XIV by Charles II was in practice the best defence option for the English Leeward Islands.

By the 1670s neither the Dutch nor the English had any real interest in conquering Spanish islands in the Caribbean on a permanent basis. Provided the Spaniards would accept them as they were in the region, there was much more profit in trading with Spain and the Spanish colonies than there was in fighting them. As early as 1667 the senior English naval administrator Samuel Pepys was saying that though he was aware that 'we have done the Spanyard abundance of mischief in the West Indys by our privateers at Jamaica', he was 'sorry for to have done it at this time'.[22] Governor Modyford of Jamaica had hoped to use the buccaneers of Port Royal primarily against the Dutch, and was simply unable to stop them from concentrating on more lucrative and easier Spanish targets instead. The buccaneer operated on a straight payment by results system: 'no prey, no pay'. When his staple diet of Spanish inter-colonial shipping was hard to find, he began to add the takings from hit-and-run raids on Spanish settlements, exploiting the extreme mobility of seaborne forces and the exceptional level of proficiency with firearms which constant practice gave him.[23] A daring and lucrative raid in 1664 on the city of Granada in Nicaragua set the pattern. Under Mansfield in 1665–66 the buccaneers raided Cuba and temporarily recaptured the old Providence Island colony off Nicaragua, but could not hold it, though they successfully reraided Granada. Henry Morgan, who had been active in these early exploits, then emerged as a charismatic leader, looting the city of Porto Bello on the north coast of the Panama isthmus in 1668, Maracaibo in 1669. In retaliation for a Spanish raid on Jamaica Modyford commissioned him in 1670, whereupon he sacked Santa Marta and Rio de la Hacha before again seizing Porto Bello early in 1671 and marching his 1400 men across to sack Panama after defeating the Spanish local forces in battle. As the Spaniards were forewarned, the expedition could steal only enough for a miserable £20 a head final pay-out. The 1670 Treaty of Madrid between England and Spain provided for suppression of piracy and mutual revocation of letters of marque and reprisal. Governor Lynch of Jamaica in the period 1671–75 discouraged buccaneering. There was a reaction later under Lords Vaughan and Carlisle, who had the now Sir Henry Morgan as their lieutenant governor. Raids started again in 1677, culminating in 1682 in another isthmus crossing by Coxon and Sawkins, who rampaged along the coasts of Chile and Peru before escaping with their loot round Cape Horn – but they were recognised as criminals, and the effect on Jamaica's trade was intolerable. Only the French persisted in filibustering raids on Spanish colonies, until other ways of penetrating Spanish America emerged after 1684. The English privateers were vulnerable if deprived of bases where they could market their loot, so Jamaica went the way of the other sugar colonies. When an earthquake destroyed Port Royal in 1692, obliterating Morgan's tomb, the old self-reliant days were long gone.[24]

Anglo–Dutch and Anglo–French competition in North America 1664–1688

The experience of Virginia during the years of the Dutch and French wars was entirely different, despite the steady development of slavery on the tidewater and the far from satisfactory state of the militia. By the 1640s most slaves had been excluded from its ranks. By the 1650s most indentured servants had been excluded, and most of the poorer freemen were to be excluded in the 1680s. After 1661 the colonial leadership was worried about the possibility of social upheaval and moved towards a smaller number

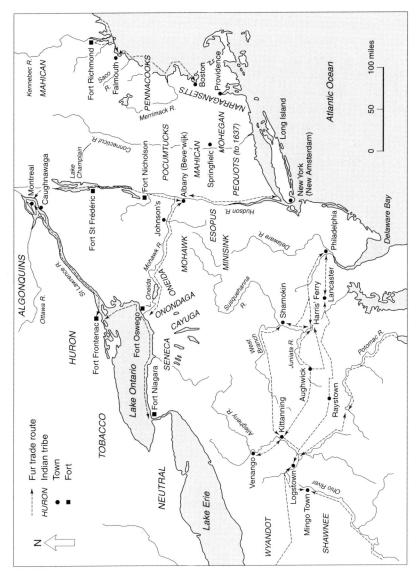

Map 7 Principal routes of the fur trade in the later seventeenth century

of elite militia units to be known as trainbands which were deliberately recruited from reliable, prosperous sections of the population. They incorporated small cavalry units. Because the militia was a force which reacted to an attack, arms and equipment had to be dispersed and held by the men in their own homes, rather than kept in a central armoury, as was the older English militia tradition. Sir William was very conscious that at a time of good prices and profitability in the tobacco export trade, making money was largely a question of securing a larger negro workforce for the fields and quays of Virginia. In peacetime he waged war primarily with the farmers (i.e. leesees of the king's customs), whom he described as 'the greatest trouble in my little Government'. They were competitors for the right to feed off the stream of tobacco profits, and war was not entirely unwelcome to the governor, for its emergencies and pressures inevitably loosened accounting controls over him. However, Berkeley knew that in 'the approaching warr with the Dutch the channel [i.e. the English Channel] will be very dangerous'. Nor could he tell whether this so predictable war had started or not in October 1664, though the lack of ships from England led him to suspect it had, 'and that for their safety they intend to come out in fleets'. That meant delay while the ships assembled, so it is a measure of Virginian perceived priorities in late 1664 that Berkeley was not obsessed with local defence but was urging a correspondent to get an order for bulk tobacco in early before the first fleet arrived and prices rose.[25]

The governor had no illusions about the forces at his disposal when he finally heard of the outbreak of war with the Dutch in 1665, but he had a plan for protecting the assets of the colony from a Dutch fleet. It involved withdrawing merchant shipping high up the rivers to four defensible anchorages, with provision for hauling them onshore if the worst came. He had 1500 mounted 'dragooners' and 2500 good infantry armed with excellent snaphance muskets, as well as a few thousand ill-equipped and ill-trained nominal militiamen. That he felt was enough to ensure that the Dutch could not go beyond the effective range of their ship guns, which in the still heavily wooded country meant less than half a mile in most places. The year 1666 saw a single Dutch privateer slip into Chesapeake Bay and capture two merchantmen. The summer of 1667 saw a very serious attack by a squadron led by Admiral Abraham Crijnsen which did do a good deal of damage, capturing a dozen tobacco ships and burning half a dozen more. Nevertheless, the raid also showed that the Virginians' protected anchorages system confined the Dutch rampage to the lower James River, and that the Dutch were likely to be destroyed in detail by fierce local opposition if they tried to land. When in the course of the third Dutch war Admiral Evertsen and Captain Binckes led a powerful Dutch squadron past the capes and into the Chesapeake, they ran into a hornets' nest, partly because of the unexpected prior arrival of two English royal frigates which led many more armed merchantmen out of the protected anchorage of Newport News to engage the enemy in a wild free-for-all action. Between that, the forts guarding the anchorages, and the swarming militia, the Dutch commanders thought better of the idea. They left to achieve what Admiral de Ruyter had failed to do in 1665, for they temporarily recaptured the colony of New Netherland, captured by the English in the second war and renamed like its capital city New York.[26]

That war had begun with an unprecedented display of active royal interest in non-European affairs, in the shape of the strong backing from the Duke of York for the surprise attack on all the Dutch trading stations in West Africa – except their seat of government, Elmina – by a squadron commanded by Sir Robert Holmes in early 1664. With the vast stakes of the Atlantic slave trade to play for, the Dutch counter-attack under De Ruyter at the end of the same year had, to use Pepys' words, ensured that the English were 'beaten to dirt at Guiny by De Ruyter with his fleet'. Oddly, the same great admiral then achieved very little when he crossed over to the Lesser Antilles, and less still when he sailed north to explore the possibility of reversing the other act of aggression committed by the English before any declaration of war, which had been the seizure of New Netherland on the back of some very specious claims. Pepys summed it all up when he heard that 'we have beat them out of the New Netherlands too' in December 1664, and opined that the English had been inflicting great mischief on the Dutch globally 'without public knowledge or reason'.[27] The Dutch West India Company, which controlled New Netherland, was financially in a bad way by 1660, and had never valued greatly the fur trade down the Hudson which was the main source of profitable exports for the inland settlement of Albany and New Amsterdam on Manhattan Island. However, the Dutch had been strong enough to subdue New Sweden, a small Swedish settlement on the Delaware, in 1655–56, and to destroy the Esopus Indians in the Hudson valley in 1663–64. Pensionary De Witt, the leading Dutch politician of his day, could see that New Netherland was potentially a vital chink in the armour of the Navigation Acts whereby Charles II was trying to exclude the Dutch from trade with his overseas dominions, but De Witt's interest came too late for Governor Stuyvesant. The latter was not even on good terms with the New Englanders, with whom he might have had a marriage of convenience based on mutual services, because of endless conflict with Connecticut, which loudly asserted its rights of jurisdiction over more and more of Long Island (where admittedly there were many English settlers). Conquering New Sweden had cost money, of which there was little available even for arms and ammunition. The fortifications of New Amsterdam were a joke, designed to hold off the Indians – with whom the Dutch were still quarrelling – rather than European forces. When an English fleet reinforced by some New Englanders appeared off New Amsterdam in the summer of 1664, Stuyvesant was persuaded by his own people not to fight but to accept the generous terms offered by the English commander Sir Richard Nicolls. The recapture of New York, formerly New Amsterdam and very briefly renamed New Orange by the Dutch in 1673, was another case of surrender to overwhelming force. Admiral Cornelis Evertsen the younger did have to mount an hour of bombardment, but it cost only one English life. There were a couple of Dutch wounded. Dutch naval power could have kept New Netherland alive and autonomous, because restoration England's naval reach had proved much too ambitious for the limited fiscal backing behind it. In the end, the United Netherlands preferred to take Surinam at the Peace of Westminster, rather than sustain New Orange as the capital of a viable colony based on western Long Island and the Hudson valley. For New England this was serious, because men unsympathetic to the ruling Congregationalist ascendancy, like the Anglican merchant Samuel Maverick, were urging imperial reorganisation. He had resided in Massachusetts and in New Amsterdam, had urged the conquest of New Netherland, and now had the ear of the Duke of York. Maverick said the New Englanders were a 'great and Considerable people' but also that 'the sooner reduced the better'.[28] By the end of the traumas of King Philip's War, the New Englanders were in an unprecedented state of shock and weakness, while the Duke of York, who had been granted the conquered Dutch territories, was a neighbour. Nor was Virginia's usually self-confident elite in good shape.

There the problem was a split within the governing class, if Nathaniel Bacon can be seen as a man whose social rank should have placed him within that magic circle. Nathaniel Bacon Jr was a scapegrace son of a Suffolk landed family who had been packed off to Virginia with £1800 sterling capital when he became too much of an embarrassment. A cousin by marriage to Governor Sir William Berkeley, who had resumed office in 1660, Bacon arrived in 1674 and had his path smoothed for him as he set up as a frontier planter and Indian trader near the falls of the James River. During the 1650s many new counties had been set up in Virginia, and the pressure to dispossess surviving Indian communities, described in one of the acts of the local assembly as 'our extreame pressures on them', led repeatedly to violence, expulsion, and extirpation for the outnumbered and outgunned Indians. That a given Indian group had a long history of alliance with the English did not spare them. The central authorities of the colony were sincerely distressed, but could not control the large landowners in the frontier counties, who organised their white tenants and humbler neighbours for aggression. When the Virginia Assembly of 1659 authorised free trade in anything (including guns and ammunition) with the Indians, it effectively gave up in despair and turned the frontier over to local county justices, who were precisely the robber barons who were generating all the trouble, out of naked greed.[29] This was the background against which the clashes with Indians in the northern marches of Virginia and Maryland which triggered Bacon's rebellion must be seen. Central in the crisis was the role of the Iroquoian-speaking Minquas – or Susquehannocks, as the English of Virginia and Maryland called them. They had moved down from the north in the sixteenth century and waged predatory warfare from their fortified villages against the other Indians of the Delaware valley. They coexisted with, and were armed by, New Sweden during its brief existence.[30] Governor Johan Risingh, the last ruler before the Dutch conquest, recorded in his diary that he arranged large land purchases from the Minquas, but on the condition that they 'should be able to buy from us cloth, guns, and all other goods that they now purchase from the Dutch and the English'. The Indians also asked that the Swedes 'establish blacksmiths and shotmakers on the land, who should make their guns and other things for good pay'.[31] New Sweden might be doomed, but the message is clear: the Indians were living in a firearms culture. The trouble was that they were economically dependent on and heavily outnumbered by their white neighbours. Clashes with other Indians over the destructive effects of European farmstock on Indian agriculture were regular on the northern bounds of the two English Chesapeake colonies, but Nathaniel Bacon appears in late 1675 to have begun to beat up and plunder Indians indiscriminately. Over a thousand Virginia and Maryland troops surrounded a Susquehannock fort defended by a mere hundred warriors in September of that year and murdered five chiefs who came out to protest their innocence and friendship to the English. By early 1676 the inevitable Susquehannock vengeance raids were hitting detached English settlements. Berkeley's policy was to ban the arms trade to Indians and rely on small garrisoned forts at the falls of the river, supplementing these with mounted patrols. Bacon suddenly emerged as the champion of those who believed literally that all Indians should be extirpated. He fed the frontiersmen's paranoid fears of betrayal by a governor who opposed all-out offensive action. His own unauthorised 'campaigns' slew almost no Susquehannocks, but did murder numbers of friendly Occaneechee and Pamunkey Indians. Eventually he challenged Berkeley's authority in a confused civil war in which he burned Jamestown and drove his rival to refuge on the eastern shore before dying unexpectedly in October 1676.

The crisis attracted royal attention, because Virginia produced £100,000 sterling of revenue annually for the king. Rebellion cut the flow of tobacco which yielded as much as the secret subsidies that Louis XIV of France was pledged to pay Charles, and that he did occasionally pay on time.[32] Charles despatched a squadron carrying no fewer than 1100 troops under Major Jeffreys to sort out the situation. They arrived late in 1676 to find Bacon dead and Berkeley fighting back, not unsuccessfully. Of course, the arrival of this large force put an end to further resistance. Most of the rebels had always stressed their loyalty to the Crown. There is no reason to doubt their words. It was Berkeley they wanted to remove, and in a sense that they did, though the governor had the pleasure of executing several of his late opponents on charges of treason to the king. He was then recalled, partly to stop him and his allies from running a more extensive vendetta motivated by hopes of confiscation of property. Any governor whose regime had ended in such shambles was likely to be removed, especially when he was as old as Berkeley. The idea that effective autonomy was terminated in Virginia in 1676 and replaced by military government rather misses the point that the troops really had nothing to do and were soon removed.[33] What King Charles wanted was his Virginia revenue, especially as he was anxious not to be beholden to parliament for grants. Once it became clear that the situation was returning rapidly to normal, the old gubernatorial structure was reinstalled. It was cheap. That it tended to lead to the governor being coopted by the local political system did not matter in so royalist and conservative a colony as Virginia, as long as the tobacco export trade was not interrupted. Bacon's rebellion was unique, because it presented the puzzled Crown with the spectacle of deep divisions in the Virginia elite. Unlike New England's shaken frontier communities, Virginians in 1676, though they feared raids, were so confident about their ability to destroy Indians that some had risen against a governor whom they saw as dragging his feet on punitive action.

New England was a different story. There the Crown had begun to move against the much abused Massachusetts charter by due legal process of *quo warranto* in the Court of the King's Bench in 1682. King's Bench ruled, very reasonably, for the Crown in 1684. To that revoked charter were soon added those of Connecticut and Rhode Island. All New England was reorganised into a dominion of New England with a royal governor, Edmund Andros, to whose jurisdiction New York and New Jersey were added in 1688. James II, who had succeeded in 1685, was undoubtedly obsessed with reducing Englishmen, and especially Protestant Englishmen, to a much more humble and obedient posture before the Crown. Though the dominion was justified to some extent by the argument that it would coordinate defence against both the Indians and French, New Englanders feared that its underlying purpose was to deprive them of basic English liberties and usher in popish absolutism. The fundamental flaw in this long overdue overhaul of the structure of an imperial monarchy was the total absence of cooperation between church and state, without which the Spanish and Portuguese Empires would have been ungovernable. With James it was worse, because he was actively hostile to the established Church of England. True, he could see no way of immediately destroying it, but peaceful coexistence was not possible. The only kind of peace the Catholic James could envisage with other churches was simply the continuation of ecclesiastical war by other means. Andros was soon being accused, like Berkeley, of being soft on Indians in a northern frontier war in the summer and fall of 1688. Much more convincing was the view that the 'treaty of peace, good correspondence, and neutrality in America' signed by James II and Louis XIV in November 1686 was an unequivocal sellout of English interests for the sake of forging a close entente between the two Catholic monarchs. It suggested that James was more interested in bullying than in defending English America. The treaty implicitly condoned recent and very sweeping French territorial claims in the trans-Appalachian region. It did not settle the boundaries of Maine or New York contested by the French. It said nothing about recent highly aggressive French behaviour in the Leeward Islands and their violent attacks on settlements of the English Hudson's Bay Company, let alone about their massive assaults on the Seneca Indian allies of New York. Better defence could have helped secure at least acquiescence in a more powerful imperial monarchy. As it was, some of James' best soldiers, like John Churchill, the future duke of Marlborough, were passionately hostile to the 1686 treaty. Not all Englishmen were as helpless in the face of superior force as the inhabitants of New Sweden or New Netherland, who by 1688 were resigned to a purely minority ethnic identity in a relatively tolerant English polity. Churchill had succeeded James as governor of the Hudson's Bay Company. His defection in the crisis which followed the invasion of England by William of Orange in 1688 was one of the many which destroyed James and made him choose to abandon the realm rather than negotiate with his subjects from a position of weakness.[34] By self-defeating political ineptitude James had squandered the moment of opportunity when a shrewder king might have at least tempered the self-reliance which successful, if punishing, Indian wars had bred in a colonial English population that Governor Berkeley had justly complained was not only inclined to disgruntlement, but also widely armed. The dominion of New England disintegrated as soon as news of the Glorious Revolution in Old England reached America.

Notes and references

1. Paul E. Hoffman, *The Spanish Crown and the Defence of the Caribbean 1535–1585* (Louisiana State University Press, Baton Rouge, LA, 1980), pp. 217–36.

2. Kenneth R. Andrews, *The Spanish Caribbean: Trade and plunder, 1530–1630* (Yale University Press, New Haven, CT, 1978), pp. 218–23.

3. Cited in Vincent T. Harlow, *A History of Barbados 1625–1685* (Clarendon Press, Oxford, 1926), p. 16.

4. Carl and Roberta Bridenbaugh, *No Peace beyond the Line: The English in the Caribbean 1624–1690* (Oxford University Press, New York, 1972), pp. 10–26 and 32.

5. John C. Appleby, 'English Settlements in the Lesser Antilles during War and Peace, 1603–1660', in Robert L. Paquette and Stanley L. Engerman (eds.), *The Lesser Antilles in the Age of European Expansion* (University Press of Florida, Jacksonville, FL, 1996), pp. 96–101.

6. Harlow, *op. cit.*, pp. 62–102.

7. Roger Hainsworth, *The Swordsmen in Power: War and politics under the English republic 1649–1660* (Sutton, Stroud, Gloucestershire, 1997), p. 195.

8. Timothy Venning, *Cromwellian Foreign Policy* (St Martin's Press, New York, 1995), Chap. 5, 'The Western Design'.

9. Betty Wood, *The Origins of American Slavery* (Hill and Wang, New York, 1997).

10. Archibald P. Thornton, *West-Indian Policy under the Restoration* (Clarendon Press, Oxford, 1956), Preface, p. v.

11. Andrew O' Shaughnessy, 'Redcoats and Slaves in the British Caribbean', in *Lesser Antilles*, eds. Paquette and Engerman, pp. 105–27.

12. Stephen Saunders Webb, *The Governors-General: The English army and the definition of the Empire, 1569–1681* (University of North Carolina Press, Chapel Hill, NC, 1979), pp. 167–210.

13. *Funk and Wagnall's Standard Dictionary* (Signet, New American Library, New York, pbk edn, 1980), is a case in point, defining buccaneer as 'a pirate'.

14. Nellis M. Crouse, *The French Struggle for the West Indies 1665–1713* (Columbia University Press, New York, 1943), remains the best general introduction to the rise of French power in the seventeenth-century Caribbean.

15. 'An Abstract of the Muster of Colonell Sir Tobias Bridges Regiment October the 20th 1668', in Blathwayt Papers, Huntington Library, San Marino, CA (hereafter BPHL), Box I, BL 374.

16. 'Petition of the Commanders and Owners of Ships that Transported the Regiment of ffoot souldiers commanded by Tobias Bridges to the Barbados ...', 21 July 1669, BPHL, Box I, BL 380.

17. 'The humble Peticon of Major Edmond Andros and Captain James Cotter in behalfe of ... Your Majesty's Regiment ... in the West Indies', BPHL, Box I, BL 381.

18. 'The humble petition of several merchants and commanders of ships which were taken up for your Majesties service in Barbados in the tyme of the late ware', BPHL, Box I, BL 387.

19. 'Memorandum Concerning the debts upon the 4 & ½ per cent', BPHL, Box I, BL 389.

20. Cornelis C. Goslinga, *The Dutch in the Caribbean and on the Wild Coast 1580–1680* (University of Florida Press, Gainsville, FL, 1971), pp. 472–82.

21. Privy Council Committee for Trade and Plantations report to the King on measures necessary to be taken for the security of the Leeward Islands, BPHL, Box II, BL 363.

22. *The Diary of Samuel Pepys*, eds. Robert Latham and William Matthews, Vol. VIII: 1667 (University of California Press, Berkeley, CA, 1974), p. 75, entry for 20 February 1667.

23. John Esquemeling, *The Buccaneers of America*, ed. George A. Williams (Stokes, New York, 1914), Chap. 5. This is a version of the first English edition of 1684.

24. Peter Earle, *The Sack of Panama* (Jill Norman and Hobhouse, London, 1981), pp. 241–44; W.L. Burn, *The British West Indies* (Hutchinson, London, 1951), pp. 42–47.

25. Sir William Berkeley to Richard Nicolls, 4 October 1664, BPHL, Box I, BL 67.

26. William L. Shea, *The Virginia Militia in the Seventeenth Century* (Louisiana State University Press, Baton Rouge, LA, 1983), pp. 86–96.

27. *Pepys' Diary*, edn cit., Vol. V, pp. 352 and 283, entries for 22 December and 29 September 1664 respectively.

28. Quoted in Henry and Barbara Van Der Zee, *A Sweet and Alien Land* (Viking Press, New York, 1978), p. 384.

29. Wilcomb E. Washburn, *Virginia under Charles I and Cromwell 1625–1660* (Clearfeld, Baltimore, MD, 1993 reprint).

30. Lorraine E. Williams, 'Indians and Europeans in the Delaware Valley, 1620–1655', in Carol E. Hoffecker *et al.* (eds.), *New Sweden in America* (University of Delaware Press, Newark, DE, 1995), pp. 112–20.

31. Entry for 6 June 1655, in *The Rise and Fall of New Sweden: Governor Johan Risingh's journal 1654–1655 in its historical context*, eds. Stellan Dahlgren and Hans Norman (Almqvist and Wiksel, Stockholm, 1988), pp. 236–37.

32. Wilcomb E. Washburn, *The Governor and the Rebel: A history of Bacon's rebellion in Virginia* (University of North Carolina, Chapel Hill, NC, 1957), pp. 92–96.

33. Stephen Saunders Webb, *1676: The end of American independence* (Alfred A. Knopf, New York, 1984).

34. Stephen Saunders Webb, *Lord Churchill's Coup: The Anglo-American Empire and the Glorious Revolution reconsidered* (Alfred A. Knopf, New York, 1995), pp. 114–23.

The fracturing of the Englishry, the marginality of colonial enterprise, and the erratic impact of war

It is too easy for modern historians to slip into glib platitudes about the nature of the early-modern 'imperial experience' for certain Western European communities, in order to construct a teleology which simply runs the history of earlier centuries into a deterministic model leading 'inevitably' to the racist, centralised overseas European empires of the age of steam power and steel. Thus 'the absolute or relative superiority of Western weaponry and Western military organisation over all others' – a concept which has to be, and has been, very carefully qualified by the best scholarship, and which only obtains during part of the nineteenth century as a defensible generalisation – is used very broadly so as to include much of the period after 1350. Marxist rhetoric about 'the primary extraction of surplus' is then used to suggest that the chartered European companies in the Orient used this 'superiority' of military technology to seize a large part of the product of that extraction process 'without the expenses, troubles and dangers of managing' it. From there the model moves rapidly through the creation of 'gradient of contempt' for lesser breeds, from Celts to Chinese, and ends with arguments about the emergence of militarised European proto-national states for whom 'the possession of overseas empire made the passage to nationhood possible or at least easier'.[1]

This sort of post-mortem broad-brush Marxism remains curiously popular in American academe but certainly for the period before 1750, especially with reference to 'civilized and prosperous Englishmen'[2] of the early-modern era, from whose alleged experience much of the model is usually derived, it is just not convincing. Some of its fundamental supports turn out to be extremely shaky when subjected to the discipline of the full range of available evidence, rather than buttressed by a selective use of those parts of the evidence which happen to fit into the model.[3] In the case of those communities which we can describe as English, certainly up to the political upheavals sparked off by the Glorious Revolution of 1688 in Old England, it is clear that colonial wars on the frontier marches of the English world display an extremely erratic pattern of success and failure. They could be seriously divisive of the unity of what for want of a better word one can call the Englishry, and many colonial peripheries which have become retrospectively matters of obsessive interest to scholars were of very little contemporary interest indeed to the core English population, even if that core be redefined as a literate elite.

The best study of books relating to the so-called 'rise of the British Empire' and published in England between 1481 and 1620 is called *Books to Build an Empire*, but its author was far too good a bibliographer and historian of print to conclude that by 1620 such books had made any significant impact. On the contrary, even after it became clear that both the Virginia Company and the EIC were established and likely to endure, 'this novel experience had not sufficiently excited the general reading public to create a demand for descriptions of New World colonies, or of the East Indies that would induce publishers to invest frequently in this type of publication'. Virginia 'was not a subject for which booksellers found a large and waiting audience'. Those who did suffer from the illusion that books might seriously help build an empire in the period 1580–1620 were a tiny, atypical minority who wrote in a 'pleading and defensive tone'. Well they might, for they were a mere fraction even of writers on geography, broadly construed. English educated minds remained oriented towards classical and Biblical scholarship, and towards domestic and European current events.[4]

Letters which were sent in 1615–17 by George, Lord Carew, an eminent figure at the Jacobean court, to his friend Sir Thomas Roe when Roe was serving as ambassador to the Great Moghul, give a clear picture of the priorities of the English elite, for these were news letters designed to keep Roe up to date. The content is overwhelmingly concerned with events at the court, with the aristocratic politics of King James' three kingdoms, and with the politics and wars of continental Europe. Overseas plantations feature minimally. Yet both men should have been prime candidates for the allegedly emerging triumphalist proto-British, Protestant 'imperial' identity. Carew had been lord president of Munster after the self-destruction of the Earl of Essex in Ireland, and had played a key role in the latter stages of the Nine Years' War. Roe was an intimate of the circle of Henry, Prince of Wales. He had made exploratory voyages to the north-east coast of mainland South America. Carew did, of course, keep him abreast of his friend Raleigh's fate, but his references to Virginia were minimal. One remarked that there was precious little news from there. Another remarked that, as with the Bermudas, a start had been made to tobacco production in

Virginia 'but yett no proffitt is retourned'. Most significant of all is Carew's side reference to Virginia in 1615 after an account of the usual massacre of every man, woman, and child in a French settlement on the Amazon which fell to a surprise attack by 800 Portuguese with 800 Indian allies: 'I pray God that Virginia may not drinke of the same cuppe.'

Carew knew full well that the French Crown would not respond with appropriate force to Portuguese provocation for, after the assassination of Henry IV by a Roman Catholic zealot in 1610, power had been transferred to the queen regent, Marie de' Medici, whose dynastic and religious sympathies ensured that she was in the Spanish interest. Similarly, Carew was aware of the passionate desire of King James for the closest possible diplomatic and dynastic ties with the Crown of Spain–Portugal. He knew that there was no way the current negotiations with commissioners from the United Netherlands, designed to settle Anglo–Dutch disputes in Arctic and Asian waters, could succeed, for in Asia 'they require that *pro-rata* we should beare equall charge of there garrisons and in there fortifications', which would mean a breach in Anglo–Spanish amity, and 'how severe the king is in performinge every article in the treatie of peace and amitie between us and Spayne you know'.[5]

The Spaniards could not be quite sure that even James would demonstrate total pusillanimity in the face of a massacre of his Virginia colony, but from the tone of Carew's remarks it seems that one of his courtiers, who knew him intimately and was a devoted subject – indeed, the son of a dean of Windsor – would not have put it past him. Most Englishmen around 1620, in so far as they thought about these matters (which probably excludes a majority) were not triumphalist about their position in the world; they were scared, with good reason. They knew that storm clouds were gathering in Europe. They feared, especially after the outbreak of what was to develop into the Thirty Years' War in 1618, that a Habsburg Counter-Reformation juggernaut would win a decisive series of victories which would undermine the viability of a Protestant Europe already substantially reduced from its peak extent by the force of Roman Catholic arms. Their monarch, James VI and I, a moderate Calvinist of strongly eirenic and ecumenical disposition, shared their alarm at the prospect of widespread sectarian warfare. European by education and almost totally European in outlook, King James was desperately anxious to further, preferably through a general council of all the churches, that reconciliation and reunification in spirit which alone would enable Europe to function as a stable comity of sovereignties.

James was proud of the title *rex pacificus*. This most learned and prayerful of monarchs was a deeply thoughtful European intellectual, and by any standard a more impressive Christian than the other kings, popes, prelates, and ministers of state with whom he dealt. He really did believe that 'The greatest gift that our Saviour gave his Apostles, immediately before his Ascension, was that hee left his Peace, with them.'[6] Most contemporary men of power were willing to wage endless, cruel war in the name of peace; to seek ideological uniformity through physical terror; and to slip only too easily along the classic terrorist track to butchery and indeed genocide when terror failed to break opponents' wills. If 'statesman' is what politicians like to call themselves, James is one of the few politicians whose motives entitle them to the title. Whether he was a sensible or effective player in the international game by 1620 is another matter. The game was to moderate Habsburg behaviour. Moderating the Counter-Reformation culture of the Austrian or Spanish Habsburgs was impossible. Ultimately James was foolish to think he could stem the flood-tide of the Counter-Reformation by suggesting through various means to the Spaniards that there was no great gap between their religion and that of the Church of England.[7] From a Roman Catholic point of view the suggestion was risible. Endless appeasement, and an apparently endless stream of concessions on specific points, merely sharpen the bloody-mindedness of those for whom bloody-mindedness appears to be paying off rather well. James never grasped the absolute cultural intolerance and triumphalism at the core of the culture he tried so hard to marry.

Englishmen, especially those in remote and dangerous parts, might well conclude that their best hope of physical security lay in their own military efforts, or in the case of the EIC on the gundecks of their ships. Of a state-sponsored 'imperial' project there was no sign under Elizabeth, and very little under James. Attempts to argue that 'From the late seventeenth century on, England began to realise the potential of imperial thinking' fly in the face of the evidence. Attempts to support such arguments by contending that 'geography was essential to the creation of an ideology of imperialism in early-modern England', and that therefore any sign of geographical or navigational studies in Oxford, Cambridge, or London shows the growth of a 'self-image as an independent and omnicompetent country' which 'had to precede the acquisition of an empire' is to cut verbal arabesques round the awkward fact that in 1620 England's overseas colonies were few and not well regarded.[8] Imperial ideologies are almost invariably retrospective rationalisations, and the academic tendency to take academic books too seriously is admirably put in its place by the splendid pilot of the Elizabethan galleon *Leicester*, who gave 'not a fart for cosmography'. Seventeenth-century Englishmen had more pressing concerns and 'the discoveries were matters of little moment'. Though its commerce broadened, without changing in essence, it is clear that before 1625 England 'was as little influenced intellectually by its experience of the outside world as was Holland'.[9]

The historian is better occupied studying the erratic impact of war than in inventing non-existent national mentalities to explain the vicissitudes of English identities between 1550 and 1688. At best an uncertain business, war on the marches of the English was in this period often further complicated by a long history of competitive coexistence with non-English cultures which bred militarisation and encouraged interchange of military techniques and technologies. The Celtic frontier was an extreme case. On the frontier between the Irish Gaelic Lordships and the feudal Anglo-Norman barons of the Lordship, Gaelic society had become deeply militarised, in an ever changing way, mainly on account of the presence of mercenary forces, originally resident gallowglass mercenaries and later the itinerant redshanks. Because of the endless fighting between the Gaels and the Anglo-Normans, the process became institutionalised. It was also stimulated by the succession conflicts in Gaelic chiefdoms, which involved the subsequent displacement of the previous ruling kindreds or septs, if they came out on the losing side. That created downward social mobility, feeding fighting men into the market as it did so. This mercenary militarisation was what distinguished Irish from Scottish Gaelic society, where the clan was a structure capable of mobilising warriors, but not a militarised society like those of the Irish Gaelic chiefdoms.[10]

Obviously, the main restriction on Irish Gaelic warlords' military technology was the cost of the more expensive items such as cannon and up-to-date artillery fortifications. Apart from that, the main external source of their mercenary manpower, which was Gaelic Scotland, was an area whose international contacts more or less guaranteed it stayed up with the military developments in continental Europe, where Scots mercenaries also sought work. A great prince of the Gaels, the Earl of Argyll – after 'trubilsome and chargeabill service against his majestys rebellis in the Ilis and against the Makgregors' – could be given 'permission by James VI and I 'to serve a forraine prince that my burdenit estate myt breath in my absence', as he put it in a message to his clan when he wanted to tell them he was coming back.[11] Since the MacGregors had been given to eking out a living by summer work as redshanks, especially in Ulster, it is interesting that when the Scots privy council wrote to Sir Duncan Campbell of Glen Orchy in August 1621 to warn him 'that some of the clangregour are now broken lous and hes begun to renew the wicked and unhappie forme of living quhairin formerlie they were brought up', they also warned him that 'they go in troupis and companyes athorte the countrey armed with unlawful and forbidden waponis'.[12] The reference is probably to firearms. There was no way on the permeable faces of interchange between Gaelic and other societies in Ireland and Scotland whereby any government could fulfil its fantasy of keeping modern hand weapons out of the hands of untrustworthy Gaels.

The upshot in Ireland was that there had been something of a military balance. The Old English nobility of the Lordship may have hoped that the proclamation of a kingdom of Ireland in 1541 would imprison the Crown in an ideological position which could not be repudiated and which would compel it to make available to them enough resources to get the frontier of conquest moving again. It did not work out so simply. In Scotland the Crown really had no military resources, so it had to work with Highland power-wielders to try to contain incipient chaos, as when it told Sir Duncan Campbell that it would hold him responsible for suppressing a threatened feud, on the grounds that those involved 'are your friendis feuaris and dependaris or at the least are such personis whoime you may command'.[13] In Ireland the Elizabethan Crown did have just enough resources to make a difference, but it had very little by way of a functional relationship with the leaders of the Gaelic principalities, to the point where, in a succession dispute, it could be genuinely puzzled as to who they were. As Elizabethan policy lurched and bungled forward, trying to do too much with too little, and fatally attracted by plausible quick fixes, it became increasingly desperate and high handed.

The resistance which nearly bankrupted the Elizabethan Crown was ultimately rooted in the old Gaelic order, especially in Ulster, where Tyrone evolved tactics which made cannon and fortifications other than field fortifications something of an irrelevance. His demand for a regality in effect asked for the repudiation of the unrepudiable claims of 1541. Given a military balance, and a non-escalation of the stakes on his part, this was not an inconceivable outcome. His truce with Essex more or less set it up, but it proved unsustainable. In the light of Tyrone's contacts with Spain and the papacy, the Elizabethan regime had to make an all-out effort to win. By the time it secured a positive military decision, the classic Gaelic chiefdoms were beyond resurrection. What was crucially important for the future was the way the waging of the war had driven the Old English not from a sense of being part of the Englishry, but into a position of political and religious alienation from their Crown which had by-passed the institutions through which it was supposed to consult them; deprived them of control over and benefit from the campaigns against the Gaelic chiefdoms; and taxed them relentlessly without consent. Only in the next century was the Counter-Reformation to provide the bridge across which the Old English, its prime patrons in Ireland, moved to a sectarian Roman Catholic national identity in Ireland which involved cooperation with the historic enemy – the Gaels.

It was only in the 1640s that that process became overt. As late as King James' death in 1625, it was incipient rather than complete. In a roughly similar period between 1622 and 1644 the new English provinces on the Chesapeake, isolated physically and with little sense of positive support from the Crown, enjoyed a bitter but ultimately far more satisfactory and profitable experience of war than the Old English of Ireland. It was bitter because, without Crown forces, they proved vulnerable to Indian attack. It was more satisfactory and profitable because the absence of Crown forces ensured they fought the war themselves and controlled it. Disease had decimated their opponents. Even in the 1640s there were limits to cross-cultural transfers of weapons technology. Superior armour, firearms, and steel blade weapons gave the English victory in the set-piece actions they could force by a feed-fight strategy. The upshot was a loyal Englishry lucratively exploiting seized agricultural assets for production of cash crops for the Atlantic trade, but also a tradition of self-reliance.

New England sat uncomfortably to the Crown from the start, basically because its dominant congregationalists had gone there to escape from the ecclesiastical authority of their king's church. The region was fortunate that, apart from the quite exceptional episode of the Pequot War, the serious Indian rising came as late as 1675. It was unfortunate in the sense that by that date there had been very extensive military technology transfer. Although heavily outnumbered, 'King Philip' and his warriors inflicted truly grievous damage on the English, setting back their settlement by decades. To some extent the English survived because some of their abler militia commanders, like Benjamin Church, were notably open to, friendly with, and willing to learn from Amerindian allies. Governor Josiah Winslow of Plymouth in July 1676 gave Captain Church a commission to raise the unit with which Church hunted down and killed Philip. The unit was specified as 'a Company of Volunteers of about 200 Men, English and Indians: the English not exceeding the number of 60'.[14] Everyone knew that Indian allies were vital.

Of course, English settlers referred to their Amerindian opponents as savages. Few communities on the globe do not abuse their mortal enemies during war, and the 1675–76 conflict in New England undoubtedly made race relations in New England much worse, but the long-term enemy the Saints of New England proved unable to fight off in the late 1670s was the Crown. Weakened by war, facing a far more resolute and interested late Stuart monarchy, this particular section of the much fissured English world did not resist the long-overdue revocation of its charters. There were a few would-be holdouts like Samuel Nowell, a warlike divine, who after acting as chaplain to Winslow's and Talcott's 'armies' in King Philip's War, entered politics. Deposed as treasurer of Massachusetts Bay Colony by a royal commission, he both privately and publicly argued for resistance to royal authority, but then he was one who tended to prove his doctrine orthodox with apostolic blows and knocks. In a sermon printed as *Abraham in Arms* (Boston, 1678), and originally delivered at the election of the prestigious (if in 1675–76 largely useless) artillery unit of the local militia, he had trumpeted: 'That the highest practice of Piety and Practice of War may agree in one person. Religion and Arms may well be joyned together; they agree so well together than the Lord assumes the name unto himself, The Lord is a Man of War, the Lord is his name.'

He would have lost had he fought. In fact he died in London in September 1688, where he had gone to assist Increase Mather in the political lobbying which, along with the Glorious Revolution, spared the religious and (covertly) political separatists of New England from the consequences of debilitating war. One reason for the sudden collapse of James II's dominion of New England was the massive indifference of King William III to the world outside Europe. He was as Eurocentric as his fellow moderate Calvinist James VI and I, but unlike James he was a soldier. The idea that English people had by 1688 developed one identity, and that a state-led riproaring imperialist one, is sheer nonsense. In so far as there was an imperial vision after 1660, it was very closely associated with the late Stuart court. Inklings of it can be seen earlier in the absurd delusions of Charles I that his subjects more or less owed him an empire like that of Portugal in the Orient. Charles did begin to develop a potential instrument of long-range power-projection in an enhanced Navy Royal. It was funded with the unpopular ship money tax which was abolished in 1641. His fleet deserted to the other side in the English Civil War, but the parliamentary navy in that war was exposed to political and commercial pressures which ensured it was affected by many of the same weaknesses that had plagued the Navy Royal.[15]

The Cromwellian regime's brief fling in the Caribbean in the shape of the 'Western Design' was basically a failure. Though executed by the sweepings of an army, it rested, as an enterprise, on a naval and military establishment which could not be funded and which self-destructed in 1660. Even at the height of its power, the Cromwellian Commonwealth of England, Ireland, and Scotland had to grant a huge measure of autonomy to West Indian islands like disaffected, royalist Barbados to keep their nominal loyalty. Only the later Stuarts, Charles II and James II, combined a navalist imperial credo with resources and a navy which made them formidable. Charles II's Dutch wars even saw 'New England' moving 'steadily, if reluctantly, towards full participation'. Partly this was because Dutch privateers, ignorant like most foreigners before and since of the complexity of English identities, chose to 'make no difference between New England and Old' (to the indignation of conservative Saints from the former). Partly it was because as New England merchants strove to screw every possible advantage out of their membership of the English community, they realised that war offered a huge market for local provisions and ship stores.[16]

Even so, Charles lost all his Dutch wars, and fighting them strained his relationship with his subjects in Old England to breaking point by 1672–73. They did not trust him. How wise they were. James II's extraordinary patronage of a war of aggression against a mighty Muslim empire 6000 miles away in India was a predictable, dismal failure. There may have been an ideological element in James' ill-judged enthusiasm. He was vaguely interested in refocusing English paranoia on the heathen Turk rather than on the most Christian king of France. It was an unlikely project. The Ottoman Turks were widely acknowledged, especially in Italian intellectual circles, as the heirs of the Eastern Roman Empire, and were a great civilised European power. Attitudes were ambiguous but '[t]he sovereigns and city-states of early modern Europe were neither politically powerful nor diplomatically cohesive enough to establish a sustained and coherent demonization of the Ottoman empire'.[17]

In 1689 the English community was scattered, but its core was emphatically European in nature and outlook, and about to be pulled into far deeper engagement with continental Europe by William III. The western peripheries of that English community were united to Old England by the Irish Sea and the Atlantic. They had been crucially scarred and shaped by war with, on balance, disruptive and distorting consequences for their relationships with the rest of the Englishry. The far-flung peripheries, in the Americas or on the trade routes of Asia, were not perceived or treated as being of central importance by the population and rulers of Old England. We must not try to plot much later shifts of identity and perception on earlier moments of history. English communities had deeply fractured mutual relationships by the later seventeenth century, but all these communities, from London to Boston, were still English in some sense, and their threatening 'Other', in so far as they were Protestant, was not some mysterious east seen through the distorting lens of villainous western 'orientalism'. It was Louis XIV. In 1689 the colonial marchlands of the English were once again posed to be buffeted by the twin forces of war and neglect.

It would be far too charitable, and to simple, to describe either their past or their future experience of such neglect as salutary. Deerfield in western Massachusetts was a small English settlement founded on a site once occupied by Pocumtuck Indians. The latter had offended the warlike Mohawks, and had been defeated and scattered by a Mohawk war party in 1664. In 1675 the new village established by white farmers was destroyed in the course of King Philip's War by a mixture of hit-and-run raids and the loss of a third of its male manpower in the Bloody Brook massacre. Re-established in the 1680s, Deerfield found itself in 1688 the nearest English settlement to Montreal and the target for Franco–Indian guerrilla bands fighting in a style 'eerily familiar' to veterans of King Philip's War. Unlike other New England colonies, it was neither destroyed nor abandoned in the first of four spasms of Anglo–French warfare in North America after 1688, though it was under virtual siege for the best part of five years. Its brief moment of historic significance was to come in the second phase of those wars when in February 1704 the French and their Abenaki Indian allies hit it with a successful surprise raid, killing, kidnapping, and burning in a spectacular way. War, which occupied half its first fifty years, kept Deerfield poor, socially conservative, and economically undynamic. It was a small consolation to its few survivors in February 1704 that their misfortune had at last shocked the New England colonies 'into unity and action'.[18] Both before and after 1688 war repeatedly modified the nature of the several varieties of Englishness, and the relationships between them, in ways which were as brutal as they were unpredictable and important.

Notes and references

1. The quotations are all from Thomas A. Brady Jr, 'The Rise of Merchant Empires, 1400–1700: A European counterpoint', Chap. 3 in James D. Tracy (ed.), *The Political Economy of Merchant Empires* (Cambridge University Press, Cambridge, 1991), pp. 117–60.

2. The phrase is cited in Brady's article, but was originally coined by Angus Calder in his *Revolutionary Empire: The rise of the English-speaking empires from the fifteenth century to the 1780s* (Cape, London, 1981).

3. *Vide* the perceptive and astringently sceptical review of James D. Tracy (ed.), *The Political Economy of Merchant Empires*, by G.V. Scammell in *History*, 79 (1994), pp. 317–18.

4. John Parker, *Books to Build an Empire: A bibliographical history of English overseas interests to 1620* (N. Israel, Amsterdam, 1965), pp. 237, 213, and 171.

5. *Letters from George Lord Carew to Sir Thomas Roe Ambassador to the Court of the Great Mogul 1615–1617*, ed. John Maclean (Camden Society, London, 1859), pp. 5–7, 27, and 36.

6. Cited from King James' *A Meditation upon the Lord's Prayer* (1619), in W.B. Patterson, *King James VI and I and the Reunion of Christendom* (Cambridge University Press, Cambridge, 1997), p. 340.

7. *Ibid.*, p. 323.

8. Lesley B. Cormack, *Charting an Empire: Geography at the English universities, 1580–1620* (University of Chicago Press, Chicago, IL, 1997), pp. 225 and 1.

9. G.V. Scammell, *The World Encompassed: The first European maritime empires c. 800–1650* (Methuen, London, 1981), pp. 500 and 498.

10. The best introduction to this is Katherine Simms, *From Kings to Warlords: The changing political structure of Gaelic Ireland in the later Middle Ages* (Woodbridge, Boydell, 1987).

11. The Earl of Argyll to his kinsmen, copy, n.d. but clearly connected with Argyll's exile in 1617–20 and from internal evidence *c.* 1621–22, Breadalbane Papers, National Archives of Scotland (hereafter NAS), GD112/39/358.

12. Privy Council to Sir Duncan Campbell, 29 August 1621, *ibid.*, NAS, GD112/39/357.

13. Same to same, n.d. but from internal evidence 1620s, *ibid.*, NAS, GD112/39/357.

14. *Diary of King Philip's War 1675–1676 by Colonel Benjamin Church with an Introduction by Alan and Mary Simpson* (Lockwood, Tiverton, RI, 1975), pp. 128–29.

15. Kenneth R. Andrews, *Ships, Money and Politics: Seafaring and naval enterprise in the reign of Charles I* (Cambridge University Press, Cambridge, 1991), Chaps. 6 and 8.

16. Bernard Bailyn, *The New England Merchants in the Seventeenth Century*, pp. 131–32.

17. Jerry Brotton, *Trading Territories: Mapping the early modern world* (Reaktion Books, London, 1997), Chap. 3, 'Disorienting the East: The geography of the Ottoman Empire'.

18. Richard I. Melvoin, *New England Outpost: War and society in colonial Deerfield* (W.W. Norton, New York, pbk edn, 1989), p. 227.

FURTHER READING

These suggestions must be limited almost exclusively to the most important modern surveys and monographs. Any attempt at a complete bibliography would be quite impractical. Books rather than articles, with the odd exception, are cited. This is partly because of the difficulty of discriminating in the boundless sea of specialist articles in academic journals, but mainly because most of these books have excellent detailed bibliographies to aid deeper study.

Imperial context

To 1630, Kenneth R. Andrews, *Trade, Plunder and Settlement* (Cambridge University Press, Cambridge, pbk edn, 1984) is useful. Thereafter Nicholas Canny (ed.), *The Oxford History of the British Empire. Vol. I: The Origins of Empire* (Oxford University Press, Oxford, 1998) provides an up-to-date survey.

Military background

The first four chapters of William H. McNeill, *The Pursuit of Power: Technology, armed force and society since AD 1000* (University of Chicago Press, Chicago, IL, 1982) are a classic introduction to his subject. Geoffrey Parker, *The Military Revolution: Military innovation and the rise of the West, 1500–1800* (Cambridge University Press, Cambridge, 1988) is largely focused on the period before 1700, as is Michael Duffy (ed.), *The Military Revolution and the State 1500–1800* (Exeter Studies in History, No. 1, University of Exeter, 1980). Useful material will be found in the first six chapters of John A. Lynn (ed.), *Tools of War: Instruments, ideas and institutions of warfare, 1445–1871* (University of Illinois Press, Urbana and Chicago, IL, 1990); as well as in Jeremy Black (ed.), *War in the Early Modern World 1450–1815* (UCL Press,

London, 1999); George N. Clark, *War and Society in the Seventeenth Century* (Cambridge University Press, Cambridge, 1958); and M.S. Anderson, *War and Society in the Europe of the Old Regime 1618–1789* (Fontana, London, pbk edn, 1988).

Naval

The following deal with broad themes: Carlo M. Cipolla, *Guns and Sails in the Early Phase of European Expansion 1400–1700* (Collins, London, 1965); Nicholas A.M. Rodger, 'Guns and Sails in the First Phase of English Colonization', in Nicholas Canny (ed.), *The Oxford History of the British Empire. Vol. I: The Origins of Empire* (Oxford University Press, Oxford, 1998), pp. 79–98; idem., *The Safeguard of the Sea. A naval history of Great Britain. Vol. 1: 660–1649* (HarperCollins, London, 1997); Peter Padfield, *Tide of Empires: Decisive naval campaigns in the rise of the west, Vol. 2: 1654–1763* (Routledge, London, 1982).

More specialised topics are covered in Kenneth R. Andrews, *Elizabethan Privateering: English privateering during the Spanish War, 1585–1603* (Cambridge University Press, Cambridge, 1964); John S. Bromley, *Corsairs and Navies 1660–1760* (Hambledon Press, London, 1987), a collection of his seminal articles; J.R. Jones, *The Anglo-Dutch Wars of the Seventeenth Century* (Longman, London, 1996); and Sari R. Horstein, *The Restoration Navy and English Foreign Trade 1674–1688* (Scolar Press, Aldershot, 1991).

Regional studies

Coverage, especially in the earlier period, tends to be most unevenly spread, but these books will be found useful.

Metropolitan background

C.G. Cruickshank, *Elizabeth's Army* (2nd edn, Oxford University Press, Oxford, 1966) provides an institutional survey, with significant Irish references. Stephen Saunders Webb has written an important trilogy whose first volume, *The Governors-General: The English army and the definition of the Empire, 1569–1681* (University of North Carolina Press, Chapel Hill, NC, 1979), presents invaluable data. The second, *1676: The end of American independence* (Alfred A. Knopf, New York, 1984) may carry its argument too far. The third, *Lord*

Churchill's Coup: The Anglo-American Empire and the Glorious Revolution reconsidered (Alfred A. Knopf, New York, 1995), certainly does.

Ireland

Cyril Falls, *Elizabeth's Irish Wars* (1950, reprint, Constable, London, 1996) was a pioneering work and remains an outstandingly good and sensible one. G.A. Hayes-McCoy, *Scots Mercenary Forces in Ireland, 1565–1603* (Burns Oates and Washbourne, Dublin, 1937) is a book of awesome erudition which has never been equalled and until recently had no successors. However, Steven G. Ellis, *Tudor Ireland: Crown, community and the conflict of cultures 1470–1603* (Longman, London, 1985) provides excellent background for studies such as Nicholas P. Canny, *The Elizabethan Conquest of Ireland: A pattern established 1565–1576* (Harvester Press, Hassocks, 1976), and Hiram Morgan, *Tyrone's Rebellion: The outbreak of the Nine Years' War in Tudor Ireland* (Royal Historical Society, Boydell Press, Woodbridge, 1993).

Asia

Historically, from 1600 Asian waters saw the earliest profitable permanent extension of English enterprise on a transoceanic basis, with the voyages and factories of the East India Company. John Keay, *The Honourable Company: A history of the English East India Company* (HarperCollins, London, 1991) provides a good large-scale synthesis. The naval conflicts with the Portuguese, Dutch, and Marathas, which were an important part of the early history of the EIC, are not well studied. The first three chapters of Charles Rathbone Low, *History of the Indian Navy (1613–1863). Vol. I* (1877; reprinted Archive Editions, n.p., 1992), provide an overview. The evolution of its Dutch and Portuguese rivals can be followed in George D. Winius and Marcus P.M. Vink, *The Merchant Warrior Pacified: The VOC (the Dutch East India Co.) and its changing political economy in India* (Oxford University Press, Delhi, 1991), and Sanjay Subrahmanijam, *The Portuguese Empire in Asia 1500–1700* (Longman, London, 1993). Ray and Oliver Strachey, *Keigwin's Rebellion (1683–4): An episode in the history of Bombay* (Clarendon Press, Oxford, 1916) deals with the early vicissitudes of the EIC's first permanent regular land garrison. The brief Anglo–Moghul War is surveyed in Bruce P. Lenman, 'The East India Company and the Emperor Aurangzeb', *History Today*, 37 (1987), pp. 23–29. Interesting material on the amphibious operations of the war at Bombay and on the nature of EIC local forces in Bengal can be found in John Burnell, *Bombay in the Days of Queen Anne* (Hakluyt Society, London, 1933; republished by Munshiram Manoharlal Publishers, New Delhi, 1997).

The Americas

Because of the subsequent wealth and power of the United States of America, there is a disproportionate emphasis not just on North America in the literature, but also on the territory covered by the thirteen states which declared their independence in 1776. It is no accident that Canadian scholarship provides a partial corrective, notably in Ian K. Steele, *Warpaths: Invasions of North America* (Oxford University Press, New York, 1994), which is by far the best currently available survey. Steele's mentor, W.J. Eccles, is the most distinguished anglophone historian of the French colonial military. Two convenient introductions to this aspect of Eccles' work are his *Essays on New France* (Oxford University Press, Toronto, pbk edn, 1987) and *The Canadian Frontier 1534–1760* (rev. edn, University of New Mexico Press, Albuquerque, NM, 1983). His first book, *Frontenac: The courtier governor* (McClelland and Stewart, Toronto, 1959) remains basic. For the Spanish colonial frontier and its sixteenth- and seventeenth-century confrontations with expanding anglophone colonies, the best current introduction is David J. Weber, *The Spanish Frontier in North America* (Yale University Press, New Haven, CT, 1992).

Francis Jennings' innovative *The Invasion of America: Indians, colonialism and the cant of conquest* (Norton, New York, pbk edn, 1976) is a very 'American' book in the narrow sense of the word, in that it is really about New England and reflects the radical alienation of some intellectuals from the predominant culture of the United States of America. Less ideological is Patrick M. Malone, *The Skulking Way of War: Technology and tactics among the New England Indians* (Johns Hopkins University Press, Baltimore, MD, pbk edn, 1993). The first eight chapters of J. Leitch Wright Jr, *The Only Land They Knew: The tragic story of the American Indians in the Old South* (The Free Press, New York, 1981), survey the dispossession of the original inhabitants of the South. Alfred A. Cave, *The Pequot War* (University of Massachusetts Press, Amherst, MA, 1996) is one of the latest contributions to a debate which the paucity and ambiguity of the sources are likely to make endless. Older studies such as Douglas E. Leach, *Flintlock and Tomahawk: New England in King Philip's War* (Macmillan, New York, 1958), and *The Northern Colonial Frontier 1607–1763* (Holt, Rinehart and Winston, New York, 1966) remain important, as does Verner W. Crane, *The Southern Frontier 1670–1732* (with new preface by Peter H. Wood, Norton, New York, pbk edn, 1981).

The West Indies are comparatively neglected as a seat of war in this earlier period, compared with the scholarship devoted to eighteenth-century conflicts in the Caribbean, but Arthur P. Newton's classic *The European Nations in the West Indies 1493–1688* (A. and C. Black, London, 1933) is essentially a study of international conflicts. It can be supplemented with

Kenneth R. Andrews, *The Spanish Caribbean: Trade and plunder, 1530–1630* (Yale University Press, New Haven, CT, 1978); and Archibald P. Thornton, *West-Indian Policy under the Restoration* (Clarendon Press, Oxford, 1956). For late seventeenth-century colonial wars in the Antilles, Arthur P. Watts, *Une Histoire des Colonies Anglaises aux Antilles* (Presses Universitaires de France, Paris, 1924), has never been superseded. Nuala Zahedieh, 'A Frugal, Prudential and Hopeful Trade: Privateering in Jamaica, 1655–89', *The Journal of Imperial and Commonwealth History*, 18 (1990), pp. 145–68, is an important modern article.

INDEX

Abbot, George 94
Abbott, Sir Morris 193
Abercorn, Earl of 165
Addison, Launcelot 204
Aguila, Don Juan del 136, 138, 139
Albert, Archduke of the Spanish
    Netherlands 129, 150, 159, 160
Alexander, Sir William the younger
    176
Alexander VI, Pope 91
Alexander, William, Earl of Stirling
    175–7
Amazon delta
    exploration and colonisation 169–71,
        173–4, 175, 177, 178
    massacre at a French settlement 285
American colonies *see* North American
        colonies; Spanish America
American identity 244
Andros, Edmund, Governor of New York
    248, 269, 278–9
Anglican Church
    and the American colonies 235–6, 237,
        279
    and the Counter-Reformation 286
    and Ireland 166–7
    in Restoration England 199
Anglo–Dutch wars (1650s–1670s)
        197–206, 262, 263, 270, 272–6,
        290–1
Annawon 248–9
Antigua 260, 263, 265, 270
Antonio, Dom (Portuguese pretender) 84,
    92
archers, in the Gaidhealtachd 45–6
Aremberg, Count 149–50
Argall, Captain Samuel 225
Argyll, Earls of 51, 52, 136–7, 287
aristocracy 13–14
    in Ireland 28–9, 30–1, 32, 33–4,
        37–8
    in Wales 14, 25

armies
    at the Battle of Bosworth 23
    in Ireland
        and composition 100–2
        retainers 30–1
    and the nobility/gentry 13
    size of 3–4
    standing 45
    Virginian militia 272–4
    see also military technology
Arnold, Nicholas 62
artillery
    forts 5–6
    and the Gaidhealtachd 44–5
Ascham, Roger 15
Asian trade
    and the Dutch 182–5, 187–8, 189–93,
        194–5, 206–7
    and the English East India Company
        182–96, 203–4, 206–7, 211
    and India 208–10
    and Islamic empires 187
    and Portugal 182, 185–7, 191, 194
Atherny, Baron of 101
Atherton Company 246
attitudes to warfare 13–17
Auragzeb, Moghul Emperor 199, 209, 210,
    211
Aviles, Pedro Menendez de 224
Ayscue, Sir George 261, 262
Aztec Empire 3, 219

Bacon, Francis, Viscount St Albans 9–10
Bacon, Nathaniel Jr 5, 276–8
Baffin, William 225
Bagenal, Mabel 126
Bagenal, Nicholas 109
Bagenal, Sir Henry 102, 109, 111, 112,
        115, 116, 122, 125, 126, 128
Ball, George 188
Baltimore, Cecilius Calvert, Lord 233
Baltinglass, Viscount 163

Banks, Sir John 208
Bannockburn, Battle of (1314) 46
Bantam, and the English East India
    Company 187–8, 190, 192,
    206
Barbados 259–60, 261–2, 264, 266, 267,
    269
Barker, Andrew 86
Beare, O'Sullivan 45
Bellingham, Sir Edward 54
Bengal 208–9
Berkeley, Sir William, Governor of
    Virginia 249, 250, 274, 276, 277,
    278, 279
Bermuda 175, 284
Bernard, Richard 15
Berrio, Antonio de 121
Best, Captain Thomas 152
Binckes, Captain 274
Bingham, George 111, 115
Bingham, Sir Richard 76–7, 101,
    103, 104, 107, 111, 112, 113,
    116
Bingley, John 165
Bingley, Richard 165
Bingley, Sir Ralph 165
Blake, Admiral 263
Bohemia 81
Boleyn, Anne 35
Bombay 199, 208, 211
Books to Build an Empire 284
Bosworth, Battle of (1485) 23–4, 26
Bradford, William 243
Brayne, Major General William 266
Brazil 91, 92, 170, 223–4, 261
Breda, Treaty of (1667) 203, 268
Brereton, John 220
Bridge, Sir Tobias 268, 269
British Empire–Commonwealth 10–11, 93,
    284
Brounker, Sir Henry 125
Buchanan, George 120
Buckingham, George Villiers, 1st Duke of
    165, 167, 174, 191
Burgh, Lord Thomas 117
Burghley, Lord see Cecil, Sir William (later
    Lord Burghley)
Burke, Edmund 1
Burke, MacWilliam 128
Burke, Richard MacRickard 107
Burke, Sir Richard 101
Burnaby, Richard 209–10
Burrough, Sir John 87
Butler, Sir Edmund 65, 163

Caesar, Sir Julius 85
Calvert, Sir George 172
Calvin, John 118
Campbell of Ardkinglas, John 45
Campbell of Calder, John 45, 156
Campbell Clan (Argyll) 48–50, 51, 136–7,
    154, 167
Campbell of Glenorchy, Colin 51–2
Campbell of Glenorchy, Sir Duncan 287,
    288
Campbell, Lady Agnes 49, 50–1, 52, 68
Campbell of Lavers, Sir John 153
Campion, Edmund 79–80
Canada 175–8
    French 4, 6, 176, 177
    Newfoundland 89, 91, 149, 172–3,
        175–6, 238
    Nova Scotia 176–7
Carew, Sir George 78, 128, 135, 137, 138,
    142, 284–5
Carew, Sir Peter 64, 67, 137
Caribbean 169, 255–72
    Antigua 260, 263, 265, 270
    Barbados 259–60, 261–2, 264, 266, 267,
        269
    and the Commonwealth 262–3, 264,
        266–7, 290
    and English privateers 85, 86, 92–3
    and the French 225, 259, 260, 265,
        267–8, 271
    Honduras 258
    Jamaica 258, 263, 264–7, 271–2
    Leeward Islands 258–9, 260, 268, 269,
        270, 271, 279
    Montserrat 263, 268, 270
    Nevis 260, 264, 270
    Nicaragua 272
    and overseas trade 82, 83
    Panama Isthmus 91, 94, 272
    Puerto Rico 258
    St Kitts 259, 260, 264, 268, 270, 271
    and Spain 255–8, 259, 260, 263–4,
        265–6, 271–2
Carlisle, James Hay, Earl of 259, 260
cartography, Crown patronage of 132
Catherine of Braganza 199
cavalry, in the Gaidhealtachd 44
Cavendish, Thomas 87, 88
Cecil, Sir Robert (later Earl of Salisbury)
    105, 121, 129, 135, 139, 162, 163,
    169
Cecil, Sir William (later Lord Burghley) 50,
    61, 67, 68, 69, 104, 105, 106, 132
Champlain, Samuel de 238, 241

Channel Islands 24
Charlemagne 12
Charles I, King 114, 175, 290
  Bishops's Wars with Scotland 165
  and the Caribbean 259, 260, 261
  and the English East India Company
    193–4, 196
  and Ireland 165–8
  and North American colonisation 230,
    246
  war with France 46, 165, 176, 177
  war with Spain 165
  and the War of the Three Kingdoms
    166, 167–8, 195, 245
Charles II, King
  and the American colonies 5, 275, 278
  and Bombay 199
  and the Caribbean 263, 265–6, 269,
    270–1
  and Dryden's *Annus Mirabilis* 201–2
  and the Dutch 198, 199, 203, 204, 205,
    206, 290–1
  and the English East India Company
    207–8
  and France 203, 204, 205
  restoration of 197, 198
Charles IX, King of France 62
Charles V, Emperor 36, 80
Charles VIII, King of France 23, 24
Chattan, Clan 155
Chesapeake colonies
  Maryland 172, 233, 234, 249–50, 277
  see also Virginia
Chichester, Sir Arthur 138, 157, 159, 164
Child, Sir John 209, 210
Child, Sir Josiah 207, 208, 209–10, 211
China 12
Chinese junks 186
Choisy, François de 208
Church, Captain Benjamin 248, 289
Churchill, John (later Duke of
    Marlborough) 279
Clanricarde, Earl of 101
Clarendon, Edward Hyde, 1st Earl of 198,
    200
Clark, Dr Bartholomew 109
Clement VIII, Pope 138–9
Clifford, Sir Conyers 116–17, 133
Clifford, Sir Thomas 198
Cobham, Lord 149–50
Cobos, Captain Alonso 127
Coen, Jan Pieterszoon 189–91, 192
Colbert, Jean-Baptiste 203, 204, 205
colonial, concept of 1–2

Colquhouns of Luss 155
Columbus, Christopher 90
Commines, Philippe de 13
Commonwealth 196–7
  and the Caribbean 262–3, 264, 266–7,
    290
  see also Rump Parliament
Connaught, composition of 101–2
conquest, patterns of 237–8
Constantine, Roman Emperor 108
Cook, Captain Richard 210
Copland, Patrick 231
Cornwall 4, 13–14, 25, 28
Cortés, Hernan 3, 219
Cotter, Captain James 269
Cotton, Sir Robert 150
Counter-Reformation
  and Ireland 73–4, 288
  and James I 285–6
  and the Netherlands 185
Courteens, William, father and son 193–4,
    259
Crijnsen, Admiral Abraham 274
Croft, Governor James 56
Cromwell, Oliver 167, 195–6, 198, 202
  and the Caribbean 263, 264
Cromwell, Thomas 34, 36
Cross, Sir Robert 87
Crusades 12
Cuba 224, 227
cultural imperialism 10–11
Cumberland, Earl of 85, 87, 221
currency, in Ireland 34–5
Cusack, Thomas, Lord Chancellor 43

Dacre, Lord 32
Dale, Sir Thomas 190, 208, 229
Danvers, Sir Charles 135
Davenport, Francis 210
Davies, Sir John 162–4
De Witt, Jan 275
Dee, John 90–1
Dee, Roland 90
Derby, Earl of 32
Dermot MacMurrough, King of Leinster
    13
Desmond, Earl of 29, 64, 75, 77, 118, 163
Desmond, James FitzThomas, Earl of 128
Desmond, Sir John of 75–6, 77
Dillon, Thomas, Chief Justice of
    Connaught 101
Discourse of Western Planting (Hakluyt) 92
*Discovery of the True Causes Why Ireland Was
    Never Entirely Subdued* 163, 164

Docwra, Sir Henry 137, 157
Dodsworth, Edward 188
Donald Clan 47, 49–50, 52, 69, 102, 103, 114, 126, 153, 164, 167
Dougal Ciar, Clan 155
Douglas, James, Earl of 47
Downing, Sir George 200–1
Downton, Captain Nicholas 152
Downton, Nicholas 187, 188
D'Oyley, Colonel Edward 266
Drake, Sir Francis 69, 84, 86, 87, 90, 91, 93, 108, 165, 221, 257
Drayton, Michael, 'To the Virginian Voyage' 233–4
Drury, Sir William 75
Dryden, John 204
    Annus Mirabilis 201–2
Dudley, Robert (illegitimate son of the Earl of Leicester) 169
Dutch East India Company 8–9, 182
Dutch Republic 6
    and the Amazon delta 170, 171, 173
    Anglo–Dutch wars (1650s–1670s) 197–206, 262, 263, 270, 290–1
    and the North American colonies 272–6
    and the Caribbean 255, 270
    and the English East India Company 182–5, 187–8, 189–93, 194–5
    Amboina episode 191–3, 195
    and North American colonisation 230
    and Spain 225
    VOC 182, 185, 188, 190, 192, 195, 199–200, 201, 203–4, 205, 206, 206–7, 211
Dutch settlers
    in the Caribbean 261, 262, 267
    in New England 237, 239, 240
Dutch West India Company 173, 275
Dyer, Edward 90

East Africa 186
East India Company see English East India Company (EIC)
East Indies 168
Edward I, King 25, 41–3
Edward III, King 24
Edward IV, King 47
Edward VI, King 25, 36, 73
    and the Reformation in Ireland 55, 58–9
EIC see English East India Company (EIC)

Elizabeth I, Queen
    and Cornwall 14
    and Crown patronage of maps 132
    death of 139, 140, 162
    and the English East India Company 8, 131, 182
    and English national identity 9, 107–8
    and English privateers 87, 88, 89, 92
    excommunication of 74
    and France 116
    and Ireland 58, 59, 60, 81, 102, 103, 105, 108, 111, 112, 113, 115, 126, 127, 128, 134, 135, 139, 140, 141–2, 164
    and the Netherlands 83–4, 116, 182–4
    'rainbow' portrait of 141–2
    and Raleigh 120, 121–2
    and religious toleration 127
    and Scotland 51, 52
    and Spenser's The Faerie Queen 119
    and Virginia 93
Elizabethan England
    attitudes to war 15
    and English identity 9
    and entrepreneurial violence on the sea frontier 82–95
    and imperialism 141–2, 286
    and Ireland 56, 58, 59–69, 73–82, 100–18, 119–20, 125–9, 132–42
Elton, Sir Geoffrey 11
Endicott, Captain John 241–2
English East India Company (EIC) 8, 131, 152, 178, 182–96, 284, 286
    and the Anglo–Dutch wars (1650s–1670s) 199, 200, 203–4, 205, 206
    and Asian trade 182–96, 203–4, 206–7, 211, 212
    and the Dutch 182–5, 187–8, 189–93, 194–5
    and India 207, 208–9
    and the Portuguese 182, 185–7, 191, 194
    and Siam 206, 209–10
English identities 291
    and the Celtic frontier 287–8
    in Elizabethan England 9, 107–8
    and Henry VIII 35–6
    and North American colonisation 234–5
    in Restoration England 204, 206
Erasmus 14, 118
Essex, Robert Devereux, 2nd Earl of 14, 89, 105, 121, 130
    Irish campaign (1599) 132–5, 284, 288

Essex, Walter Devereux, 1st Earl of 52, 67–9
Evertsen, Admiral 274, 276

The Faerie Queen 118, 119, 120
Falkland, Viscount 172–3
Falmouth, Charles Berkeley, Earl of 198
feudal society, and conquest 12
Fife Adventurers 154
Fitzgerald, Gerald, ninth Earl of 5
Fitzgerald, Sir James Fitzmaurice 64, 67, 74, 75, 76, 78, 128
Fitzgerald, Sir Thomas 27
FitzThomas, James, Earl of Desmond 128
Fitzwalter, Lord 56
Fitzwilliam, Sir William 59–60, 67, 69, 76, 77, 104, 107, 110, 112, 113
Flodden, battle of (1513) 4
Florida 224, 225, 228, 255
Ford of the Biscuits, Battle of the 112
France
  artillery forts 5–6
  and Asian trade 203–4, 208
  and the Caribbean 225, 259, 260, 265, 267–8, 271
  Catholic League 108, 116
  and Charles II 203, 204, 205
  Charles I's wars with 46, 165, 176, 177
  and the Crown of England 23, 24
  and Elizabethan England 73, 116
  French East India Company 205
  and Henry VIII 35–6, 38
  and Ireland 59
  and North America 222, 228, 291–2
    French Canada 4, 6, 176, 177
  and Scotland 73
  and Siam 210
  and Spain 84, 285
  trade with Spanish America 83
Frederick, Elector Palatine 174
Frederick the Great, King of Prussia 4
French Canada 4, 6, 176, 177
French West India Company 268

Gaidhealtachd (Ireland) 4, 28, 30, 34, 35, 36, 37, 38, 43–59, 79, 81, 137, 168
  and military technology 44–6
Gaidhealtachd (Scotland) 46–53, 73, 114, 137
gallowglasses, in the Gaidhealtachd 44, 45, 81, 101, 114
Gardiner, Bishop 237–8
Gates, Sir Thomas 225

Gilbert, Sir Humphrey 62, 64–5, 74–5, 76, 77
  and American colonisation 88–90, 92, 95, 217
  and John Dee 90–1
Glorious Revolution (1688) 211, 279, 284, 290
Goa 149, 194
gold, and Spanish America 94
Gondomar, Diego Samiento de Acuña, Conde de 170, 171, 174–5
Gordon, Clan 152, 154, 155, 157
Gorges, Sir Ferdinando 236
Grantham, Sir Thomas 208
Great Northern War 6
Gregor, Clan 155
Gregory XIII, Pope 74
Grenville, Sir Richard 64, 78–9, 88, 93, 221
Grey, Lord Leonard 34, 36, 38
Grey of Wilton, Lord 76
Griggs, Thomas 91
Grossart, Alexander 119
Guiana
  English Guiana Company 173
  exploration and colonisation 169, 170
  Raleigh's account of 120–2

Habsburg Empire 148–9, 285, 286
Hagen, Steven van der 189
Hakluyt, Richard the elder 86–7, 89, 91, 92, 184, 217–20
Hakluyt, Richard the younger 90, 91–2, 93, 94–5
Harman, Sir John 268–9
Harmenszoon, Wolpert 185
Harrington, Sir Henry 133
Harriot, Thomas 223
Harrison, William 247
Harvey, John, Governor of Virginia 235
Hatton, Sir Christopher 111
Hawkins, John 82, 83, 165, 257
Hawley, Henry, Governor of Barbados 260
Hayes, Edward 89
Heemskerk, Jacob van 185
Henry II, King 13, 24, 28
Henry II, King of France 13
Henry III, King 24
Henry III, King of France 13, 108
Henry IV, King of France (Henry of Navarre) 89, 108, 116, 160, 285
Henry, Prince of Wales (son of James I) 284
Henry V, King 4, 5, 35–6

Henry VII, King 12, 23–4, 26
    and Ireland 26, 27, 28, 29–30, 55, 128,
        163
Henry VIII, King 5, 90, 100, 108
    and English national identity 35–6
    and France 35–6, 38
    and imperialism 147–8
    and Ireland 31–8, 41–3, 58
    and the navy 6, 7
    and Scotland 50
    and Spain 82
    and Wales 25, 37
Henty, G.A. 10
Herbert, Sir William 14, 106
Holmes, Sir Robert 200, 275
Holy Roman Empire 147
Howard of Effingham, Charles 85–6, 95,
    121
Howard, Lord Thomas 220–1
Hudson, Henry 225, 238
Hudson's Bay Company 279
humanism
    and pacifism 14–15
    and Spenser 118–19, 120
Huntly, Earl (later Marquess) of 152, 153,
    157

imperialism 9–11, 286
    and James I 147–8, 286
    in Restoration England 197
Inca Empire 3
India
    and Asian trade 208–10
    Bengal 208–9
    Bombay 199, 208, 211
    and the English East India Company
        207
    Goa 149, 194
    Moghul empire 152, 187, 188, 189, 199,
        208, 208–9, 284, 291
    Surat 186, 187, 199, 208
Ireland
    and Charles I 165–8
    coinage 34–5
    conquest of 12–13
    and cultural imperialism 11
    Elizabethan 14, 59–69, 73–82, 100–18,
        119–20, 125–9, 132–42, 163
        and composition 100–2
        and demilitarisation 106–7
        and English identity 107–8
        Essex's campaign (1599) 132–5, 284
        fall of Enniskillen Castle 111–12, 113,
            115

    and the Munster plantation 77–8
    and the Munster revolt 64–5, 74–7
    and the English Reformation 33
Gaidhealtachd 4, 28, 30, 34, 35, 36, 37,
    38, 43–59, 79, 81, 137, 168
and Henry VII 26, 27, 28, 29–30, 55,
    128, 163
and James I 139–40, 141, 142, 149,
    156–65, 288
    and Common Law 161, 162, 163
    Ulster plantation 164–5, 168
Kildare rebellion (1534–35) 32–3, 34
Lordship of 13, 25–7, 28–9, 30–1, 32,
    33–5, 37–8, 41–3, 287, 288
New English 56, 64, 80, 100–1, 106–7,
    108, 110, 127, 139, 166–7
Old English 56, 59, 63–4, 69, 73, 75,
    79, 80, 100, 101, 108, 117–18, 120,
    129, 159, 288, 289
    and overseas exploration and
        colonisation 171–2
parliaments 26, 30–1, 33, 55–6, 100–1
and Poynings' Law 29, 30–1
and religion
    Anglican Church 166–7
    Counter-Reformation 73–4, 288
    the Reformation 33, 55, 58–9, 80
    Roman Catholicism 100, 129–9, 134,
        159, 166, 288
    toleration 127, 159
and Scotland 49–53, 57–8, 69, 102–3,
    114
and Spain 100, 105–6, 111, 116, 126,
    135–6, 137, 138–9, 142
and the Spanish Armada 76–7, 103–4
and the Treaty of Mellifont (1603)
    139–40, 149, 156, 157, 160
and Tudor England 5, 25–38, 51–49
and Yorkist pretenders 26–8, 30
Islamic empires, and Asian trade 187

Jackson, Andrew (US President) 16–17,
    245
Jahangir, Moghul emperor 152, 189, 193
Jamaica 258, 263, 264–7, 271–2
James I, King 14–15, 147–78, 284, 290
    Basilikon Doron 152, 161
    and the Counter-Reformation 285–6
    Counterblast to Tobacco 230
    death of 173
    and the Dutch 201
    and the English East India Company
        188–9, 191, 192, 196
    and imperial kingship 147–8, 286

James I, King (*continued*)
 and Ireland 139–40, 141, 142, 149,
  156–65, 288
 as James VI of Scotland 50, 52, 104,
  119, 135
 and North American colonisation 224,
  225, 230, 232
 and overseas expansion and colonisation
  168–78
 and Scotland
  Anglo-Scottish union 148–9
  Highlands and Islands 152–6, 287
 and Spain 149–50, 168, 173, 174, 258,
  285
 and the triple monarchy 142, 160–1
 The True Law of Free Monarchies 147
James II, King (formerly Duke of York and
  Albany)
 and the American colonies 275, 276,
  278–9, 290
 and the Caribbean 268
 and the Dutch 198, 199, 201, 203
 and the English East India Company
  207, 208
 and imperialism in Asia 209–10
 and the Turks 204, 291
James IV, King of Scotland 27, 47
Jeffreys, Major 278
Johnson, Dr Samuel 1
Jonson, Ben 89, 234
Jourdain, John 190

Keigwin, Richard 208
Kildare, Earls of 5, 26, 29, 30, 34, 41, 53,
  60
Kildare rebellion in Ireland (1534–35)
  32–3, 34
Kildare, 'Silken Thomas' 32, 37
Kinsale, Battle of (1601) 138, 139

Lacy, Ambrose 53
Lancaster, James 131
Lancaster, Sir James 184, 185
Lane, Sir Ralph 78–9, 80, 94, 128, 221,
  223
languages 27–8
Leeward Islands 258–9, 260, 268, 269,
  270, 271, 279
Leicester, Robert Dudley, Earl of 61, 67,
  79, 111
Levant Company 199
Lewis (Hebrides) 153–4
Lincoln, Earl of 27
London, Great Fire of (1666) 201

London, Treaty of (1604) 150, 169, 224,
  257–8
Louis XIII, King of France 177
Louis XIV, King of France 5, 6, 199, 201
 and the American colonies 278, 279
 and the Caribbean 268, 271
 and the Dutch 201, 202, 203, 204, 212
 and Roman Catholicism 206
Louth, Lord 159
Ludwell, Philip 249
Luna, Tristan de 228
Lynch, Governor of Jamaica 272

MacBaron, Cormac 112
MacCarthy, Florence 137
Macdonald, Alasdair MacColla 167–8
MacDonald of Glengarry 168
Macdonald of Islay, Angus 48
McDonald of the Isles, James 102
MacDonald, Sir James of Dunyveg 153,
  156
MacDonalds of Dunyveg 156
MacDonnell, Alexander 102
MacDonnell, Alexander Carragh 103
MacDonnell, Angus James 103
MacDonnell, Donnell Gorme 102, 103,
  154
MacDonnell, James, sixth of Dunyveg and
  the Glynnes 49, 51
MacDonnell, James Sorley 117
MacDonnell, Randal (later Marquis of
  Antrim) 167
MacDonnell, Sorley Boy 50–1, 51–2, 52–3,
  58, 61, 63, 69, 86, 102, 103
MacGregor, Alasdair 155
MacGregor Clan 51–2, 287
Macguires of Fermanagh 56–7
Mackellar, Gillipatrick Oig 45
Mackenzie, Colin, Earl of Seaforth 154
Mackenzie, Kenneth, Lord Kintail 154
Mackenzie, Professor John 10
Mackenzie, Roderick 154
Mackintosh, Lachlan of Dunnachton 155
Maclean, Hector 48
MacLeod, Ruari Mor of Dunvegan 153,
  154
MacQuillan, Rory 103
MacRory, Owen 127
Madrid, Treaty of (1670) 266, 272
Magellan, Ferdinand 87
Magellan, Strait of 91–2
Magennis, Catherine 126
Maguire, Coconaught, Lord of Fermanagh
  161

Maguire, Connor Roe 111–12
Maguire, Hugh 111, 137
Malbie, Sir Nicholas 50–1
Maldive Islands 185
Man, Isle of 32
Marie de' Medici, Queen of France 285
maritime trade 2, 3
  and the East India Company 8–9,
    182–212
  and Elizabethan England 82–4
  and plantations 2
Marvell, Andrew 202, 203
Marxism 283
Mary of Guise 58
Mary I, Queen, and Ireland 54, 56, 58, 59
Mary, Queen of Scots 50, 51, 58, 83, 159
Maryland 172, 233, 234, 249–50, 277
Mason, Captain John 242
Mather, Cotton 238
Maverick, Samuel 276
M'Cabbe, Melaghlin 103
Medici, Marie de', Queen of France 285
Mellifont, Treaty of (1603) 139–40, 149,
    156, 157, 160
Mendoza (Spanish Ambassador) 95
Menendez de Aviles, Pedro 92, 93, 225,
    227
Metacomet 246–8
Mexico, conquest of 3, 12, 80, 81, 219,
    227, 255
Miantonomi (Narragansett chief) 245
Middleton, Sir Henry 187
military technology 12
  in Elizabethan Ireland 114–15
  and the Irish Gaidhealtachd 44–6
  and native Americans (Indians) 241,
    243–4, 289
  and naval warfare 130–1
  in Tudor Ireland 33
  Western 283
Milton, John 167
Modyford, Sir Thomas 267, 272
Monck, General 197, 198
Montcalm, Marquis de 4
Montrose, James Graham, Marquis of 167,
    168
Moore, Caleb 247
Moray, Earl of 51
More, MacCarthy 45, 64
Morgan, Henry 267, 272
Mountbatten, Lord Louis 88
Mountjoy, Charles Blount, Lord 135, 136,
    137–8, 139, 140, 141, 149, 156
Mun, Thomas 201

Namier, Sir Lewis 11
Narai, King of Siam 206, 209
Narvaez, Panfilo de 228
naval warfare, in Elizabethan England 130,
    131–2
navalist imperialism 197
Navigation Acts 195, 262, 275
navy
  English 6–9
  Spanish 7–8
Neale, Sir John 108
Netherlands
  and Elizabethan England 83–4, 108,
    116, 182–4
  and the Pilgrim Fathers 236
  see also Dutch Republic
Nevis 260, 264, 270
New England 235–49, 250, 260, 278–9,
    289–90
  Deerfield (Massachusetts) 291–2
  and the Dutch 237, 239, 240
  Hartford Agreement (1638) 239–40
  Massachusetts Bay Colony 236–7, 240,
    244, 245, 289
  and native Americans (Indians) 236, 237,
    245–9, 250, 279, 291–2
    disease and epidemics 238, 239
    and indigenous culture 244–5
    and the Pequot War (1637) 239–43,
      245, 289
    and weapons 241, 243–4
  Plymouth 236, 237, 239, 241, 245, 246,
    249
  Rhode Island 240, 244, 246, 247, 278
  United Colonies of 245, 248
Newbolt, Sir Henry 10
Newfoundland 89, 91, 149, 238
  exploration and colonisation 172–3,
    175–6
Newport, Christopher 86, 87
Nijmegen, Peace of (1678/79) 270
Noell, Martin 262
Nonsuch, Treaty of (1585) 182–3
Norman Conquest 4, 11, 12, 24, 41, 237–8
Norris, John 69
Norris, Sir Henry 116
Norris, Sir John 116, 118
Norris, Sir Thomas 116
North American colonies 1, 4, 175–8,
    217–50, 288–90
  and the Anglican Church 235–6, 237,
    279
  and English identity 234–5
  establishing claims to 222–3

North American colonies (*continued*)
  Florida 224, 225, 228, 255
  Humphrey's Gilbert's plans for
    settlement 89, 90–1
  Long Island 275, 276
  Maryland 172, 233, 234, 249–50, 277
  and native Americans (Indians) 220, 223
    and the Iroquois–Susquehannock war
    249–50
    in Virginia 6, 226–30, 231–3
  New Sweden 275–6, 279
  New York 248, 275, 276
  and patterns of conquest and migration
    237–8
  plans for Catholic colony 95
  and sea traffic 217–19, 235
  War of the American Revolution 244
  see also Canada; New England; Virginia
north of England 25, 64
North, Roger 170, 175
Northampton, Henry Howard, Earl of 150,
  159
Nottingham, Earl of 258
Nowell, Samuel 289–90

O'Brien, Sir Turlough 101
O'Cahan, Manus 106, 159
O'Cahan, Shane Carragh 162
Ochiltree, Lord 153
O'Connor, Sir Donogh 133
O'Donnell, Calvagh 51, 60
O'Donnell, Hugh 63, 109
O'Donnell, Hugh Roe 110, 111, 112, 115,
  126, 128
O'Donnell, Ineen Dubh 110
O'Donnell, Niall Garve 137, 140
O'Donnell, Rory *see* Tyrconnell, Rory
  O'Donnell, Earl of
O'Dougherty, Sir Cahir 162
O'Flaherty, Murrough na Doe 107
O'Neill, Conn Bacagh, Earl of Tyrone 43,
  103
O'Neill, Cormac 113
O'Neill, Hugh *see* Tyrone, Hugh O'Neill,
  second Earl of
O'Neill, Hugh Gavelach 126
O'Neill, Owen Roe 166
O'Neill, Shane 57, 58, 60–1, 62–3, 73, 163
O'Neill, Sir Arthur 140
O'Neill, Sir Brian McPhelim, Lord of
  Clandeboy 67, 68
O'Neill, Turlough Luineach 45, 50, 52, 63,
  68, 86, 102–3, 109
Openchancanough 230, 231, 232

O'Reilly, Pilib 110
O'Reilly, Sir John 110
Ormonde, Earls of 29, 64, 67, 76, 110,
  117, 125, 137
O'Rouke, Brian 107
O'Rouke, Brian Oge 133
O'Rouke, P.J. 11
Ottoman Empire 204, 291
Owain Gwynedd (Welsh prince) 90
Oxenden, Sir George 199

pacifism 14–15
Pakenham (Irish general) 16
Panama Isthmus 91, 94, 272
papacy
  and Elizabeth I 74, 80
  and James I 148
Papillon, Thomas 208
Parente, Bento Maciel 171
Parkhurst, Anthony 91
Penn, Admiral 262, 264
Pepys, Samuel 271, 275
Pequot War (1637) 239–43, 245, 289
Perrot, Sir John 14, 52, 53, 74, 75, 100,
  101, 102, 103, 104–5, 110
Persia, and the English East India
  Company 191, 203
Peru, conquest of 3, 80, 81
Peter Martyr 238
Phaulkon, Constantine 206, 209, 210
Philip II, King of Spain 7, 8, 54, 74, 238
  and the Armada 105
  and the Catholic League 108
  and conflict with Elizabethan England
    82–3, 84, 85, 88, 108, 121, 184
  and the Dutch 199
  and Ireland 127, 135, 136
  and Portugal 182
Philip III, King of Spain 168, 175
  and the Americas 223, 225
  and Ireland 138–9, 139
Pilgrim Fathers 236
Pius V, Pope 74
plantation, concept of 1–3
Pocahontas 228, 229
Ponce de Leon, Juan 228
Porter, Endymion 194
Portugal
  and the Amazon delta 170–1, 173, 285
  and Asian trade 182, 185–7, 191, 194
  and Bombay 208
  and Brazil 261
  conquests in the East Indies 149
  and Cromwell 263

Portugal (*continued*)
and the Dutch VOC 199–200
naval warfare with 130, 131–2
Spanish takeover of 84
Postlethwayt, Malachy 2
Powell, Captain John 259
Poynings' Law 29, 30–1
Poynings, Sir Edward 29–30
Pring, Martin 190
privateers
in Elizabethan England 85–95, 130
and James I 149
Protestantism
and English identity 291
and English privateers 85–6, 89–90
in Ireland 166–7
and the Reformation 33, 55, 58–9
and New England 278–9
and oversees settlement 95
in Scotland 108
see also Anglican Church
Puerto Rico 258
Purcell, Philip 170

Radcliffe, Sir Thomas 56
Raleigh, Sir Walter 76, 77, 78, 79, 87, 88,
129, 130, 152
and Carew's letters 284
and claims to North American colonies
222
and the colonisation of Virginia 93, 94,
220, 221
*Discoverie of the Large, Rich and Bewtiful
Empyre of Guiana* 120–1, 122
and James I 149–50, 169, 174
plan of County Cork estate 132
Real, Laurens 189
Reformation
and English national identity 107, 108
in Ireland 33, 55, 58–9, 80
religious toleration
and the Dutch 202
and Ireland 127, 159
Rich, Penelope, Lady 135
Richard, Duke of York 26, 27
Richard III, King 23, 24, 25
Richelieu, Cardinal 177
Risingh, Governor Johan 277
Robert the Bruce, King of Scotland 46, 51
Roberts, Henry 184
Robinson, Reverend John 236
Roe, Sir Thomas 152, 169, 189, 193, 194,
284
Rolfe, John 229, 230

Rolt, Thomas 203
Roman Britain 237
Roman Catholicism
Catholic League in France 108, 116
and the Counter-Reformation 73–4,
185, 285
in Elizabethan England 95
and English exploration and colonisation
172, 174
in Ireland 100, 129–9, 134, 159, 166
in Restoration England 199, 206
Rump Parliament
and the Dutch war 197, 198
and the English East India Company
195
and the Navigation Act (1651) 262, 266
Russell, Sir William 113, 114, 116
Ruyter, Admiral Michiel de 200, 201, 202,
267, 275
Rycaut, Sir Paul 204

St Helena 211
St Kitts 259, 260, 264, 268, 270, 271
St Leger, Sir Anthony 34, 43, 56
Sanderson, William 132
Saravia, Hadrian 147
Schwartz, Martin 27
Scotland
borders 4, 46–7
and Charles I 165
and the Commonwealth 197
and the Crown of England 23, 24, 25
and France 73
Gaelic society in 287, 288
Gaidhealtachd 46–53, 73, 114, 137
and Ireland 49–53, 57–8, 69, 102–3,
114
and James I
Anglo-Scottish union 148–9
Highlands and Islands 152–6
Lordship of the Isles 47–50, 53
Protestantism in 108
Scots settlement in Nova Scotia 176–7
and the Spanish Armada 104
and Spenser's *The Faerie Queen* 119
and the Ulster plantation 165, 167
wars of independence 46
Scott, Edward 188
Scott, Thomas 168
sea voyages
and Elizabethan English privateers
85–95, 130
to the American colonies 217–19, 235
Searle, Governor of Barbados 262

Sebastian of Portugal 74
Shakespeare, William 23, 24, 133
Sherley, Robert 191
shipping
  Asian ships 186
  navies 6–9
  Portuguese ships 186
  Spanish corsairs 255–7
Siam 206, 208, 209, 209–10
Sidney, Sir Henry 62, 63, 64, 67, 69, 79,
    137
Sidney, Sir Philip 13, 95
Simnel, Lambert 26–7
Siol Torquil of Lewis 153, 154
Sitric, Viking King 27
Skeffington, Sir William 32–3, 34
slave trade 83
slaves, in the Caribbean 261, 264–5
Smith, Captain John 15, 227, 233
Smith, Sir Thomas 66–7, 82
Soto, Hernando de 228
Southampton, Earl of 132–3, 134, 135,
    140
Spain
  and the Caribbean 255–8, 259, 260,
      263–4, 265–6, 271–2
  Charles I's wars with 165
  and the Dutch 182, 184, 225
  and Elizabethan England 14, 73, 82–5,
      88, 116, 121, 129–30
  and English exploration and colonisation
      170
  and France 84, 285
  and Ireland 100, 105–6, 111, 116, 126,
      135–6, 137, 138–9, 142
  and James I 149–50, 173, 174, 285
  naval power 7–8
  and North American colonisation 95,
      223–5
Spanish America 2–3, 6, 81, 91–2
  Amazon delta 169–71, 173–4, 175, 177,
      178, 285
  Brazil 91, 92, 170, 223–4
  conquistadores 188, 219
  and Cromwell 263
  English trade with 82, 83
  Isthmus of Panama 91, 94, 272
  Mayan resistance in 248
  Mexico 3, 12, 80, 81, 219, 227, 255
  Peru 3, 80, 81
  Sir Robert Cotton on 150
Spanish Armada 7, 8, 76–7, 80, 95,
    103–4, 108, 184
Spenser, Edmund 118–19, 120, 128

Spielberg, Joris van 185
Spotswood, Alexander, Lieutenant
    Governor of Virginia 234–5
Sri Lanka 186
Standish, Miles 236, 241, 242
Stanley, Sir John 32
Stanley, Sir William 102
Stapleton, Colonel 270, 271
Stirling, William Alexander, Earl of 175–7
Strafford, Thomas Wentworth, Earl of 119,
    166, 167
Stukeley, Thomas 74, 77
Stuyversant, Peter 275
Surat 186, 187, 199, 208
Surrey, Earl of 32, 41–3
Susquehannock Indians 277
Sussex, Earl of, policy in Ireland 56, 57–8,
    59–61, 67
Sweden 3, 6

Talbot, Sir Robert 172
Tantallon Castle, East Lothian 33
taxation, and the Irish parliament 26, 55
Teixeira, Pedro de 173
Temple, Sir William 8–9
Thirty Years' War (1618) 285
Thomond, Earl of 101, 128
Thompson, Maurice 262
Thornton, Archie 16
Thorpe, George 231
Throckmorton, Bess 77, 120
tobacco 229–30, 232, 250, 274, 284–5
Towerson, Gabriel 191
trade see maritime trade
Trinidad 121, 170
Tudor England 4–5, 11–14, 23–38
  and Ireland 25–38, 51–49
  navy 6–8
  see also Elizabeth I, Queen; Henry VII,
      King; Henry VIII, King
Twitt, John 87
Tyrconnell, Rory O'Donnell, Earl of 140,
    141, 158–60, 161
Tyrone, Hugh O'Neill, second Earl of 109,
    110–11, 112–14, 115, 116, 117,
    126–9, 137–8, 142, 288
  and the Battle of Kinsale 138, 139
  and the Battle of the Yellow Ford 125,
      126
  death 166
  and Essex's campaign 133, 134
  flight from Ireland 158–60
  and James I 156–61
  and Spain 135–6

Tyrone, Hugh O'Neill, second Earl of
  (*continued*)
  and the Treaty of Mellifont (1603) 139,
    140, 149
Tyrrel, Richard 127

Underhill, Captain John 242
United Netherlands *see* Dutch Republic
United States of America 16–17, 245

Vauban, Marshall 5
Venables, General 262, 264, 266
Vera, Domingo de 121
Vervins, Peace of (1598) 130
A View of the Present State of Ireland 118, 119,
    120, 164
Virginia 10, 15, 26
  Bacon's rebellion 5, 276–8
  and Carew's letters 284–5
  colonisation of 26, 93, 94, 175, 220–3,
    224–35, 249, 250
  and the Dutch wars 274–5
  and English national identity 234–5
  militia 272–4
  and native Americans (Indians) 276, 277
    Algonquin 6, 226
    Powhatans 226–30, 231–3
  representative assembly in Jamestown
    230–1
  and tobacco 229–30, 232, 250, 274,
    284–5
Virginia Company 165, 223, 224–5, 229,
    230, 231, 233, 284

Wales 4
  conquest of 12, 43
  Council of Wales and the Marches 14,
    25, 62
  and Henry VIII 25, 37
  nobility and gentry 14, 25, 28
  union with England (1536–43) 25, 37
Wallop, Sir Henry 78, 80
Walsh, Nicholas 100

Walsingham, Sir Francis 50, 105, 107,
    111
Warbeck, Perkin 27–8, 29, 30
Ware, Sir James 63, 119
Warner, Sir Thomas 259, 260
Warwick, Earl of 264
Washington, George 265
weaponry *see* military technology
West Indies 168
White, George 206, 210
White, John 93, 221
White Mountain, Battle of the (1620) 81
White, Nicholas 101
White, Samuel 206, 209–10, 210
Whyte, Edward 103
William I, King (the Conqueror) 24
William III, King (William of Orange)
    211–12, 279, 290, 291
Williams, Roger 240, 243
Williamson, Sir Joseph 247
Willis, Captain Humphrey 111
Willoughby, Lord 268
Willoughby, William 268
Wingfield, Sir Richard 162
Wingfield, Sir Thomas 126
Winslow, Governor Josiah 289
Winter, Admiral 76
Winter, Edward 200
Winter, John 91
Winthrop, John Jr 237, 240–1
Witt, Johan de 201
Wolfe, General James 4
Wolstenholme, Sir John 225
Woodhead, Abraham 204

Yale, Elihu 210
Yale, Thomas 210
Yellow Ford, Battle of the 125–6, 127,
    128, 141
Yorkist pretenders, and Ireland 26–8, 30

Zubiaur, Don Pedro 138
Zuñiga, Pedro de 224, 225